Lecture Notes of the Institute for Computer Sciences, Social Informatics and Telecommunications Engineering 382

More information about this series at http://www.springer.com/series/8197

Dragan Perakovic · Lucia Knapcikova (Eds.)

Future Access Enablers for Ubiquitous and Intelligent Infrastructures

5th EAI International Conference, FABULOUS 2021
Virtual Event, May 6–7, 2021
Proceedings

 Springer

Editors
Dragan Perakovic ⓘ
University of Zagreb
Zagreb, Croatia

Lucia Knapcikova ⓘ
Technical University of Košice
Prešov, Slovakia

ISSN 1867-8211   ISSN 1867-822X (electronic)
Lecture Notes of the Institute for Computer Sciences, Social Informatics
and Telecommunications Engineering
ISBN 978-3-030-78458-4   ISBN 978-3-030-78459-1 (eBook)
https://doi.org/10.1007/978-3-030-78459-1

This Springer imprint is published by the registered company Springer Nature Switzerland AG
The registered company address is: Gewerbestrasse 11, 6330 Cham, Switzerland

Preface

We are delighted to introduce the proceedings of EAI FABULOUS 2021 – the 5th EAI International Conference on Future Access Enablers of Ubiquitous and Intelligent Infrastructures.

The event aims to bring together leading academic scientists, researchers, and research scholars to exchange and share their experiences and research results on all aspects of innovative and sustainable solutions for ubiquitous and intelligent communication infrastructures. The theme of EAI FABULOUS 2021 was "Security of innovative services and infrastructure in traffic/transport/logistic ecosystem".

The technical program of EAI FABULOUS 2021 consisted of 30 full papers and 2 invited talks in video presentation sessions, all in full online conference format. The conference topics were as follows: Future access networks; Internet of Things and Smart City/Smart Environment applications; Communications and Computing Infrastructures; Security aspects in communications and data processing; and Signal processing and Multimedia.

Aside from the high-quality paper presentations, the program also featured two invited keynote speeches presented by Kim-Kwang Raymond Choo, Cloud Technology Endowed Professorship at The University of Texas at San Antonio (UTSA), USA, and Prof. Aleksandar Jevremović, Faculty of Informatics and Computing/Singidunum University, Serbia and guest lecturer at Harvard University, USA.

Coordination with the steering chair, Imrich Chlamtac, and all EAI team members was essential for the success of the conference. We sincerely appreciate their constant support and guidance. It was also a great pleasure to work with such an excellent Organizing Committee team. Full thanks for their hard work in organizing and supporting the conference. In particular, we are grateful to the Technical Program Committee (TPC), led by our TPC Co-chairs, Marko Periša, Marko Krstić, Anca D. Jurcut, and Dr. B. B. Gupta, who completed the peer-review process for the papers and put together a high-quality program. Additionally, our thanks go to General Co-Chair Goran Marković and Web Chairs Ivan Cvitić and Alexandru Vulpe for all their support.

We are also grateful to Conference Manager, Natasha Onofrei for her support and all the authors who submitted their papers to the EAI FABULOUS 2021 conference.

We strongly believe that the EAI FABULOUS conference series provides a good platform for all researchers, developers, and practitioners to discuss all science and technology aspects that are relevant to Future Access Enablers of Ubiquitous and Intelligent Infrastructures. We also expect that the future EAI FABULOUS conferences will be as successful and stimulating as EAI FABULOUS 2021, as indicated by the contributions presented in this volume.

Last but not least, we especially thank our colleague Ivan Cvitić (Local Chair) for all the effort invested in the organization and preparation of the conference in Zagreb.

Unfortunately, the impact of mobility restrictions and new measures caused by the COVID-19 pandemic meant that we could not hold this year's conference in person.

Certainly, we hope that EAI FABULOUS 2022 will take place in Zagreb, Croatia.

May 2021

Dragan Peraković
Lucia Knapčíková

Organization

Steering Committee

Chair

Imrich Chlamtac   University of Trento, Italy

Co-chairs

Dragan Peraković   University of Zagreb, Croatia
Lucia Knapcikova   Technical University of Košice, Slovakia

Organizing Committee

General Chairs

Dragan Peraković   University of Zagreb, Croatia
Goran Marković   University of Belgrade, Serbia
Lucia Knapcikova   Technical University of Košice, Slovakia

Technical Program Committee Chairs

Marko Periša   University of Zagreb, Croatia
Marko Krstić   RATEL Beograd, Serbia
Anca D. Jurcut   University College Dublin, Ireland
B. B. Gupta   National Institute of Technology Kurukshetra, India

Web Chairs

Ivan Cvitić   University of Zagreb, Croatia
Alexandru Vulpe   Politehnica University of Bucharest, Romania

Publicity and Social Media Chair

Rossi Kamal   Xaria ICT, Bangladesh

Workshops Chair

Gordana Jotanović   University of East Sarajevo, Bosnia and Herzegovina

Sponsorship and Exhibits Chair

Marko Periša   University of Zagreb, Croatia

Publications Chairs

Dragan Peraković	University of Zagreb, Croatia
Lucia Knapcikova	Technical University of Košice, Slovakia
Ivan Cvitić	University of Zagreb, Croatia

Posters and PhD Track Chair

Dragan Peraković	University of Zagreb, Croatia

Local Chair

Ivan Cvitić	University of Zagreb, Croatia

Technical Program Committee

Alberto Huertas	University of Murcia, Spain
Alessandro Ruggiero	University of Salerno, Italy
Alexandru Vulpe	Politehnica University of Bucharest, Romania
Arcangelo Castiglione	University of Salerno, Italy
Arianit Maraj	AAB College, Kosovo
Anca D. Jurcut	University College Dublin, Ireland
Anna Otsetova	University of Telecommunications and Post, Bulgaria
B. Gupta	National Institute of Technology Kurukshetra, India
Dalibor Dobrilović	University of Novi Sad, Serbia
Dharma P. Agrawal	University of Cincinnati, USA
Dragan Peraković	University of Zagreb, Croatia
Dražan Kozak	University of Osijek, Croatia
Dušan Šimšik	Technical University of Košice, Slovakia
Goran Marković	University of Belgrade, Serbia
Imran Razzak	Deakin University, Australia
Ivan Cvitić	University of Zagreb, Croatia
Ivan Grgurević	University of Zagreb, Croatia
Ján Piteľ	Technical University of Košice, Slovakia
Lucia Knapcikova	Technical University of Košice, Slovakia
Marko Matulin	University of Zagreb, Croatia
Martin Straka	Technical University of Košice, Slovakia
Milan Čabarkapa	University of Belgrade, Serbia
Michael Herzog	Technical University of Applied Sciences Wildau, Germany
Mirjana Stojanović	University of Belgrade, Serbia
Miroslav Vujić	University of Zagreb, Croatia
Marko Periša	University of Zagreb, Croatia
Marko Krstić	RATEL Beograd, Serbia
Peter Kolarovszki	GS1 Slovakia/FPEDAS Zilina, Slovakia
Phuc Do	Vietnam National University Ho Chi Minh City, Vietnam
Štefica Mrvelj	University of Zagreb, Croatia

Contents

Internet of Things and Smart City/Smart Environment Applications

Information and Communications Technology

Smart Health Applications

Sustainable Communications and Computing Infrastructures

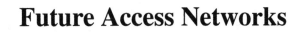

Future Access Networks

Effectiveness of Mobile Wiping Applications

Kevin Jochims, Andres Bello, and Kim-Kwang Raymond Choo$^{(\boxtimes)}$ (iD)

Department of Information Systems and Cyber Security,
University of Texas San Antonio, San Antonio, TX 78249, USA
{kevin.jochims,ren574}@my.utsa.edu,
raymond.choo@fulbrightmail.org

Abstract. Given the considerable amount of data (including sensitive and personal information) collected, stored, disseminated by mobile devices, there is a need to ensure that such devices can be securely wiped when they are misplaced, stolen or disposed. Hence, in this paper we evaluate the effectiveness of three categories of wiping applications: Factory Reset, Remote Reset, Data Wiping Applications (apps). Specifically, we study two popular wiping apps (i.e., Shreddit – Data Eraser by PalmTronix, and Secure Wipe by Pinellas CodeWorks) and install both apps on three test devices, namely: Samsung S5 (Android 6.0.1), Samsung S5 Active (OS version 6.0.1), and an iPhone 6S (iOS 13.2.2). We then study the extent of data that can be recovered, from the three categories of wiping, using two popular commercial mobile forensic software, namely: Mobile Phone Examiner Plus (MPE+) from Accessdata, and MOBILedit from Compelson labs.

Keywords: Remote wiping · NAND memory · Mobile forensics · Secure data deletion · Android forensics · iOS forensics

1 Introduction

Advances in mobile device technologies (e.g. processing speeds, and memory capacity) have partly contributed to significant growth in the sales of mobile devices, particularly smartphones [1–5]. Contemporary mobile devices are capable of collecting, accessing, storing and disseminating a broad range of information (e.g. user physiological data, user credentials, and other personal identifiable information – PII) [6–8]. However, leakage or unauthorized access to such information can be (ab)used to facilitate criminal activities such as identity theft [9, 10]. For example, there has been a growing trend of individuals taking compromising or nude photos with their mobile devices, as evidenced by a number of studies [7], such as the Pew Internet study. The latter study found that an increasing number of young adults are now using their smartphones to exchange sexual pictures and sexual conversations (also referred to as sexting) [7]. In 2011, sexting was identified as one of the top 10 major health concerns for youth [7]. As of 2019, over 27% of adolescences (aged between 13 and 15) have either sent or received nude pictures from sexting [11], and according to a Cosmopolitan Magazine poll [12], up to 90% of the Millennial women admitted to taking nude photos of themselves. Milne's [13] study

D. Perakovic and L. Knapcikova (Eds.): FABULOUS 2021, LNICST 382, pp. 3–24, 2021.
https://doi.org/10.1007/978-3-030-78459-1_1

shows the effects and trauma from loss of sensitive and personal information can resulted in monetary, social, physical, and psychological harms or damages. Associated consequences also include loss of self-esteem or sense of worth, and in some cases fatality. The fast pace of users replacing their mobile devices (estimated to be approximately every two years) reinforce the importance of ensuring users are able to securely wipe data from such devices, particularly sensitive information.

Newer Android and iOS devices, for example, have built in encryption and factory reset features. The latter feature is used to wipe a device of user data and return it to a sanitized state. This feature only works if the individual has direct access to the device, but with theft and loss, users need the ability to perform a remote initiated wipe of user data from the device. There are times where a user wishes to only wipe recently deleted data that can be carried out using third-party mobile apps.

However, there are a number of questions associated with the utility of these third-party mobile apps. For example, how effective are such third-party apps, have factory resets improved enough to prevent data recovery, and are remote initiated wipes as good as a factory reset? This is the focus of this paper. Specifically, in this paper we study two popular wiping apps namely: Shreddit – Data Eraser by PalmTronix, and Secure Wipe by Pinellas CodeWorks. Data, programs (apps). We attempt data recovery following a factory reset, using two popular commercial mobile forensic software, namely: Mobile Phone Examiner Plus (MPE+) from Accessdata, and MOBILedit from Compelson labs.

In the next section, we will briefly introduce data deletion and the extant literature.

2 Background and Related Work

2.1 Data Deletion

There are two main categories for deleting files on a digital device: namely: deletion and secure data deletion [3, 5, 14–17]. For most operating systems, when a user "deletes" a file, just the metadata for that file (e.g. in the Master File Table (MFT) for a NT file system (NTFS)), is changed, and the drive space the old data bits occupy is marked as unallocated. Using forensic tools can potentially allow a user to recover the deleted data [3, 5, 15–17]. A secure data deletion, on the other hand, is designed to compound the challenge of recovering deleted data.

There are three ways to accomplish a secure data deletion of a smartphone with no physical impact to the device; providing the device is available to the user. The first option is to use a third-party software (e.g. app) that focuses on wiping just the unallocated areas/space on the device. The next option is to perform a factory reset of the device. The last option is to encrypt the data on the phone (and deleting the decryption key) [15–32].

Smartphones read and write data slightly different than other computer systems, and generally store data in three partitions, namely: system data, internal flash data storage, and external data storage (e.g. SD card) [19]. The internal data is a form of flash media called NAND. It is designed with multiple blocks filled with tiny memory cells [15, 16, 20]. When the device wants to write new data, bits are stored in the empty cells of a block and a logical address pointer is created and mapped to the file. When a delete command is made for a file, the logical address pointer for that file is redirected to an empty space in a block, making the data available for erasure. With no moving parts NAND memory is very fast and allows for higher storage capacity [3, 15, 16, 20].

There is one limitation associated with NAND; whereas disk drives can be re-written on the fly, the data marked for deletion must be erased prior to writing new data in that cell, [3, 16–20] with NAND the erasure is done on the block level, not bit by bit [15, 20]. The erasing function in NAND memory is hard on the cells creating a limit to how many times data can be erased and written to it. Yang et al. [15] express that failure is typically after 104 to 105 cycles, and the block use is balanced through wear levelling.

Prior to transferring ownership of a phone, additional steps should be taken to ensure all PII is removed. For use with third-party wiping apps, manually locate and delete data, with PII, and delete any installed apps that may contain PII. Third-party software only wipes the data blocks that are marked as unallocated; not active data locations. Since deletion is performed at the block level, fragments of old data may still be present in un-erased blocks, although these data fragments may not be visible without the use of appropriate forensic tools. A factory reset is designed to return the phone to a generic initial state, with all user apps and user data removed. Both iOS and Android devices have the ability to perform a factory reset.

Prior literature on factory resets has shown that Apple iOS has performed well since version 4.0, with very minimal or no data recovered. In Android devices running versions 2.3 to 7.0, varying amounts of deleted data could be recovered after factory reset [12, 15, 16, 19, 25–27, 30]. For example, Khramova [12] tested 68 Android phones from nine different manufacturers, running versions from 2.3 to 7.0, and was able to recover data from these phones after a factory reset.

2.2 Remote Wiping Apps

When a device is misplaced or stolen, the user will not be able to physically activate the factory reset option. In circumstances like this, a remote wiping app could be used. Such an app can be downloaded from the manufacture's website (Samsung, Apple, Google, HTC, etc.), the official OS site (Google for Android, Apple for iPhones, etc.), or a third-party app store. The first two options usually come by default as the phone is activated and the user sets up their accounts with the OS or manufacture's website [33].

A number of major anti-malware companies have also put out remote wipe apps like Norton's Mobile Security, Avast's Anti-theft, or Bitdefender's Anti-Theft. These apps do require a purchase, but there are free apps available. Such free apps require some software installed on the phone prior to use. Research has shown there is extensive data on factory resets of smartphones running OS versions prior to 2014, but limited data is available on the effectiveness of remote wiping applications [33].

In the next section, we will briefly explain how remote wiping apps work.

3 Remote Wiping Apps and Their Effectiveness

3.1 How Remote Wiping Apps Work

Remote wiping capabilities are commonly available from the mobile device manufacturer or through third-party apps that can be enabled by the device's user or managed services with access to the device. The objective of remote wiping is to securely delete user data stored in the mobile device whether it is stored in the manufacturer's delivered applications or third-party apps installed and enabled by the device user.

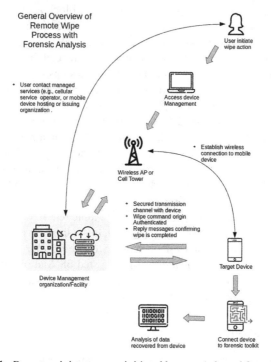

Fig. 1. Remote wiping process initiated by user (adapted from [34]).

Figure 1 illustrates the general request process for remote wiping of mobile devices. The user can access management utilities (typically provided by the organization managing the cellular service, or hosting the device such as the case of organizations that issue mobile devices to employees, or third-party apps) through another device. The user could select predefined options for the wiping functions such as low-level formatting, factory reset, data deletion, removal of header only or full clearing of dedicated storage areas in the device including unallocated areas. Alternatively, the user can contact the device management organization/facility directly to initiate the wiping process. Once a secured connection is established between the device and the management organization or facility the wipe commands are authenticated between the device and the device management organization/facility [27, 34]. Reply messages confirming the completion of phases of the wiping process or summary message indicating the full completion of the process are transmitted to the device management organization/facility. These messages would be sent back to the user in case (s)he is the origination point and logged-in at the device management organization.

An example of a manufacturer wiping process is the patented process of Apple [35], which starts with accessing the remote management account facility. In the process, it is assumed that the commands can be initiated from devices connected to a network, for example a web service. The web service accessing the remote account functions is able to generate and transmit command messages. Additionally, it is able to receive transmitted messages from the remote devices to acknowledge the completion or failure of the original command transmitted. The centralized device management system will display the mobile devices available to the user for the wiping functions. Once a device selection is made, the user can select the commands that will execute a specific wiping command. A remote command message is generated that will instruct the remote device to execute the wiping function. It should be noted that the remote command is generated and transfer to a server that will publish it thru the available network and reach the device selected. Once the wiping command is executed in the remote device, a message is generated and transmitted back to the management account facility via the available network and routing server to the web service that originated the initial command. The message will carry the completion status of the wiping process (success or failure). Once complete, the user is able to select other remote commands for the same device or select a different device and start the same process again.

In addition to manufacturer's wiping applications, mobile users can install third party applications in their mobile devices to execute wiping commands [28]. For example, the process patented by Air Watch LLC [36] establishes connection with the mobile device and start a two-command process: backup data from the mobile device and issue a wipe command. Through a centralized management facility, that can be accessed by a web service, the user can select to back up the data from the remote device and wipe it, back up the data from the remote device, or just wipe the data without backing it up. Once the user has made a command selection, based on the network availability, the command is issued and routed to a server for publishing. If the user selects the backup and wiping functions, a separate message is generated for each command. In this scenario, the backup command is executed first to ensure that the data is transmitted from the remote device and backed up by the centralized management facility. Once the backup confirmation is received; then, the second command to wipe the data is generated and transmitted to the remote device. Finally, once the data has been wiped out, the remote device generate and transmit a message confirming that the data wiping has been completed [27].

3.2 Effectiveness of Remote Wiping Apps

In the last two patented processes reviewed, on remote data wipe of devices, the user relies on messages generated and transmitted by the remote device to verify that data wiping took place [37]. b However, detailed information on the deletion method is not readily available from the messages transmitted from the remote device. It is not speci- fied whether the wiping process performed a physical or logical deletion of the user data, and whether traces of user data are left behind. Therefore, to verify the wiping process was effective and to identify user data that might have been left behind on the device, forensic toolkits are required to perform in depth analysis. Previous research conducted have determined that in addition to user data, residual network and cloud storage appli- cation data can still be found and in devices that were remotely wiped. Furthermore, there could be significant differences among devices and whether the remote wipe was executed using a manufacture's wiping process or a third-party application [26]. Other considerations in the effectiveness of remote wiping include security of the transmission of command messages generated to wipe information in remote devices, and the receiving messages confirming completion of the wiping command. Additionally, the handling of interrupted messages and capabilities to regenerate, re-transmit command messages in case of network disruptions or power failures from the mobile device. Similarly, capabilities from the mobile device to report on incomplete wiping command executed [34].

Evaluating the effectiveness remote wiping by using forensic toolkits can help law enforcement resources manage time used in research when investigating a crime involving mobile devices. For example, knowing that manufacturer's-based wiping from a particular device might have different results from third party applications and what traces of user data is left behind could help law enforcement identify important forensic evidence based on device, wiping process or forensic toolkit utilized.

Research on the effectiveness of data recovery after wiping commands are executed on remote devices is limited. Current research has relied on the availability of forensic toolkits with limited functionality or non-commercial licenses, and older device releases used for research. Forensic tools functionality relies on software, hardware tools, or a combined software/hardware approaches. We observe that most research has been conducted using the software approach only. Available research shows a similar methodology with the following steps when evaluating results from different remote wiping processes utilized: Identify forensic toolkit to be utilized; backup user application data from the devices to be used for testing; identify the categories of data available on the device and the number of files associated with each category; identify the wiping process to be utilized (manufacturer or third party); select and execute wiping commands; record and evaluate results; using forensic toolkit to recover, identify and categorize user data left behind after wiping process; and compare the number of files before and after executing remote wiping for each category identified [7, 10, 23].

4   Proposed Evaluation and Methodology

Remote wiping capabilities are commonly available from the mobile device manufacturer or through third-party apps that can be enabled by the device's user or managed services with access to the device. The objective of remote wiping is to securely delete user data stored in the mobile device whether it is stored in the manufacturer's delivered applications or third-party apps installed and enabled by the device user.

Forensic data recovery/retrieval starts with two main focal points, namely: the "Specialized Tool(s)" used for data recovery, and the "Deletion Process" used to delete or wipe the data.

Additional points to consider for the effectiveness of data recovery relies on an understanding of the following: (1) What type of data can be recovered?; (2) Where the data is stored (e.g. location the data is stored on a device, or if not on the local device where is the physical location of the data, such as network or cloud based)?; (3) What is the format of the data stored as (e.g., text, media, standard data exchanging formats such as Extensible Markup Language (XML), Data Base (DB), and JavaScript Object Notation (JSON))?; and (4) Whether files are encrypted?.

Our proposed research focuses on data that can be recovered after a remote delete/wipe process has completed on a mobile device. The scenario for all mobile devices used in our research require the following: (1) Smartphone(s) for testing data recovery; (2) Data objects to attempt recovery of on the smartphone(s): email, images, different application data, calendar objects, and text messages; (3) Network availability: Wi-Fi or Cellular; (4) A network-based account to allow for backing up the smartphone(s); (5) Network-based ability to initiate/execute the remote delete/wipe; (6) Forensic tool(s) to recover data; and (7) Forensic reports to allow for data analysis.

The equipment used include three smartphones, without sim cards or external SD cards: Android – Samsung S5, Model # SAMSUNG-SM-G900A, running OS version 6.0.1 (hereafter referred to as Samsung G900 or as G900), Android – Samsung S5 Active, Model # SAMSUNG-SM-G870A, running OS version 6.0.1 (hereafter referred to as Samsung G870 or as G870), and Apple- iPhone 6S, Model # MN1K2, running iOS version 13.2.2 (hereafter referred to as iPhone 6S). All three smartphones had a Wi-Fi access account added to allow for network/Internet access. For both G900 and G870, a Google account was created and added to allow for backup and remote wipe ability. For the iPhone 6S, an Apple ID and iTunes account was created to allow for backup and remote wipe capability.

Data installed included multiple instances of the following: Four (4) contacts, two (2) emails, three (3) SMS texts, four (4) pictures, four (4) documents, 506 calendar events, three (3) audio files, one (1) video, four (4) random web pages were opened and two (2) pictures from those web pages were downloaded. We also installed the following applications: Shreddit – Data Eraser by PalmTronix, and Secure Wipe by Pinellas CodeWorks.

We also used Mobile Phone Examiner Plus (MPE+) from Accessdata, and MOBILedit from Compelson labs, on computers running Windows 10 OS. The evaluation methodology will follow the forensics investigation model of [34], which is also described below.

Preservation: Smartphones will be selected for research, data baseline will be established, and a data backup will be performed. Baselining will consist of sanitizing/removing any personally identifiable information (PII) currently on the phone and then installing, or adding, selected data and apps to each phone. Backup will be performed using a manufacturer online account to store a device-initiated backup. There will also be a logical copy of the baseline imaged device, stored on a laptop; this is only a failsafe in case the online backup fails.

Acquisition: Forensic tool(s) will be selected that allow for mobile phone examination. The tool will be used to extract the data from the smartphones at different acquisition points. Data acquisition reports, if not provided by the forensic tools, will be created after each of the different analysis tests. There are four proposed different data acquisition points: After initial baseline of the device; After a factory reset is performed; After a restore of the device to baseline; After a remote delete/wipe is performed. Prior to performing the factory reset, a locally installed data wiping app will be used to remove any prior residual deleted data or data fragments remaining after baselining the device. Data acquisition tests will be used to validate the effectiveness of the app. This is to ensure the tests focus on residual data of freshly deleted items.

Examination Analysis: All of the acquisition reports will be created in the same manner as to allow for data comparison on two levels. The first comparison will of the all data recovery reports for each individual device to see how what data could be recovered. The second comparison will be to look for differences in the data recovery ability of the three different devices.

Reporting: Explanation and summary of forensic reports findings are included and written in this paper with a conclusion of our findings and identified areas for further research.

5 Case Study

5.1 Data Installation and Preservation

The smartphones, selected for this research, were found to still contain the previous user's data; not wiped/reset. Each phone was examined and PII that was discovered was deleted. This included all deleting previous accounts, deleting internet history, and browser form filling data. Online accounts were created for the phones to allow for backup, restore, and remote delete/wipe ability. The reason for using new accounts were to avoid possible data spillage or cross deletion with our personal phones. Both Android phones, G870 and G900, were able to use a single Google account. An Apple account was created for the iPhone 6S.

The selection of Apple for the iPhone and Google for the Androids was to create a condition that the majority of users would find themselves in if needing to remotely wipe their devices. Third-party apps were available but would require additional steps such as downloading, installing, and configuring an account. The majority of third-party apps that allow remote wiping required a cost. The additional data selected was copied onto the device. The online accounts were used to update all installed apps and to download the two third-party local data erasing apps: Shreddit-Data Eraser and Secure Wipe. These were selected due to high recommendations in different electronic review sites and high ratings on the Google Play Store.

The two wiping apps will be used prior to performing the factory reset test. Their purpose is to remove any of the previously deleted data, or residual data fragments, remaining after baselining the device. The old deleted data would not be backed up to the online account or copied to a folder on the laptop being used, unless a physical image could be obtained. These unallocated data fragments may cause variances in the expected data acquisitions. A logical copy of the files and folders on the phone were copied to folder on a laptop as an emergency backup in the event of a crash.

These steps were to ensure and establish repeatable baseline images allowing for initial data consistency prior to the different analysis tests, or recovery in the event of data corruption due interrupted forensic scans or device malfunctions. Once all data and apps were installed and updated, an online backup was initiated through the phones setting options. Once completed, the Wi-Fi was disabled to prevent the data from changing. The phone was now ready for the acquisition phase.

5.2 Data Acquisition

This section will describe how the data acquisitions were performed. The first step after baselining the device, was to create a baseline data acquisition report with the use the forensic tools. Several varying steps were required based on the type of phone analysed, Android vs. Apple, and different issues occurred while using the different forensic tools. Both of the selected forensic tools were full versions and required a paid licence for use. They were installed in UTSA's computer lab.

After preparing the phones for examination, the forensic software tool will be started and the smartphone plugged into the computer or laptop running the software. If the software tool or operating system (OS) does not recognize the phone, a set of phone drivers or speciality software may need to be downloaded and installed. It could also mean additional steps with the phone is needed to be recognized.

Documentation from both tools showed that Android phones need to be placed in the debugging mode for them to work. Debug mode is not turned on by default due to security issues. MPE+ recommends using a third-party tool to root the phone if unable to turn on debugging mode. MOBILedit does have some options available to access a locked phone if access to the phone's system menu was not available. The software documentation discussed that using these options will or may overwrite the internal software; based on the method used to access the phone. To prevent damage to the phones, and since we had access to the phones interface, we selected the manual way of putting the phones in to debug mode. For this reason, the phones examined were not rooted, and the screens were unlocked, during the whole data acquisition process.

To place the phones in debug mode, the hidden Developer Option button must be unlocked. First, locate the Build Number in Settings, most likely in the About options. Tap on the Build Number multiple times, most phones take seven times, then go back into Settings to find the Developer Option button visible. In there, select debug mode, select stay awake while charging, and deselect verify apps via USB.

The first data recovery tool attempted was MPE+. Due to licensing, the software could only be installed on select computers in the computer lab and had to be run with administrator privileges. Multiple attempts were made to use this tool but none were successful. None of the phones were identified by the software, manual selection of the phones still did not allow the software to recognize the phones. Going through the different screen pages displayed, it was obvious that the Androids were being seen but only as a device in Media Transfer Protocol (MTP) mode. The phone was recognized in Windows. MTP mode does not allow for data recovery or viewing of all the internal files. The iPhone was not recognized by MPE+ at all. Due to the multiple issues only the MOBILedit software was used for data extraction in this research.

Compelson Labs had issued our forensic class a limited number of MOBILedit full access licences, that would expire after 60 days. This allowed MOBILedit to be loaded on two personal laptops, eliminating the administrative mode issues. MOBILedit is a specialized forensic tool for smartphones. The installation was straight forward with an easy to use interface. The iPhone was recognized right away by the software as an iPhone, and displayed a menu to allow the user to select which version the iPhone was; we used the 6S version for all tests. The Android devices did require that the debug mode be enabled for the software to effectively work. MOBILedit has additional options to connect to the phones by Bluetooth or Wi-Fi; these connection methods were not used during this research. The software allows for different data recovery configurations (such as full, deleted only, user specified and others) and it has the ability to create different reports or data backups based on the selections made.

There are four (4) different data acquisition points required for the test data to be relevant. The first is after the initial baseline of the device is created. This data acquisition test is needed to create a data acquisition baseline. The results can be used to validate if the backup restore process worked, and helps identify how much data is restored from the backup; 100% or less. The second acquisition point is after a factory reset is performed. This data acquisition test is needed to identify if any previous data or user PII can be recovered, and establishes a data acquisition reset baseline. The test results allow for a comparison of the factory reset option vs. a remote reset option. The third acquisition point is after the device is restored from the back up to the baseline. The fourth acquisition point is after the remote delete/wipe is performed.

There were six additional tests with the Android phones, and four additional tests with the iPhone. All proposed tests are as follows: (1) Full content - Baseline (without debug mode enabled) (Android only); (2) Full content – Baseline; (3) Deleted data only – Baseline; (4) Deleted data only – After running Shreddit with default settings; (5) Deleted data only – After running Secure Wipe with default settings; (6) Full content – After Factory Reset (without debug mode enabled and without a user account); (7) Full content – After Factory Reset (without a user account); (8) Deleted data only – After Factory Reset (without a user account) (Android Only); (9) Full content – After phone restored from backup; and (10) Full content – After Remote Delete/Wipe (without a user account) (with debug mode enabled).

Android Devices

The Samsung G870 was selected as the first device for data acquisition. The following is the data, steps, and findings for the Samsung G870 only. The Samsung G900 results were very similar and the differences will be explained at the end of this section.

Since the Android devices required the extra step of turning on the debug mode, the first data acquisition test with MOBILedit was performed with the phone in the same configuration as a normal user; without the debug mode option. The phone was recognized but only as an MTP device, and little data was discovered during the test; only 314 files. The debug mode was enabled and the phone was properly recognized. MOBILedit did request an extra step to allow it to install its software on the phone. As it installed, it requested access to five areas: device location, contacts, calendar, photos/media/files, and SMS messages. A full content data acquisition of the baseline with the debug enabled was conducted. Comparing this report against the no-debug report of baseline showed a significant increase in data recovered; 3,687 files/data. See Table 1 for a comparison of the data from the summary reports.

The next three data acquisitions were for deleted data only. Once the baseline data acquisition was recorded, the next step was to try and wipe the deleted items found using Shreddit. This application is used directly on the phone to delete unallocated data on smartphones. It has the ability to perform multiple passes, but was run with the default setting selected. Once started, Shreddit required access to the smartphones' photos, media, and files. After it finished, the Android device was restarted and a data acquisition test was performed. MOBILedit found the same deleted items as were found in the full report. There was no change, it was as if Shreddit was ever run.

This same process was performed using the Secure Wipe app. Once again, the same previously identified deleted data was discovered. It was only after a factory reset was performed that the deleted data was no longer found. The failure to delete the unallocated data may be due to the way NAND memory cells work. Deletion only happens when all data in the cell is marked for deletion and deletion is done on the cell level, not the file or bit level. If any data is still relevant in a cell, the unallocated data in that cell will not be wiped. All three deleted data only acquisitions are found to be redundant since the deleted data is already displayed in the full report. Table 2 shows an extract of deleted data found during five consecutive data acquisitions.

Table 1. Comparison of the data from the MOBILedit summary reports

FileSystems	No Debug	Baseline	Factory Reset
Internal Filesystem	314 files	17 files	17 files
External Filesystem		419 files	17 files
Application System		2645 files	1447 files
Extra Filesystem		275 files	222 files
Misc Filesystem	0 file	1 file	0 file
System Logs		91 files	90 files
Bluetooth Pairings		0	0
Contact Analysis		0	0
Cookies		169	0
Loactions			
GPS Locations	0	0	1
Notifications		2	4
Passwords			
Password from Chrome (Saved Passwords)		1	
Passwords SAMSUNG-SM-G870A (Wi-Fi)		1	
Screen Unlocking History		3	7
User Dictionary		0	0
Wi-Fi-Networks		2	1
Web			
Web Browsing History		56	0
Web Search History		5	0
Bookmarks		0	0

Table 2. Extract of deleted data found during five consecutive data acquisitions

Download Manager	Baseline-Full	Delete Only	Shreddit	Secure Wipe	Factory Reset
Downloaded Files	10 (8 deleted)	(8 deleted)	(8 deleted)	(8 deleted)	
Account Kaa80@gmail.com					
Contacts	68 (67 deleted)	(67 deleted)	(67 deleted)	(67 deleted)	
Circles	27 (25 deleted)	(25 deleted)	(25 deleted)	(25 deleted)	

The factory reset was carried out natively within the phone setting options, with the option to erase all the data on the phone selected. After the factory reset was complete a data acquisition test was performed. Two data acquisition were performed without any user account being entered: one data acquisition with no-debug, another with debug enabled. The Google account was installed and a backup sync was requested from the phone's settings. All apps were updated and the two data delete/wipe apps were installed. When complete the wireless connection was turned off and full content data acquisition was performed. This was done to validate the restore function worked, and to allow comparison with the baseline on how much data does not get restored. The last step was to perform a remote deletion of the phone. The wireless connect function of the phone was turned back on. Using the laptop, the user Google account was accessed. The phones for this account were found in the managing your account section, in the security option. By selecting the G870 phone, and then the find my phone option, a window will appear which allows the user different options to include remotely erasing the phone's data called "Consider erasing your device".

If the Android device was not connected to a Wi-Fi or cellular network at the time the remote wipe was requested, the reset request will wait and the next time the device is connected the process will be carried out. After the phone finishes restarting, a data acquisition test was performed. This data acquisition was performed without any user account being entered, and with debug enabled. The Samsung G900 was then selected and put through the same steps and tests that the G870 was put through. There were a few minor differences in how some of the apps were handled in the report, and how much data was retrieved after the resets. The most significant finding was that the Google account for this phone, did not provide an option to remotely delete the data on the phone. The process to find the phone on the web page was the same but the final popup window displayed different options.

In order to facilitate a remote delete/wipe of the phone, a Samsung account had to be created. Through the Samsung website the remote delete option was available. It performed similar to the Google account remote wipe. Figure 2 depicts the process flow used for the Android smartphones, to prepare the devices, data acquisitions, factory reset, and remote wiping.

Apple Device

The iPhone 6S was recognized right away by MOBIL edit as an iPhone as it was plugged in. The difference in how MOBILedit recognized the phone. With the Androids,

MOBILedit recognized the make and version right away, with the iPhone the version of iPhone had to be selected from a provided list. The same action and steps taken with the Androids, were performed with the iPhone except: debug enabling was not required and the two downloaded delete/wipe apps were not used. A similar delete/wipe app was not found in the iTunes store. This reduced the number of data acquisitions from ten (10) to four (4).

The final step of remote delete/wipe was performed slightly different than the Androids. With the iPhone 6S this task was performed through the iCloud website. Once the website was accessed, using the Apple account, the proper iPhone was selected. The website will attempt to locate the iPhone and the option to erase all content and settings in the iPhone data accessible. Once the phone finishes resetting a full data acquisition is performed. Figure 3 depicts the process flow followed with the iPhone to prepare the device and the scanning actions followed by executing the remote wiping functions.

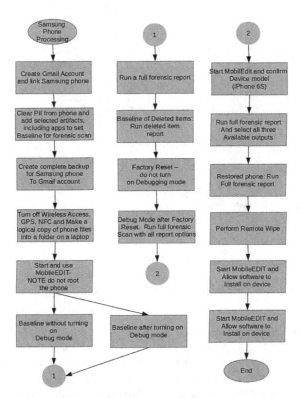

Fig. 2. Samsung devices – Processing and forensic scan process flow

6   Discussion

Data collected, during the data acquisitions tasks, were performed requesting all three report formats and all four exports available, from the MOBILedit forensic software package used. The purpose was to have more options with how to analyse the collected data. The easiest report format to collect the data from was the pdf reports. Copies of the first three sections of each report (Screenshots of Report Settings, Summary, and Deleted Data) were extracted. The final section, Data Extraction Log, was also extracted.

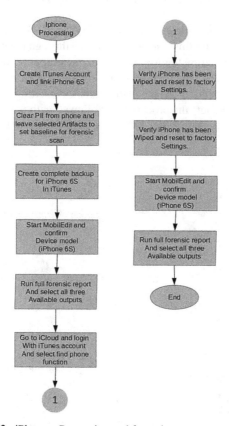

Fig. 3. iPhone – Processing and forensic scan process flow

The extracted data presented in each of the baseline's data report Summary section, was used to create an Excel spreadsheet for that specific phone. The data displayed in the Summary section from each of the 10 Android tests, 4 Apple tests, was transferred to a corresponding line in that phone's spreadsheet. The data from each of the Data Extraction Log sections of the reports, was similarly transferred to a spreadsheet for that phone.

Each column of the spreadsheets represented the data from one of the 10 acquisition tests, discussed earlier in this report. From here it was easily seen that the four deleted data only reports were not needed. The data displayed in the "deleted data only" reports is already listed in the full content reports and the downloaded wiping apps were unsuccessful; these four columns were hidden. The next redundant report found was comparing the two data acquisitions where the debug mode was not enabled. Since these two reports were identical, the no debug report after the factory reset column was hidden. The remaining columns, five (5) for the Android phones and four (4) for the Apple phone, were used for evaluating the data acquired. The extra column for the Android phones is the data from first acquisition test (no-debug), since this shows a valid contrast to the other reports. Similarly, the Data Extraction Log section spreadsheets were adjusted to match the four identical column identifiers for both phones; the no-debug report was not used when analysing the data from this section.

The bulk of the MOBILedit data acquisition report is detailed breakouts for each application and the system files. Most have a link to open the corresponding data/file for a more detailed inspection. These detailed data sections were reviewed to examine if any relevant, or PII, data remained and was captured in the data acquisition but hidden from easy visibility.

The baseline amount of data for each phone was recorded as: G870 = 4,207 (Table 3); G900 = 3,338 (Table 4); and the iPhone 6S = 6,188 (Table 5). It is understandable why the iPhone differed from the Androids, but both Androids should have been closer. This information shows that even a slight change to the phone (a regular S5 to a S5 Active) can create a significant data change. This was further demonstrated with examination of how much data extraction change there was, after each acquisition event, against the baseline data for each of the phones.

The percent of data change against the baseline was examined next. Comparing of the baseline data numbers to the amount of data recovered following the factory reset showed 41–84% reduction of data. Comparison of baseline data to the amount of data found after a restore action showed a 10–30% reduction in data. Comparison of the amount of data found after the factory reset to the amount of data found after the remote wipe showed less than a .2% data reduction change for each phone: G870 = .1% loss, or 2 data objects; G900 = .2%, or 4 data objects; iPhone 6S 0% with no data reduction (See Table 6).

The G870 showed the highest reduction in recoverable SQL, XML, and JSON data following the remote wipe, with 74% reduction of SQL data, 36% reduction of XML data, and 100% reduction of JSON data. The iPhone showed the lowest reduction percentage for these three data types with 64% reduction of SQL data, 19% reduction of XML data, and 94% reduction of JSON data.

The iPhone also had the highest data restore percentage rate with only 10% loss of all data after the restore operation, −1% loss for SQL, 1% loss for XML, and 0% loss of JSON. Unsure why there was a slight SQL increase; this should be examined further in a later research project. The lower part of the Summery section of the G870 data reports, show similar reduction percentages with the recovered filesystems data (See Table 7).

The data acquired after both the factory reset and the remote reset, showed all previously deleted data was sanitized and no longer recoverable with the software. Additionally, examination of the detailed section and the two summaries (Summary and Data Extraction sections) for these two acquisition tasks, did not reveal any of the users PII or any of the user relevant data that was installed on the phones to achieve a baseline.

Table 3. Data extraction numbers for G870

G870	Base	Factory Reset	Restored	Remote Delete
Phone Books	4	1	4	1
Messages	1	1	2	1
Events	506	0	297	0
Phone call	0	0	0	0
Archive Files	15	1	6	1
Documents	13	3	3	3
Certificates	1	1	1	1
Audio	3	1		1
Image	500	402	407	402
JSON	90	XXX	13	XXX
Sqlite	122	33	89	32
Video	1	0	0	0
XML	683	439	603	437
Other Files	1	1	1	1
All Other files	1937	822	1175	823
Applications	330	321	326	321
Totals	4207	2026	2927	2024

The downloaded third-party apps, for wiping the unallocated data space were, ineffective on the phones. They were chosen as highly recommended by review sites and had a high user feedback rating. They were used with the default settings, which only completes one wipe pass, but this should have at least reduced the number of recoverable deleted items.

The failure of the third-party wiping apps, might be discovered examining the amount of time they spent performing their tasks. The deletion down time with the two third-party apps was just about 10 s each. The deletion down time for the factory reset and remote reset was 2–5 min each. Based on the results it appears the two events (factory reset and remote reset) performed a wipe similar in results to a low-level format of a hard drive. Justification for this line of thinking is that the previously identified deleted data was no longer seen in the acquisition reports after these two tasks.

It is unsure what the two third-party wiping apps did. There are two possibilities for their failure, the structure of the NAND cells prevents completing a secure wipe of all unallocated data in an active cell. The other possibility could be that the algorithms in MOBILedit allows for greater data recoverability.

Table 4. Data extraction numbers for G900

G900	Base	Factory Reset	Restored	Remote Delete
Phone Books	4	1	4	1
Messages	0	0	0	0
Events	506	0	298	0
Phone call	0	0	0	0
Archive Files	7	1	11	1
Documents	4	3	3	3
Certificates	1	1	1	0
Audio	3	1	3	1
Image	405	397	407	397
JSON	85	XXX	67	XXX
Sqlite	92	28	78	27
Video	0	0	0	0
XML	596	425	546	423
Other Files	1	1	1	1
All Other files	1312	792	1228	792
Applications	322	316	326	316
Totals	3338	1966	2973	1962

Table 5. Data extraction numbers for iPhone 6S

iPhone 6S	Base	Factory Reset	Restored	Remote Delete
Archive Files	2	XXX	1	XXX
Documents	7	1	7	1
Image Files	XXX	104	XXX	104
Auddio	404	0	404	0
Extracted	2491	267	2098	267
JSON	49	3	49	3
plist	967	382	1023	382
sqlite	156	56	158	56
Realm databases	2	1	2	1
Video	186	0	88	0
XML	118	96	117	96
Binary coockies	33	XXX	33	XXX
Other files	1656	0	1469	0
Applications	117	96	116	96
Totals	6188	1006	5565	1006

Table 6. Percentage of data change to the baseline, for each phone

Baseline Total Change	G870	G900	iPhone S6
% Change after FR	52%	41%	84%
% Change after restore	30%	11%	10%
% Change after remote	52%	41%	84%
% Difference between base and restore events	41%	41%	N/A
% Difference between base and restore SQL	27%	15%	-1%
% Difference between base and restore XML	12%	8%	1%
% Difference between base and restore JSON	86%	21%	0%
% Difference between base and remote SQL	74%	71%	64%
% Difference between base and remote XML	36%	29%	19%
% Difference between base and remote JSON	N/A	N/A	94%
Count difference between base and restore	1280	365	623
Count difference between FR and remote	2	4	0

Table 7. G870 spreadsheet data

Filesystems	No-Debug	Baseline	Factory Reset	Recovery	Remote Delete
Internal Filesytem	314 files	17 files	17 files	17 files	17 files
External Filesystem		419 files	17 files		17 files
Applications Filesystem		2645 files	1447 files	2010 files	1445 files
Extra Filesystem		275 files	222 files	271 files	222 files
Misc Filesystem	0 file	1 file	0 file	1 file	0 file
System Logs		91 files	90 files	91 files	90 files

7   Conclusion

Previous studies on recovering data from smartphones, mostly focused on extracting PII and relevant user data after executing wiping commands from the devices themselves by using OS available functions or third-party apps. There were multiple studies conducted using Android phones, but almost all of them were version 5.0 or earlier; very few studies were found using iPhones and those found used iOS 4.0 and earlier. There were a few studies found that addressed data recovery after a factory reset, but they were also conducted with the early version of smartphones just addressed. Their tests also showed that some of the smartphones, Apple iOS prior to version 4.0 and Android OS prior to version 7.0, had faulty factory reset ability, allowing varying amounts of data to be recovered; the amount of data varied with different models. Research showed that Android OS version 5.0 and Apple iOS version 4.0 allowed for encrypting the device's data, but encryption was not turned on by default until 2014. The smartphones displayed great factory reset ability, although this does not address the problem of deleting data in the event of a lost or stolen phone. It is acknowledged that encrypted data is not useful without the key, so in this instance the data is considered sanitized.

The focus of this study was to see the effectiveness of a remote delete/wipe, and if any relevant or PII data remains on a smartphone after the wipe. Based on the results found, from the different data acquisition attempts, it appears that the remote wipe and factory resets on these smartphone devices are effective in sanitizing PII data and other user data. However, the findings could also be due to the fact that the data acquisition methods chosen had limited visibility into the devices used. Hence, future research should include the use of other mobile forensic software. It was also noticed that data backup/sync functions do not completely restore a phone to its previous state, and may be a good basis for another research project in the future as to why.

Continued research should be performed using a larger variety of devices from different manufacturers and running different operating systems, to test if the effectiveness of the remote wiping commands might vary. Additional research should be done to examine the contents of the XML, SQL, and JSON files. The data size suggests minimal data is present; many are listed less than 1kb. Due to time and tool restraints, this was not performed during this research project.

Encryption on by default allows for a quick recovery following a factory or remote reset since only the encryption token needs to be wiped. Additional research should be conducted on trying to recover the deleted encryption tokens. This will allow law enforcement access to encrypted data. Future tests should review the ability to access locked phones of newer makes and models without firmware, software, or hardware damage to the phones.

Acknowledgement. We would like to express our gratitude to Compelson Labs for the support and making MobilEdit available to our research. We would also like to acknowledge the contributions of Andrew Mendoza in the research of background and related work, and testing.

References

1. Jones, B.H., Chin, A.: On the efficacy of smartphone security: a critical analysis of modifications in business students' practices over time. Int. J. Inf. Manag. **35**(5), 561–571 (2015). https://doi.org/10.1016/j.ijinfomgt.2015.06.003. Accessed 17 Oct 2019
2. Allam, S., Flowerday, S., Flowerday, E.: Smartphone information security awareness: a victim of operational pressures. Comput. Secur. **42**, 56–65 (2014). https://doi.org/10.1016/j.cose.2014.01.005. Accessed 17 Oct 2019
3. Cardwell, G.: Residual Network Data Structures in Android Devices, Masters, Naval Postgraduate School (2011)
4. Yao, M., Chuang, M., Hsu, C.: The kano model analysis of features for mobile security applications. Comput. Secur. **78**, 336–346 (2018). https://doi.org/10.1016/j.cose.2018.07.008. Accessed 17 Oct 2019
5. Blancco Technology Group: Analysis of Data Remanence After Factory Reset, and Sophisticated Attacks on Memory Chips. Blancco Technology Group (2019)
6. Bransfield-Garth, S.: Mobile phone calls as a business risk. Network Secur. **2010**(9), 4–11 (2010). https://doi.org/10.1016/s1353-4858(10)70114-8. Accessed 17 Oct 2019
7. Korenis, P., Billick, S.: Forensic Implications: adolescent sexting and cyberbullying. Psychiatric Quart. **85**(1), 97–101 (2013). https://doi.org/10.1007/s11126-013-9277-z. Accessed 17 Oct 2019
8. Ehatisham-ul-Haq, M., Azam, M., Naeem, U., Rèhman, S., Khalid, A.: Identifying smartphone users based on their activity patterns via mobile sensing. Procedia Comput. Sci. **113**, 202–209 (2017). https://doi.org/10.1016/j.procs.2017.08.349. Accessed 17 Oct 2019
9. Narayanan, S.V.: Myths and fallacies of "Personally Identifiable Information". Commun. ACM **53**(6), 24 (2010). https://doi.org/10.1145/1743546.1743558. Accessed 17 Oct 2019
10. Wilbanks, L.: The impact of personally identifiable information. IT Professional **9**(4), 62–64 (2007). https://doi.org/10.1109/mitp.2007.77. Accessed 17 Oct 2019
11. Gámez-Guadix, M., Mateos-Pérez, E.: Longitudinal and reciprocal relationships between sexting, online sexual solicitations, and cyberbullying among minors. Comput. Hum. Behav. **94**, 70–76 (2019). https://doi.org/10.1016/j.chb.2019.01.004.. Accessed 17 Oct 2019
12. Barker, Cosmo Survey: 9 out of 10 Millennial Women Take Naked Photos. Cosmopolitan (2014). https://www.cosmopolitan.com/sex-love/advice/a30675/ninety-percent-millennial-women-take-nude-photos-cosmo-survey/. Accessed 17 Oct 2019
13. Milne, G., Pettinico, G., Hajjat, F., Markos, E.: Information sensitivity typology: mapping the degree and type of risk consumers perceive in personal data sharing. J. Consumer Affairs **51**(1), 133–161 (2016). https://doi.org/10.1111/joca.12111. Accessed 17 Oct 2019
14. Tankard, C.: The security issues of the Internet of Things. Comput. Fraud Secur. **201**(9), 11–14 (2015) https://doi.org/10.1016/s1361-3723(15)30084-1. Accessed 17 Oct 2019
15. Yang, L., Wei, T., Zhang, F., Ma, J.: SADUS: secure data deletion in user space for mobile devices. Comput. Secur. **77**, 612–626 (2018). https://doi.org/10.1016/j.cose.2018.05.013.Accessed 17 Oct 2019

16. Reardon, J., Basin, D., Capkun, S.: SoK: secure data deletion. In: 2013 IEEE Symposium on Security and Privacy (2013). https://doi.org/10.1109/sp.2013.28. Accessed 17 Oct 2019
17. Di Leom, M.: Remote Wiping in Android. University of South Australia, Masters (2015)
18. Kissel, R., Regenscheid, A., Scholl, M., Stine, K.: Guidelines for Media Sanitization (2014). https://doi.org/10.6028/nist.sp.800-88r1. Accessed 17 Oct 2019
19. Simon, L., Anderson, R.: Security Analysis of Android Factory Resets. University of Cambridge (2015)
20. Patel, N.: Utilisation of Flash Storage Memory, no. 2018 (2018). https://doi.org/10.13140/RG.2.2.35672.34565.. Accessed 17 Oct 2019
21. Brown, Almost ALL iPhones Are Encrypted, Almost ALL Android Smartphones Are NOT, Express.co.uk (2019). https://www.express.co.uk/life-style/science-technology/653099/iPhone-iOS-Encryption-Android-OS-Google-Smartphone. Accessed 17 Oct 2019
22. Miller, J.: Google and Apple to Introduce Default Encryption, BBC News (2014). https://www.bbc.com/news/technology-29276955. Accessed 17 Oct 2019
23. Gómez-Miralles, L., Arnedo-Moreno, J.: Hardening iOS devices against remote forensic investigation. Security and Resilience in Intelligent Data-Centric Systems and Communication Networks, pp. 261–283 (2018). https://doi.org/10.1016/b978-0-12-811373-8.00012-4. Accessed 17 Oct 2019
24. Kingsley-Hughes, Here's How to Securely Wipe Your Android Smartphone for Resale, ZDNet (2019). https://www.zdnet.com/article/heres-how-to-securely-wipe-your-android-smartphone-for-resale/. Accessed 17 Oct 2019
25. Altuwaijri, H., Ghouzali, S.: Android data storage security: a review. J. King Saud University – Comput. Inf. Sci. (2018). https://doi.org/10.1016/j.jksuci.2018.07.004. Accessed 17 Oct 2019
26. Meckley, T.: An Empirical Comparison of Smartphone Factory-Resets to Remote Deletion Applications. University of South Alabama, Masters (2019)
27. UZ, The Effectiveness of Remote Wipe as a Valid Defense for Enterprises Implementing a BYOD Policy, Masters, University of Ottawa (2019)
28. Pollitt, M., Shenoi, S. (eds.): DigitalForensics 2005. ITIFIP, vol. 194. Springer, Boston (2005). https://doi.org/10.1007/0-387-31163-7
29. Barmpatsalou, K., Cruz, T., Monteiro, E., Simoes, P.: Current and future trends in mobile device forensics. ACM Comput. Surv. 51(3), 1–31 (2018). https://doi.org/10.1145/3177847. Accessed 17 Oct 2019
30. Thomas, D.: How to delete files on android so they can't ever be recovered. Gadget Hacks (2016). https://android.gadgethacks.com/how-to/delete-files-android-so-they-cant-ever-be-recovered-0169550/. Accessed 17 Oct 2019
31. Bilić, D.: How to delete your smartphone data securely before selling your device. WeLiveSecurity (2016). https://www.welivesecurity.com/2016/06/03/how-do-you-delete-your-data-securely-before-selling-your-cell-phone/. Accessed 17 Oct 2019
32. Glisson, W., Storer, T., Blyth, A., Grispos, G., Campbell, M.: In-the-wild residual data research and privacy. J. Digital Forens. Secur. Law 11(1) (2016). https://doi.org/10.15394/jdfsl.2016.1371
33. Yu, X., Wang, Z., Sun, K., Zhu, W., Gao, N., Jing, J.: Remotely wiping sensitive data on stolen smartphones. In: Proceedings of the 9th ACM Symposium on Information, Computer and Communications Security - ASIA CCS 2014, no. 2014, pp. 537–542 (2014). https://doi.org/10.1145/2590296.2590318.. Accessed 17 Oct 2019
34. Di Leom, M., Choo, K., Hunt, R.: Remote wiping and secure deletion on mobile devices: a review. J. Foren. Sci. 61(6), 1473–1492 (2016). https://doi.org/10.1111/1556-4029.13203. Accessed 17 Oct 2019
35. Apple Inc. Remotely Locating and Commanding a Mobile Device, US 2018/0337974 A1 (2018)

36. AirWatch LLC, Device Back and Wipe, US 2019 / 0073271 A1 (2019)
37. Hoffman, Why Deleted Files Can Be Recovered, and How You Can Prevent It. How-To Geek (2019). https://www.howtogeek.com/125521/htg-explains-why-deleted-files-can-be-recovered-and-how-you-can-prevent-it/. Accessed 17 Oct 2019

A Self-organized Adaptation of Spreading Factor for LoRa Radio Layer Based on Experimental Study

Victor Casas[1], Mehdi Harounabadi[2(✉)], and Andreas Mitschele-Thiel[1]

[1] Integrated Communication Systems Group, Ilmenau University of Technology, Ilmenau, Germany
{victor-fernando.casas-melo,mitsch}@tu-ilmenau.de
[2] Fraunhofer Institut für Integrierte Schaltungen (IIS), Erlangen, Germany
mehdi.harounabadi@iis.fraunhofer.de

Abstract. LoRa technology provides low power, long range and low data rate communication solution for sensor nodes on Internet of the Things (IoT) applications. In this work, we study experimentally the performance of LoRa radio for a device-to-device communication with different spreading factors. A measurement campaign is carried out under different scenarios such as outdoor, indoor, different altitudes, and different distances. In all scenarios, we measure Packet Delivery Ratio (PDR) and Signal to Noise Ratio (SNR). The results show that the distance between a transmitter and a receiver is not the only effective parameter determining the SNR but also environmental conditions and the altitude of a receiver impact on the SNR. We show also that the PDR depends on the applied spreading factor. Besides, we derive a mapping between the SNR to a proper spreading factor of the LoRa radio for different PDR requirements using our empirical results. Applying this mapping, we propose a self-organized algorithm that adapts the spreading factor in LoRa radio to achieve a required PDR. The results show that the proposed adaptive scheme adapts the LoRa radio to provide a given 80% PDR requirement between two LoRa nodes.

Keywords: LoRa nodes · Arduino · Self-organization · Experimental study

1 Introduction

LoRa is a technology developed for low power wide area networks. It can be applied mainly in Internet of the Things (IoT) such as smart homes, intelligent transportation systems [1], UAV based networks [2,3], or sensor networks. A LoRa network consists of LoRa devices that work based on the specifications of the physical layer which were patented by Semtech Corporation [4] and the MAC layer of LoRaWAN protocol [5].

© ICST Institute for Computer Sciences, Social Informatics and Telecommunications Engineering 2021
Published by Springer Nature Switzerland AG 2021. All Rights Reserved
D. Perakovic and L. Knapcikova (Eds.): FABULOUS 2021, LNICST 382, pp. 25–36, 2021.
https://doi.org/10.1007/978-3-030-78459-1_2

This experimental study focuses only on the LoRa physical layer. The LoRa physical layer uses the frequency range of 902–928 MHz in the United States, 863–870 MHz in Europe and the ISM band of 433 MHz and 169 MHz [4]. Its coverage rage is from 10 to 15 km in rural areas and up to 5 km in urban areas [6]. The radio modulation scheme used by LoRa is Chirp Spread Spectrum. Chirp spreading factor provides robustness against the channel degradation due to multipath, fading or interference [4]. By employing the orthogonal spreading factors, signal robustness can be increased depending on the coverage range and the transmission power. On the other side, data rate decreases when the robustness of the signal increases.

In this paper we present the results of our study on the LoRa physical layer and the experimental evaluations of its performance. For this purpose, we implemented a device-to-device communication between the RN2483 LoRa nodes from the Microchip [6]. The idea of device-to-device communication has been proposed in LTE networks [7], but it is applied to LoRa nodes for an experimental study in this paper. Three scenarios were considered for our experiments. In the first scenario, the receiver was placed about 15 m higher than the ground and the transmitter was located at different distances from 250 m up to 3000 m. The second scenario is similar to the first one, but the receiver was located on the ground. In the third scenario, the transmitter was located at a distance of 480 m from the receiver and was sending packets over 24 h. For each scenario three spreading factors (7, 9 and 12) were applied in the physical layer of LoRa nodes and the Packet Delivery Ratio(PDR) and Signal-to-Noise-Ratio (SNR) were measured.

Based on the experimental results, we derived a table that maps SNR to PDR for each Spreading Factor (SF). The mapping table can be used to decide the spreading factor according to the SNR of the received packets and a given PDR requirement. By utilizing the mapping table, we propose a self-organized algorithm which dynamically adapts the spreading factor over the time for a device-to-device communication between two LoRa nodes based the state of communication (SNR) and the PDR requirements. The results show that the proposed adaptive algorithm achieves a given requirement of 80% PDR in a communication between two LoRa nodes.

This paper is organized as follows. Section 2 presents related work. Section 3 describes the hardware specifications of LoRa nodes and scenarios for the experiments. In Sect. 4, the results of the measurement campaign are presented and analyzed. A self-organized algorithm to adapt the spreading factor in the LoRa nodes is proposed in Sect. 5. Finally, the conclusion and future work is presented in Sect. 6.

2   Existing Work

Since the release of the LoRa specifications version 1.0 in 2015 [8], some performance evaluations and experimental analyses have been carried out. In [9], the authors derived experimentally the minimum required Received Signal Strength

Indicators (RSSI) to receive a packet using spreading factors 7, 9 and 12 in the 868MHz frequency band. The experiment was conducted in the suburb of Paris using a LoRa gateway and an end-node. The authors transmitted packets from five different locations with a transmission power. The article did not provide any information about PDR during the experiment.

A similar experiment was described in [10]. This time, the authors took measurements in the city of Glasgow. The transmitter was moved through the streets up to a distance of 2.2 km from the receiver, while sending beacons. For every received beacon, the RSSI was measured. However, the paper did not provide any information about the applied spreading factor for the transmissions and the achieved PDR.

Authors in [11] assessed the QoS that a LoRa network can provide in the 868.1 MHz frequency band. In their experiment, the authors considered two scenarios. In the first scenario, the transmitter was mobile in a suburban scenario, while sending packets using the spreading factor 12. The packet was received by different receivers. In the second scenario, transmitter sent packets using spreading factors 7, 9 and 10 and eight receivers were located at a distance of 3 km to the transmitter. In both scenarios the authors measured Packet Error Rate (PER), RSSI and SNR.

In [12], another performance evaluation was done for LoRa in the 863–870 MHz frequency band. It was an indoor scenario in a 570 m x 320 m area. In their first experiment the transmitter sent packets using spreading factor 12 in different channels, while moving at the speed of 5 km/s. The results showed a PDR of 95%. In the second experiment, PER and RSSI for spreading factors 7, 8, 9 and 10 were measured using different distance to the receiver.

Authors in [13] presented a comprehensive experimental work where RSSI, SNR and PER were evaluated for the 868MHz frequency band. The author used a single measurement point for its experiment with a line of sight scenario, indoor and urban scenarios. In this work, the author presented the minimum SNR values for each spreading factor, which are required for receiving a packet. Additionally, it was suggested that further experiments should be carried out, in order to clarify more the relation between SNR and the spreading factor.

In this paper, we contribute with an experimental analysis of the LoRa performance applying spreading factors 7, 9 and 12 in the 433MHz frequency band that complements previous studies. Our scenarios focus on the impact of distance between a transmitter and a receiver, location of nodes and the impact of environmental conditions. Our goal is to experimentally define the spreading factor that should used based on the SNR of received packets and a given PDR requirement.

3 Experimental Setup

This section describes the hardware and static parameters that were used for the experimental study on LoRa radio layer. Then, we present three scenarios that we considered for our measurements. At the end of this section, we describe the scenario where our proposed adaptive SF algorithm was tested.

3.1 Hardware

The experiments were carried out using the Microchip's LoRa module RN2483. This module can operate in the 433 MHz and 868 MHz frequency bands. Its transmitter (TX) power can be configured up to +14 dB and it can use FSK, GFSK or the LoRa modulation scheme [6]. According to [6], the module RN2483 has a coverage up to 15 km in rural areas and up to 5 km in urban areas. The module RN2483 was connected to an Arduino board by using the cooking hacks multi-protocol shield for Arduino [14]. The complete node is presented in Fig. 1.

The configuration of the LoRa module RN2483 and packet generation is made by the Arduino. For the following experiments we used the LoRa radio layer and module was controlled using the radio commands presented in the module commands reference user's guide [15].

In our experiments, the transmissions were done at 433.375 MHz frequency with the highest possible TX power which is +14 dB. LoRa nodes used the LoRa modulation scheme and 4/8 coding rate in their physical layer.

Fig. 1. The LoRa node used in the experiments.

3.2 Scenarios

Our measurements took place in the city of Ilmenau, in Germany. The considered scenarios are as follows:

Packet Delivery for Different TX/RX Distances with Receiver at 15 m Height. The first scenario for the measurements is presented in the Fig. 2. In this scenario the receiver position is represented by the star and was located 15 m above the ground outside of a building. The black dots represent the transmitter location for each measurement. In each position, the transmitter sent 50 packets using each of spreading factors 7, 9 and 12. No ACKnowledgment (ACK) packet was used for this scenario. On the receiver side, the SNR value for each received packet and the total PDR for each SF were measured.

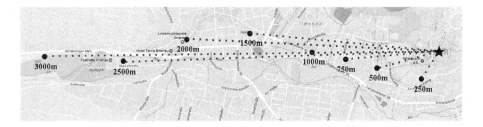

Fig. 2. Measurement points

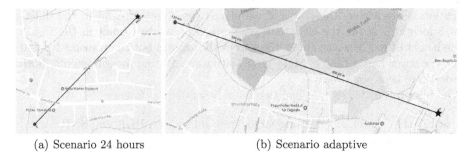

(a) Scenario 24 hours   (b) Scenario adaptive

Fig. 3. Scenarios

Packet Delivery for Different TX/RX Distances with Receiver at Ground Level. In our second scenario, we put the receiver at the same place of the star in Fig. 2, but this time we located it on the ground level. For this experiment, 50 packets were transmitted at each one of the 8 black points in Fig. 2. For each transmission only SF12 was used.

Packet Delivery over 24 h. In the third scenario, the receiver and transmitter were located as Fig. 3(a). The receiver is represented by the star and the transmitter by the black point. The distance among receiver and transmitter was 480 m and it was fixed over the whole experiment. Every hour, the transmitter sent 100 packets using SF7, SF9 and SF12 and no ACK was used. On the receiver side, the SNR and PDR were measured.

Test Scenario for the Proposed Adaptive SF Algorithm. The proposed adaptive algorithm was tested using the scenario of Fig. 3(b). Again, the star represents the position of the receiver and the black point is the position of the transmitter. The distance between the receiver and transmitter was 1.3km. In this scenario, the transmitter sends groups of 10 packets and waits 5 s for the ACK. The receiver waits for the group of packets to arrive, measures the SNR and returns an ACK. The test was run continuously for one hour. PDR and average SNR were measured over the hour.

4   Results and Analysis

In this section, we present and analyze the results of the experiments described in Sect. 3.

4.1   Packet Delivery for Different TX/RX Distances

We measured the PDR and SNR of received packets in a device-to-device communication between two LoRa nodes in scenario 1. The nodes were placed in different distances from 250 m to 3000 m, as it is shown in Fig. 2. The receiver's location is marked by the star and we placed the transmitter in to the different 8 locations inside the city, that are marked by a black point in the Fig. 2. The height of receiver was about 15 m from the ground but the transmitter and receiver never had a Line of Sight (LoS) situation. During measurements, both nodes were kept stationary.

Our study in this section had two main objectives as follows:

– Study the impact of spreading factor and distance on PDR and SNR
– Study the impact of a receiver altitude

Next we describe in details each of studies.

Study on the Impact of Spreading Factor and Distance. To see the impact of different spreading factors in a communication between two LoRa nodes, we sent 50 packets applying spreading factors 7, 9 and 12 in each distance between the LoRa transmitter and receiver. Figures 4 and 5 illustrate the performance of LoRa nodes for the scenario 1. Figure 4 shows that SF9 and SF12 have similar PDR and SF7 is the least robust spreading factor. By the distance of 1000 m, all spreading factors have PDR of 80% or more. Beyond 1000 m, SF7 faces several fluctuations in PDR, but generally speaking, the distance only impacted SF7 while SF9 and SF12 can deliver all packets even in 3000 m. Figure 5 presents fluctuations in SNR of received packets for all spreading factors. These fluctuations show that the distance is not the main factor in SNR. The location of transmitter and obstacles between the nodes have a bigger impact than the distance. However, fluctuations in SNR impacts the PDR of the weakest spreading factor, but others can tolerate a high amount of degradation in SNR.

Comparison Between Performance with Receiver on Ground Level and 15 m Height. In our second scenario, we compared the PDR and SNR for two different heights of the receiver applying the most robust spreading factor which is SF12. This time, we repeated the first experiment but this time the receiver was at the ground level. Figures 6 and 7 demonstrate the PDR and SNR of received packets for two different altitudes of the receiver. By increasing the altitude of the receiver, the SNR increases dramatically and therefore PDR

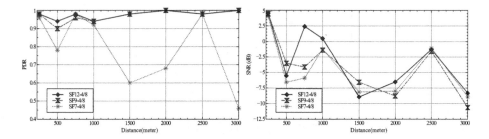

Fig. 4. Packet delivery ratio for different spreading factors and distances.

Fig. 5. Signal to noise ratio of different spreading factors and distances.

increases. The results show a big difference in PDR for most of the distances by elevating the location of a receiver for several meters from the ground even if there is no LoS transmission between two nodes. By locating the receiver in an altitude of 15 m from the ground, the PDR changes from 30% to 100% for 3000 m distance between the transmitter and receiver.

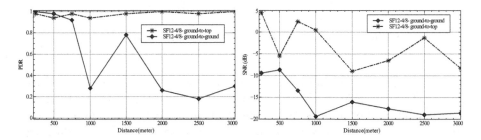

Fig. 6. Impact of different receiver altitudes on the packet delivery ratio.

Fig. 7. Impact of different receiver altitudes on the signal to noise ratio.

4.2   Packet Delivery over 24 h

We study in this section the influence of environmental conditions in communication between two LoRa nodes. For this reason, we placed two LoRa nodes inside two different buildings as shown in Fig. 3(a) and kept them stationary for 24 h. Every hour, the transmitter sent 100 packets using SF7, 100 packets using SF9 and 100 packets using SF12. The distance between nodes, their location and the spreading factor was constant during the 24 h measurement. Therefore, any change on PDR and SNR may be caused by the weather conditions such as rain, humidity, temperature change or due to the noise and interference. Figure 8 shows the PDR for different repeats of our measurements with different spreading factors. SF12 was tolerant to the environmental changes and most of the

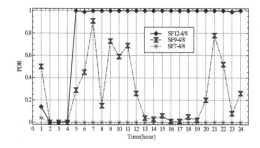

Fig. 8. Packet delivery ratio in 24 h with different spreading factors.

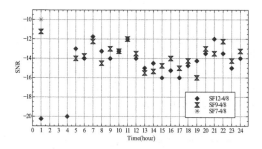

Fig. 9. Signal to noise ratio in 24 h with different spreading factors.

times was able to receive all packets. On the other hand, SF7 did not receive any packet mostly. SF9 shows a fluctuating behavior over time. However, it can receive about 80% of packets some times, but for several hours had a PDR of zero. In Fig. 9, we can see many changes in SNR for SF9 and SF12 in different times of a day. However, SF12 tolerated them, but SF9 lost many or all of the packets.

4.3 SNR Table

Based on our measurements in the mentioned experiments above, we derive a mapping between SNR and PDR for each spreading factor of LoRa. Table 1 illustrates the PDR for each spreading factor based on the average SNR of received packets. The mapping table provides us the spreading factor that should be applied in LoRa nodes for any PDR requirement having an average SNR in received packets. This table will be used in the next section to adapt the spreading factor for a given PDR requirement in a device-to-device LoRa communication.

Table 1. Mapping SNR to PDR for different spreading factors.

Spreading factor	PDR (80–100)%	PDR (30–80)%	PDR $\leq 30\%$
SF7	SNR ≥ -6.5	$-6.5 >$ SNR ≥ -9	$-9 >$ SNR ≥ -10.5
SF9	SNR ≥ -12	$-12 >$ SNR ≥ -14	$-14 >$ SNR ≥ -16
SF12	SNR ≥ -16	$-16 >$ SNR ≥ -17.5	$-17.5 >$ SNR ≥ -21

5 Self-organized Spreading Factor Adaptation for Device-to-device Communication of LORA Nodes

In this section, we propose a self-organized algorithm which adapts the spreading factor in a device-to-device communication between two LoRa nodes to achieve a PDR requirement. The proposed scheme applies the mapping table between SNR and PDR for different spreading factors that was presented in Sect. 4.3. In the self-organized spreading factor adaptation scheme, LoRa nodes start their communication with the most robust spreading factor which is SF12. Then, when some packets have been received in the receiver, the average SNR is calculated in the LoRa receiver and based on the mapping table (Table 1), both nodes adapt their spreading factor to achieve the required PDR.

Having a static spreading factor during a communication may degrade PDR, as we showed in our 24 h measurements. As an example, LoRa nodes may be tuned to SF7 to have the fastest packet transmission, but the PDR can be very low in some scenarios (as we showed in our experimental results). However, if LoRa nodes are tuned to the most robust spreading factor to have the best PDR, they may loose the opportunity of using lower spreading factors and faster transmission of packets if there is a high SNR in received packets. Therefore, an adaptive scheme is a reasonable solution to define the spreading factor between two LoRa devices on-the-fly and based on the observations of nodes from the state of communication. Figure 10 shows the adaptive spreading factor algorithm in a LoRa transmitter and receiver pair. As mentioned, both nodes start with SF12 to do the adaptation based on the measurements from SNR of received packets on the receiver side. The reason that we chose SF12 is due to the high sensitivity of LoRa receivers in this spreading factor which can receive packets with a very low SNR (-21 dB as the minimum SNR for packet reception). If any other spreading factor is used for the start of adaptive scheme, the receiver may receive no message and the spreading factor adaptation fails in this case. Now, we describe steps in the algorithms in both transmitter and receiver sides. Steps in the transmitter side are as follows:

1. Set SF12: The transmitter tunes itself to SF12 to start the adaptation procedure.
2. Transmit data packets: 10 data packets are sent continuously without waiting for any acknowledgment.

3. Wait for ACK: After sending the packets, the transmitter waits at SF12 to receive an acknowledgment from the receiver. The ACK message is always sent in SF12 to increase the probability of its reception.
4. Tuning spreading factor: After reception of ACK, the transmitter tunes its spreading factor based the information in the ACK message.
   – If the ACK is not received during a time window, the spreading factor for data transmission will be set to SF12.
5. Goto the step 2.

In the receiver side, the algorithm has the following steps:

1. Set SF12: The receiver tunes itself to SF12 to start the adaptation procedure.
2. Receive, measure and make decision: By receiving data packets, the receiver measures the average SNR of the packets and decides about the spreading factor based on Table 1.
   – If the receiver does not receive any packet in a specific time window, it will choose SF12 as the next spreading factor.
3. Send ACK: The receiver sends an ACK to the transmitter and informs it about its decision for the spreading factor. The receiver uses always SF12 for transmission of ACK.
4. Tuning the spreading factor: The receiver tunes its spreading factor based on its decided spreading factor in step 2.
5. Goto the step 2.

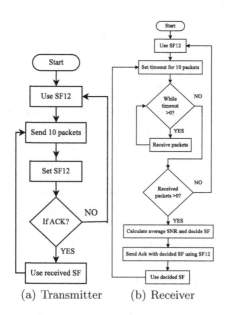

(a) Transmitter   (b) Receiver

Fig. 10. Adaptive algorithm in LoRa nodes.

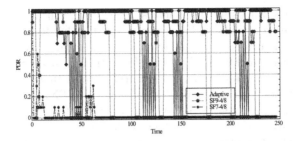

Fig. 11. Packet delivery ratio for different spreading factors and the adaptive approach.

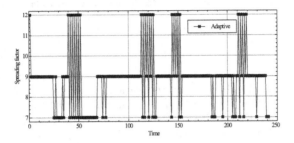

Fig. 12. Adaptation of spreading factor in the proposed approach.

Figure 11 shows the PDR for 3 different spreading factors in the scenario that was presented in Fig. 3(b). The nodes was placed outdoor in the second floor of two buildings inside the city but they had no LoS condition. The transmitter was transmitting data packets for 1 h using SF7, SF9, SF12 and the proposed adaptive algorithm of this paper. We set a requirement of 80% PDR for our transmission. As the PDR for SF12 was always 100%, we do not show the results for SF12 in the figure. As it can be seen in Fig. 11, SF7 can transmit a few or no packets in most of the time. SF9 was the best spreading factor for this scenario and it had more than 80% of PDR in most of the times. However, SF12 had always 100% PDR but due to its low throughput it is not the best choice is this scenario. Figure 12 demonstrates the changes in the spreading factor using the adaptive algorithm. We can see that the proposed algorithm adapts to SF9 which is the best spreading factor in this scenario. However, sometime the algorithm tries to use SF7 when the SNR increases, but when it does not receive any packet with SF7 it changes to SF12. Additionally, Fig. 11 shows that the proposed algorithm achieve an average PDR of 83%, which is a bit more than our initial requirement.

6   Conclusion

In this paper an experimental study on the LoRa radio layer was presented. We used the 433MHz frequency band and tested a device-to-device communication between two nodes using spreading factors 7, 9 and 12. During our experiments, we proved that, in non line of sight scenarios, the TX-RX distance is not a good parameter for configuring the spreading factor of the LoRa radio layer. Instead of that, SNR measurements gives better information for selecting the spreading factor. Based on our results, we derived a mapping table that allows us to decide which spreading factor should be used according to the SNR of received packets and a given PDR requirement. Based on this table, a self-organized algorithm for on-the-fly adaptation of the spreading factor in a transmitter and receiver was proposed. We validated experimentally our algorithm and showed its capability in achieving a required PDR. A study on the performance of the self-organized algorithm in a scenario with mobile LoRa devices is considered as a future work.

References

1. Ferrari, P., et al.: On the use of LoRaWAN for the internet of intelligent vehicles in smart city scenarios. In: Sensors Applications Symposium (2020)
2. Casas, V., et al.: On the emergence of virtual roundabouts from distributed force/torque-based UAV collision avoidance scheme. In: 13th IEEE International Conference on Control and Automation (ICCA) (2017)
3. Harounabadi, M., et al.: Evolutionary path planning for multiple UAVs in message ferry networks applying genetic algorithm. In: 29th Annual International Symposium on Personal, Indoor and Mobile Radio Communications (PIMRC) (2018)
4. Semtach: LoRa Modulation Basics, rev.2 (2015)
5. LoRa Alliance: LoRaWAN Specification, v1.0.2 (2016)
6. Microchip: Low-Power Long Range LoRa Technology Transceiver Module, rev. A. (2015)
7. Soleymani, D.M., et al.: Implementation aspects of hierarchical radio resource management scheme for overlay D2D. In: 9th International Congress on Ultra Modern Telecommunications and Control Systems (2017)
8. LoRaWAN r1.0 open standard releases for the IoT, Wireless News (2015)
9. Augustin, A., et al.: A study of LoRa: Long range and low power networks for the internet of things, Sensors (2016)
10. Wixted, A.J., et al.: Evaluation of LoRa and LoRaWAN for wireless sensor networks. IEEE Sensors (2016)
11. Petric, T., et al.: Measurements, performance and analysis of LoRa FABIAN, a real-world implementation of LPWAN. In: 27th Annual International Symposium on Personal, Indoor, and Mobile Radio Communications (PIMRC) (2016)
12. Petäjäjärvi, J., Mikhaylov, K., Yasmin, R., Hämäläinen, M., Iinatti, J.: Evaluation of LoRa LPWAN technology for indoor remote health and wellbeing monitoring. Int. J. Wirel. Inf. Networks **24**(2), 153–165 (2017). https://doi.org/10.1007/s10776-017-0341-8
13. Ruano, E.: LoRa protocol. Evaluations, limitations and practical test. Institut national polytechnique de Grenoble (2016)
14. https://www.cooking-hacks.com, Multiprotocol Radio Shield v2.0 Tutorial for Arduino
15. Microchip: RN2483 LoRa Technology Module Command Reference User's Guide, Microchip Technology Inc. (2018)

A Design of Energy Efficient Nanorouting Protocol Using Greedy Algorithm

Iqra Iqbal[1] (ID), Anca D. Jurcut[3](✉), and Muhammad Mohsin Nazir[2] (ID)

[1] University of Education, Township Campus Lahore, Lahore, Pakistan
iqra.iqbal@ue.edu.pk
[2] Lahore College for Women University, Lahore, Pakistan
mohsin.nazir@lcwu.edu.pk
[3] University College Dublin, Dublin, Ireland
anca.jurcut@ucd.ie

Abstract. Nanonetwork has given rise to many other disciplines like agriculture, defense, health care, and industrial applications. With nanonetwork there exist tiny nanodevices or nanomachines. The interconnection of tiny nanodevices with internet helps to make an entire network i.e. the next generation of network, named nanonetwork. Nanodevices, due to their small sizes, have several limitations like communication range, frequency range, energy consumption rate, limited amount of memory and many others. Developing protocols and routing framework is quite a challenging task for nanonetworks. This research work will explore the scarce availability of energy in nanonetworks by digging in the existing routing protocols, especially on the ones designed to cater the energy constraint. The opportunities and challenges of existing work will be investigated and discussed. Furthermore, a solution will be devised and its effectiveness will be stated that will pave its way in the future activities of energy efficient nanorouting protocols.

Keywords: Nanodevice · Nanonetwork · IoNT · WSN · NanoRouter · NanoBattery · NanoInterface · NanoCluster · NnaoAntenna · Geographical routing · Greedy algorithm · Energy efficient nanorouting protocols

1 Introduction

Nanotechnology is the transition from IoT (Internet of Things) to IoNT (Internet of NanoThings) in which the backbone of IoT is modern wireless communication devices. Those devices can connect other devices like sensors, actuators, mobile phones, tablets and other intractable objects [1]. The IoT helps to give birth to another advance domain of networking named IoNT. As the name suggest, the nanodevice, due to its nano scale, have some unique characteristics like nanobatteries, nanoantennas, nanorouters, small communication ranges, limited communication distance etc. Nanosensors were the earliest devices explored and can be used within human body for drug delivery, monitoring air pollution, and protection against chemical attacks to the soldiers. There are four communication technologies to communicate at nanoscale and these are: mechanical, electromagnetic, acoustic, and molecular [2]. The first communication technology

© ICST Institute for Computer Sciences, Social Informatics and Telecommunications Engineering 2021
Published by Springer Nature Switzerland AG 2021. All Rights Reserved
D. Perakovic and L. Knapcikova (Eds.): FABULOUS 2021, LNICST 382, pp. 37–47, 2021.
https://doi.org/10.1007/978-3-030-78459-1_3

requires the nanodevices to be connected to each other physically. Hence, these methods are not feasible. Electromagnetic technology did not get specific attention from the researchers in the past, because the electronic nanocomponents of nanodevices have not been manufactured yet. The acoustic waves are absorbent in the human body hence; this technology cannot be headed further for IoNt [2]. However, all the innovations like nanobatteries, nanoantennas, and nanoscale circuits are due to molecular technology and the new generation of grapheme based electronic has been evolved.

With the limitations mentioned above, there is an urgent need for efficient methodologies for each layer of nanonetwork to ensure successful communication of data. The routing protocols help to deliver the data from its source to its destination by choosing the best routing path. The routing protocol of WSN (Wireless Sensor Network) also does the needful as well as it helps to deliver the required information to its destination. This can be done with optimum energy usage and by keeping the constraints under observation. Usually WSN keeps track of the energy consumption and energy usage data, but the protocols with efficient performance typically use more energy and processing power [3]. This is the reason the WNN (Wireless Nano Network) cannot use the classical routing protocols for the WSN and is paramount to design new protocols for the stack of nanonetwork. Mostly, the routing protocols of nanonetwork use flooding based technology, where the receiving node blindly forwards the data. This action leads to conflicts and redundancy of data [4].

The rest of this paper is as follows: Sect. 2 presents a relevant study of the existing protocols that have been designed for nanonetworks. An energy efficient routing protocol is proposed and its efficiency is analysed in the form of comparison graphs in Sect. 3. Finally, a conclusion is drawn and the future research directions are discussed in Sect. 4.

2   Routing Protocols in Nanonetwork

It was observed that the nanonodes have been made with various limitations like highly dense and small memory nanodevices, low processing nanodevices and energy inefficient nanodevices. Therefore, studies are majorly focused on reducing the complexity and improving the energy constraint of these devices [5]. Several protocols were manufactured for this purpose. In this research review we discuss the existing routing protocols and classify them on the bases of energy efficient or energy aware routing protocols. For example, the ECR is a type of energy efficient routing protocols, while the SLR and LSDD are energy inefficient routing protocols for the named network.

2.1   Energy Efficient Routing Protocols in Nanonetwork

Single path and multipath are two subdivisions of routing protocols in nanonetwork. The energy efficient routing protocols are mostly single path in nanonetwork. The reason is obvious that single path routing consumes less energy comparative to multipath routing. In multipath routing protocol, we always try to find the best and optimized path to route the networking traffic, while in case of single path routing protocol, the information is routed to the only path, thus optimizing the energy of overall network [6]. This makes the below discussed routing protocols energy efficient.

2.1.1 Energy Conserving Routing (ECR)

Energy Conserving Routing (ECR) is a protocol paradigm specifically designed for Wireless Body Sensor Network (WBSNs) [7]. WBSN is another application of nanonetwork in which the communication within human body tissues is possible using Terahertz (Thz) waves. The path loss for this type of transmission may include spreading loss, shadowing impact, and absorption attenuation. WBSNs mainly follow hierarchical network architecture for efficient communication between nanointerface and nanonodes. The ECR protocol follows the same strategy, it comprises of nanointerface, nanonodes, and nanocontroller that follows a specific hierarchy to make the transmission possible. ECR performs two different types of communication, namely intercluster and intracluster communication. This protocol use multilayers to make the communication possible. The width of these layers is one half of the distance of single hop. This division is based on the distance from nanointerface to nanonodes and the single hop transmission range of these nanonodes.

When the layers are divided, next task is to select the nanocontroller for the first round with the left over energy. The selected nanocontrollers start broadcasting the message and the nanonodes on receiving side measure the strength of the signal with the help of Received Signal Strength Indicator (RSSI) [8]. The nanocontroller with highest RSSI is then selected and nanonodes start sending joining requests to the selected nanocontroller. The nanocontrollers start sending the data in the lower layers if it is an intercluster communication, but in most of the cases in WBSN it used to be intracluster. The nanointerface plays a major role in ECR transmission by sorting the transmission order of each layer with the help of total transmission time. The transmission time is allocated to each cluster in each layer. As nanonodes are closer to the nanocontroller in intercluster communication, only one hop or double hop transmission is considered. If nanonode has data to send, it prefers direct communication instead of double hop transmission as it maximizes energy efficiency. The intracluster or cross layer transmission needs more energy, so the remaining energy of nanocontroller is always lower than nanonodes. That is why nanocontroller has to be reselected after each transmission.

This cross layer transmission and time allocation of nanonodes make the transmission of ECR collision free and it consumes less energy in WBSNs, but the intercluster communication needs huge quantity of nanocontroller as it only requires one hop or double hop transmission.

2.1.2 Multihop Deflection Routing-Reinforcement Learning (MDR-RL)

The Multihop Deflection Routing Algorithm based on Reinforcement Learning (MDRRL) has been proposed as an energy efficient routing algorithm that dynamically explores the routing path with data packet transmission [9]. The deflection and routing table has been implemented such that the nanonodes can deflect data packets if the entries are invalid. To upload the table entries one forward (on policy) and two feedbacks (off policy) updating algorithms have been proposed. The routing table deflects the data packets if there are any issue of memory and energy in table entries, also considered as invalid entries. The table is initially empty and the data will be filled in it once the transmission process starts. An arbitrary network with several nanonodes is considered in which every nanonode will have this deflection and routing table. Upon receiving or generating any data packet the annonode will check its routing table to find the next hop. To reach to the destination the MDRRL route table has only one route entry. The route entry has the following contents:

- Destination nanonode ID
- Next hop nanonode ID
- Time for the route entry updation
- QValue to destination nanonode
- Flag of route validity
- Recovery rate to next nanonode
- Lifetime
- Hop Count to destination nanonode

The QValue is the weight of routing path, which means the higher is the QValue the more resources will be consumed by the routing path. The routing validity specifies the validity of route entry. The flag is enabled when the nanonode receives a data packet or acknowledgment (ACK) from its neighboring nanonode, otherwise it will be disabled upon receiving negative acknowledgment (NACK) or time out. Recovery rate to the next nanonode is to check whether the nanonode will recover to its original state or not, by harvesting energy from the environment. The lifetime is the time of a route entry that can stay in the routing table for a specific amount of time, as the table is used to get updated during the transmission process [10]. The entry may become invalid due to some conditions, including:

1. The next hop nanonode don't have sufficient energy
2. The next hop nanonode is busy with another nanonode and don't have more memory/buffer or energy to communicate with new data packets.
3. An error occurs during transmission process due to several reasons like modulation error or channel congestion.

All or any of the above mentioned reasons may cause failure in the packet transmission and to overcome this issue another table has been introduced in MDRRL, named as deflection table. The deflection table can help other nanonodes to deflect to other nanonodes to complete the packet transmission process if the next hop is invalid. As the nanonodes have limited energy capacity; therefore to deal with this energy constraint, the MDRRL introduced an energy prediction scheme that predicts the energy level of next hop with maximum amount of energy. The nanonodes are allowed to share their energy levels, its energy harvesting rates, and energy consumption rates. Based on simulation results the MDRRL has been proved to have the best performance in terms of packet delivery ratio with energy awareness.

2.2 Energy Inefficient Routing Protocols

Almost all the routing protocols that are not energy efficient are multi path and flood based routing protocols. Only the TTL based efficient Forwarding (TEForward) routing protocol that is single path routing protocol is part of this category. In multi path routing protocols each reachable nanonode is allowed to forward the data that may cause redundancy and consume lots of energy. These are basically comprised of two common schemes named as limit flood area based and dynamic infrastructure based routing schemes. The limit flood area based routing forward the data packets only in the partial area between the sender and receiver nanonodes; hence is consumes less energy in comparison with the dynamic infrastructure based routing in which the nanonodes dynamically classify themselves as "user" or "infrastructure". This is further based on the quality of received packet which eventually increases the computational complexity at every nanonode.

2.2.1 RADAR Routing

Nanonodes in the RADAR routing protocol is distributed in circular area [11]. An entity which is placed at the center of the circle constantly emits radiations at a specific angle. The nanonodes that come in that radiation range, are active nodes and the rest are inactive nodes. Upon sending the information packet, the area is flooded with radiation that overall minimize the number of transmitted packets. The drawback of this routing protocol is packet loss, as the receiver of the nanonode may be inactive. To overcome this issue, the angle of radiation is very important to consider. If the angle of radiation is increased, then the energy consumption rate will increase. Hence, this issue should be optimized in different scenarios. Another aspect to be considered is the packet loss that is possible if the energy level of nanonode is sufficienet, but the nanonode itself is inactive due to the angle of radiation. Another drawback of RADAR routing is that it increases the number of active nanonodes as it moves away from central entity that may cause collision among data packets. The RADAR routing becomes more problematic if the network is of large scale.

2.2.2 Coordinate and Routing System for Nanonetwork (CORONA)

A coordinate and Routing System for Nanonetwork (CORONA) uses a coordinate system to assign addresses to the nanonodes [12]. These addresses are designed for the nanonodes elaborated in Software Defined Metamaterials (SDM). The metamaterials are artificial materials used in combination of nanonodes and cannot be found in natural environment. The SDM provides energy resources to nanonetwork that introduces new fields in the engineering and industrial domain which also includes renewable efficient energy resources for the nanonodes. The main target of SDM protocol is to reduce the number of data packets and hence, to reduce the collision and redundancy among the data packets. In CORONA, every nanonodes dynamically derives coordinates and it is assumed to be placed equally distant in a rectangular area. Four nodes are placed in four corners of the rectangular area in the setup phase. Every nanonode sends the packet in a specific sequence and sets it hop count from the anchor nodes as its specific coordinate.

When a nanonode A wants to send the data to nanonode B, all the nanonodes retransmit the data packets of whose coordinates are between A and B. This retransmission is possible with the help of flooding mechanism, but the two facing anchor nodes cannot be selected at once; otherwise the transmission will not be completed. The hop count from a nanonode to its four anchor nodes is considered to be the coordinates in CORONA and the flooding is limited to the arc shape. This communication is possible for point to point communication in a restricted environment to make it energy efficient [13]. Table 1, given below, provides a detailed comparison of the exiting work for these routing protocols. Most of them are energy efficient routing protocols in nanonetworks. The focused issues, and energy management techniques have been considered here.

Table 1. Comparison of existing routing protocols

Work	Network method	Type of application	Focused issues	Energy management technique	Simulation/real time
[14]	Random	Event based	Residual batterypower andradio links	Energy storage	Simulation
[15]	Nanorectennas	Periodic	Total harvesting efficiency	Energy harvesting	Simulation
[16]	Nanorectennas	Event driven	Optimization	Energy harvesting	Simulation
[17]	Dynamic	Event based	Time synchronization	Energy consumption	Simulation
[18]	Fixed	Periodic	Energy transferefficiency	Energy consumption	Simulation
[19]	Random	Distributive and adaptive	Energy transfer	Energy consumption	Simulation
[20]	Cluster	Query based	Scalability	Energy recharge	Simulation
[21]	Random	Event based	Efficient wireless power transfer	Energy consumption	Simulation
[13]	Cluster	Query based	Optimization of energy harvesting and consumption process	Energy harvesting	Simulation
[22]	Static and dynamic	Event driven	Delivery rate of data packets	Energy consumption	Simulation
[23]	Random	Periodic	Quantification ofMCs	Energy consumption	Simulation
[24]	Random	Event based	Optimization of energy transfer	Energy consumption	Simulation
[7]	Cluster	Event Driven	Maximizing energy utilization	Energy harvesting and energy consumption	Simulation

3   Proposed Protocol for Energy Efficient Routing

In our proposed work we have considered the scenario of an environment, where different nanoclusters, nanorouters, nanonodes/nanomembers, a nanointerface and a remote server is considered, as can be seen in Fig. 1. It is assumed that nanointerface and the nanorouters are fixed, but the nanonodes are moving. Reclustering in this work has been prohibited; moreover, it is assumed that the nanonodes constrained by energy are moving with a constant velocity. This work follows a typical hierarchy in which the remote server will communicate with the nanointerface. This interaction is assumed to be a simple request/response process through and from the external entity and the nanointerface. Then the nanointerface will deliver the request to the nanorouters, and these nanorouters then will communicate and receive answers from their corresponding nanoclusters. The response generated from a subset of nanonodes will be forwarded to the remote server in the opposite direction via internet/intranet.

It is also considered that the number of requests generated from the remote server can be too high or the requests might arrive too fast with respect to time. Hence, the nanonodes may not always be available to fulfill the requests and to answer them accordingly.

Four messages have been defined to make this work possible:

(1) *ND message*: a message conveyed from nanorouters to discover its nanocluster's available nanomembers. The size expressed in bits is represented by nanoND.

(2) *EF message:* a response message of ND message generated by nanomembers having its energy level stored in them. The size expressed in bits is represented by nanoEF.

(3) *R message:* a query/request message generated by remote server and forwarded through nanointerface to all the subsequent nanorouters and to its nanocluster controller that have been selected by routing mechanism. The size expressed in bits is represented by nanoR.

(4) *A message:* an answer message of R, generated by specific nanocluster controller back to the nanointerface and the remote server. The size expressed in bits is represented by nanoA.

3.1   Nanocluster Formation

For the above mentioned messages and for better communication purpose, the nanoclusters are composed. A nanocluster will have nanocluster members/nodes. The nanocluster will be chosen on the basis of available energy levels. The nanocluster helps to aggregate the data and to send it to the nanorouters. It also helps with the intercluster and intracluster communication with high power transmission range and low power transmission range, respectively. The nanocluster will be chosen for every next round using round robin technique, depending on its residual energy i.e.

$$WNC = Energy_{residual}/Energy_{max} \qquad (1)$$

If nanocluster could not find another nanomember larger than the Weight nanocluster (WNC) it will again select itself as a nanocluster. The newly selected nanocluster then multicast its message to the nearby non-member nanonodes and they will send the join request to the respective nanocluster having high RSSI (Received Signal Strength Indicator). The procedure continues until the formation of a nanocluster and re-clustering is avoided to prevent from the communicational complexity and clustering overhead.

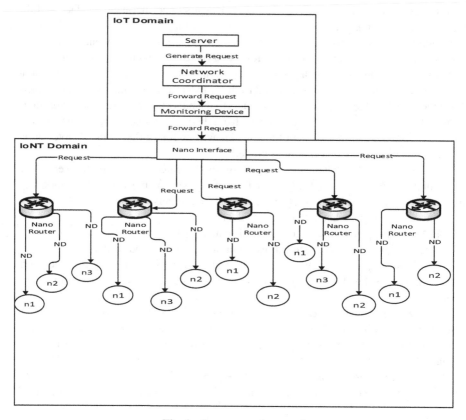

Fig. 1. Our proposed protocol

3.2 Geographic Routing Protocol Using Greedy Algorithm

The nanonetwork is a resource limited network. Our proposed communication model should use fewer resources in terms of memory consumption, computational power and energy utilization. Flooding is not a suitable option for this type of networking with scarce availability of resources. Therefore, to avoid resource wastage, the proposed model forwards the data packets from nanointerface to the nanodevices, i.e. more precisely using minimal energy, memory and computations [10]. Inspired from geographical routing protocols used in IoT and WSN, in this work we propose a forwarding scheme that reduces the number of relaying nanonodes for a said transmission. Initially, all the nanorouters broadcast messages and the nanonode choose the nearest nanorouter by the broadcasted messages in the medium. The nearest nanorouter based on its location will forward the data packet through nanocluster, and this procedure continues until it reaches to the nanointerface. This protocol is divided into three steps to make it easier to understand. (1) First is the selection of nanorouter, (2) second is the selection of next hope nanonode from the nanocluster, and (3) last is the transmission phase of data.

The important result shown here is the amount of energy available in nanonodes and the number of requests per cluster. Figure 2a, 2b shows that the available energy decreases with the increase in request rate. The reason is quite clear; the nanonodes use more energy to fulfill the increased rate of requests. Moreover it shows that if there will be an increase in the nanonodes per cluster then it will lower the amount of energy stored in them.

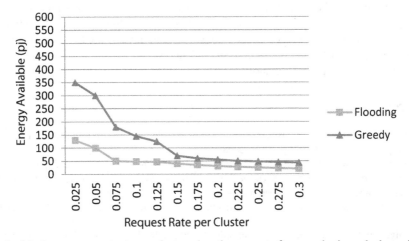

Fig. 2. (a). Average request rate per cluster when the amount of nanonodes in each cluster is 50

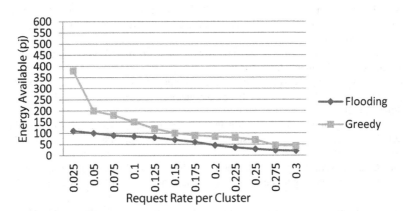

Fig. 2. (b). Average request rate per cluster when the amount of nanonodes in each cluster is 100

4 Conclusion

In this work the feasibility of energy efficient system has been discussed to measure the total energy of nanoclusters. This proposed process works on the basis of energy efficiency, as well as it will have greedy moves to choose the best route of nanocluster that will eventually move towards nanodevices. The designed model is evaluated and the behavior of proposed system is observed in detail. The results show that if the number of nanomachines increase in each cluster the transmission rate increase gradually with a low amount of the energy consumed. This work is implemented on a descriptive example to evaluate the efficiency of the introduced model. The output obtained is shown in the form of graph with varying parameter values.

These results will constitute a base for future work conducted to obtain better optimized results in near future. The behavior of the devised solution will be investigated with several parameters. The nanotechnology and nanodevices are the components of next evolutionary world that is still in its making and we are planning to investigate it in a more realistic and specific scenarios.

References

1. Akyildiz, I.F., Brunetti, F., Blázquez, C.: Nanonetworks: a new communication paradigm. Comput. Netw. **52**(12), 2260–2279 (2008)
2. Drexler, K.E.: Molecular engineering: assemblers and future space hardware. Paper AAS-86-415, presented at Aerospace XXI, the 33rd Annual Meeting of the American Astronautical Society, Boulder, CO, 26–29 October 1986 (1986)
3. Drexler, E.: Nanosystems: Molecular Machinery, Manufacturing, and Computation. Wiley (1992)
4. Deligeorgis, G., Coccetti, F., Konstantinidis, G., Plana, R.: Radio frequency signal detection by ballistic transport in y-shaped graphene nanoribbons. Appl. Phys. Lett. **101**(1), 013502 (2012)
5. Otsuji, T., Boubanga Tombet, S., Satou, A., Ryzhii, M., Ryzhii, V.: Terahertz-wave generation using graphene— toward new types of terahertz lasers. IEEE J. Sel. Top. Quantum Electron. **19**(1), 8400209 (2013)
6. Sensale-Rodriguez, B., et al.: Broadband graphene terahertz modulators enabled by intraband transitions. Nat. Commun. **3**, 780 (2012)
7. Afsana, F., Asifurrahman, M., Ahmed, M.R., Mahmud, M., Kaiser, M.S.: An energy conserving routing scheme for wireless body sensor nanonetwork communication. IEEE Access **6**, 9186–9200 (2018)
8. Tamagnone, M., Gomez-Diaz, J.S., Mosig, J.R., Perruisseau-Carrier, J.: Reconfigurable terahertz plasmonic antenna concept using a graphene stack. Appl. Phys. Lett. **101**(21), 214102 (2012)
9. Wang, C.C., Yao, X., Wang, W.L., Jornet, J.M.: Multi-hop deflection routing algorithm based on reinforcement learning for energy-harvesting nanonetworks. IEEE Trans. Mobile Comput. (2020)
10. Akyildiz, I.F., Jornet, J.M.: Electromagnetic wireless nanosensor networks. Nano Commun. Netw. **1**(1), 3–19 (2010)
11. Neupane, S.R.: Routing in resource constrained sensor nanonetworks. Master's thesis (2014)
12. Tsioliaridou, A., Liaskos, C., Ioannidis, S., Pitsillides, A.: CORONA: a coordinate and routing system for nanonetworks. In: Proceedings of the Second Annual International Conference on Nanoscale Computing and Communication, pp. 1–6, September 2015

13. Wang, P., Jornet, J.M., Malik, M.A., Akkari, N., Akyildiz, I.F.: Energy and spectrum-aware MAC protocol for perpetual wireless nanosensor networks in the Terahertz Band. Ad Hoc Netw. **11**(8), 2541–2555 (2013)
14. Dhondge, K., Shorey, R., Tew, J.: HOLA: heuristic and opportunistic link selection algorithm for energy efficiency in industrial internet of things (IIoT) systems. In: 2016 8th International Conference on Communication Systems and Networks (COMSNETS), pp. 1–6. IEEE, January 2016
15. Anjum, S.S., et al.: Energy management in RFID-sensor networks: taxonomy and challenges. IEEE Internet Things J. **6**(1), 250–266 (2017)
16. Ma, Z., Vandenbosch, G.A.: Optimal solar energy harvesting efficiency of nano-rectenna systems. Sol. Energy **88**, 163–174 (2013)
17. Chen, X., Li, J., Zhu, P., Tang, R., Chen, Z., He, Y.: Fragmentation-aware routing and spectrum allocation scheme based on distribution of traffic bandwidth in elastic optical networks. IEEE/OSA J. Opt. Commun. Netw. **7**(11), 1064–1074 (2015)
18. Xie, L., et al.: A mobile platform for wireless charging and data collection in sensor networks. IEEE J. Sel. Areas Commun. **33**(8), 1521–1533 (2015)
19. Angelopoulos, C.M., Nikoletseas, S., Raptis, T.P.: Wireless energy transfer in sensor networks with adaptive, limited knowledge protocols. Comput. Netw. **70**, 113–141 (2014)
20. Farris, I., Militano, L., Iera, A., Molinaro, A., Spinella, S.C.: Tag-based cooperative data gathering and energy recharging in wide area RFID sensor networks. Ad Hoc Netw. **36**, 214–228 (2016)
21. Wu, J., Chi, K.T., Lau, F.C., Ho, I.W.: Analysis of communication network performance from a complex network perspective. IEEE Trans. Circuits Syst. I Regul. Pap. **60**(12), 3303–3316 (2013)
22. Lu, X., Wang, P., Niyato, D., Kim, D.I., Han, Z.: Wireless charging technologies: fundamentals, standards, and network applications. IEEE Commun. Surv. Tutor. **18**(2), 1413–1452 (2015)
23. Dai, H., Wu, X., Chen, G., Xu, L., Lin, S.: Minimizing the number of mobile chargers for large-scale wireless rechargeable sensor networks. Comput. Commun. **46**, 54–65 (2014)
24. Madhja, A., Nikoletseas, S., Raptis, T.P.: Distributed wireless power transfer in sensor networks with multiple mobile chargers. Comput. Netw. **80**, 89–108 (2015)

Flash Crowd Management in Beyond 5G Systems

Valentin Rakovic$^{(\boxtimes)}$, Hristijan Gjoreski, Marija Poposka, Daniel Denkovski, and Liljana Gavrilovska

Faculty of Electrical Engineering and Information Technologies, Ss. Cyril and Methodius University in Skopje, Skopje, North Macedonia
{valentin,hristijang,poposkam,danield,liljana}@feit.ukim.edu.mk

Abstract. Wireless network (radio) virtualization and its synergy with ML/AI-based technologies is a novel concept that can efficiently address problems of legacy networks, such as flash crowds. This paper discusses the integration aspects of intelligence-based technologies with Sate-of-the-Art end-to-end reconfigurable, flexible and scalable network architecture, capable of handling demands in flash crowd scenarios. The presented results, demonstrate that advanced solutions based on ML can significantly improve the network proactivity and adaptivity by reliably predicting flash crowd scenarios. The results also show that in case of low dataset fidelity, conventional statistical models are a more suitable option.

Keywords: Flash crowd · Radio virtualization · Machine learning

1 Introduction

Conventional network architectures are characterized by static deployment and configuration, rendering them uncapable for managing geographical and spatio-temporal variations of users' capacity demand. The network inflexibility presents a challenging problem in the attempt to satisfy the service demands for the increased number of flash crowd scenarios in the recent years, especially emergency situations such as terrorist attacks and natural disasters. The overall scenarios' outcome depends on the ability to reliably and promptly exchange information between the first team responders and the victims.

The strict requirements imposed by the flash crowd scenarios demand a sheer transformation from future mobile systems. These scenarios introduce specific service requirements that traditional network architectures cannot provide on-the-fly and in a manner that operators would be willing to support (i.e. low-cost, efficient and real-time service demand satisfaction). However, the emerging 5G systems [1] and the associated aspect of radio virtualization promises to address these challenges.

Some of the focal aspects of 5G are the radio network virtualization and softwarization that enable flexible, scalable, agile network architectures, which address the demands

---

The original version of this chapter was revised: The family name of the first author was corrected. The correction to this chapter is available at https://doi.org/10.1007/978-3-030-78459-1_31

D. Perakovic and L. Knapcikova (Eds.): FABULOUS 2021, LNICST 382, pp. 48–57, 2021.
https://doi.org/10.1007/978-3-030-78459-1_4

in flash crowds. Radio virtualization [2] allows isolated coexistence of multiple virtual radio networks on the same physical infrastructure, and has ability to dynamically create heterogeneous virtual networks. Network softwarization, represented through Software Defined Networking (SDN) [3, 4], enables network programmability by decoupling data and control planes. It also decouples the network functions from the hardware where they commonly run and implements them in software manner. It brings an opportunity to place the network functions in a virtualized environment (i.e. cloud platform).

Recently the radio virtualization has started to evolve towards the concept of Open-RAN (O-RAN) [5]. O-RAN is fostering more open and smarter radio access networks by relying on openness and Intelligence. To address the complexity issues, operators and vendors cannot rely on conventional human intensive means of deploying, optimizing and operating the mobile networks. Instead, the mobile networks must be able to facilitate new intelligence-based technologies (i.e. ML/AI), hence facilitating automated operational network functions that will reduce the operational costs.

This paper discusses the aspects of flash crowd scenarios and presents a promising solution for its effective mitigation. Specifically, the paper presents the requirements for an end-to-end reconfigurable, flexible and scalable network architecture, capable of addressing the demands in flash crowd scenarios. The emphasis is on the design and performance analysis of a self-autonomous network entity called Virtual Resource Manager (VRM) capable of orchestrating the different underlying radio access technologies, in case of flash crowd occurrence.

The paper is organized as follows. Section 2 provides an insight on the flash crowd specific, and consequently the underlying system requirements and design. Section 3 focuses on different algorithms for flash crowd prediction, based on the underlying network information. Section 4 presents the performance analysis of the algorithms presented in Sect. 3. It also discusses the potential applicability and deployment for real-world scenarios. Section 5 concludes the paper.

2   Flash Crowd Scenarios

2.1   Flash Crowd Aspects

Flash crowd scenarios are becoming important due to the increased requirement for providing a reliable communication and ubiquitous access infrastructure for a large number of active users and devices. The given scenarios are characterized by a substantial increase of user connectivity and/or traffic demand, as a result of high concentration of users per unit area (e.g. sport events, concerts etc.) or by a high volume of required user connections (e.g. tele-voting, emergency situations, etc.). The flash crowd scenarios can affect many system's characteristics, such as cell densification and self-organization, resource reconfiguration, system outages and failures, etc. The most demanding and important flash crowd scenarios involve emergency situations that arise either from out of natural (e.g. earthquakes, floods) or man-made (e.g. terrorist attacks, industrial accidents, transportation failures) disasters.

The fifth generation of mobile systems, 5G, envisions a paradigm shift by introducing very high carrier frequencies with massive bandwidths, dynamic softwarization and virtualization, high reliability, low latency and very high number of connected users. A number of ongoing activities focus on system architecture and initiates standardization of various aspects of 5G, such as ML/AI integration into the system [6]. However, applying advanced algorithms such as ML/AI in flash crowd-aware future wireless networks is very limited. The remainder of the section presents the generic system architecture capable of addressing the issues related to flash crowds in mobile systems.

2.2 System Design

In order to provide reliable and efficient communication in flash crowd scenarios the wireless systems, such as 5G, should focus on virtualization and autonomous decision-making algorithms (e.g. based on ML/AI). Virtualization and autonomous decision-making can facilitate optimized virtual resource allocation for wireless network environments, leveraging a highly flexible and adaptable wireless network.

The flash crowd-aware system should aim at supporting the operation of various underlying wireless technologies and to dynamically and optimally allocate the cloud hardware resources onto the available wireless network resources, depending on the environment and the traffic demands. There have been several recent works that propose the integration of virtualization and autonomous decision-making algorithms in mobile systems. However, only the FALCON-based wireless system focuses on the aspects of flash crowd scenarios [7]. The remainder of the section will specifically elaborate on the FALCON system architecture and its flash crowd-aware design.

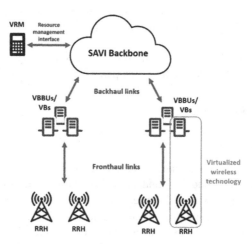

Fig. 1. Generic FALCON architecture

Figure 1 depicts the generic FALCON system architecture. The generic FALCON architecture integrates the Radio Access Network and the backbone core network in a single reconfigurable system entity. The RAN segment incorporates the Cloud-RAN (C-RAN) paradigm, comprising of Remote Radio Heads (RRHs) that are located at remote sites. They transmit and receive wireless signals, but do not perform any base-band signal processing. The digital baseband signal is forwarded, via a high speed/low latency fronthaul links, to the Virtual BaseBand Units (VBBUs)/Virtual Base Stations (VBSs) housed in the centralized processing pools. The VBBUs/VBSs control the RRHs and perform the baseband processing of the digital signals to retrieve the essential data from the respective virtualized wireless communication system. The communication between the RRHs and VBBUs can be provided by Software Defined Network (SDN) equipment that can dynamically adapt to the underlying scenario requirements and conditions. Moreover, the FALCON architecture incorporates aspects of Multi-Access Edge Computing (MEC) [8] to support a distributed cloud deployment (C-RAN). The MEC aspect improves the performance, the scalability and the agility of the C-RAN platform by bringing the centralized processing pools closer to the wireless nodes [9].

Based on the data traffic/user connectivity demands, as well as on the virtualized wireless network technology, the Virtual Resource Manager (VRM) computes the hardware resources in the MEC processing pool (CPU load, memory allocation, etc.) providing optimal performance and resource allocation. The FALCON architecture integrates the proposed MEC based C-RAN with the SDN-based SAVI Backbone platform via backhaul links. SAVI acts as the core facilitator of the backbone communication and services in the C-RAN system, leveraging advanced network management [10].

The VRM is the focal entity in the FALCON system architecture responsible for the optimal system reconfiguration under particular flash crowd occurrences. The VRM's main objective is to proactively detect and predict the underlying flash crowds in the network. The following section presents the key VRM functionalities responsible for the flash crowd prediction.

3   Flash Crowd Prediction

In order to facilitate the detection process, the VRM utilizes particular prediction algorithms that can be applied over a large plethora of scenarios. Specifically, these scenarios vary in the type and content of available network information (i.e. dataset) that the VRM utilizes for its decision-making process.

Specifically, the scenarios and the applied algorithms vary with respect to the information size in the dataset. When utilizing large amount of historical information from the dataset, the optimal approach is to exploit advanced prediction algorithms based on ML. However, in many real-world situations mobile operators operate with limited historical data, rendering the ML algorithms unusable. In this case it is more efficient to apply conventional statistical algorithms.

The remainder of the section elaborates on the dataset aspects and the optimal algorithms that can be applied in the VRM for the particular scenarios of interest.

3.1   The Dataset

The traffic characteristics over time are an important aspect of cellular networks in consideration of resource provisioning, traffic engineering and system optimization. There has been some progress in revealing temporal dynamics and spatial inhomogeneity of cellular traffic, however there is quite a limited knowledge about traffic dependence, and statistics analysis about the load of the network: number of users, number of data packets, size of the data transfer, etc. One of challenges is the lack of relevant data collected in real-life conditions. The City Cellular Traffic Map (C2TM) dataset [11, 12] is the only one that contains such data, and additionally provides analysis on week-long traffic generated by a large population of people in a median-size city of China.

The dataset is collected over 8 continuous days [11, 12]. The data represents request-response records extracted from HTTP traffic at the city scale, consisting of individuals' activities, with accurate timestamp and location information indicated by connected cellular base stations (BS). The hashed International Mobile Subscriber Identity (IMSI) detects each individual. To conserve the traffic characteristics and also to preserve user privacy, only hourly statistics at base-station granularity is available. This means a maximum of N × M records (N the number of base stations, M the number of recording hours).

The dataset contains two types of data: traffic and topology. The former provides hourly traffic statistics for each base station, while the latter stores the relative topology of underlying cellular network. The relative location of base station is in longitude/latitude form to facilitate some analysis with standard geographic processing about great circle distance.

In our analysis we used only the traffic related data, since we were interested only in the traffic frequency characteristics. This data contains:

- timestamp
- base station ID
- number of active users associated with specific base station and hour
- number of transferred packets associated with specific base station and hour
- number of transferred bytes associated with specific base station and hour.

In total, there are 13.269 base stations and 1.625.680 data rows (hours), in the presented dataset. However, the dataset is not evenly distributed, i.e., there is missing data for some of the base stations. In the first step, we filtered the dataset in in order to leave only the base stations that contain complete data, i.e., 192 h of data (8 days). This resulted in keeping 1.983 base stations, i.e., 380.736 data rows (hours).

Then, we used this dataset to develop two approaches that predict the number of users one hour in advance. The first one is based on machine learning regression algorithms and predicts the number of users for an individual base station, i.e., it uses the characteristics of that particular base station to predict the number of users in the next hour. The size of the dataset is 380.736 data samples. The second approach uses other more generic statistical algorithms to predict the number of users on aggregated level, i.e., in all of the base stations. It utilizes only 192 data samples (the same as the number of hours), which is too small dataset that can be applied to advanced ML.

3.2 Individual Base Station Prediction

This approach is based on machine learning, regression models that predict the number of users at a particular base station in one-hour interval. The model takes as input the current and the historical (last 24 h) traffic data from the particular base, then calculate numerous statistical features, and finally provide the prediction for the next hour.

The first step in the development of the machine learning model is the features extraction. In our case we use as input the current and the historical (last 24 h) traffic data from the particular base station, and then calculate numerous statistical features. We calculated the following statistical features for the last 24 h for each of the characteristics: number of users, number of packets, and number of bytes: mean value, max value, min value, kurtosis, standard deviation, skewness. Additionally, as a separate feature we use the previous value of each of the 3 characteristics.

In, the next step we trained 4 regression models: Decision Tree [13], KNN [14], Random Forest [15], and Xtreme Gradient Boost [16] models. Additionally, we used Dummy Regressor [17] as a baseline model. This model is simple statistical model that predicts a constant, i.e., the mean value of the users in the train data.

3.3 Aggregated Prediction

Since cellular traffic manifests usual time series behavioral model, including seasonal and trend patterns, statistical models can be utilized for forecasting the future outcomes in regard to past statistics. In order to identify a pattern or formula that may apply in future data prediction, many researchers have developed statistical analysis methods for time series [17]. The paper analyses 4 statistical analysis models, i.e. Moving Average (MA) [18], Exponential Smoothing (ES), i.e., Single Exponential Smoothing (SES) and Double Exponential Smoothing (DES) [19] and SARIMA [20]. These models are trained to predict the number of users on aggregated level for all base stations.

Moving Average Model
MA is a simple model that aims to predict trend-cycle elements by smoothing past data. A future data point is estimated as average of the k previous equally weighted data points. The MA data point estimate Y_t^{MA} is given by the following formula:

$$Y_t^{MA} = \frac{X_t + X_{t-1} + \ldots + X_{t-(k-1)}}{k} \tag{1}$$

where X_t is data point value at time t and k represents the number of past data points used in the MA model. Choosing this number properly is of great importance. Specifically, very small values will not capture the trend present in the time series, while very large values will impair the forecasting accuracy.

Exponential Smoothing Model
Since the most recent data observations yield the best reference for the future, there is need for schemes that have decreasing weights in time, as the observations get older. ES models are example for weighted schemes that have exponentially decreasing weights. Although there are many ES models, they all weight recent observations more significantly than the older values by using smoothing parameters. In our case, we use SES where the most recent observation is the most weighted DES, which takes into account the possibility of trend and seasonal components by introducing one more term in the observation. The equation for next predicted value Y_{t+1}^{SES} for SES model is given by:

$$Y_{t+1}^{SES} = \alpha X_t + (1 - \alpha) Y_t^{SES}, \tag{2}$$

where Y_t^{SES} is present predicted value, X_t is present actual value and α is smoothing parameter, $0 \leq \alpha \leq 1$.

In case of DES, the forecast value Y_{t+1}^{DES} is given by:

$$Y_{t+1}^{DES} = \alpha X_t + (1 - \alpha)(Y_t^{DES} + b_t), \tag{3}$$

$$b_{t+1} = \beta\left(Y_{t+1}^{DES} - Y_t^{DES}\right) + (1 - \beta)b_t, \tag{4}$$

where Y_t^{DES} is present predicted value, X_t is present actual value and α is level smoothing parameter $(0 \leq \alpha \leq 1)$, β is trend smoothing parameter $(0 \leq \beta \leq 1)$ and b_t s estimate of the slope of the time series at time t.

SARIMA Model

Seasonal Autoregressive Integrated Moving Average, known as SARIMA is actually modified ARIMA that supports data with seasonal component. The model consists of trend elements and seasonal elements that can be chosen through thorough analysis of autocorrelation function and partial autocorrelation functions of the time series. Trend elements are represented by the following parameters:

p: Trend autoregression order.
d: Trend difference order.
q: Trend moving average order
On the other hand, there are 4 seasonal parameters:
P: Seasonal autoregressive order.
D Seasonal difference order.
Q: Seasonal moving average order
m: seasonal length in the data

This hyperparameters are used to specify the seasonality (S), autoregression (AR), differencing (I) and moving average (MA), so *SARIMA (p, d, q)(P, D, Q)m* is applied to the time series x_t with the following equation [21]:

$$\Phi\left(L^m\right)\phi(L)\Delta^d \Delta_m^D x_t = \theta_0\Theta\left(L^m\right)\theta(L)w_t, \tag{5}$$

where L is the lag operator and w_t is assumed to be Gaussian white-noise process with mean zero and variance σ^2. Δ^d and Δ_m^D are assumed to be difference operator and seasonal difference operator. This operators aim to transform the non-stationary time series x_t to the stationary process x_t^*:

$$x_t^* = (1 - L)^d (1 - L)^D y_t. \tag{6}$$

Further, $\phi(L)$ and $\theta(L)$ are defined as the following polynomials in the lag operator:

$$\phi(L) = 1 - \phi_1 L - \ldots - \phi_p L^p, \tag{7}$$

$$\theta(L) = 1 + \theta_1 L + \ldots + \theta_q L^q. \tag{8}$$

The seasonal polynomials $\Phi(L^m)$ and $\Theta(L^m)$ in the lag operator are defined as:

$$\Phi(L^m) = 1 + \Phi_1 L^m - \ldots - \Phi_p L^{Pm}, \tag{9}$$

$$\Theta(L^m) = 1 + \Theta_1 L^m + \ldots + \Theta_p L^{Qm}. \tag{10}$$

The following section analyses the prediction performance of the presented algorithms, in the case of flash crowd occurrences.

4 Performance Analysis

This section evaluates the prediction accuracy and reliability of the presented algorithms, for both the individual and aggregate base station predictions. The analysis is performed by examining the Mean Absolute Error (MAE), as a metric for evaluation and comparison between the different algorithms. To evaluate the models the dataset was divided 70% for training, and 30% for evaluation.

Figure 2 depicts the MAE results for the ML-based algorithms used in the per base station prediction. The figure shows that all of the models significantly outperform the baseline. This suggests that ML algorithms are more reliable and suitable for flash crowds' predictions compared to conventional prediction algorithms, when the system has large volumes of historical information. As a result, the ML algorithms were able to learn a model that uses the characteristics of the dataset to better predict the number of users. The figure also shows that the best performing model is the Random Forest. It achieves MAE of 7.1 users, which means that on average the model will under- or over-estimate the number of users by 7.

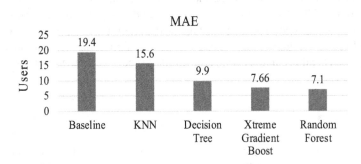

Fig. 2. Individual prediction of the number of users. Comparison of models.

Random Forest and Xtreme Gradient Boost induce the highest computational complexity of all analyzed models. In particular, they consist of hundreds of Decision Trees. In scenarios where the virtual RAN is computational capabilities are limited or computationally heavy loaded, Decision Tree can be more suitable because of their significantly lower computational complexity and relatively high accuracy. Another advantage of the Decision Tree is that it is understandable model, i.e., an expert can check and evaluate the model visually. This is something that we plan to further exploit in future work.

Figure 3 depicts the results and the comparison between the statistical models used for the aggregate base station prediction. The results show that the MA model shows worst performance, since it is the simplest time series model. Between the SES and DES, it is clear that DES model performs better due to the fact that it takes into account the trend and seasonality characteristics of the time series. It is also evident that the SARIMA model outperforms all of the previous models as a result of its complexity and the numerous trend and seasonal parameters that play a big role in the prediction process.

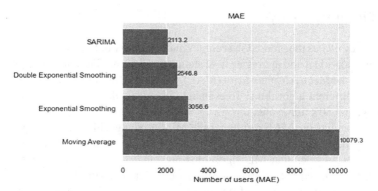

Fig. 3. Aggregated prediction of the number of users. Comparison of models

Taking into consideration that the average value of the data set in the aggregate prediction case, which is 56 815.4 users, SARIMA achieves less than 4% error in the prediction process. In the case of the individual base station prediction, the average number of users is 29, thus Random Forest achieves 24% error. However, the distribution of the number of users among the base stations varies a lot, i.e., the standard deviation is 28, resulting in the higher error percentile. For example, the Baseline model, that reflects the statistical predictors, has significantly higher prediction error compared to the Random Forest.

5   Conclusion

As a result of their inflexibility and static configuration, existing network architectures are failing to provide service in the most critical periods related to flash crowd situations. The 5G, as a promising technology, still do not address properly the utilization of the network virtualization and its dynamicity with respect to flash crowds.

This paper discusses the potential applicability of RAN virtualization and its synergy with new intelligence-based technologies, such as ML, that can address the issues related to flash crowd scenarios. The results in the paper clearly show that advanced solutions based on ML can significantly improve the network performance and its proactive adaptivity by reliably predicting flash crowd scenarios. The ML-based solutions are especially efficient when the available historical information is large and when the number of active users has significant variation. The paper also discusses that in case of low dataset fidelity or limited computational capabilities, conventional statistical models are a more suitable option.

Future work will extend the analysis to specific flash crowd scenarios, such as emergency situations. Moreover, it will focus on practical implementation of the proposed algorithms and foster real-world trials.

References

1. 5GPPP Architecture Working Group: View on 5G Architecture (2017)
2. Chowdhury, N.M.M.K., Boutaba, R.: A survey of network virtualization. Comput. Netw. Int. J. Comput. Telecommun. Netw. **54**(5), 862–876 (2010)
3. Kreutz, D., Ramos, F.M.V., Veríssimo, P.E., Rothenberg, C.E., Azodolmolky, S., Uhlig, S.: Software-defined networking: a comprehensive survey. Proc. IEEE **103**(1), 14–76 (2015). https://doi.org/10.1109/JPROC.2014.2371999
4. European Telecommunications Standards Institute: Network Functions Virtualisation (NFV), NFV#17 Plenary meeting, Bilbao, Spain (2017)
5. Gavrilovska, L., Rakovic, V., Denkovski, D.: From cloud RAN to open RAN . Wireless Pers. Commun. **113**, 1523–1539 (2020). https://doi.org/10.1007/s11277-020-07231-3
6. ITU Focus Group on Machine Learning for Future Networks including 5G (2020). https://www.itu.int/en/ITU-T/focusgroups/ml5g/Pages/default.aspx
7. Marinova, S., et al.: End-to-end network slicing for flash crowds. IEEE Commun. Mag. **58**(4), 31–37 (2020). https://doi.org/10.1109/MCOM.001.1900642
8. Gavrilovska, L., Rakovic, V., Denkovski, D.: Aspects of resource scaling in 5G-MEC: technologies and opportunities. In: IEEE Globecom 2018 (2018)
9. European Telecommunications Standards Institute: MEC in 5G networks, Sophia Antipolis, France (2018)
10. Kang, J.M., Lin, T., Bannazadeh, H., Leon-Garcia, A.: Software-Defined Infrastructure and the SAVI Testbed. In: Leung, V., Chen, M., Wan, J., Zhang, Y. (eds.) Testbeds and Research Infrastructure: Development of Networks and Communities. Springer, Cham (2014)
11. The dataset: https://github.com/caesar0301/city-cellular-traffic-map
12. Chen, X., Jin, Y., Qiang, S., Hu, W., Jiang, K.: Analyzing and modeling spatio-temporal dependence of cellular traffic at city scale. In: 2015 IEEE International Conference on Communications (ICC) (2015)
13. Hssina, B., Merbouha, A., Ezzikouri, H., Erritali, M.: A comparative study of decision tree ID3 and C4.5. Int. J. Adv. Comput. Sci. Appl. **4**(2), 13–19 (2014)
14. García-Laencina, P.J., Sancho-Gómez, J.L., Figueiras-Vidal, A.R., Verleysen, M.: K nearest neighbours with mutual information for simultaneous classification and missing data imputation. Neurocomputing **72**(7–9), 1483–1493 (2009)
15. Breiman, L.: Random forests. UC Berkeley TR567 (1999)
16. Chen, T., He, T., Benesty, M., Khotilovich, V., Tang, Y.: Xgboost: extreme gradient boosting. R package version 0.4-2, pp. 1–4 (2015)
17. Makridakis, S., Wheelwright, S.C., Hyndman, R.J.: Forecasting Methods and Applications. Wiley Student Edition, 3rd edn. ISBN 9780-471-532330
18. Box, G.E.P., Hunter, J.S., Hunter, W.G.: Statistics for Experimenters: Design, Discovery, and Innovation, 2nd edn. Wiley, Hoboken (2005). 13 978-047 J -71813
19. Gardner, E.: Exponential smoothing: the state of the art—part II. Int. J. Forecast. **22**, 637–666 (2006). https://doi.org/10.1016/j.ijforecast.2006.03.005
20. Fuller, W.A.: Introduction to Statistical Time Series, 2nd edn. Wiley, New York (1996)
21. Brockwell, P.J., Davis, R.A.: Time Series: Theory and Methods. Springer, New York (1991)

Mutual Authentication Protocol for Secure VANET Data Exchanges

Vincent Omollo Nyangaresi[1](✉), Anthony J. Rodrigues[2], and Nidhal Kamel Taha[3]

[1] Tom Mboya University College, Homabay, Kenya
vnyangaresi@tmuc.ac.ke
[2] Jaramogi Oginga Odinga University of Science and Technology, Bondo, Kenya
tonyr@jooust.ac.ke
[3] The World Islamic Science and Education University, Amman, Jordan
nidhal.omari@wise.edu.jo

Abstract. The initial signaling and data exchanges over open wireless transmission channels in vehicular ad hoc networks (VANETs) renders these networks susceptible to security and privacy violation attacks such as impersonation and packet replays. To curb this, a number of protocols have been proposed such as Public Key Infrastructure (PKI) based schemes, identity (ID) based schemes, anonymity based approaches and password or biometric based schemes. However, PKI based schemes have high computational overheads while ID based schemes are vulnerable to denial of service attacks (DoS). On the other hand, password and biometric based schemes employ the long term shared secrets stored in tamper proof devices (TPD) as the sole authentication factor, rendering them vulnerable to side-channel attacks. On their part, anonymity based approaches employ either digital certificates, pseudonyms or group signatures. However, these schemes do not offer trajectory privacy, conventional signature signing and verification is inefficient, and certificate storage or revocation leads to high storage and computation costs. In this paper, a multi-factor mutual authentication protocol that addressed some of these attacks is proposed. This scheme eliminates the requirement for long term storage of secret keys on TPD and remained secure even in the face of on-broad unit (OBU) active physical attack. Simulation results showed that the proposed protocol is robust against attacks such as privileged insider, masquerade and packet replay. It also preserved backward key secrecy, forward key secrecy, password secrecy and anonymity. Its performance evaluation revealed that it exhibited average computation and communication overheads, in addition to average beacon generation and verification latencies.

Keywords: Key management · Mutual authentication · Nonce · Time stamp · Privacy · Security · Session · VANETs

1 Introduction

A typical Vehicular ad-hoc network (VANET) consists of roadside units (RSUs), a trusted thirty part (Trust Authority-TA), vehicle on-broad units (OBUs), wheel rotation sensors and radars which employ IEEE 802.11p as the wireless access standard.

D. Perakovic and L. Knapcikova (Eds.): FABULOUS 2021, LNICST 382, pp. 58–76, 2021.
https://doi.org/10.1007/978-3-030-78459-1_5

Whereas sensors continually monitor driving data such as position, direction and speed, OBUs facilitate communication among vehicles as well as with RSUs through Dedicated Short Range Communications (DSRC). On the other hand, TA has to register RSUs and vehicles in addition to establishing the real identity of malicious vehicles. On its part, the RSU bridges both TA and OBU. VANETs proliferation can be attributed to emergence of smart cities and a surge in the number of vehicles, which necessitate communication among vehicles to obtain information such as traffic congestions and road conditions. Although this intelligent transportation system (ITS) offers road safety, their safety-critical communication is via open unsecured access wireless channels and hence the security of the transmitted data is a major concern [1]. In addition, authors in [2–4] and [5] explain that VANETs have numerous security and privacy (location and identity) issues owing to their open access. Further, security and privacy of communication over open wireless channels has been cited as a big challenge in VANETs [6]. As explained in [7], these open channels are susceptible to both active and passive attacks such as message interception or modification. Although numerous privacy preservation and secure authentication schemes have been developed to address these issues, majority of them have massive communication or computation overheads and have other privacy and security issues [8–10].

Researchers in [2] explain that security issues in these networks revolve around information confidentiality and integrity and hence the need for secure and user friendly authentication schemes. Moreover, authors in [11] concur that VANETs present novel security challenges that need to be addressed. Authors in [5] explain that efficient authentication among communicating entities, message integrity and preservation of privacy are key issues in VANETs, but which conventional security solutions do not fully satisfy. Further, although the fifth-generation (5G) cellular communication technology promotes the development of VANETs due to its higher capacity and data rates, and ultra-low latency, challenges such as security, privacy and efficiency remain unresolved [12]. Since 5G-VANET interfaces cyberspace and real space, attacks such as traffic analysis and privacy violation can lead to traffic accidents [13].

Although authentication can be deployed to address security issues in these networks [14], owing to the relatively high speed of vehicles and their resource-constrained OBUs, only lightweight authentication algorithms are ideal [5]. As explained in [9], conditional privacy preserving authentication (CPPA) schemes have been employed to solve privacy and security of VANETs. However, these schemes require highly tamper-proof devices (TPDs) to be installed in vehicles, which may be infeasible [9]. These authors explain that all VANET entities and transmitted messages should be authenticated to prevent attacks such as replay and masquerade that may endanger pedestrians or drivers' lives. Most TPD-based approaches require the storage of long-term secret sensitive data in TPDs. These secret key, password or biometric-based authentication techniques either employ the shared secret or stored sensitive data as the sole authentication factor, which is not adequate in VANET environment. The authentication secret information stored in TPDs is assumed to be robust against any attack since it is the axiom of these schemes that TPDs are robust against side-channel or cloning attacks and can never be compromised [15], which is unrealistic. For instance, TPDs might erase all secrets due to uneven road surfaces that may be mistakenly interpreted as malicious tampering [16]. In addition, side-channel attacks exampled by electromagnetic radiation and power consumption analysis may be employed to learn secret information stored in TPDs.

To protect privacy in VANETs, anonymous communication is key, in which pseudonyms are deployed instead of real identities. Authors in [17] explain that the provision of efficient anonymous authentication in VANETs is very challenging. High communication and computational costs of the conventional pseudonymous authentication techniques has been cited by [18] as being detrimental to this process. Researchers in [19] point out that key management is another major issue in VANETs. Although Public Key Infrastructure (PKI) based schemes have been deployed for key management [20, 21], these schemes rely on a centralized TA which is susceptible to single point of failure [22], and require Certificate Revocation List (CRL) that generates immense communication overheads. Owing to the distributed nature and dynamic topology of VANETs, PKI based schemes are inefficient.

Identity-based signature schemes have been deployed in these networks to uphold privacy via mutual authentication. However, these approaches fall short of user privacy protection, are susceptible to attacks or have high computational complexity [23]. As pointed out in [24] and [25], the open nature of VANET environment calls for the development of robust authentication and privacy preserving techniques. Authors in [26] explain that majority of ID-based schemes are inefficient and have both high communication and computational overheads. As such, these schemes require some improvements. The contributions of this paper include the following:

I.	A protocol that leverages pseudo-identities and dynamic intermediary security parameters is developed to offer both identity and location privacy.
II.	Nonce and timestamps are deployed to protect the communication network against replay attacks.
III.	We stochastically update pseudo-identities, intermediary security parameters and session keys to resist side-channel attacks.
IV.	We utilize lightweight elliptic curve cryptography, hash functions and XOR operations in our protocol to lessen both computation and communication overheads.
V.	We show that I-III above eliminate the need for TPD and by extension the single point of failure.

The rest of this paper is organized as follows: Sect. 2 discusses related work while Sect. 3 expounds on the system model employed to achieve the paper objectives. On the other hand, Sect. 4 presents results, discusses them and evaluates the developed protocol. Lastly, Sect. 5 concludes this paper and gives future direction in this research area.

2 Related Work

Security and privacy issues in VANETs have attracted a lot of attention both in the industry and academia and hence numerous schemes have been developed or proposed. Authors in [5] proposed a lightweight multi-factor authentication technique for VANETs using pseudo-identities and physically unclonable functions. However, this scheme employs certificate authority which can be a single point of failure. In addition, the assumption that RSUs are structured into domains with each of these domains enjoying autonomous regional private materials may not always hold. Techniques based on PKI and TPD are some of the conventional security and privacy preserving approaches for VANET security but as pointed out in [27], PKI based schemes exhibit high computational and communication costs. On the other hand, TPD based schemes employ static information stored in them for authentication, but this information can be captured by adversaries through side channel attacks. For instance, PKI –based schemes developed in [16] and [28] have not only high communication overheads but also complex certificate management. Authors in [28] developed a scheme that achieved anonymous authentication and privacy tracking but which had reduced efficiency due to frequent applications for anonymous certificates from RSUs. In [29], an identity-based authentication protocol is developed for VANETs which still lacks non-repudiation and is also susceptible to replay attacks.

Authors in [30] developed an authentication technique which researchers in [31] demonstrated to offer very weak security levels. The batch verification technique developed in [32] is susceptible to both tracking and forgery attacks while the group key agreement approaches in [33] and [34] are vulnerable to tracking attacks. To reduce computation overheads, researchers in [35] proposed batch verification technique, but which is susceptible to bogus message injection attacks. Although the cryptographic puzzle based technique in [17] can prevent Denial of Service (DoS) attacks, the initial certificate verification is computationally intensive. Authors in [36] develop a lightweight privacy-preserving authentication technique that upheld both privacy and security but is still vulnerable to insider attacks, privacy breaches and masquerade attacks. To curb these issues, researchers in [37] developed an Elliptic Curve Cryptographic (ECC) based mutual authentication for VANETs, but this technique cannot assure user anonymity and is susceptible to both identity guessing and impersonation attacks.

Symmetric cryptosystem based techniques developed in [38–40] achieved fast message authentication and verification but vehicles are unable to authenticate messages independently, requiring the incorporation of RSUs. Researchers in [41] proposed group signature based schemes for privacy protection but signature verification require high computation costs. Identity based cryptography has been employed in [18] and [42] to achieve conditional privacy while alleviating certificate management issues but have high time complexities due to bilinear pairing operations. Authors in [43] developed a lightweight mutual authentication, which is susceptible to location tracking attacks. Researchers in [15] developed a lightweight message authentication scheme to thwart DoS but it exhibits long message verification delays and fails to implement mutual authentication between vehicles. Blockchain based key management techniques have been proposed for VANETs in [44–46]. However, these approaches lack automatic key update in fast and highly dynamic applications. As pointed out in [11], although blockchain boosts trust through its tamper proof nature, it renders key update and revocation cumbersome. Authors in [47] propose an RSU based authentication scheme for regular updating of the master key. However, the scheme in [47] is susceptible to both privacy attacks and impersonation attacks and is computationally intensive due to bilinear pairings. To reduce complexity in bilinear pairing, ECC based scheme has been developed in [48], which is however vulnerable to impersonation attacks and cannot offer privacy protection [49].

A privacy-preserving authentication method has been proposed in [50], which is inefficient due to bilinear pairings. Similarly, researchers in [51] proposed a bilinear based anonymous authentication method which is still vulnerable to replay and tracking attacks and cannot ensure both forward and backward security. To boost anonymity and integrity, authors in [49] proposed an authentication scheme which is still susceptible to tracking attacks. A two-factor authentication scheme has been proposed in [52] to improve authentication efficiency. However, the scheme in [52] is still vulnerable to DoS, masquerading attack and privacy leaks. The security technique in [53] is not robust against side channel attacks and as such, authors in [42] developed a scheme to address these attacks through periodic update of data stored in TPDs. However, as pointed out by [50], signature verification in [42] generates high communication overheads.

3 System Model

Provisions for malicious vehicle certificate revocation, packet source authentication, data integrity, conditional privacy in which vehicle private information is only known by authorized entities, and non-repudiation are characteristics of robust VANET authentication protocol [54]. It has been pointed out that most of the conventional VANET authentication schemes depend on system key and long-term secret keys stored in highly secured TPD. These approaches are therefore not ideal for resource-constrained OBUs. Consequently, a robust authentication protocol should take into consideration the resource constrained nature of OBUs [5]. In addition, user's private data such as real identity and trajectory have to be protected from eavesdropping. This calls for a robust vehicle authentication protocol that is also lightweight to satisfy efficiency requirements. To attain, these goals, lightweight pseudonyms-based protocol based on ECC is developed. Elliptic Curve Cryptographic (ECC) provides robust level of security with shorter keys and hence ECC based mathematical problems have been deployed in VANET authentication schemes. As such, this paper deployed ECC discrete logarithm for security enhancement. In particular, the Elliptic Curve Discrete Logarithm (ECDL) problem and Elliptic Curve Computational Diffe-Hellman (ECCDH) problem are complex problems for any Probabilistic Polynomial Time (PPT) algorithm to solve with non-negligible probability. For both EDL and ECCDH problems, the following hold:

Definition-1: Taking $\mathfrak{f}$ as an elliptic curve group defined by prime numbers ζ and generator ϱ, E as an elliptic curve $y^2 = x^3 + ax + b \bmod \zeta$, and $a, b \in_R Z_\zeta^*$, then given two random points ϱ and $\varkappa$ of group $\mathfrak{f}$ on E, the objective of the ECDL is to find an integer $a \in_R Z_\zeta^*$ that satisfies $\varkappa = a\varrho$, where the unknown number a is difficult to calculate. Consequently, the problem of ECDL is assumed to be computationally infeasible for any PPT algorithms to solve.

Definition-2: Given two random points R and $\varkappa$ of group $\mathfrak{f}$ on E, where R $= a\varrho$ and $\varkappa = b\varrho$, the goal of ECCDHP is to compute point $ab\varrho \in \mathfrak{f}$, where $a, b \in_R Z_\zeta^*$ are two unknown integers. Since point $ab\varrho \in \mathfrak{f}$ is difficult to compute, it is assumed that the problem of ECCDH is computationally infeasible for any PPT algorithms to solve.

Definition 3: Taking point ϱ on E, scalar point multiplication of E is computed by repeated addition of this point. Let $\mathrm{M} \in_R Z_\varsigma^*$, then $\mathrm{M}\varrho = \varrho + \varrho + \cdots + \varrho(\mathrm{M}$ times), where $\mathrm{M} > 0$.

Definition 4: The discriminant of the elliptic curve is $4a^3 + 27b^2 \neq 0$, and E forms a cyclic additive group $\mathfrak{f}$ under point addition operation $\varrho + \varkappa = \mathrm{R}$.

Definition 5: Hash algorithms $h(.)$ encode data into fixed digits digital signatures in such a way that it is infeasible to compute original data from the enciphered digits. Any $h(.)$: (a)generates fixed-length enciphered digits for any length of input data. (b) it is straightforward to generate $K = h(\chi)$ from χ but infeasible to generate $\chi = h^{-1}(K)$ from K. (c) Given χ and K, finding $h(\chi) = h(K)$ can be computationally infeasible.

As shown in Fig. 1, the simulated VANET consisted of one AS which acted as TA, two OBUs, two RSUs, and two vehicles (V_S and V_T) all communicating through the IEEE 802.11p protocol. The OBUs recorded vehicle data such as velocity and location while RSUs connected vehicles to the internet, in addition to information exchange with passing vehicles to establish road conditions.

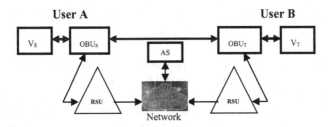

Fig. 1. VANET structure

In conventional authentication schemes, authentication of vehicles is through private keys stored in TPD which are used to generate digital signatures for each vehicle. In these schemes, TA provides RSUs and vehicles with public and private key pairs. However, the proposed protocol eliminated the requirement for the storage of private keys stored in TPD and instead, these keys were dynamically generated and refreshed using lightweight hashing functions and XOR operations. Table 1 gives the notations used in this paper and their brief descriptions.

The proposed mutual authentication protocol comprised of five major phases: *AS* parameter setting, V_i registration, login phase, session authentication, and data exchange phases. Each of these major phases had sub-steps that realized the objectives of the major phases.

AS Parameter Setting, V_i Registration & Login Phase: The first step in the proposed protocol is for the authentication server (*AS*) to register V_i (step -1) after which the *AS* selects $\mathcal{S} \in_R Z_\varsigma^*$ stochastically as its secret key. It then employs one way hash chain technique to compute secure key-sets as shown in step-2, which are sent to UBU_i together

Table 1. Notations

Notation	Description	Notation	Description
AS	Authentication server	$\mathcal{P}_T$	Target *OBU* public key
Ş	*AS* secret key	z_i	Protects security of $ħ_i$
SKS	Secure key-sets	d_i	Validation parameter
V_i	i^{th} vehicle	q_i	Parameter for computation of d_i
V_S	Source vehicle	έ	Session key
V_T	Target vehicle	tmp_c	Current time stamp of OBU_i
ƥ	$i^{th}V_i$ password	OBU_S, OBU_T	Source *OBU*, target *OBU*
l_i	$i^{th}V_i$ pseudo-identity	tmp_S	Current time stamp of OBU_S
l_j	$j^{th}V_i$ pseudo-identity	tmp_T	Current time stamp of OBU_T
n_1	*AS* nonce	tmp_v	Current time of V_i
h	Hash function	‖	Concatenation operator
$ħ_i$	User of V_i private key	$\oplus$	Exclusive OR (XOR) operator
$ħ_S$	Source *OBU* private key	$\mathcal{P}_i$	Public key of V_i
$ħ_T$	Target *OBU* private key	$\mathcal{P}_S$	Source *OBU* public key

with public parameters $\{ tf, \varrho, \zeta \}$ (phase-3) for storage (step-4). Afterwards, the V_i registration begins with the selection of its password ƥ and computation of its pseudo-identity l_j (step-5) which are utilized to compute $\mathcal{G}$ (phase -6). In step 7, $\mathcal{G}$ is sent to *AS* which then selects nonce n_1 that is used to compute parameters q_i, $ş_i$, $б_i, ɛ_i$ (step 8), where parameter $ş_i$ is only known to the *AS*. In phase 9, these security parameters $\{б_i, ɛ_i, n_1, h(), tf, \varrho, \zeta \}$ are sent to OBU_i for buffering (step 10, the user in V_i supplies l_j and ƥ to OBU_i after which nonce $ħ_i$ is selected as user of V_i's private key. This is followed by the computation of V_i's public key $\mathcal{P}_i$ as well as security parameter z_i at UBU_i (phase-11) as shown in Fig. 2. In step 12, OBU_i employs ƥ and $б_i$ to retrieve q_i that is used to derive the validation parameter d_i (phase-13), before buffering $\{ \mathcal{P}_i, z_i, l_j, ƥ \}$. Here, z_i protects $ħ_i$ from side channel attacks.

In phase 14, the user commences the VANET login process by inputting $\{ l_j, ƥ \}$ into the OBU_i which, together with the re-computed q_i using $б_i$ (step 15) are used to derive Ұ for authenticating user of V_i (phase -16). On condition that Ұ and d_i are equivalent, the user in V_i is successfully authenticated, otherwise the login request is rejected (step-17).

Session Authentication: The next procedure is session authentication between OBU_S and OBU_T which starts by having OBU_S generate nonce R_i, re-compute security key sets, *SKS* (step 18), compute beacon $\bar{Q}$, followed by security parameters $Ł_1$ and $Ł_2$ (phase 19). In step 20, the authentication message $\{ \bar{Q}, ɛ_i, n_1, Ł_1, Ł_2, tmp_c \}$ is sent to OBU_T which then checks its freshness. If timestamp tmp_c is beyond the set range, the message is flagged as replay attack (phase-22). If this is not the case, OBU_T re-computes security parameter $ş_i$ and retrieves R_i (step-23). This is followed checking of the validity

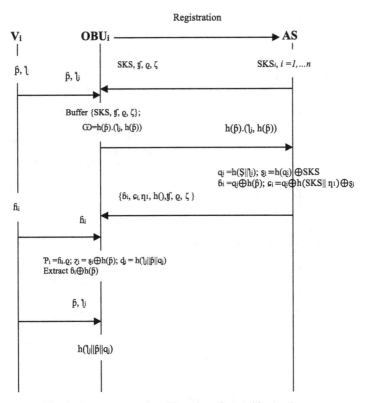

Fig. 2. Parameter setting, V_i registration and login phases

of security parameter $Ł_2$ such that if it is not valid, session authentication is rejected (phase -24). However, if it is valid, OBU_T generates nonce R_j used to derive security parameter z and session key $\acute{e}$ (step-25). This is followed by the computation of security parameters $Ł_3$, $Ł_4$, and verification message $Ł_5$ (phase-26) after which message $\{z, Ł_3, Ł_4, Ł_5, tmp_v\}$ is sent to the OBU_S (step-27). In phase 28, the validity of timestamp tmp_v is checked such that if it is invalid, the request is flagged as replay attack (step-29). However if tmp_v is within the set range, OBU_S re-computes security parameters R_j, s_i and session key $\acute{e}$ (phase-30). To fully trust OBU_T, verification message $Ł_5$ is re-computed and employed (step-31) such that if it is not valid, session authentication is terminated (phase-32). However, if it is valid, security parameter $Ł_6$ and c_i^* are computed (step-33) before replacing security parameters c_i and η_I with c_i^* and R_i respectively (phase-34). In step 35, OBU_S extracts SKS and computes security parameter ϑ before buffering them as shown in Fig. 3. This ensures that an adversary cannot obtain data that can facilitate side channel attacks.

In phase 36 through 40, OBU_S sends security parameters $\{h^*(R_j||z)\}$ and $\{\acute{e} \oplus Ł_6\}$ to OBU_T which is used to verify that OBU_S is not malicious. This marks the end of the session authentication phase and the onset of data exchange.

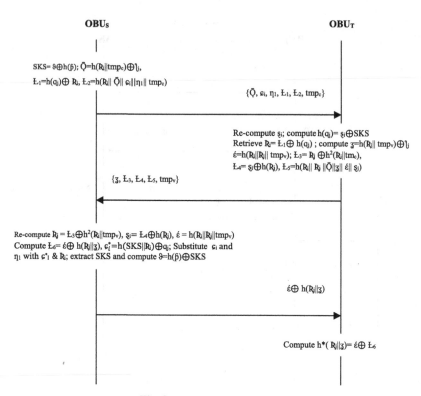

Fig .3. Session authentication

Data Exchanges: In step 41, OBU_S generate nonce R_S and beacon $\bar{Q}_S$ before computing security parameters r, $Ł_S$ and verification message $Ł_V$. Thereafter, message $\{Ł_S, Ł_V, \bar{Q}_S, tmp_S\}$ is sent to OBU_T (phase 42) where time stamp is validated (step 43 and 44) as before. If this time stamp is within the set range, OBU_T re-computes security parameter r using its own private key fi_T and OBU_S' public key P_S (phase- 45) as shown in Fig. 4. In step 46, the connection request is authenticated using $Ł_V$ such that it is rejected if $Ł_V$ is invalid (phase-47). However, provided it is valid, OBU_T chooses nonce R_T and calculates security parameters z_T, $Ł_3$, $Ł_4$ and session key $é$ (phase 49) before sending response message $\{Ł_3, Ł_4, z_T, tmp_T\}$ to OBU_S (step-50). In phase 51, time stamp tmp_T is validated by OBU_S as before while security parameters R_T, l_T and session key $é$ are re-calculated in step 53 at the OBU_S, provided tmp_T is within set range. In phase 54, the equivalence of message $\{h(l_T \| é)\}$ to verification message $Ł_4$ is checked as before and if it is valid, response message $Ł_5$ is generated (step-56) and sent to OBU_T (phase -57).

Upon receipt of $Ł_5$, OBU_T confirms its validity by re-calculating message $\{h(R_T \| é)\}$ (step-58). If it is valid, V_S and V_T can start data exchanges (phase-61). To ensure robust security, upon completion of data exchanges, SKS is re-generated as shown in Fig. 5.

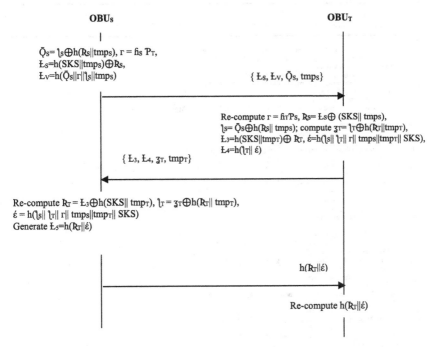

Fig. 4. Secure data exchanges

4   Results and Discussion

To simulate the proposed protocol, the parameters in Table 2 were employed. The vehicle speed was varied from 10 m/s to 50 m/s over the 4 km^2 by 4 km^2 simulation area. The number of vehicles lay between 50 and 250 while the communication range was between 200 m to 350 m. On the other hand, the simulation duration of 5 min was established to be optimum for the measurement of the required data.

Regarding the wireless communication protocol, IEEE 802.11p was deployed. The performance of the proposed protocol was then analyzed in terms of key performance indicators in VANETs. This included end-to-end (E2E) packet latency and packet delivery ratio (PDR), beacon signing and verification latencies. Afterwards, its performance was further compared with that of other mutual authentication schemes in [5, 15] and [52].

E2E Packet Latency: we sought to investigate how the number of vehicles and their speeds in the VANET environment affected network delays. To accomplish this, the generated beacon transmission under three vehicle speed scenarios were considered which included slow speed (20 m/s), average speed (30 m/s) and high speed (40 m/s) as shown in Fig. 6. It can be observed that under a particular vehicle speed scenario, as the number of vehicles increases, so does E2E latencies.

This can be attributed to the fact that an increase in the number of vehicles in VANETs lead to increased packet congestion which then increase the processing and delivery time

INPUT: $\S, \beta, \mathfrak{f}, \varrho, \zeta, \eta_1, \mathfrak{f}_i, \mathfrak{R}_i, \mathfrak{R}_S, \mathfrak{R}_T$

OUTPUT: $\mathfrak{l}_j, \text{CD}, q_j, \mathfrak{s}_i, \delta_i, \varrho_i, \mathcal{P}_i, z_j, d_j, \chi, \text{SKS}, \bar{Q}, \acute{\varepsilon}, \mathfrak{z}, \text{Ł}_1, \text{Ł}_2, \text{Ł}_3, \text{Ł}_4, \text{Ł}_5, \text{Ł}_6, \varrho_i^*, \vartheta, \bar{Q}_S, r, \text{Ł}_S, \text{Ł}_V, \mathfrak{l}_S, \mathfrak{z}_T, \mathfrak{l}_T$

BEGIN:

1. AS registers V_i via a secure channel /* *start of AS parameters setting* */
2. Randomly select $\S$ and compute secure key sets $\{SKS_i, i = 1,...n\}$
3. $AS \rightarrow OBU_i$: $\{SKS, \mathfrak{f}, \varrho, \zeta\}$
4. Buffer $\{SKS, \mathfrak{f}, \varrho, \zeta\}$ in OBU_i /* *End of AS parameters setting* */
5. V_i selects its β and computes its pseudo-identity $\mathfrak{l}_j$ /* *start of V_i registration* */
6. Compute $\text{CD} = h(\beta).(\mathfrak{l}_j, h(\beta))$
7. $OBU_i \rightarrow AS$: $\{h(\beta).(\mathfrak{l}_j, h(\beta))\}$
8. AS chooses nonce η_1 and computes $q_j = h(\S||\mathfrak{l}_j), \mathfrak{s}_i = h(q_j) \oplus SKS, \delta_i = q_j \oplus h(\beta), \varrho_i = q_j \oplus h(SKS||\eta_1) \oplus \mathfrak{s}_i$
9. $AS \rightarrow OBU_i$: $\{\delta_i, \varrho_i, \eta_1, h(), \mathfrak{f}, \varrho, \zeta\}$
10. V_i inputs $\mathfrak{l}_j$ and β to OBU_i and selects $\mathfrak{f}_i$
11. Calculate $\mathcal{P}_i = \mathfrak{f}_i.\varrho$ and $z_j = \mathfrak{s}_i \oplus h(\beta)$
12. Using β and δ_i, OBU_i extracts $q_j = \delta_i \oplus h(\beta)$
13. Compute the validation parameter $d_j = h(\mathfrak{l}_j||\beta||q_j)$ /* *end of V_i registration* */
14. $V_i \rightarrow OBU_i$: $\{\mathfrak{l}_j, \beta\}$ /* *start of VANET login phase* */
15. Re-compute q_j using δ_i and calculate $\chi = h(\mathfrak{l}_j||\beta||q_j)$
16. **IF** $\chi != d_j$ **THEN:**
17. Reject login request /* *End of VANET login phase* */
18. **ELSE:** OBU_S generates nonce $\mathfrak{R}_i \in Z_i^*$ & compute $SKS = \vartheta \oplus h(\beta)$ /* *Start of session authentication* */
19. Calculate $\bar{Q} = h(\mathfrak{R}_i||tmp_c) \oplus \mathfrak{l}_j, \text{Ł}_1 = h(q_j) \oplus \mathfrak{R}_i, \text{Ł}_2 = h(\mathfrak{R}_i|| \bar{Q} || \varrho_i||\eta_1|| tmp_c)$
20. $OBU_S \rightarrow OBU_T$: $\{\bar{Q}, \varrho_i, \eta_1, \text{Ł}_1, \text{Ł}_2, tmp_c\}$
21. **IF** tmp_c not within range **THEN:**
22. Flag as replay
23. **ELSE:** Re-calculate $\mathfrak{s}_i$ using $\varrho_i \oplus h(SKS||\eta_1), h(q_j) = \mathfrak{s}_i \oplus SKS$ & retrieve $\mathfrak{R}_i = \text{Ł}_1 \oplus h(q_j)$
24. **IF** $\text{Ł}_2 = h(\mathfrak{R}_i|| \varrho_i||\bar{Q}_i||\eta_1|| tmp_c)$ **THEN:** Terminate session authentication request
25. **ELSE:** Generate nonce $\mathfrak{R}_j \in Z_i^*$ and compute $\mathfrak{z} = h(\mathfrak{R}_j|| tmp_v) \oplus \mathfrak{l}_j$ & $\acute{\varepsilon} = h(\mathfrak{R}_i||\mathfrak{R}_j|| tmp_v)$
26. Compute $\text{Ł}_3 = \mathfrak{R}_j \oplus h^2(\mathfrak{R}_i|| tm_c), \text{Ł}_4 = \mathfrak{s}_i \oplus h(\mathfrak{R}_i), \text{Ł}_5 = h(\mathfrak{R}_i|| \mathfrak{R}_j || \bar{Q} || \acute{\varepsilon} || \mathfrak{s}_i)$
27. $OBU_T \rightarrow OBU_S$: $\{\mathfrak{z}, \text{Ł}_3, \text{Ł}_4, \text{Ł}_5, tmp_v\}$
28. **IF** tmp_v not within range **THEN:**
29. Flag as replay
30. **ELSE:** Re-compute $\mathfrak{R}_j = \text{Ł}_3 \oplus h^2(\mathfrak{R}_i|| tmp_v), \mathfrak{s}_i = \text{Ł}_4 \oplus h(\mathfrak{R}_i), \acute{\varepsilon} = h(\mathfrak{R}_i|| tmp_v)$
31. **IF** $\text{Ł}_5 != h(\mathfrak{R}_i||\mathfrak{R}_j||\bar{Q}||\mathfrak{z}|| \acute{\varepsilon}|| \mathfrak{s}_i)$ **THEN:**
32. Terminate authentication process
33. **ELSE:** Trust OBU_T & compute $\text{Ł}_6 = \acute{\varepsilon} \oplus h(\mathfrak{R}_i||\mathfrak{z}), \varrho_i^* = h(SKS||\mathfrak{R}_i) \oplus q_j$
34. Substitute ϱ_i and η_1 with ϱ_i^* & $\mathfrak{R}_i$
35. Using $\mathfrak{s}_i \oplus h(q_j)$, extract SKS and compute $\vartheta = h(\beta) \oplus SKS$
36. $OBU_S \rightarrow OBU_T$: $\{\text{Ł}_6\}$
37. Calculate $h^*(\mathfrak{R}_i||\mathfrak{z}) = \acute{\varepsilon} \oplus \text{Ł}_6$
38. **IF** $h^*(\mathfrak{R}_i||\mathfrak{z}) != h(\mathfrak{R}_i||\mathfrak{z}||)$ **THEN:**
39. Flag as replay
40. **ELSE:** Trust OBU_S /* *End of session authentication* */

/* *Start of V_S & V_T Data Exchanges* */

41. OBU_S randomly chooses $\mathfrak{R}_S$ and computes $\bar{Q}_S = \mathfrak{l}_S \oplus h(\mathfrak{R}_S|| tmps), r = \mathfrak{f}_S \mathcal{P}_T, \text{Ł}_S = h(SKS|| tmps) \oplus \mathfrak{R}_S, \text{Ł}_V = h(\bar{Q}_S|| r||\mathfrak{l}_S|| tmps)$
42. $OBU_S \rightarrow OBU_T$: $\{\text{Ł}_S, \text{Ł}_V, \bar{Q}_S, tmps\}$
43. **IF** $tmps$ not within range **THEN:**
44. Flag as replay
45. **ELSE:** Re-compute $r = \mathfrak{f}_T \mathcal{P}_S, \mathfrak{R}_S = \text{Ł}_S \oplus (SKS|| tmps), \mathfrak{l}_S = \bar{Q}_S \oplus h(\mathfrak{R}_S|| tmps)$
46. **IF** $h(SKS|| tmps) \oplus \mathfrak{R}_S != \text{Ł}_V$ **THEN:**
47. Reject connection request
48. **ELSE:**
49. Randomly choose $\mathfrak{R}_T$ and compute $\mathfrak{z}_T = \mathfrak{l}_T \oplus h(\mathfrak{R}_T|| tmp_T), \text{Ł}_3 = h(SKS|| tmp_T) \oplus \mathfrak{R}_T, \acute{\varepsilon} = h(\mathfrak{l}_S|| \mathfrak{l}_T|| r|| tmps|| tmp_T|| SKS), \text{Ł}_4 = h(\mathfrak{l}_T|| \acute{\varepsilon})$
50. $OBU_T \rightarrow OBU_S$: $\{\text{Ł}_3, \text{Ł}_4, \mathfrak{z}_T, tmp_T\}$
51. **IF** tmp_T not within range **THEN:**
52. Flag as replay
53. **ELSE:** Re-compute $\mathfrak{R}_T = \text{Ł}_3 \oplus h(SKS|| tmp_T), \mathfrak{l}_T = \mathfrak{z}_T \oplus h(\mathfrak{R}_T|| tmp_T), \acute{\varepsilon} = h(\mathfrak{l}_S|| \mathfrak{l}_T|| r|| tmps|| tmp_T|| SKS)$
54. **IF** $h(\mathfrak{l}_T|| \acute{\varepsilon}) != \text{Ł}_4$ **THEN:**
55. Reject connection request
56. **ELSE:** Generate response $\text{Ł}_5 = h(\mathfrak{R}_T||\acute{\varepsilon})$
57. $OBU_S \rightarrow OBU_T$: $\{\text{Ł}_5\}$
58. Re-compute $h(\mathfrak{R}_T||\acute{\varepsilon})$
59. **IF** $h(\mathfrak{R}_T||\acute{\varepsilon}) != \text{Ł}_5$ **THEN:**
60. Reject connection request
61. **ELSE:** Commence data exchange /* *Secured by $\acute{\varepsilon}$* */
62. **IF** sender window is empty **THEN:**
63. Re-compute SKS and close session

END

Fig. 5. Proposed VANET mutual authentication protocol

at the *OBUs* and *RSUs*. Considering all the three vehicle speed scenarios, it is evident that as the vehicle speed increases, E2E latencies also increase. This can be attributed to the intermittent connectivity among the vehicles and RSUs resulting from very fast motion of the vehicles.

Table 2. Simulation parameters

Parameter	Value
Vehicle speeds	10–50 m/s
Area	4 by 4 km^2
Number of vehicles	50–250
Communication range	200-350 m
Simulation duration	5 min
Wireless protocol	802.11p

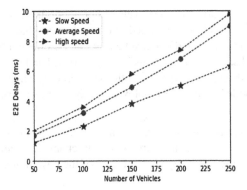

Fig. 6. E2E delays comparisons

PDR: To assess how PDR in the proposed protocol was affected by the increase in vehicle density, the same setting as that of E2E was employed. As shown in Fig. 7, the value of PDR is reduced when the number of vehicles in a VANET environment is increased.

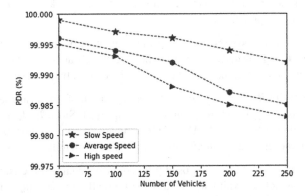

Fig. 7. PDR comparisons

The rationale for this observation is that congestion crops in with the high density of vehicles which overwhelms both *RSUs* and *OBUs*. Consequently, some of the packets may be dropped when the receiver window is full to its maximum capacity. It is clear from Fig. 7 that in all the three vehicle speed scenarios, the values of PDR remained well above 99%.

Stability: To analyze the stability of the proposed protocol, the number of vehicles in a VANET environment was increased from 50 to 250 as the value of PDR was measured. The obtained results are shown in Fig. 7, from which it is clear that PDR remained above 99.984% even in the presence of a very high vehicle density.

4.1 Security Analysis

To analyze the security features of the developed protocol, the Random Oracle model was employed. In this model, it is assumed that an adversary has access to all oracles and hence both authentication and data exchanges can be effectively controlled by an attacker. Insider attacks, attacks against anonymity, forward and backward key secrecy, password secrecy, and resilience against both masquerading and replay attacks were the specific attack models that were employed to assess the security of the proposed protocol.

Insider Attack: In this attack, it was assumed that *AS* stores β in plaintext. Although V_i sends $\{h(\beta).(\}_i, h(\beta))\}$ to *AS* over the communication channel, an attacker is unable to re-compute β owing to the one –way characteristic of the hash function $h()$ and hence β cannot be misused.

Anonymity: In the proposed protocol, both location and identity privacy are safeguarded by the utilization of pseudo-identities $\}_i$, timestamps (tmp_C, tmp_S, tmp_T), random nonce (η, R_i, R_j, R_S, R_T), XOR operations ($\oplus$) and hashing $h()$. As such, the interception of the transmitted parameters cannot yield location and real identity of the users.

Forward and Backward Key Secrecy: The session key $\acute{e}$ is generated from random parameters such as R_i and R_j, incorporates time stamps and is finally hashed. As such, its value is dynamically changed and consequently, an attacker with the present $\acute{e}$ is unable to discern the previous session key nor can the session key for the subsequent communication be computed.

Password Secrecy: The password β is encapsulated in other parameters such as pseudo-identity $\}_i$ before being hashed and sent to the *AS*. Consequently, even if an attacker captures the hash value, its value cannot be determined from the one way hash.

Masquerading Attacks Resilience: During the computation of the session key $\acute{e}$, random parameters such as R_i, R_j, $\}_i$ and time stamps are employed. Since R_i, R_j are enciphered using key q_j which is only known to *AS* and *OBU*, an adversary is unable to compromise the session key to access the communication entities' real identities.

Replay Attack Resilience: In the proposed protocol, all exchanged messages have current time stamps which are validated against the mutually agreed range. Due to these time stamp freshness checks, replayed messages are easily detected.

4.2 Performance Evaluation

To assess the performance of the developed protocol against other similar schemes, performance metrics such as computation costs, communication overheads, beacon generation and beacon verifications latencies were used.

Computation Costs: The execution times presented in [52] were adopted for this evaluation. Here, the SHA-256 hash function operation (T_{hash}) takes 0.006 ms, while the hash-based message authentication code, HMAC (T_{HMAC}) takes 0.0167 ms. Then, the goal here was to establish the duration that the proposed protocol took to login, sign and verify a single beacon. Let beacon generation be BG and a single beacon verification be BV. To login, the V_i computed the validation parameter d_i from l_i, β, and q_i which were then hashed. Since q_i computation also involves hashing, d_i generation required two $h()$ operations. Afterwards, for the login phase, OBU_i had to re-compute q_i which required one $h()$ operation. For message $\bar{Q}$ signing, one $h()$ operation was required. As such, login and message signing required 4 $h()$. To verify message $\bar{Q}$, $Ł_2$ was employed which required 3 $h()$ operations. Therefore, BG and BV required a total of 7 $h()$ operations. This value was then compared with those of schemes in [5, 15] and [52] as shown in Table 3.

Table 3. Computation costs comparisons

Scheme	BG	BV	BG + BV(ms)
Scheme in [5]	0.018	0.006	0.024
Scheme in [15]	0.0587	0.0227	0.0814
Scheme in [52]	0.0287	0:0167	0.0454
Proposed protocol	0.024	0.018	0.042

In the proposed protocol, the computation cost for BG needs four hash function operations, so the overall cost of BG is $4T_{hash} = 0.024$ ms; On the other hand, BV needs three a hash function, so the BV overall cost is $T_{HMAC} = 0.018$ ms. On the other hand, the scheme in [15] requires 7 T_{hash} and one T_{HMAC} for BG computation and hence the overall cost of BG is $7T_{hash} + T_{HMAC} = 0.0587$ ms. On the other hand, the message verification BV requires one T_{hash} and one T_{HMAC} and hence total BV is 0.0227 ms. For the scheme in [52], BG needs two T_{hash} and one T_{HMAC} and hence total BG cost is $2T_{hash} + T_{HMAC} = 0.0287$ ms. The BV phase requires only one T_{HMAC} and hence its cost is 0.0167 ms. Regarding the scheme in [5], BG needs only three T_{hash}, and hence total cost of BG is $3T_{hash} = 0.018$ ms, while BV needs only one T_{hash}, implying that BV cost is $T_{HMAC} = 0.006$ ms.

Communication Overhead: In this evaluation, the developed protocol was analyzed in terms of the size of the beacons transmitted across the VANET. In our protocol, a single beacon $\bar{Q}$ consisted of pseudo-identity, hash signature, nonce, and time stamp of sizes 20,

20, 2, and 4 bytes respectively, leading to an overall size of 46 bytes. This communication cost was then compared with costs for schemes in [5, 15] and [52] as shown in Table 4.

Table 4. Communication overheads comparisons

Scheme	Beacon components	Beacon Size (Bytes)
Scheme in [5]	pseudo-identity, h(), time stamp	44
Scheme in [15]	pseudo-identity, MAC sig., time stamp	47
Scheme in [52]	pseudo-identity, a truncated MAC sig., index no., time stamp	60
Proposed protocol	h(), R_i, tmp_c, l_i	46

The single beacon scheme in [5] has a total of 44 bytes, which consists of pseudo-identity, hash signature, and time stamp of sizes 20, 20, and 4 bytes respectively while a single beacon for the scheme in [15] has a total size of 47 bytes comprising of pseudo-identity, MAC signature and time stamp of sizes 23, 20, and 4 bytes respectively. On the other hand, a single beacon for the scheme in [52] has a total size of 60 bytes, consisting of pseudo-identity, a truncated MAC signature, index number, and time stamp of sizes 40, 12, 4 and 4 bytes respectively, leading to an overall size of 60 bytes.

Beacon Generation and Beacon Verifications Latencies: The schemes in [5, 15] and [52] have been evaluated in terms of beacon generation and verification latencies. As such, the beacon generation and verification of the proposed protocol was compared to these schemes as shown in Fig. 8(a) and Fig. 8(b). As shown in Fig. 8(a), the scheme in [5] had the least beacon generation latency while the scheme in [15] had the greatest beacon generation latency. On the other hand, the proposed protocol's beacon generation latency was slightly higher than that of the scheme in [5] but lower than the values for both [15] and [52].

Regarding beacon verification latencies, Fig. 8(b) shows that the scheme in [5] had the least latency while the scheme in [15] had the longest latency. This observation can be attributed to the increase in the computation costs as the number of T_{hash} and T_{HMAC} operations increases in all the four schemes. Although the scheme in [5] has better performance than the proposed protocol, this scheme employs certificate authority which can be a single point of failure. Moreover, its assumption that *RSUs* are structured into domains with each of these domains enjoying autonomous regional private materials may not always hold. In addition, the scheme in [5] employs time stamps as the only technique for replay attack prevention while our protocol further introduces nonce as another layer of pseudonomy during the session key generation. The security on the scheme in [15] is mainly dependent the system key, rendering it susceptible to attacks such as man-in-the-middle and common key compromising attacks. On the other hand, the scheme in [52] is vulnerable to attacks such as DoS, masquerade and privacy leaks.

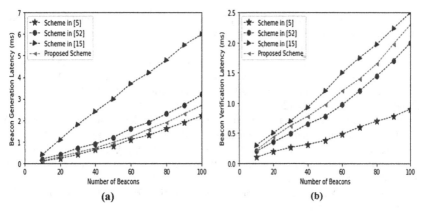

Fig. 8. (a) Beacon generation latency (b) Beacon verification latency

It further assumes a totally secure TPD that is immune against side channel attacks, an assumption that is too idealistic. Moreover, since schemes in [15] and [52] permanently store sensitive private information *TPD,* practically this information is vulnerable due to both cloning and side channel attacks against TPD.

5   Conclusion and Future Work

Many schemes have been proposed to offer security and privacy in VANET environment. However, it has been shown that these approaches either have high communication and computation overheads or are still vulnerable to other security or privacy violations. In this paper, a mutual authentication protocol for VANET entities has been developed and simulated. The results have indicated the robustness of the proposed protocol against privileged insider, masquerade and packet replay attacks. Moreover, the security analysis has shown that this protocol offers backward key secrecy, forward key secrecy, password secrecy and anonymity, which are key for the protection of sensitive data being transmitted over VANETs. Although the lightweight multi-factor authentication technique for VANETs using pseudo-identities and physically unclonable functions performed relatively better than our protocol, it is prone to single point of failure and does not assure robust pseudonomy. Future work in this area involves the deployment of the proposed protocol in a real VANET environment so that its security and performance can be evaluated in real-time.

References

1. Li, X., Liu, T., Obaidat, M.S., Wu, F., Vijayakumar, P., Kumar, N.: A lightweight privacy-preserving authentication protocol for VANETs. IEEE Syst. J. **14**(3), 3547–3557 (2020)
2. Wu, L., et al.: An efficient privacy-preserving mutual authentication scheme for secure V2V communication in vehicular ad hoc network. IEEE Access **7**, 55050–55063 (2019)
3. Sari, A., Onursal, O., Akkaya, M.: Review of the security issues in vehicular ad hoc networks (VANET). Int. J. Commun. Netw. Syst. Sci. **8**(13), 552–566 (2015)

4. Zhang, Z., Han, B., Chao, H.C., Sun, F., Uden, L., Tang, D.: A new weight and sensitivity based variable maximum distance to average vector algorithm for wearable sensor data privacy protection. IEEE Access **7**, 104045–104056 (2019)
5. Alfadhli, S.A., Lu, S., Chen, K., Sebai, M.: Mfspv: a multi-factor secured and lightweight privacy-preserving authentication scheme for vanets. IEEE Access **8**, 142858–142874 (2020)
6. Cheng, H., Liu, Y.: An improved RSU-based authentication scheme for VANET. J. Internet Technol. **21**(4), 1137–1150 (2020)
7. Bagga, P., Das, A.K., Wazid, M., Rodrigues, J.J., Park, Y.: Authentication protocols in internet of vehicles: taxonomy, analysis, and challenges. IEEE Access **8**, 54314–54344 (2020)
8. Al-Shareeda, M.A., Anbar, M., Hasbullah, I.H., Manickam, S., Hanshi, S.M.: Efficient conditional privacy preservation with mutual authentication in vehicular ad hoc networks. IEEE Access **8**, 144957–144968 (2020)
9. Wang, B., Wang, Y., Chen, R.: A practical authentication framework for VANETs. Secur. Commun. Netw. **2019**, 1–12 (2019)
10. Cui, J., Xu, W., Han, Y., Zhang, J., Zhong, H.: Secure mutual authentication with privacy preservation in vehicular ad hoc networks. Veh. Commun. **21**, 100200 (2020)
11. Ma, Z., Zhang, J., Guo, Y., Liu, Y., Liu, X., He, W.: An efficient decentralized key management mechanism for VANET with blockchain. IEEE Trans. Veh. Technol. **69**(6), 5836–5849 (2020)
12. Wang, P., Chen, CM., Kumari, S., Shojafar, M., Tafazolli, R., Liu, Y.N.: HDMA: hybrid D2D message authentication scheme for 5G-enabled vanets. IEEE Trans. Intell. Transp. Syst., 1–10 (2020)
13. Huang, Z., Liu, S., Mao, X., Chen, K., Li, J.: Insight of the protection for data security under selective opening attacks. Inf. Sci. **412–413**, 223–241 (2017)
14. Wang, D., Li, W., Wang, P.: Measuring two-factor authentication schemes for real-time data access in industrial wireless sensor networks. IEEE Trans. Ind. Inf. **14**(9), 4081–4092 (2018)
15. Wang, F., Xu, Y., Zhang, H., Zhang, Y., Zhu, L.: 2FLIP: a two factor lightweight privacy-preserving authentication scheme for VANET. IEEE Trans. Veh. Technol. **65**(2), 896–911 (2016)
16. Raya, M., Hubaux, J.-P.: Securing vehicular ad hoc networks. J. Comput. Secur. **15**(1), 39–68 (2007)
17. Sun, C., Liu, J., Xu, X., Ma, J.: A privacy-preserving mutual authentication resisting DoS attacks in VANETs. IEEE Access **5**, 24012–24022 (2017)
18. Liu, J., Yong, Y., Zhao, Y., Jia, J., Wang, S.: An efficient privacy preserving batch authentication scheme with deterable function for VANETs. In: Man Ho, A., et al. (eds.) NSS 2018. LNCS, vol. 11058, pp. 288–303. Springer, Cham (2018). https://doi.org/10.1007/978-3-030-02744-5_22
19. Qu, F., Wu, Z., Wang, F.-Y., Cho, W.: A security and privacy review of vanets. IEEE Trans. Intell. Transp. Syst. **16**(6), 2985–2996 (2015)
20. Kang, J., Elmehdwi, Y., Lin, D.: Slim: secure and lightweight identity management in vanets with minimum infrastructure reliance. In: Lin, X., Ghorbani, A., Ren, K., Zhu, S., Zhang, A. (eds.) SecureComm 2017. LNICSSITE, vol. 238, pp. 823–837. Springer, Cham (2018). https://doi.org/10.1007/978-3-319-78813-5_45
21. Xiong, W., Tang, B.: A cloud based three layer key management scheme for vanet. In: Yuan, H., Geng, J., Liu, C., Bian, F., Surapunt, T. (eds.) GSKI 2017. CCIS, vol. 849, pp. 574–587. Springer, Singapore (2018). https://doi.org/10.1007/978-981-13-0896-3_57
22. Albarqi, A., Alzaid, E., Al Ghamdi, F., Asiri, S., Kar, J.: Public key infrastructure: a survey. J. Inf. Secur. **6**(1), 31 (2015)
23. Wu, L., Wang, J., Choo, K.R., He, D.: Secure key agreement and key protection for mobile device user authentication. IEEE Trans. Inf. Forensics Secur. **14**(2), 319–330 (2019)

24. Kumar, S., Mann, K.S.: Prevention of dos attacks by detection of multiple malicious nodes in VANETs. In: International Conference on Automation, Computational and Technology Management (ICACTM), pp. 89–94. IEEE (2019)

25. Yao, Y., et al.: Multi-channel based Sybil attack detection in vehicular ad hoc networks using RSSI. IEEE Trans. Mobile Comput. **18**(2), 362–375 (2018)

26. Tzeng, S.-F., Horng, S.-J., Li, T., Wang, X., Huang, P.-H., Khan, M.K.: Enhancing security and privacy for identity-based batch verification scheme in VANETs. IEEE Trans. Veh. Technol. **66**(4), 3235–3248 (2017)

27. Zhang, L., Men, X., Choo, K.R., Zhang, Y., Dai, F.: Privacy- preserving cloud establishment and data dissemination scheme for vehicular cloud. IEEE Trans. Depend. Secure Comput., 1–14 (2018)

28. Lu, R., Lin, X., Zhu, H., Ho, P.-H., Shen, X.: Ecpp: efficient conditional privacy preservation protocol for secure vehicular communications. In: Proceedings of IEEE 27th Conference Computing Communications, pp. 1229–1237 (2008)

29. Zhang, C., Lu, R., Lin, X., Ho, P.-H., Shen, X.: An efficient identity-based batch verification scheme for vehicular sensor networks. In: Proceedings of 27th Conference Computing Communiations (INFOCOM), pp. 246–250 (2008)

30. Shim, K.-A.: Cpas: an efficient conditional privacy-preserving authentication scheme for vehicular sensor networks. IEEE Trans. Veh. Technol. **61**(4), 1874–1883 (2012)

31. Liu, J.K., Yuen, T.H., Au, M.H., Susilo, W.: Improvements on an authentication scheme for vehicular sensor networks. Expert Syst. Appl. **41**(5), 2559–2564 (2014)

32. Lee, C.-C., Lai, Y.-M.: Toward a secure batch verification with group testing for VANET. Wirel. Netw. **19**(6), 1441–1449 (2013)

33. Islam, S.H., Obaidat, M.S., Vijayakumar, P., Abdulhay, E., Li, F., Reddy, M.K.C.: A robust and efficient password-based conditional privacy preserving authentication and group-key agreement protocol for VANETs. Future Gener. Comput. Syst. **84**, 216–227 (2018)

34. Cui, J., Tao, X., Zhang, J., Xu, Y., Zhong, H.: HCPA-GKA: A hash function-based conditional privacy-preserving authentication and group key agreement scheme for VANETs. Veh. Commun. **14**, 15–25 (2018)

35. Jiang, S., Zhu, X., Wang, L.: An efficient anonymous batch authentication scheme based on HMAC for VANETs. IEEE Trans. Intell. Transp. Syst. **17**(8), 2193–2204 (2016)

36. Chuang, M.C., Lee, J.F.: TEAM: trust-extended authentication mechanism for vehicular ad hoc networks. IEEE Syst. J. **8**(3), 749–758 (2014)

37. Zhou, Y., Zhao, X., Jiang, Y., Shang, F., Deng, S., Wang, X.: An enhanced privacy-preserving authentication scheme for vehicle sensor networks. Sensors **17**(12), 2854 (2017)

38. Zhang, C., Lin, X., Lu, R., Ho, P.-H.: RAISE: an efficient RSU-aided message authentication scheme in vehicular communication networks. In: Proceedings of IEEE International Conference on Communication, pp. 1451–1457 (2008)

39. Lyu, C., Gu, D., Zeng, Y., Mohapatra, P.: PBA: prediction based authentication for vehicle-to-vehicle communications. IEEE Trans. Depend. Secure Comput. **13**(1), 71–83 (2016)

40. Shen, J., Zhou, T., Wei, F., Sun, X., Xiang, Y.: Privacy preserving and lightweight key agreement protocol for v2g in the social internet of things. IEEE Internet Things J. **5**(4), 2526–2536 (2018)

41. Zhu, X., Jiang, S., Wang, L., Li, H.: Efficient privacy preserving authentication for vehicularAdHoc networks. IEEE Trans. Veh. Technol. **63**(2), 907–919 (2014)

42. Zhang, L., Wu, Q., Domingo-Ferrer, J., Qin, B., Hu, C.: Distributed aggregate privacy-preserving authentication in VANETs. IEEE Trans. Intell. Transp. Syst. **18**(3), 516–526 (2016)

43. Cespedes, S., Taha, S., Shen, X.: A multihop-authenticated proxy mobile IP scheme for asymmetric VANETs. IEEE Trans. Veh. Technol. **62**(7), 3271–3286 (2013)

44. Lu, Z., Liu, W., Wang, Q., Qu, G., Liu, Z.: A privacy-preserving trust model based on blockchain for vanets. IEEE Access **6**, 45 655-45 664 (2018)
45. Lasla, N., Younis, M., Znaidi, W., Arbia, D.B.: Efficient distributed admission and revocation using blockchain for cooperative ITS. In: 2018 9th IFIP International Conference on New Technologies, Mobility and Security (NTMS), pp. 1–5. IEEE (2018)
46. Lei, A., Cruickshank, H., Cao, Y., Asuquo, P., Ogah, Z., Sun, C.P.A.: Blockchain-based dynamic key management for heterogeneous intelligent transportation systems. IEEE Internet Things J. **4**(6), 1832–1843 (2017)
47. Bayat, M., Pournaghi, M., Rahimi, M., Barmshoory, M.: NERA: a new and efficient RSU based authentication scheme for VANETs. Wirel. Netw. **26**, 1–16 (2019)
48. Lo, N.-W., Tsai, J.-L.: An efficient conditional privacy-preserving authentication scheme for vehicular sensor networks without pairings. IEEE Trans. Intell. Transp. Syst. **17**(5), 1319–1328 (2016)
49. Alazzawi, M.A., Lu, H., Yassin, A.A., Chen, K.: Efficient conditional anonymity with message integrity and authentication in a vehicular ad-hoc network. IEEE Access **7**, 71424–71435 (2019)
50. Zhong, H., Han, S., Cui, J., Zhang, J., Xu, Y.: Privacy-preserving authentication scheme with full aggregation in VANET. Inf. Sci. **476**, 211–221 (2019)
51. Shao, J., Lin, X., Lu, R., Zuo, C.: A threshold anonymous authentication protocol for VANETs. IEEE Trans. Veh. Technol. **65**(3), 1711–1720 (2016)
52. Hakeem, S.A.A., El-Gawad, M.A.A., Kim, H.: A decentralized lightweight authentication and privacy protocol for vehicular networks. IEEE Access **7**, 119689–119705 (2019)
53. He, D., Zeadally, S., Xu, B., Huang, X.: An efficient identity-based conditional privacy-preserving authentication scheme for vehicular ad hoc networks. IEEE Trans. Inf. Forensics Secur. **10**(12), 2681–2691 (2015)
54. Cui, J., Zhang, J., Zhong, H., Xu, Y.: SPACF: a secure privacy preserving authentication scheme for VANET with cuckoo filter. IEEE Trans. Veh. Technol. **66**(11), 10283–10295 (2017)

Analysis of MPLS and SD-WAN Network Performances Using GNS3

Ivan Grgurevic[1(✉)], Gabriela Barišić[1], and Adam Stančić[2]

[1] Faculty of Transport and Traffic Sciences, Department of Information and Communications Traffic, University of Zagreb, Vukelićeva 4, 10000 Zagreb, Croatia
`ivan.grgurevic@fpz.unizg.hr`
[2] Karlovac University of Applied Sciences, Ivana Meštrovića 10, 47000 Karlovac, Croatia
`adam.stancic@vuka.hr`

Abstract. MPLS and SD-WAN are technologies which ensure the quality of service in a different way. MPLS is a network technology which, with its method of routing the network packets, ensures the end-to-end service to users. On the other hand, SD-WAN ensures the global overview of the entire network and central managing thus enabling easy configuration or exchange of the already existing configuration system. The topic of this paper is analysis of these two network technologies by having them configured and simulated in the software tool GNS3. After that the analysis of the traffic network has been carried out. Regarding the ever-increasing development of the network technologies, an overview of the SD-WAN technology has been provided, as the new paradigm and its potential future applications.

Keywords: MPLS · SD-WAN · GNS3 · Software-defined networks · Network performances · Network simulation · Network traffic analysis

1 Introduction

Multi-Protocol Label Switching (MPLS) is a network technology which provides a new method of routing IP packages and it also satisfies the level of service quality at the same time. Since scalability and reliability have become an increasing concern for businesses, especially those with data centres, MPLS has provided the users with setting priorities within the service.

SD-WAN (Software Defined WAN) is a new paradigm which uses the characteristics of software-defined networks in the data centres, but with the application to a wide area network of the company and its affiliates. SD-WAN and SDN virtualize the resources in order to provide better performance, greater availability and automatic network management. At the same time, the costs are significantly reduced, especially compared to the MPLS technology.

By configuration and simulating MPLS and SD-WAN technologies and subsequent comparative analyses of various network parameters such as quality of service,

D. Perakovic and L. Knapcikova (Eds.): FABULOUS 2021, LNICST 382, pp. 77–90, 2021.
https://doi.org/10.1007/978-3-030-78459-1_6

bandwidth and delay, an analysis of their performances and their application has been made.

The motivation for choosing MPLS and SD-WAN technologies for comparison is their rapid development and expected potential future applications of SD-WAN.

The purpose of the paper is to determine the applicability and manageability of the software-defined WAN as a concept of software-defined networks.

The aim of the paper is to conduct an analysis of MPLS and SD-WAN network performances according to various recognised factors (management, latency, quality of service, etc.). The paper has been divided into eight sections. After the introduction, a brief overview has been given about the existing relevant research of the topic of this paper. Section 3 defines the MPLS technology and the mechanisms of routing MPLS technology that ensure reliable traffic transmission. Section 4, Characteristics of SD-WAN, describes the software-defined networks as the basis of SD-WAN and its characteristics have been defined. Section 5, Case study: Configuration and simulation of MPLS and SD-WAN networks in the GNS3 software tool, a network simulation was made using the GNS3. Section 6, MPLS network performance analysis, an analysis of the MPLS technology network traffic was made using a Wireshark network analyser, which collected data over endpoints in a previously simulated network. In Sect. 7, Analysis of SD-WAN network performances, the functionalities of the Mininet environment were used to define and analyse the network parameters. The last Section, Conclusion, shows the main elements of the work and a conclusion is made based on the conducted research.

2   Related Research

In paper [1], the performance of MPLS and traditional IP routing was measured in order to make a comparative analysis based on delays, missed packets and bandwidth in the OPNET network simulator.

According to research [2], the effectiveness of MPLS was compared with the use of the OpenFlow protocol. The study compared the scalability and interoperability with the emphasis on performance comparison. The test environment was created using routers and Hyper-V technology together with the Mininet environment for the SDN experiments.

According to studies [3] and [4], an overview has been given of the application of the software-defined networks in the WAN technology as well as an overview of the current research on this topic. The advantages of SD-WAN technology implementation as well as the challenges and the future of SD-WAN have been defined. Also, a layered architecture of the software-defined WAN has been defined.

In paper [5], a test environment was created by using *open-source* technology such as OpenvSwitch and OpenDaylight to set up a network monitoring and path selection based on the defined policies. The results have shown new features and benefits for the companies, particularly in resource optimisation.

In paper [6], the authors suggest the so-called *HOMA* approach to SD-WAN topology and routing management, based on the linear programming, and the results show cost reduction and overall efficiency.

In a report by the Frost & Sullivan Company [7], the telecommunication operator AT&T presents their vision of implementing SD-WAN network technology. The emphasis of this work lies on hybrid solutions, i.e. maintaining of the existing Ethernet and MPLS technologies with additional application of SD-WAN solution.

Furthermore, a hybrid solution of SD-WAN and MPLS has been proposed with a combination of OpenFlow routers on the edges of the network whereas the core network consists of MPLS routers. The results of the research showed that the hybrid architecture in network engineering has better efficiency compared to traditionally implemented MPLS networks [8].

3 MPLS Features

Multi-Protocol Label Switching (MPLS) is an IETF standard based on Cisco tag switching and allows interoperability with other network equipment manufacturers [9].

MPLS allows packet forwarding through the network so that the information in the packet header is analysed only once, and further forwarding is based on label checking, [10, 11]. Labels represent packet identification tags, and they are of fixed length. An MPLS tag is a 32-bit field with a specific structure [12]. An MPLS domain consists of one or several MPLS Label Switch Routers (LSRs) that scan and replace MPLS packet labels in order to forward them through the network [13].

The LSR that is on the edge of an MPLS domain and forwards the traffic inside and outside the MPLS domain is called a Label Edge Router (LER). The Label Switched Path (LSP) is a series of LSRs that switch the labelled packets through an MPLS network or a part of a MPLS network. That is, the LSP is the path through the MPLS network. The first LSR for a LSP is the input LSR and the last LSR for this LSP is the output LSR. LSP is a one-way communication. LSP is established for the first time by using the Label Distribution Protocol (LDP) [14].

The Forwarding Equivalence Class (FEC) is a group or flow of the packets that are forwarded the same way and treated equally in terms of forwarding. All the packets that belong to the same FEC have the same label. However, not all packets that have the same label do necessarily belong to the same FEC, since their forwarding treatment may differ [15].

For the packets to be transmitted via LSP through the MPLS network, the LDP is run on the LSR. When LSRs have labels for each FEC, the packets can be forwarded to the LSP. Label operations (addition, replacement and removal) are known to each LSR according to the LFIB table. The Label Forwarding Information Base (LFIB) is a table for forwarding labelled packets, and it consists of input and output labels for LSP [16–18].

4 SD-WAN Features

SD-WAN is a specific application of the software-defined networks technology on the WAN connections such as the broadband Internet or Long Term Evolution (LTE). It connects the corporate networks, including branches and datacentres, over long geographical distances [19].

SDN is a new network paradigm that is an example of software networks whose basic idea is to separate the control plane from the data plane. The control plane is all the logic which decides what needs to be done and gives instructions to the data plane on how to implement the decision. The control plane contains the control and routing behaviour such as topological change tracking, forwarding rule installation, route calculation, etc. The data plane forwards the traffic based on the rule specified by the control plane. The centralized control part is called the controller and it manages all the data planes and is software-installed in the hardware [20].

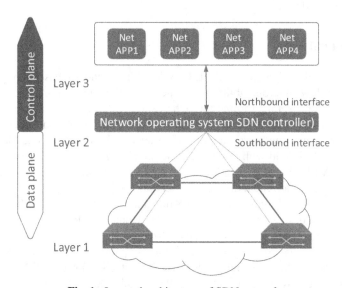

Fig. 1. Layered architecture of SDN network

Figure 1 shows the SDN network architecture. The first layer is the infrastructure layer that is called data plane, and it consists of network forwarding elements. The responsibilities of this layer are data forwarding, local information following and statistics collection. The layer above is the control plane. It is responsible for programming and management of the forwarding layer. OpenFlow, which is one of the most frequently used southbound interface consists mostly of switches, where some other SDN solutions use also routers [21].

The last layer is the application plane which contains network applications. They can introduce new network features such as security and management, forwarding schemes or help in the control part of the network configuration. The interface between the application plane and the control plane is called the northbound interface [21].

4.1 Definition of SD-WAN

SD-WAN is a part of a wider SDN technology which was described in the previous section. Both are software-defined technologies, but SD-WAN uses similar software-defined concepts of separating the control and the data plane on WAN network. Gartner defines SD-WAN with four characteristics:

1. Supports various types of connections like MPLS, Internet, LTE, etc.;
2. Has the ability to dynamically select the route, i.e. load sharing on WAN connections;
3. Provides a simple network management interface;
4. VPNs as well as other third-party service should be supported, [22].

Another important feature of SD-WAN technology is Zero touch provisioning (ZTP). This is a characteristic of the switch that allows automatic configuration. That is, when the switch is turned on, it sends a DHCP request in order to get the location of the centrally stored image and configuration, which it then downloads and runs [23].

4.2 SD-WAN and Network Virtualization

Network Functions Virtualization (NFV) is a technology that enables the separation of network functions from their assigned hardware devices and the implementation of these functions as software components into fully virtualized network infrastructures. NFV avoids manufacturer exclusivity and provides resource flexibility of upper layers (L4–L7) [24].

NFVs are Virtual Network Functions (VNFs) that manage the specific network functions. Individual VNFs can be connected or merged as building blocks to create a fully virtualized environment. VNFs run on Virtual Machines (VM) on the network infrastructure hardware [25].

The controller maintains the global network overview and programs the edges that can be custom or generic (VNF) hardware deployed to remote locations. The edges learn the routes, which enables central decision-making with remote execution by the edge. This architecture ensures the availability if the controller or the gateway is unavailable, and the edge device can make a local decision based on the latest instructions [26].

5   Case Study: Configuration and Simulation of MPLS and SD-WAN Networks in the GNS3

Graphical Network Simulator-3 (GNS3) is a network software emulator that allows the combination of virtual and real devices in order to simulate a complex network. GNS3 is used by many organizations and telecommunication networks specialists for their studies and the greatest advantage of GNS3 is the ability to collaborate with real networks. The configuration requires the Cisco Operating System (IOS) images on network devices, and in order to accomplish this, GNS3 uses Dynamips emulation software [27]. Version 2.2.9 of the GNS3 was used in the simulation, and the Cisco C3725 router with the image *c3725-adventerprisek9-mz.124–15.T14* was used for the MPLS network topology. Further in the text the following is described: the configuration and simulation of the MPLS core network (5.1), the configuration of user locations and VRF (5.2), and the configuration and simulation of the SD-WAN network (5.3).

5.1   MPLS Core Network Configuration and Simulation

The first part of the MPLS network simulation is the core network configuration consisting of three Cisco C3725 routers. The routers are assigned loopback addresses and interface IP addresses. An OSPF routing protocol is started on each router and LDP is enabled. Between the edge routers, a Multi Protocol BGP session is started with the vpnv4 configuration. Figure 2 shows the topology of the core network.

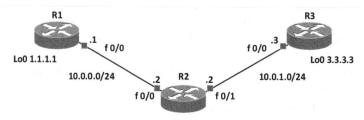

Fig. 2. MPLS core network topology

First, the IP address is configured for a loopback interface that is always running (state *up*); so the OSPF protocol will recognize it as a Router ID, and OSPF is started with the last line of the code and it is assigned process 1, and the area is 0 for the MPLS core network.

MPLS LDP is enabled under the OSPF process, and MP-BGP is configured on all Provider Edges (PEs).

5.2 Configuration of User Locations and VRF

It is necessary to configure two user locations that will also run the OSPF protocol, and Virtual Routing and Forwarding (VRF) will be configured on the PE routers. Figure 3 shows the selected MPLS network topology.

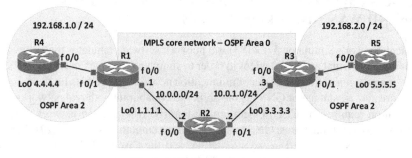

Fig. 3. MPLS network topology

The f0/1 interface with IP address 192.168.1.1/24 is configured on R1. After this step, the VRF needs to be configured. VRF is a technology included in the IP routers that allows multiple instances of routing tables within a router and their simultaneous operation. The VRF provides automatic traffic segregation which is applicable in creating separate virtual private networks (VPN) for the users. Hence, PE routers are able to store routes and to forward packets even if the users use identical addressing [28].

The final step for complete connectivity over the MPLS core is the redistribution of OSPF routes to R1 and R3 in MP-BGP and MP-BGP in OSPF. After configuration of the routers the MPLS core network is built which runs the OSPF with loopback addresses. R1 and R3 have peering with MP-BGP. LDP is enabled on all internal interfaces, and the external interfaces of the MPLS core network are set in VRF under the name RED which is also joined by local routers. The final step for complete connectivity via MPLS core is the redistribution of OSPF routes to R1 and R3 in MP-BGP and MP-BGP in OSPF.

5.3   Configuration and Simulation of SD-WAN Network

To begin with, the configuration of the physical part of the SD-WAN network was made, and it consists of four Cisco c3725 routers between which there is the OpenvSwitch, as presented in Fig. 4. As seen in Fig. 4, according to the network topology, two routers each form separate networks that are interconnected by OpenvSwitch.

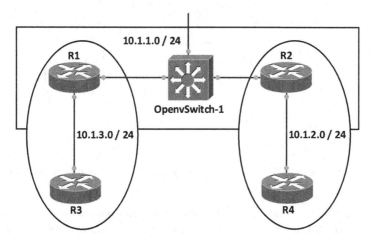

Fig. 4. Topology of physical routers connected by OpenvSwitch in SD-WAN network

The routers are interconnected by RIP routing protocol and end-to-end communication is achieved, and no additional configuration on OpenvSwitch was required, which shows the simplicity of the SD-WAN network configuration itself.

The next step in configuring the software-defined networks is to add a Mininet controller to the network topology, as shown in Fig. 5. After having configured the OpenvSwitch, the communication of the Mininet controller with the physical part of the network is established. With this, the centralised management of the entire simulation has been achieved, which will be also evident from the network traffic analysis.

The next part of the paper describes the simulation of SD-WAN network. A GNS3 simulator has been used as the basic simulation program, in which the physical Cisco c3725 router, OpenvSwitch and Mininet controller were run.

OpenvSwitch is a virtual switch designed for the network automation through program extensions, while still providing standard interfaces and protocols. It's a multilayer software switch and it's suited for virtual environment to function as virtual switch, [29]. Furthermore, the Mininet virtual environment enables the management of software-defined networks and supports the OpenFlow protocol [30].

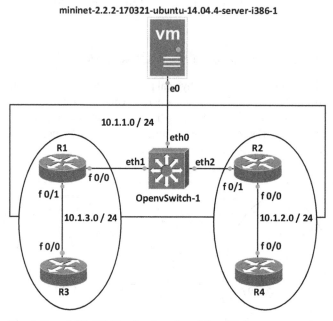

Fig. 5. Simulation of SD-WAN technology by adding Mininet as network controller

Mininet is a free network emulator hosting standard Linux network software with flexible custom routing and support of Software Defined Networking, [30]. The following sections will present an analysis of the traffic and the SD-WAN network parameters and their comparison with the MPLS.

6   Analysis of MPLS Network Performances

In order to analyse the end-to-end MPLS network performances in the software tool GNS3, a large quantity (<10,000) of ping packets between the end devices has been generated.

Figure 6 shows the MPLS network performance statistics when analysing the collected packets at the destination device. From graph in Fig. 7, one can see the average, maximal and minimal response times to ICMP packets.

As can be seen from Graph 7, the average response time of a ping packet is stable all the time and the maximal value is 0.66 ms.

Statistics

Measurement	Captured	Displayed
Packets	13098	11474 (87.6%)
Time span, s	5762.292	5743.598
Average pps	2.3	2.0
Average packet size, B	97	98
Bytes	1268754	1124452 (88.6%)
Average bytes/s	220	195
Average bits/s	1761	1566

Fig. 6. Statistics of MPLS network performances

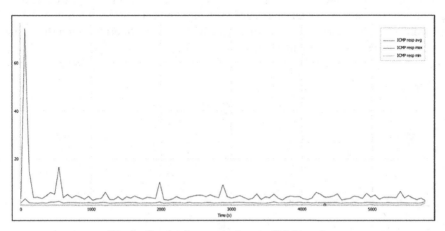

Fig. 7. Graph of response times to ICMP packets

Furthermore, the next packet collection was done between core and edge MPLS router, and according to Fig. 8, by using the network analyser *Wireshark,* the exchange of messages between these two routers is visible [17].

Fig. 8. Packets of LDP MPLS protocol between two routers

Figure 8 shows the communication of the LDP protocol which is responsible for the distribution of labels in the network. After the hello messages have been successfully sent in the network, and TCP connection between the core and the edge router has been established, the exchange of messages between these two routers began. Through LDP messages it is visible that the ID of the router is the loopback address that we had configured on the router. The LDP messages exchange information on the routes, labels and address families. The second filtering is the filtering of the BGP protocol which shows the label replacement mechanism, as shown in Fig. 9.

Through the LDP messages the router ID is the loopback address that we had configured on the router. The LDP messages exchange information on the routes, labels and address families. The second filtering is the BGP protocol filtering which shows the mechanism of label replacement, shown in Fig. 9.

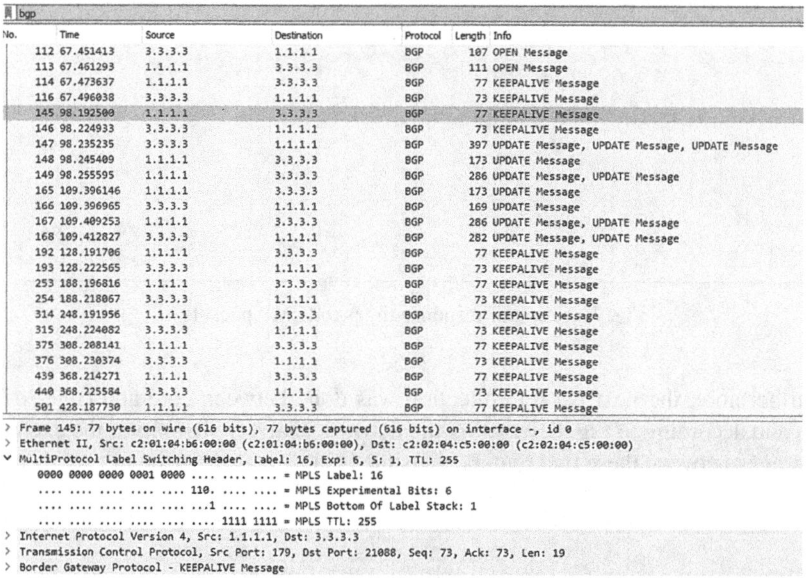

No.	Time	Source	Destination	Protocol	Length	Info
112	67.451413	3.3.3.3	1.1.1.1	BGP	107	OPEN Message
113	67.461293	1.1.1.1	3.3.3.3	BGP	111	OPEN Message
114	67.473637	1.1.1.1	3.3.3.3	BGP	77	KEEPALIVE Message
116	67.496038	3.3.3.3	1.1.1.1	BGP	73	KEEPALIVE Message
145	98.192500	1.1.1.1	3.3.3.3	BGP	77	KEEPALIVE Message
146	98.224933	3.3.3.3	1.1.1.1	BGP	73	KEEPALIVE Message
147	98.235235	3.3.3.3	1.1.1.1	BGP	397	UPDATE Message, UPDATE Message, UPDATE Message
148	98.245409	1.1.1.1	3.3.3.3	BGP	173	UPDATE Message
149	98.255595	1.1.1.1	3.3.3.3	BGP	286	UPDATE Message, UPDATE Message
165	109.396146	1.1.1.1	3.3.3.3	BGP	173	UPDATE Message
166	109.396965	3.3.3.3	1.1.1.1	BGP	169	UPDATE Message
167	109.409253	1.1.1.1	3.3.3.3	BGP	286	UPDATE Message, UPDATE Message
168	109.412827	3.3.3.3	1.1.1.1	BGP	282	UPDATE Message, UPDATE Message
192	128.191706	1.1.1.1	3.3.3.3	BGP	77	KEEPALIVE Message
193	128.222565	3.3.3.3	1.1.1.1	BGP	73	KEEPALIVE Message
253	188.196816	1.1.1.1	3.3.3.3	BGP	77	KEEPALIVE Message
254	188.218067	3.3.3.3	1.1.1.1	BGP	73	KEEPALIVE Message
314	248.191956	1.1.1.1	3.3.3.3	BGP	77	KEEPALIVE Message
315	248.224082	3.3.3.3	1.1.1.1	BGP	73	KEEPALIVE Message
375	308.208141	1.1.1.1	3.3.3.3	BGP	77	KEEPALIVE Message
376	308.230374	3.3.3.3	1.1.1.1	BGP	73	KEEPALIVE Message
439	368.214271	1.1.1.1	3.3.3.3	BGP	77	KEEPALIVE Message
440	368.225584	3.3.3.3	1.1.1.1	BGP	73	KEEPALIVE Message
501	428.187730	1.1.1.1	3.3.3.3	BGP	77	KEEPALIVE Message

```
> Frame 145: 77 bytes on wire (616 bits), 77 bytes captured (616 bits) on interface -, id 0
> Ethernet II, Src: c2:01:04:b6:00:00 (c2:01:04:b6:00:00), Dst: c2:02:04:c5:00:00 (c2:02:04:c5:00:00)
v MultiProtocol Label Switching Header, Label: 16, Exp: 6, S: 1, TTL: 255
    0000 0000 0000 0001 0000 .... .... .... = MPLS Label: 16
    .... .... .... .... .... 110. .... .... = MPLS Experimental Bits: 6
    .... .... .... .... .... ...1 .... .... = MPLS Bottom of Label Stack: 1
    .... .... .... .... .... .... 1111 1111 = MPLS TTL: 255
> Internet Protocol Version 4, Src: 1.1.1.1, Dst: 3.3.3.3
> Transmission Control Protocol, Src Port: 179, Dst Port: 21088, Seq: 73, Ack: 73, Len: 19
> Border Gateway Protocol - KEEPALIVE Message
```

Fig. 9. MPLS label replacement presented in *Wireshark*

It can be seen from Fig. 9 that MPLS label 16 was used, and that the experimental bit used to determine the class of service is set to the binary value 110 which marks the high importance of the packet (network control). Also, label 16 is the last label in the stack, which is seen from the value of MPLS Bottom of Label Stack with the value 0 except if the label is the last one in the stack [31, 32].

7   Analysis of SD-WAN Network Performances

In this part of analysing the network performances, an analysis of the SD-WAN network technology has been made. The SD-WAN network technology and its performances can be analysed directly on the network controller, and the analysis has been made on the previously used Mininet controller.

For the analysis of network performances, the performances are used with which the quality of service in the networks is measured, and these are: availability, throughput capacity, delay and loss of packet.

Mininet enables checking the availability among all the hosts by simple command *pingall* by which for every host ping packets are sent to all hosts in the network. Figure 10 shows that there are no losses in the network and that the reachability is 100%.

```
*** Ping: testing ping reachability
h1 -> h2 h3 h4
h2 -> h1 h3 h4
h3 -> h1 h2 h4
h4 -> h1 h2 h3
*** Results: 0% dropped (12/12 received)
```

Fig. 10. Checking reachability of all hosts in the network

With this check it is in fact clear how much the checking of mutual reachability of hosts is simplified. In traditional network, such checking would require connecting with each host individually and generating ping packets towards every host in the network.

Furthermore, Fig. 11 shows how it is possible with the command *iperf* to analyse the TCP network bandwidth and network capacity on the link between *h1* and *h2*. Such an analysis in traditional networks would require an analysis of the traffic generated in a tool like *Wireshark* in order to calculate the average link bandwidth.

```
mininet> iperf
*** Iperf: testing TCP bandwidth between h1 and h4
*** Results: ['20.0 Gbits/sec', '20.0 Gbits/sec']
```

Fig. 11. Analysis of network bandwidth and throughput capacity on the link

Figure 12 shows the delays that are caused by delay of 10 ms on three links between two hosts resulting in the average Round Trip Times (RTTs) of 60 ms.

The loss of packet is one of the most important parameters of the quality of service in real-time applications where it is important that the loss of packets is as low as possible.

Figure 13 shows that by defining the loss of packet of 15% on every link, out of twenty ping packets between hosts *h1* and *h2* the loss is as much as 70% of packets.

Considering conducted analysis of MPLS and SD-WAN network traffic, it's visible that without real network traffic, there isn't many QoS parameters to be gathered from MPLS network traffic in GNS3 simulation. Using Wireshark, analysis of MPLS network traffic showed no packet loss and low response time to ping requests. As opposed to MPLS, utilizing Mininet in SD-WAN simulation, it's possible to manipulate and analyse network parameters from centralized point which simplifies real-life troubleshooting.

```
mininet> h1 ping -c10 h2
PING 10.0.0.2 (10.0.0.2) 56(84) bytes of data.
64 bytes from 10.0.0.2: icmp_seq=1 ttl=64 time=134 ms
64 bytes from 10.0.0.2: icmp_seq=2 ttl=64 time=64.5 ms
64 bytes from 10.0.0.2: icmp_seq=3 ttl=64 time=63.7 ms
64 bytes from 10.0.0.2: icmp_seq=4 ttl=64 time=64.3 ms
64 bytes from 10.0.0.2: icmp_seq=5 ttl=64 time=62.2 ms
64 bytes from 10.0.0.2: icmp_seq=6 ttl=64 time=62.8 ms
64 bytes from 10.0.0.2: icmp_seq=7 ttl=64 time=64.1 ms
64 bytes from 10.0.0.2: icmp_seq=8 ttl=64 time=64.4 ms
64 bytes from 10.0.0.2: icmp_seq=9 ttl=64 time=62.9 ms
64 bytes from 10.0.0.2: icmp_seq=10 ttl=64 time=64.4 ms

--- 10.0.0.2 ping statistics ---
10 packets transmitted, 10 received, 0% packet loss, time 9011ms
rtt min/avg/max/mdev = 62.252/70.843/134.618/21.273 ms
```

Fig. 12. Checking of RTT between two hosts

```
mininet> h1 ping -c20 h2
PING 10.0.0.2 (10.0.0.2) 56(84) bytes of data.
From 10.0.0.1 icmp_seq=1 Destination Host Unreachable
From 10.0.0.1 icmp_seq=2 Destination Host Unreachable
From 10.0.0.1 icmp_seq=3 Destination Host Unreachable
64 bytes from 10.0.0.1: icmp_seq=6 ttl=64 time=63.4 ms
64 bytes from 10.0.0.1: icmp_seq=9 ttl=64 time=64.4 ms
64 bytes from 10.0.0.1: icmp_seq=10 ttl=64 time=65.2 ms
64 bytes from 10.0.0.1: icmp_seq=16 ttl=64 time=64.0 ms
64 bytes from 10.0.0.1: icmp_seq=17 ttl=64 time=63.0 ms
64 bytes from 10.0.0.1: icmp_seq=20 ttl=64 time=66.1 ms

--- 10.0.0.2 ping statistics ---
20 packets transmitted, 6 received, +3 errors, 70% packet loss, time 19058ms
rtt min/avg/max/mdev = 63.002/64.402/66.111/1.073 ms, pipe 4
```

Fig. 13. Test of packet losses through ping packets

8 Conclusion

The MPLS network technology was created as Cisco response to provide the users with an end-to-end service ensuring the quality of service. However, with the development of advanced technologies such as cloud computing, the applications no longer need to run on local servers, but can be accessed anywhere and anytime. The MPLS does not have a technical solution for the ever-increasing presence of cloud services.

On the other hand, a software-defined network is a newly created technological solution that offers simplified management of complex network systems by separating the control and the data parts. This enables a global overview of the entire system and centralized management of all network elements. SD-WAN is an extension of SDN technology where the application of SDN solutions to WAN is defined, and where the service providers and their transformation from traditional technologies into software networks play a major role.

The conducted configuration and simulation of network technologies in the software tool GNS3 has shown the complexity and depth of the necessary knowledge required to configure the MPLS networks. It can be therefore concluded that in the large systems the process of implementing the MPLS technology can take time. Furthermore, in order to analyse the network traffic in the MPLS network, it was necessary to generate a certain traffic and to analyse it using the *Wireshark* network analyser.

Unlike the MPLS, the configuration and simulation of SD-WAN technology is simpler and the configuration itself of all the network elements is possible centrally by using the Mininet controller from which later a complete traffic analysis was made. By comparing the ease of performing the traffic analysis, the software-defined technologies provide a much simpler solution where different parameters of the quality of service (e.g. delay, bandwidth, packet loss, etc.) can be defined and checked with a single command. In contrast, the analysis of the traffic and performances of the MPLS network required the collection of data and their detailed analysis in order to verify the success of the simulation.

The SD-WAN network technology allows adjustment of network parameters in real time, which can be extremely useful during large video conferences, etc., where the performances on the links are adapted to the current traffic flows without too much expense for the user. Such approach to network engineering and flexible adaptation to user requirements can transform the way the network service is understood as opposed to the traditional approach.

It is evident from the conducted research that both technologies have their benefits and drawbacks. Since many users already have implemented technologies such as MPLS, the future research should be based on achieving the interoperability of the traditional routing technologies with an SD-WAN solution. Furthermore, by using the analyses and the application of the artificial intelligence in the field of network engineering, the models of optimisation and prediction of network traffic will be made, and this will lead to an overall improvement of the level of the quality of service.

References

1. Nousyba, E., Elrasoul, H., Algasim, A., Babiker, A., Mustafa, A.N.: MPLS Vs IP Routing and its Impact on QoS Parameters. Int. J. Eng. Tech. Res. **11**, 179–180 (2014)
2. Terefenko, D.: A Comparison of Multiprotocol Label Switching (MPLS) and OpenFlow Communication Protocols. Institute of Technology Tallaghtno, Dublin, Ireland (2018)
3. Mine, G., Hai, J., Jin, L., Huiying, Z.: A design of SD-WAN-oriented wide area network access. In: International Conference on Computer Communication Networking Security, pp. 174–177 (2020). https://doi.org/10.1109/ccns50731.2020.00046
4. Yang, Z., Cui, Y., Li, B., Liu, Y., Xu, Y.: Software-defined wide area network (SD-WAN): architecture, advances and opportunities. In: Proceedings of International Conference Computer Communiacation Networks, ICCCN, vol. 2019-July (2019). https://doi.org/10.1109/ICCCN.2019.8847124
5. Troia, S., Zorello, L.M.M., Maralit, A.J., Maier, G.: SD-WAN: an open-source implementation for enterprise networking services. In: International Conference on Transparent Optics Networks, vol. 2020-July, pp. 1–4 (2020). https://doi.org/10.1109/ICTON51198.2020.9203058
6. Zad Tootaghaj, D., Ahmed, F., Sharma, P., Yannakakis, M.: Homa: an efficient topology and route management approach in SD-WAN overlays. In: Proceedings IEEE INFOCOM, vol. 2020-July, pp. 2351–2360 (2020). https://doi.org/10.1109/INFOCOM41043.2020.9155503
7. Hoonachari, R.: The Critical Role of Hybrid Networks in SD-WAN Deployments. Frost & Sullivan, USA (2018)
8. Tajiki, M. M., Akbari, B., Mokari, N., Chiaraviglio, L.: SDN-based resource allocation in MPLS networks: A hybrid approach. In: Concurrency and Computation Practice and Experience, pp. 1–11 (2018)

9. Cisco Community. https://community.cisco.com/t5/networking-documents/how-to-Config ure-tag-switching-and-mpls/ta-p/3128570, Accessed 16 Aug 2020
10. Ferdous, J.: The Basic Concept of Multiprotocol Label Switching (MPLS). Daffodil International University Dhaka, Bangladesh (2019)
11. Ridwan, M.A., Radzi, N.A.M., Wan Ahmad, W.S.H.M., Abdullah, F., Jamaludin, M.Z., Zakaria, M.N.: Recent trends in MPLS networks: technologies, applications and challenges. IET Commun. **14**(2), 177-185 (2020). https://doi.org/10.1049/iet-com.2018.6129
12. Cisco certified expert. https://www.ccexpert.us/mpls-network/mpls-and-the-osi-reference-model.html, Accessed 16 Aug 2020
13. Nadeau, T.D.: MPLS Network Management, Label-Switching Router. https://www.sciencedi rect.com/topics/computer-science/label-switching-router, Accessed 16 Aug 2020
14. Nadeau, T.D.: MPLS Network Management, Label Switched Path. https://www.sciencedi rect.com/topics/computer-science/label-switched-path, Accessed 17 Aug 2020
15. De Ghein, L.: MPLS Fundamentals. Cisco, Indianapolis, USA (2007)
16. Semantic Scholar – LIB. https://www.semanticscholar.org/topic/Label-Information-Base/ 2763152, Accessed 24 Aug 2020
17. Yasin, W., Ibrahim, H.: Improving triple play services using multi protocol label switching technology label switching technology. J. Comput. Sci. (2010)
18. MPLS Fundamentals: Forwarding Labeled Packets. http://www.ciscopress.com/articles/art icle.asp?p=680824&seqNum=2, Accessed 25 Aug 2020
19. SDxCentral. https://www.sdxcentral.com/networking/sd-wan/definitions/software-defined-sdn-wan/, Accessed 27 Aug 2020
20. Ranjan, P., Pande, P., Oswal, R., Qurani, Z.: A survey of past, present and future of software defined networking. Inst. Electric. Electron. Eng. **7782**, 238–248 (2014)
21. Braun, W., Menth, M.: Software-defined networking using openflow: protocols, applications and architectural design choices. Futur. Internet **6**(2), 302–336 (2014)
22. Network World. https://www.networkworld.com/article/3031279/sd-wan-what-it-is-and-why-you-ll-use-it-one-day.html, Accessed 13 Sept 2020
23. Juniper, https://www.juniper.net/documentation/en_US/junos/topics/topic-map/zero-touch-provision.html, Accessed 16 Sept 2020
24. Prashanth, M., Manthena, V., Lucent, A.: Network-as-a-service architecture with SDN and NFV: a proposed evolutionary approach for service provider networks network-as-a-service architecture with SDN and NFV, Netherlands (2016)
25. SDxCentral. https://www.sdxcentral.com/networking/nfv/definitions/virtual-network-fun ction, Accessed 16 Sept 2020
26. VeloCloud, Guide to SDN, SD-WAN, NFV, and VNF, VeloCloud (2016)
27. GNS3. https://docs.gns3.com/docs/, Accessed 17 Sept 2020
28. Plixer   VRF.   https://www.plixer.com/blog/what-is-vrf-virtual-routing-and-forwarding, Accessed 20 Sept 2020
29. Openvswitch. http://www.openvswitch.org, Accessed 17 Sept 2020
30. Mininet. http://www.mininet.org, 17 Sept 2020
31. Cisco MPLS QOS classification overview. https://www.cisco.com/c/en/us/td/docs/ios/qos/ configuration/guide/12_2sr/qos_12_2sr_book/classification_oview.html, Accessed 17 Sept 2020
32. IETF MPLS label stack encoding. https://tools.ietf.org/html/rfc3032, Accessed 18 Sept 2020

The Role of CNN for Intrusion Detection Systems: An Improved CNN Learning Approach for SDNs

Mahmoud Said Elsayed[1], Hamed Z. Jahromi[1], Muhammad Mohsin Nazir[2], and Anca Delia Jurcut[1(✉)]

[1] University College Dublin, Dublin, Ireland
{mahmoud.abdallah,hamed.jahromi}@ucdconnect.ie, anca.jurcut@ucd.ie
[2] Lahore College for Women University, Lahore, Pakistan
mohsin.nazir@lcwu.edu.pk

Abstract. An intrusion detection system (IDS) is an essential component of computer networks to detect and secure the system and environment from malicious activities and anomalous attacks. The convolutional neural network (CNN) is a popular deep learning algorithm that has been broadly applied in the field of computer vision. More recently, several researchers attempted to apply CNN for IDSs. However, the majority of these ignore the influence of the overfitting problem with the implementation of deep learning algorithms, which can impact the robustness of CNN-based anomaly detection systems. In this paper, we investigate the use of CNN for IDSs and propose a technique to enhance its performance by using two popular regularization techniques to address the overfitting problem. Our technique improves the capability of IDSs in detection of unseen intrusion events. We use InSDN benchmark dataset to train and evaluate the performance of our technique. The experimental results demonstrate that the regularization methods can improve the performance of CNN-based anomaly detection models for the software-defined networking (SDN) environment.

Keywords: Intrusion · Intrusion Detection System (IDS) · Machine learning · Software-defined Networking (SDN) · Convolutional Neural Network (CNN) · Overffiting problem

1 Introduction

Intrusion Detection Systems (IDSs) detect network intrusions (i.e., anomalies) by inspecting the network traffic flows to classify them as normal or anomalous. IDS employs preventive measures for anomalous activities and protect the environment from possible disruptions.

IDS commonly performs classification based on heuristics or rules. The system learns about the normal network activities and classify a particular traffic

© ICST Institute for Computer Sciences, Social Informatics and Telecommunications Engineering 2021
Published by Springer Nature Switzerland AG 2021. All Rights Reserved
D. Perakovic and L. Knapcikova (Eds.): FABULOUS 2021, LNICST 382, pp. 91–104, 2021.
https://doi.org/10.1007/978-3-030-78459-1_7

flow as malicious when it falls out of the normal conditions. However, it is challenging to distinguish and classify the attacks from the normal network traffic with regular traffic characteristics. An intruder may generate several network attacks similar to the normal traffic without being detected.

Researchers have been working actively to improve the IDS capabilities in detecting and classifying anomalous activities. However, reducing the false alarm rate and improving the detection rate is still an open research area.

More recently, machine learning techniques have been employed in IDS and proved to be effective for detecting anomalous activities [1–5]. For instance, algorithms such as Logistic Regression (LR), Naïve Bayes (NB), and Support Vector Machine (SVM) are widely used to identify various network-based attacks. These aforementioned techniques are known as shallow learning due to its learning characteristics based on pre-defined features. These approaches uses features engineering as domain knowledge to extract features using data mining techniques. However, the feature selection is a challenging process and requires the domain of knowledge experts. For example, a feature that may exist is an important characteristic for one attack class, but irrelevant to other types of attacks [6]. Besides, the nature of data takes the behavior of non-linearity, and the shallow learning methods provide low accuracy when the data account the high degree of non-linearity. As a result, the researchers have started to use deep learning techniques for attack recognition tasks [7–12].

Deep learning (DL) techniques can automatically extract the high-level features from the network traffic without using feature engineering or knowledge of domain experts. The CNN is broadly applied for various classification and recognition tasks in computer vision and other research domains (e.g., identifying key chemical structures in various drug developments, weather phenomena and video surveillance). The strength of CNN as compared to the others DL models lies in it's ability to extract high-level features from raw data with low number of parameters(i.e., the concept of weight sharing). Furthermore, the CNN significantly outperforms the traditional feature selection algorithms in obtaining the best representative features.

The success of CNN in various domains is encouraging for the network researchers to investigate it's effectiveness for the intrusion detection tasks. The features learning capability of CNN makes it suitable for today's explosive network environment. However, the overfitting problem of CNN has been hitherto neglected in the majority of intrusion detection studies. The performance of the neural networks (NN) relies on the input data and a set of parameters. Therefore, to produce an expressive model with a capability of learning complicated relationships between inputs and outputs features, a complex network architecture with multi-hidden layers can be used. The complex network architecture, however, requires a large amount of training data, which is not always available. Consequently, training large neural networks with limited data can cause the model to describe the random error in the data rather than the relationships between variables. This problem leads to model overfitting issues. This model can perform well during the training but perform poorly in a real test data (even if they come from the same distribution).

Several methods exist to address the overfitting problem, and one of the effective methods uses the regularization techniques. The key idea behind the regularization is to impose a large number of restrictions on the learning model or simply control the model's ability to learn. Although it sacrifices some flexibility to fit the training data effectively, it avoids the model to become complex. Hence, it's ability to predict unseen data can be increased efficiently (i.e., anomaly detection). In this paper, we investigate the use of CNN for IDSs, and propose a technique to enhance it's performance using two popular regularization techniques i.e., L2 regularization and the dropout methods.

2 Background

This section briefly introduces the background related to the proposed work. The first subsection presents the current challenges of the conventional networks, the motivation for the SDN to overcome such limitations and the current security flaws of SDN. The second subsection introduces the component of the CNN and it's working operation. The last subsection discusses the overfitting problem, the theoretical background and the existing techniques to address similar kind of problems.

2.1 Software-defined Networking (SDN) Environment

In the conventional distributed networks, the routers and the switches operate independently. Each device makes an independent decision on how to handle or treat the network traffic. Consequently, a change in the network policy or routing configuration requires access to each device individually. The aforementioned caveat of the distributed networks is due to the existence of control plane (responsible for decision making) and the data plane (responsible for forwarding packets/frames from one interface to another) within a same network device. Thus, the network management and the orchestration is often complex and relatively exposed to errors. For example, in a large scale environment with various network equipment and connectivities, it is a complex process to develop innovative services without jeopardizing the network stability.

The emergence of SDN and programmable networks with centralized architecture facilitates network research studies to explore, develop and implement a new level of network security and management applications [13,14]. A SDN environment offers full control and visibility over the network, and facilitates the collection of end-to-end network heuristics from a centralized point [15]. SDN controllers interact with the network devices using southbound interface (SBI), and provide network application programming interfaces (APIs) to the applications using northbound interface (NBI).

SDN allows the developers to create network applications and implement it directly through API, avoiding the high cost of hardware devices. For instance, an IPS/IDS system can utilize SDN's NBI to advise the controller on how to deal with a malicious traffic flows. Despite the advantage of SDN environments, the centralized architecture can produce new attack vectors that are specific to SDNs. For example, SDN controller is the brain of the network, and is a single point of failure. If an attacker exhaust the controller resources by sending a massive amount of malicious traffic (e.g., Denial of Service (DoS) or Distributed Denial of Service (DDoS)), the network operation might be impacted and cause a significant damage. Similarly, a compromised SDN controller gives the attacker a chance to modify or redirect the network traffic [16].

2.2 Convolutional Neural Network (CNN)

CNNs are organized in different architectures compared to the traditional neural networks. We can find that each layer in the traditional neural network consists of a group of neurons, which are connected to all neurons in the previous layer. In contrast, in CNN, each layer is attached only to a small portion of the neurons instead of fully connected neurons with the previous layer. A typical structure of the CNN is constructed from three layers of convolution, pooling, and fully connected layer [17]. In convolutional layer, a filter or kernel passes through the input image and forms a conclusion of an array of numbers. Multiplying the kernel across the portion of the input produces a single number, by moving the filter through the whole image. A metric of multiple numbers is generated, which refers to a feature map. Using multiple kernels produces a number of feature maps, which represent different characteristics of the input tensors. The mathematical description of the convolution layer is described in the following equation:

$$M_i = f(M_{i-1} \otimes W_i + b_i) \tag{1}$$

Where M_i describes the feature map at layer i and $M_0 = $X (input layer), W_i represents the weight vector of the convolution filter at layer i, while the b_i and f represent the bias vector and activation function, respectively. One of the typical non-linear function used in the CNN is rectified linear unit (ReLU) activation function [18]. Compared to the regular neural network, the dominant CNN is using less number of parameters by sharing the same weight and bias vector. It also does not require hand-crafted feature extraction as compared to conventional machine learning classifiers. The second layer is the pooling layer i.e., downsampling operation, and aims to reduce the dimensionality of the feature map.

There are two types of pooling operation: Max pooling and average pooling [19]. The final convolution or polling layer's output is passed through one or more fully-connected layers for classification tasks to get the final outputs. The number of nodes or neurons in the last output layer is equal to the number of output classes.

2.3   Overfitting Prevention and Regularization

Overfitting is a serious problem in machine learning techniques due to high number of parameters. With the occurrence of overfitting, learning model performs well during the training phase, but provides a poor result on unseen data. A predominant solution to deal with overfitting problem is by applying some model selection algorithm to choose the features with greater importance. However, these techniques may cause some loss of valuable information. An alternative solution is using regularization methods to control the model complexity to reduce the burden on the parameters complexity (i.e. weights & biases). The regularization techniques penalize the features by imposing a constraint on the magnitude of the coefficients without any loss. Controlling the value of parameters can eliminate overfitting and enhance the performance of the model on unseen data. The L2 regularization is a method which adds a penalty to the square of the weight coefficient values. As a result, it poses the large parameters be close to zero. During the training process, we try to minimize the following cost function:

$$j(w^1, b^1, ..., w^L, b^L) = \frac{1}{m} \sum_{i=1}^{m} L(\hat{y}^{(i)}, y^{(i)}) \tag{2}$$

where, L is the loss function, w is the wight and b is the bias. Now, using L2 regularization, the loss function will become:

$$j(w^1, b^1, ..., w^L, b^L) = \frac{1}{m} \sum_{i=1}^{m} L(\hat{y}^{(i)}, y^{(i)}) + \frac{\lambda}{2m} \sum_{l=1}^{L} \left\| w^L \right\|^2 \tag{3}$$

where, λ is a parameter that can be tuned to control the regularization effect. Using large λ, the weight penalty will be large. Similarly, small λ will reduce the effect of regularization. This is trivial, because the cost function must be minimized. By adding the squared norm of the weight matrix and multiplying it by λ, large weights will be driven down in order to minimize the cost function.

Hinton et al. proposed dropout method to reduce the risk of the overfitting [20]. The key idea behind dropout is to randomly ignore some units from the network with probability p during training, but use all these units in testing. The best value of the probability is usually between 0.5 and 0.8.

An example of the dropout process is illustrated in Fig. 1 and Fig. 2. In this work, we combine L2 regularization (i.e. weight decay) and dropout techniques together to improve the performance of our proposed detection model.

3   Related Work

Khan et al. applied CNN for intrusion detection on the KDD'99 dataset [21]. The model architecture composed of three hidden layer. Each hidden layer contains a convolutional layer followed by a pooling layer. They demonstrated that their proposed CNN model outperforms support vector machine (SVM) and deep

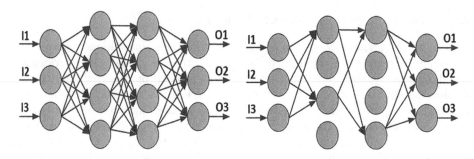

Fig. 1. A typical feedforward ANN.   **Fig. 2.** The dropout of p = 0.5 applied.

belief network (DBN) with an accuracy of 99.23%. The estimated accuracy for SVM and DBN are 98.20% and 98.59%, respectively.

Yong et al. used batch normalization to improve the performance of the CNN model for intrusion detection on KDD' 99 dataset [22]. The best model performance was obtained using two convolutional layers with kernel dimensions of 12, and 24, respectively. Their experimental results reveals that CNN is more effective for intrusion detection compared to SVM and neural network algorithms.

HU et al. improved convolutional neural network (CNN) by using adaptive synthetic sampling (ADASYN) algorithm [23]. The ADASYN aims to deal with unbalanced data by adding new samples for minor classes and prevent the model from being biased towards frequent samples. In addition, to improve the diversity of features, the split convolution module SPC-CNN method is used to overcome the problem of inter-channels information redundancy. The enhanced CNN model (SPC-CNN) achieved an accuracy of 83.83% on the NSL-KDD testing data, with 4.35% higher than the traditional CNN.

XIAO et al. proposed an intrusion detection approach based on CNN model using KDDcup99 dataset [24]. The architecture of the CNN based method was constructed from two convolutional layers, two Max pooling and one fully connected layer. They have used the principal component analysis (PCA) and the autoencoder reduction techniques to reduce the feature of the input data and to prepare the dimensional input for the CNN requirements. Two sets of feature reduction, 100 and 121 are obtained using PCA, while different sets of 100, 121, 81, and 64 are extracted from the autoencoder. From their experimental results it can be understood that the autoencoders have been more effective in feature reduction, in comparison to the PCA technique.

JIANG et al. proposed a hybrid intrusion detection model (CNN-BiLSTM). The model integrates the CNN and the Bi-directional long short-term memory (BiLSTM), in order to learn the spatial and temporal features [25]. The synthetic minority oversampling technique (SMOTE) algorithm is used to tackle the problem of minority classes in the unbalanced data. Similarly, the one-side selection (OSS) algorithm is used to reduce the major class samples. Two datasets NSL-KDD and UNSW-NB15 are used to evaluate their proposed model.

The CNN-BiLSTM model achieved an overall accuracy of 82.74% and 77.16% for NSL-KDD and UNSW-NB15, respectively.

4   Proposed CNN-Based Technique

This section introduces the solution methodology of the proposed CNN model. The first subsection introduces the dataset, which is used to verify the proposed detection model. The second subsection shows the various steps to prepare the dataset for the model training. In the last subsection, we discuss the structure of the CNN model and the used parameters to set up our proposed method.

4.1   Dataset

In this work, we use InSDN dataset to evaluate the performance of the proposed CNN approach [6]. InSDN dataset allows researchers to investigate and develop intrusion detection models specific to SDN networks. The dataset includes normal traffic (e.g., HTTP, HTTPS, DNS, Email, FTP and SSH), attacks related to traditional networks and SDN related attacks. The attack types include DoS, DDoS, Probe, Botnet, Exploitation, Password-Guessing, and Web attacks. The dataset was produced using a virtual SDN network, which was constructed from four virtual machines. The first machine acts as an attacker and the second machine is the Metasploitable-2 vulnerable Linux server. The other two machines are used to represent the OVS switch and SDN controller. In addition, the dataset's attacks come from several sources, i.e., internal and external, to reflect the real attack cases.

The dataset is available in both PCAP file and .CSV file format and divided into three groups. The first group i.e., OVS group, includes the attacks coming from outside to SDN internal network. The second group contains the attacks against Metasploitable 2 server. The last group represents the normal traffic. The dataset has more than 80 features generated using the CICFlowMeter tool. In this work, we only utilize a subset of 48 features to train our CNN model. More details about these features are discussed in [6].

Furthermore, the attack samples, which were used during the testing phase are from different distribution from those used in the training. The number of data records for training and testing datasets is 135,870 and 50,230, respectively.

4.2   Data Preprocessing

The following pre-processing steps are performed before feeding the input data into the deep learning model:

1. The normalization technique is applied to map the value of features between 0 and 1, using the standardization method (i.e., Z-score normalization) according to the Eq. 4.
2. The 1D-dimensional network traffic is translated into image format with a dimension of 8×6.
3. the Symbolic feature is converted into numerical data.

The label column has several attack classes and a normal class. It is also important to note that this study preforms a binary classification and set the normal label to 0 and all attack labels to 1.

$$y = \frac{y - MIN}{MAX - MIN} \tag{4}$$

4.3   Proposed CNN Architecture

The proposed CNN architecture is depicted in Fig. 3. The network architecture is constructed from two convolutional layers with 32, 64 filters, where each filter has a size of 3×3 and a stride of 1. Each convolutional layer is followed by a max-pooling layer with a size of 2×2. The 'same' padding is used in the convolutional layers to make the output same as the input. Thus, the input image gets fully covered by the filter and the specified stride. A fully connected layer is used with a number of units equal to 128. The final layer is the softmax layer to classify the network traffic into normal (0) or malicious traffic (1).

The binary cross-entropy is used as a loss function in the output layer, while the non-linear ReLU activation function is used for all layers except the last layer. The drouput method is used after the second Max pooling layer and the fully connected layer. The probability (p) of 0.2 is used in prior after the softmax layer, while p = 0.5 is used after the fully layer.

Since the dropout causes some information loss, hence any loss in the first layers will propagate to the whole network. Therefore, a common practice is to start with low dropout and then gradually increase it. In addition to the dropout layer, the weight decay technique is used to further improve the performance of the model, and to reduce the error rate. L2 regularization method is applied in this experiments, as it provides high performance than the L1 method.

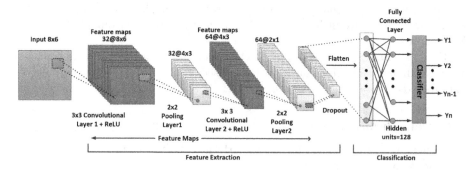

Fig. 3. The structure of CNN model.

5   Evaluation

This section discuss the experimental results of the proposed model.

5.1   Evaluation Criteria

To evaluate our CNN model, four performance indicators of Accuracy (Acc), Precision (Pre), Recall (Rec) and F1 measure are used. The mathematical representation of these indicators are calculated based on Eqs. 5, 6, 7, and 8, respectively.

$$\text{Acc} = \frac{TP + TN}{TP + TN + FP + FN} \tag{5}$$

$$\text{Pre} = \frac{TP}{TP + FP} \tag{6}$$

$$\text{Rec} = \frac{TP}{TP + FN} \tag{7}$$

$$\text{F1} = \frac{2 \times \text{Pre} \times \text{Rec}}{\text{Pre} + \text{Rec}} \tag{8}$$

TP, TN, FP and FN denote true positives, true negatives, false positives, and false negatives, respectively.

5.2   Experimental Results

We use Keras Library with Python programming language to perform all our experiments. The experiments are conducted on a machine with Intel core I7-8650U CPU @ 1.90 GHz (8 cores), Window 10 operating system. The InSDN is the benchmark dataset used for all classification experiments to perform 2-class anomaly detection.

We compare the performance of the CNN model with various classification algorithms, including k-nearest neighbor classifier (KNN), naive Bayes (NB), support vector machines (SVM), Adaptive Boosting (AdaBoost), logistic regression (LR), random forest (RF), decision tree (DT). Besides the aforementioned classifiers, we use deep neural network (DNN) to further evaluate our CNN model. The used parameters of the DNN is depicted in Fig. 1, while the default parameters from the scikit-learn are used for all other classifiers.

The experiment results are represented in Table 2, Fig. 4 and Fig. 5. It can be seen that the proposed CNN algorithm performs well compared to all other existing classifications. Table 2 and Fig. 4 show that the classical ML algorithms have low performance compared to the deep learning models, except the KNN algorithm, with its performance slightly higher than the DNN model. The average accuracy of the KNN and DNN is 89.06% and 88.32%, respectively. The NB algorithm performed very poor in all evaluation metrics followed by RF and AdaBoost. On the other side, we can see that the CNN model generally outperforms the classical ML algorithms.

In addition, the classification of normal class in all models is relativity lower than the attack class. This is due to the low size of the normal class during training and testing phases. The low amount of samples is not enough for the classifier to learn the behavior of raw data significantly. To further evaluate our proposed CNN based model, the receiver operating characteristics (ROC) curve (Fig. 5) is used to represent how the model performs in general. The ROC curve represents the relation between the true-positive and false-positive rates, and the area under the curve (AUC), as a measure of the model's capability. The CNN has a higher AUC with a value of 0.928, followed by the KNN and DNN algorithms with values of 0.89 and 0.88, respectively. In contrast, all other classifiers provide low AUC values, which indicate a low performance for these algorithms in network anomaly detection (Table 1).

Table 1. The hyper-parameters used in multi-layer perceptron approach.

Traffic type	Detection rate
Hidden nodes (HN)	3
Number of neurons	100, 100, 100
Number of epoch	10
Batch size	128
Classification function	Softmax
Activation function	ReLU

Table 2. Precision, Recall, and F1-score of the different methods.

Model	Precision (%)		Recall (%)		F1-Score (%)	
	Normal	Attack	Normal	Attack	Normal	Attack
NB	50.21	63.87	90.30	16.05	64.53	25.66
RF	52.02	75.00	93.03	19.58	66.73	31.05
AdaBoost	52.68	65.08	82.53	30.51	64.31	41.54
DT	81.36	59.91	33.78	92.74	47.74	72.79
LR	96.89	59.95	29.36	99.11	45.07	74.71
SVM	81.34	75.58	70.78	8478	75.69	79.92
DNN	96.47	83.00	78.73	97.30	86.71	89.58
KNN	89.62	88.56	87.52	90.50	88.56	89.52
Proposed CNN Model	**98.67**	**88.82**	**86.71**	**98.91**	**92.31**	**93.59**

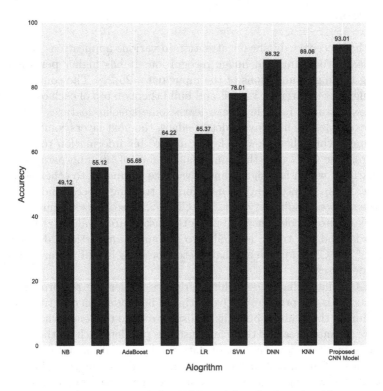

Fig. 4. Comparison of the CNN model and other algorithms

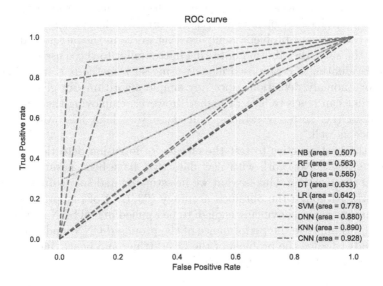

Fig. 5. Receiver operating curve (ROC) of different IDS approaches.

6   Discussion

The CNN has received significant attention in various applications such as natural language processing and image recognition. It has higher performance in discovering the high-dimensions of the input data [26,27]. The convolution layers are using a set of filters or kernels and build them on top of each other to learn the complex features. Each layer can learn some specific features of the input data. For example, the first layers detect edges, the next layers combine them to detect shapes, while the following layers merge this information to detect that as a feature. The CNN uses the minimum number of training parameters (i.e., weight sharing), which is a significant advantage compared to other deep learning models. It can reduce the time used for the training process and also able to classify the network traffic very fast. The CNN can also be used comprehensively for network environments since the network packets are similar to the structure of the words, and the traffic is similar to sentences and articles. However, the adoption of the CNN for the anomaly detection area is still at early stage and needs further research.

One of the main challenges, which seriously hinder the performance of the ML/DL models is the problem of Overfitting. The model can effectively perform very well during the training but fails to display a good tendency with the unseen data. There are many reasons that can cause this problem such as, the complexity of the model and the low amount of data used to create a suitable approach. However, most of machine learning algorithms are data-hungry and collecting a large amount of training data can be considered one of the significant challenges, especially in the network intrusion domain. The availability of network data or creating a new dataset can be subjected to several challenges including privacy or illegal issues. The network data includes customer information or sensitive data, and the availability of such data can reveal this information to the public. Adding to the previous problem, many existing works in the intrusion detection area, used the same distribution of testing data similar to those used during the training. Evaluating the proposed models using such methods is not a reliable method for anomaly detection, since any simple algorithm can give very high accuracy that can reach to 99% or higher. However, employing the same model for new data (i.e. zero-day attacks) will cause very high false rates and low performance as well.

Thus, the best practice to test the efficacy of intrusion detection models is to evaluate how it can work with new data that have been never seen before and during the training. This is what we investigated and successfully achieved in this work. Although the obtained accuracy (93.01%) of our proposed CNN based technique is not convincing enough to be applied in real SDN networks, we are working to improve the performance of the proposed CNN model by finding new methods to solve the problem of the Overfitting, and hence, increasing the ability of the model for the outlier detection.

7   Conclusion

The innovative features of the SDN speed up replacing the current network architectures, especially in the recent days since cyber-attacks are becoming more prevalent. With a growing number of people working remotely, the traditional network architecture is starting to fall short of satisfying the essential network needs. On the other hand, the SDN paradigm generates security risks that still need to be addressed before securely deploying it in the current networks. In this work, we investigated the role of the CNN to tackle the security issues of the SDN by proposing an improved CNN-based IDS technique. The dropout and L2 regularization techniques are used to overcome the problem of overfitting and to enhance the technique functionality to detect unseen anomalies. The experimental results indicated that the CNN could effectively be used to detect the new anomalies compared to other classifiers. In our future work, we will work to improve the performance of the CNN for IDS by proposing further techniques to enhance its ability for anomaly detection.

References

1. Çavuşoğlu, Ü.: A new hybrid approach for intrusion detection using machine learning methods. Appl. Intell. **49**(7), 2735–2761 (2019). https://doi.org/10.1007/s10489-018-01408-x
2. Halimaa, A., Sundarakantham, K.: Machine learning based intrusion detection system. In: 2019 3rd International Conference on Trends in Electronics and Informatics (ICOEI), pp. 916–920. IEEE (2019)
3. Abdulhammed, R., Musafer, H., Alessa, A., Faezipour, M., Abuzneid, A.: Features dimensionality reduction approaches for machine learning based network intrusion detection. Electronics **8**(3), 322 (2019)
4. Alkasassbeh, M., Almseidin, M.: Machine learning methods for network intrusion detection. arXiv preprint arXiv:1809.02610 (2018)
5. Taher, K.A., Jisan, B.M.Y., Rahman, M.M.: Network intrusion detection using supervised machine learning technique with feature selection. In: 2019 International Conference on Robotics, Electrical and Signal Processing Techniques (ICREST), pp. 643–646. IEEE (2019)
6. Elsayed, M.S., Le-Khac, N.-A., Jurcut, A.D.: InSDN: a novel SDN intrusion dataset. IEEE Access **8**, 165 263–165 284 (2020)
7. Althubiti, S.A., Jones, E.M., Roy, K.: LSTM for anomaly-based network intrusion detection. In: 2018 28th International Telecommunication Networks and Applications Conference (ITNAC), pp. 1–3. IEEE (2018)
8. Elsayed, M.S., Le-Khac, N.-A., Dev, S., Jurcut, A.D.: DDoSNet: a deep-learning model for detecting network attacks. In: 2020 IEEE 21st International Symposium on "A World of Wireless, Mobile and Multimedia Networks" (WoWMoM), pp. 391–396. IEEE (2020)
9. Elsayed, M.S., Le-Khac, N.-A., Jurcut, A.D.: Detecting abnormal traffic in large-scale networks. In: 2020 International Symposium on Networks, Computers and Communications (ISNCC), pp. 1–7. IEEE (2020)
10. Said Elsayed, M., Le-Khac, N.-A., Dev, S., Jurcut, A.D.: Network anomaly detection using LSTM based autoencoder. In: Proceedings of the 16th ACM Symposium on QoS and Security for Wireless and Mobile Networks, pp. 37–45 (2020)

11. Shone, N., Ngoc, T.N., Phai, V.D., Shi, Q.: A deep learning approach to network intrusion detection. IEEE Trans. Emerg. Top. Comput. Intell. **2**(1), 41–50 (2018)
12. Al-Qatf, M., Lasheng, Y., Al-Habib, M., Al-Sabahi, K.: Deep learning approach combining sparse autoencoder with SVM for network intrusion detection. IEEE Access **6**, 52 843–52 856 (2018)
13. Elsayed, M.S., Le-Khac, N.-A., Jurcut, A.D.: Dealing with covid-19 network traffic spikes [cybercrime and forensics]. IEEE Secur. Priv. **19**(1), 90–94 (2021)
14. Jahromi, H.Z., Hines, A., Delaney, D.T.: Towards application-aware networking: ML-based end-to-end application KPI/QoE metrics characterization in SDN. In: 2018 Tenth International Conference on Ubiquitous and Future Networks (ICUFN), pp. 126–131. IEEE (2018)
15. Jahromi, H.Z., Delaney, D.T.: An application awareness framework based on SDN and machine learning: defining the roadmap and challenges. In: 2018 10th International Conference on Communication Software and Networks (ICCSN), pp. 411–416. IEEE (2018)
16. Scott-Hayward, S., O'Callaghan, G., Sezer, S.: SDN security: a survey. In: 2013 IEEE SDN for Future Networks and Services (SDN4FNS), pp. 1–7. IEEE (2013)
17. Vedaldi, A., Lenc, K.: MatConvNet: convolutional neural networks for MATLAB. In: Proceedings of the 23rd ACM International Conference on Multimedia, pp. 689–692 (2015)
18. Zhou, D., Yan, Z., Fu, Y., Yao, Z.: A survey on network data collection. J. Netw. Comput. Appl. **116**, 9–23 (2018)
19. Yamashita, R., Nishio, M., Do, R.K.G., Togashi, K.: Convolutional neural networks: an overview and application in radiology. Insights Imaging **9**(4), 611–629 (2018). https://doi.org/10.1007/s13244-018-0639-9
20. Hinton, G.E., Osindero, S., Teh, Y.-W.: A fast learning algorithm for deep belief nets. Neural Comput. **18**(7), 1527–1554 (2006)
21. Khan, R.U., Zhang, X., Alazab, M., Kumar, R.: An improved convolutional neural network model for intrusion detection in networks. In: 2019 Cybersecurity and Cyberforensics Conference (CCC), pp. 74–77. IEEE (2019)
22. Yong, L., Bo, Z.: An intrusion detection model based on multi-scale CNN. In: 2019 IEEE 3rd Information Technology, Networking, Electronic and Automation Control Conference (ITNEC), pp. 214–218. IEEE (2019)
23. Hu, Z., Wang, L., Qi, L., Li, Y., Yang, W.: A novel wireless network intrusion detection method based on adaptive synthetic sampling and an improved convolutional neural network. IEEE Access **8**, 195 741–195 751 (2020)
24. Xiao, Y., Xing, C., Zhang, T., Zhao, Z.: An intrusion detection model based on feature reduction and convolutional neural networks. IEEE Access **7**, 42 210–42 219 (2019)
25. Jiang, K., Wang, W., Wang, A., Wu, H.: Network intrusion detection combined hybrid sampling with deep hierarchical network. IEEE Access **8**, 32 464–32 476 (2020)
26. Gu, J., et al.: Recent advances in convolutional neural networks. Pattern Recogn. **77**, 354–377 (2018)
27. Khan, A., Sohail, A., Zahoora, U., Qureshi, A.S.: A survey of the recent architectures of deep convolutional neural networks. Artif. Intell. Rev. **53**(8), 5455–5516 (2020). https://doi.org/10.1007/s10462-020-09825-6

Automation of Network Device Configuration Using Zero-Touch Provisioning - A Case Study

Ivan Šimunić and Ivan Grgurević[✉]

Faculty of Transport and Traffic Sciences, University of Zagreb, Vukelićeva 4,
10000 Zagreb, Croatia
ivan.simunic@combis.hr, igrgurevic@fpz.unizg.hr

Abstract. The installation of new network devices in the production environment represents a process of several steps. First of all, it is necessary to connect the hardware and then define all the necessary global and local parameters by using the Command Line Interface (CLI) and so for each device in the implementation separately. With the development of automation models within the concept of Software Defined Networks (SDN), the Zero Touch Provisioning (ZTP) occurs as a potential solution to reduce the complexity of installation of a new network infrastructure. The ZTP model can be used to reduce time and costs of installing new devices in the network. This paper presents a case study of implementing the ZTP model on the example of Cisco CSR1000v network device in the local area network. The initial step was the creation of the network environment in the emulation software Emulated Virtual Environment Next Generation. In the network environment the necessary servers were defined and the device that supports the ZTP model was assigned. Then it was necessary to create a script in the Python programming language and upload it to the appropriate server. At startup the device downloads the script from the server. The script is then executed, and as the result of this process, the appropriate configuration on the device is applied. After the implementation of the ZTP model and review of the results, the potential that enables such a solution in networks of much larger scales is evident. The application of this model would certainly simplify the process of installing new devices on the network. The applied ZTP model and the created one's own script have proven significant saving in the installation time (over 95%), at the same time achieving also a saving in the costs of employees, and affecting a reduction in human error. The results of this paper can contribute to better understanding of the process of implementing the ZTP model with the aim of its more widespread application.

Keywords: Zero-touch provisioning · Software defined networking · Cisco IOS XE

1 Introduction

Computer networks today support significantly different IT environment compared to several years ago. The network is becoming the critical component in the overall infrastructure of the company, and the end users expect it to follow the technological evolution

© ICST Institute for Computer Sciences, Social Informatics and Telecommunications Engineering 2021
Published by Springer Nature Switzerland AG 2021. All Rights Reserved
D. Perakovic and L. Knapcikova (Eds.): FABULOUS 2021, LNICST 382, pp. 105–119, 2021.
https://doi.org/10.1007/978-3-030-78459-1_8

and support the constant growth of the network requirements [1]. The configuration of such networks is usually a complex and time-consuming process, and automation models and response mechanisms are virtually non-existent [2]. Although the network experts have managed to adapt the existing networks to new challenges by continuous optimization, implementing new approaches in network design and introducing new features, computer networks are still based on traditional and inflexible infrastructure [3].

The idea of Software Defined Networks (SDN) is being developed as a potential solution to these problems. SDN provides a programmable network infrastructure with centralized approach which would enable automation of end-to-end services in the network, such as customer segmentation, quality of service, and analytics [4].

Furthermore SDN provides the possibility of automation of the user policy for appropriate access control and of the user experience quality when using applications [5]. Also, within the SDN concept, the model of configuration automation is being developed when installing new devices on the network (Day-Zero Automation). By introducing automation and enabling multipoint auto configuration of network devices, the Zero Touch Provisioning (ZTP) concept emerges as a possible alleviation of the complex network provisioning and infrastructure services deployment process.

The aim of this research is to automate the configuration process of Cisco IOS XE network device when implementing the device into the network according to the ZTP model. The device automation will be based on downloading the configuration script from the appropriate servers which will then be executed on the device and with the help of the configuration file, also located on a certain server, perform the configuration. The implementation of this research will require the establishment of a laboratory with appropriate network devices and servers and the development of a script in the *Python* programming language. The purpose of this research is to use the process of ZTP model implementation in an environment founded on the existing solutions, to present all the benefits whose application would significantly reduce the network installation time for the network experts (research focus), reduce the financial costs and the likelihood of human error.

The remainder of the paper is organized as follows. Section 2 deals with the related research. Section 3 shows the Zero-Touch Provisioning overview. Section 4 describes the environmental development for the Zero-Touch Provisioning model, such as network topology and Python script development. Section 5 shows the results of implementing the Zero-Touch Provisioning model. The paper concludes with the remarks on the future development in Sect. 6.

2 Related Research

The configuration automation has the potential of significantly reducing the device implementation time, but also the costs that occur during such a process. In the world of technology today, the method of automating the provisioning of devices is becoming more and more common. Thus, the term ZTP has been increasingly appearing. ZTP is a term that includes an automation solution developed to reduce the likelihood of error and save administrators time in implementing new devices. This term has been present for some time in the networking world in the domain of the service provider. The author

[6] in his paper investigates and proposes multi-service procedures for activating the ZTP procedure for telecom operating operators using network virtualization.

Often this process has been used precisely in cases of providing a large device when maintained efficiency is required, not referring to a single network. Thus, the authors [7] described the examples of ZTP methodology in the context of providing IoT devices. The author of this paper states that ZTP is an appropriate solution to reduce the probability of error and reduce the time required to train new devices and the proposed conclusion about the advantages.

Paper [8] explores the options for the tactical deployment of network automation with NetZTP to provide maximum return on investment as organizations explore strategic approaches to network automation.

In paper [9] the authors present the results of the ongoing development of the Cloud Services Delivery Infrastructure (CSDI) that provides a basis for infrastructure centric cloud service provisioning, operation and management in multi-cloud multi-provider environment defined as a Zero Touch Provisioning, Operation and Management (ZTP/ZTPOM) model.

The authors in [10] in defining a new Meto-Haul architecture based on the SDN concept and network virtualization incorporate ZTP functionality as an appropriate solution to enable the installation and provisioning of new hardware automatically. In addition, this functionality is cited as an integral part of their demo.

Research like the one from Cisco suggests that Day-Zero Automation can reduce the implementation costs by as much as up to 79% [11]. Also, due to lower probability of configuration failure it is possible to reduce the time spent in finding the problem by 50%. Besides, 70% of all network errors and 35% of total time during which the network was not functional were caused by human inconsistency in configuration which could be significantly reduced by introducing automation models for the implementation of network devices [11].

ZTP is a model developed within the SDN concept and represents a solution for automating the configuration of new network devices. Several authors have evaluated the possibilities of the ZTP model in various environments and highlighted its advantages. In research [12] the authors state the advantages of the ZTP model in configuration automation, where the authors emphasize as a special advantage the possibility of configuring a large number of devices simultaneously. Thus, it is possible to centralize an otherwise distributed network model using a single point of integration, which opens up additional opportunities for the implementation of complex network services throughout the network domain.

Other authors also mention the characteristics of the ZTP model and its advantages in large-scale environments and in the use of cloud-based applications. The authors in paper [13] state the orientation of network vendors such as Cisco and Juniper towards the development of this concept and they state the possibilities of implementing the ZTP model by individual vendors. Also, the possibility of implementing this model with the already existing network solutions and technologies is stated.

Under the influence of these trends it can be concluded that it is possible to achieve various advantages by implementing the ZTP model when installing new devices in the network. Also, in a review of the existing literature it has been found that there are documents that have evaluated the ZTP model and its characteristics in cloud computing [12, 13], but there is still a lack of research dealing with the development of the environment and the application of the ZTP model in access networks.

Therefore, the purpose of this case study, in addition to demonstrating the functionality, is to use the process of ZTP model implementation in an environment founded on the existing solutions, to present all the benefits whose application would significantly reduce the network installation time for the network experts in the production environment, reduce the financial costs and the likelihood of human error.

3   Zero-Touch Provisioning Overview

ZTP provides open bootstrap interfaces to automate network device provisioning in heterogeneous network environments [14]. The holistic approach to the definition of the ZTP model suggests that the network devices that are connected to the network should be configured automatically. In more detail, ZTP could be described as the automation solution developed in order to reduce the probability of the occurrence of error and time saving for the network experts in the implementation of the new network infrastructure [15]. The ZTP model makes it possible for the network device to be automatically provisioned by obtaining the necessary information from the network, eliminating most of human interventions [16].

The ZTP process has its roots in the automated server setup process, which is a typical process that has been part of the IT world since the first Linux server [13]. However, in the networking world, the idea of the ZTP process appeared only a few years ago with the development of the SDN concept. When using the ZTP approach for network device configuration, the network administrator receives the device and then installs it physically into the network cabinet, conducts appropriate cabling and connects the device to the network. After connecting the device to the network, the device is started and with the help of standard network protocols the necessary information is obtained in order to download the configuration script. Then the script is downloaded and executed on the device, after which the device is ready to be used on the network [17]. A detailed process of the ZTP model operation usually includes the following steps:

1. Connecting the device to the network and starting it.
2. The device locates the DHCP server and sends a query and in response gets the IP address, network mask, default gateway and if necessary DNS server address, and
3. DHCP server will also provide the device with the TFTP server address or Uniform Resource Locator (URL) to access the HTTP server from which the system image and the configuration script are downloaded.

Before starting the ZTP process it is necessary to set the script to an available TFTP or HTTP server on the network. Besides, it is necessary to configure the DHCP server to assign the appropriate information.

When the device is connected to the network it receives the IP address of the TFTP server or the URL for access to the HTTP server and the file path to the configuration file, which requires two options to be configured on the DHCP server [14]:

- Option 150 – contains a list of IP addresses that point to the TFTP or HTTP server, and
- Option 67 – contains the file path to the configuration file or script on the TFTP or HTTP server.

Consequently, in this paper one's own script has been developed in the Python programming language whose application will serve to test its advantage, in compliance with the observation range – number of device installations within the ZTP model.

3.1 Guest Shell

Guest Shell is a virtualized Linux-based environment developed with the purpose of running custom Linux applications, including Python for automated control and management of Cisco devices. Using the Guest Shell environment, it is possible to install, upgrade and manage third-party applications. It is primarily intended for certain device management tools and applications [14].

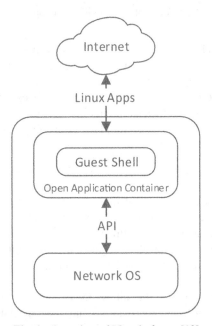

Fig. 1. Overview of IOx platforms [18]

Guest Shell shares the kernel with the network device operating system; in this case IOS XE, version 16.6.7. The users are given access to the Guest Shell environment and are allowed to edit scripts and to upgrade the software packages. Guest Shell container is managed using IOx (Fig. 1). IOx represents an end-to-end application framework that provides application-hosting capabilities for different types of applications on Cisco network platforms, and Guest Shell represents one such application [18].

Within the Guest Shell environment Cisco devices support Python version 2.7 (newer versions support only version 3.6). The possibility of Python scripting provides programmatic access to the CLI of the device to perform various tasks, but also the ability to implement the ZTP model [14].

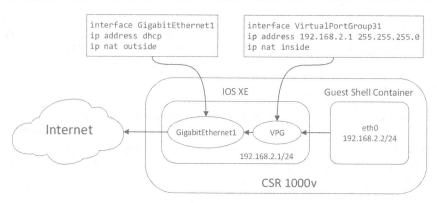

Fig. 2. Guest shell environment configuration for application hosting [19]

When running the ZTP process IOx is first enabled, which manages various applications, including the Guest Shell environment. In the case of routing platform which uses the VirtualPortGroup for front panel networking, as in the case of this paper, the configuration of GigabitEthernet and VirtualPortGroup interfaces is performed first. Guest Shell uses VirtualPortGroup as the source interface to connect to the outside network through NAT (Network Address Translation) [14]. The interface configuration is shown in Fig. 2.

3.2 Python CLI Module

Python is an interpreted, object-oriented, high-level programming language with dynamic semantics. Its high-level built-in data structures, combined with dynamic typing and dynamic binding, make it very attractive for rapid application development, as well as for the use as a scripting or glue language to connect the existing components together. Python supports modules and packages which encourages modularity and code reuse [20].

Cisco provides Python module that allows the execution of CLI commands in the Guest Shell Python environment. There are six functions available in the Python CLI module for executing various CLI commands and an additional help() function that displays features of the Cisco CLI module. To use these functions, it is necessary to first import the module with the import cli module command. The argument of these functions is the string of particular CLI commands. The following functions are available [14]:

- cli.cli(command) – The function takes any IOS command as an argument, parsing is performed and the command is executed, and after that the resulting text is returned. If an invalid command is issued, Python exception occurs.

- cli.clip(command) – This function behaves the same as the previous one, except that the resulting text is printed. The functions cli and clip provide the possibility of forwarding multiple commands.
- cli.execute(command) – This function individually executes the user and privileged EXEC level commands and returns the output.
- cli.executep(command) – Like the previous command, this function executes individual EXEC level commands, but the result of executing the function is printed unlike the previous case where the result is returned.
- cli.configure(command) – This function configures the network device according to the passed commands in the function argument. The function returns a list containing the submitted command, the success of the execution of the command, and information about error if it exists. It is possible to pass a series of commands separated by commas.
- cli.configurep(command) – This function behaves identically as the previous one, except that it prints the output of executing the function.

4   Environment Development for Zero-Touch Provisioning Model

The process of developing the environment in which the case study will be presented requires a two-step approach. First, it will be necessary to define the network topology in which the ZTP process will be performed and to configure the network devices and servers in it. Second, the development of the script in the Python programming language which will be executed on a Cisco CSR1000v router. This is followed by starting the device and applying the configuration.

4.1 Development of Network Topology

The ZTP model will be tested in the emulated network by using the Emulated Virtual Environment Next Generation (EVE-NG) software, version 2.0.3-110. Thus Router1, Switch1, Linux server and Cisco CSR1000v router on which the ZTP model is tested, are connected to the local network (Fig. 3).

Linux server with Ubuntu 20.04. operating system hosts DHCP, TFTP and HTTP servers.

The configuration of the aforementioned servers on Linux required the Internet access to install the necessary upgrades. Thus, Router1 is configured to allow access to external networks. The configuration of DHCP server on Ubuntu OS is presented in Fig. 4.

4.2 Python Script Development

The Guest Shell environment within the device comes with the support for Python 2.7 that allows access to the device CLI to perform various processes, including also the ZTP process. The idea when developing the script was to create a single script that could be executed on multiple devices on the network, and a configuration file would be available on a specific server to be downloaded by the script, containing variable values for each device. The configuration file would be written in an easy-to-understand JavaScript Object Notation (JSON) format (Fig. 5) whereby the values could be entered

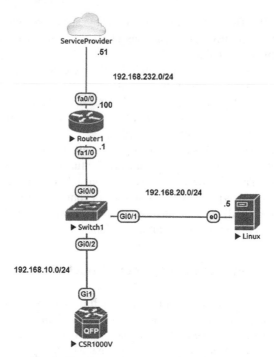

Fig. 3. Topology of test network environment

```
subnet 192.168.10.0 netmask 255.255.255.0 {
range 192.168.10.10 192.168.10.254;
option bootfile-name "ZTP_python.py";
option tftp-server-name "192.168.20.5";
option subnet-mask 255.255.255.0;
option routers 192.168.10.1;
option broadcast-address 192.168.10.255;
default-lease-time 600;
max-lease-time 7200;
```

Fig. 4. Configuration of DHCP server on Ubuntu OS

by anyone, and not just the developer. In this way, it is possible to configure a large number of devices in a very efficient way.

The script imports three Python modules, and these are re, cli and json. Module re or Regular Expression represent a string of characters which create a pattern to search a particular string. Then cli module which, as already mentioned, is used for passing commands to the network device from the Python environment. The script defines three functions for every step of the device configuration, which are called at the end of the script.

```
[
    {
        "SN": "9KZE846DMPS",
        "hostname": "ZTPDevice1",
        "ipaddress": "192.168.10.10",
        "netmask": "255.255.255.0",
        "secret": "admin"
    }
]
```

Fig. 5. Configuration file in JSON format

```
def get_serials():
    print '\nSerialNo parsing...\n'
    inventory = cli('show inventory')
    invetoryList = inventory.split('\n\n')
    for chassis in invetoryList:
            if (re.search('NAME: "Chassis"',chassis)):
                match = re.findall('SN:\s(.*)', chassis)
    serialNo = match[0]
    print '\nSerial number: {}\n'.format(serialNo)
    return serialNo
```

Fig. 6. Function within the script to obtain a serial number of the network device

The first function, i.e. get_serials(), has the task to use re module to parse the serial number of the network device that is obtained on it by submitting an adequate command via cli module. This function eventually returns the variable which contains the requested serial number (Fig. 6).

```
def get_config():
    url = 'http://192.168.20.5/device_config.json'
    print '\nDownloading configuration from URL: {}'.for-
mat(url)
    clip('copy http://192.168.20.5/device_config.json
flash')
    config = cli('more flash:device_config.json')
    json_config = json.loads(config)
    print '\nConfiguration commands: Collected!\n'
    return json_config
```

Fig. 7. Function within the script to download the configuration file from HTTP server

Furthermore, the function get_config() has been defined for the purpose of downloading a configuration file in JSON format from an HTTP server. A unique URL is first defined, which is then passed along with the rest of the corresponding file download command via the cli module. After the download, the JSON form is converted into a dictionary data type, i.e. in the list of dictionary data which is then returned by the function (Fig. 7).

```
def configure_device(config, serial):
    print '\nConfiguring device...\n'
    for line in config:
        if line["SN"] == serial:
            device_config = line

            configurep(['hostname {}'.format(device_con-
fig['hostname'])])

            configurep(['int GigabitEthernet1', 'ip add
{} {}'.format(device_config['ipaddress'],
                            device_config['netmask']), 'no
shut', 'end'])
            configurep(['line con 0', 'logging synchro-
nous', 'no exec-timeout', 'end'])
            configurep(['ip domain-name domain.com'])
            configurep([crypto key generate rsa modulus
1024'])
            configurep(['username user password admin'])
            configurep(['enable secret {}'.format(de-
vice_config['secret'])])
            configurep(['line vty 0 4', 'transport input
ssh', 'login local'])
```

Fig. 8. Function that performs device configuration

Finally, the function configure_device() has been defined, which retrieves the corresponding values of variables from the list of dictionaries and passes them through the cli device configuration module. The configuration in this case is for the purpose of displaying the ZTP model and the arbitrary commands are selected (Fig. 8).

5   Results of Implementing Zero-Touch Provisioning Model

After developing the network environment that allows the implementation of the ZTP process and the creation of a script and the necessary configuration file, it is possible to begin with the implementation of the specified process. Once the Cisco CSR1000v router with the IOS XE operating system is connected to the network, it can be started.

The Cisco device begins the startup process by checking certain components, such as the processor, Random Access Memory (RAM) and Non-Volatile Random Access Memory (NV-RAM). After the tests have been performed, the bootstrap program is copied from Read-Only Memory (ROM) into RAM memory. After copying, the processor executes the instructions from the bootstrap program. The main task of the bootstrap program is to locate the Cisco IOS and to load it into RAM. The last step in booting the device is to check the existence of the startup configuration in the NVRAM memory.

When the device starts and checks for the absence of a startup configuration in the NVRAM memory, it enters the ZTP operating mode. The device then finds the DHCP server and then receives a DHCP offer which includes the option 150 and 67, respectively. The device receives information on the location of the TFTP server and the file path to the script which is located on that server and downloads the script and stores it in the flash memory. The enabling of the Guest Shell environment starts then, preceded by enabling of the IOx platform.

After the process of starting the Guest Shell environment is completed, the script can be executed in the Python environment. The device in this process obtains the configuration file from the HTTP server, parses the values of the variables and commands are passed by means of the cli module. With the submission of commands, the ZTP process ends and the device is configured and ready for use online. By entering the show running-configuration command it is possible to see the applied configuration on the CSR1000v router. Figure 9 shows the hostname configuration on the device. Further in the same display it is possible to see the encrypted configured password which is used to enter the privileged EXEC level. Finally, there is a display of configured domain name for the purpose of allowing access via the SSH protocol. The hostname and the password values were parsed from the JSON file.

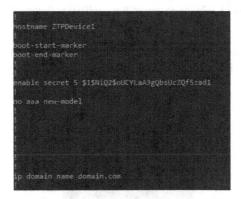

Fig. 9. Configured hostname, password and the domain name

Figure 10 shows the configuration of the VirtualPortGroup interface, whose configuration is automated when enabling the Guest Shell environment. In addition, the script configures the GigabitEthernet1 interface to which an IP address is associated which is parsed from a JSON file.

Figure 11 shows the configuration of IOx application framework. The configuration of the IOx framework is followed by the configuration of NAT where the role of the inside interface is played by the VirtualPortGroup, and the outside by GigabitEthernet1. NAT is configured automatically when enabling the Guest Shell environment.

```
interface VirtualPortGroup31
 ip address 192.168.2.1 255.255.255.0
 ip nat inside
 no mop enabled
 no mop sysid

interface GigabitEthernet1
 ip address 192.168.10.10 255.255.255.0
 ip nat outside
 negotiation auto
 no mop enabled
 no mop sysid
```

Fig. 10. Configured Virtual Port Group and interface

```
iox
ip nat inside source list NAT_ACL interface GigabitEthernet1 overload
ip forward-protocol nd
ip http server
no ip http secure-server
ip http client source-interface GigabitEthernet1



ip access-list standard NAT_ACL
 permit 192.168.0.0 0.0.255.255
```

Fig. 11. Configuration of IOx application framework

Finally, Fig. 12 shows the configuration of the console port and the configuration of the Virtual Terminal lines, thus enabling the remote access by means of the SSH protocol.

```
line con 0
 logging synchronous
 stopbits 1
line vty 0 4
 login local
 transport input ssh
```

Fig. 12. Configuration of console port and Virtual Terminal lines

This type of automation results in the saving of time, costs of employees – reflected in the saving of engineer-hours and reduction of human error. The result of savings depends on the number of installations, i.e. the increase in the number of devices causes an increase in the efficiency in relation to the traditional method. Also, the difference in the saving is reflected in the dependence on the kind and type of the device, implementation environment and end user requirements. With the done research, for instance, the time savings for the selected 100 arbitrary installations amounts to more than 95% time, which represents a much greater saving in relation to the analyzed research [11]. Additionally, the time saving depends directly on the reduction of engineer-hours, which results in financial savings.

Below is the conclusion about the carried out case study and the proposal for further research.

6 Conclusion

Today's computer networks encounter challenges of rapid development and implementation of new services in order to satisfy the ever stricter user requirements. In order to satisfy the user expectations for fast, elastic and scalable networking, fundamental changes in the method in which heterogeneous networks support a wide spectrum of applications are needed. New paradigm of Software Defined Network (SDN) with programmable infrastructure appears as a promising solution.

Until now, in traditional networks, the process of implementing new devices into the network represented a time-consuming and financially demanding process with the always present possibility of human error. As consequence of the increasing need for automation of the network processes and the development of the SDN concept, the Zero-Touch Provisioning model has been presented.

ZTP is an automation solution that allows reduction of time and costs of implementing new devices into the network. Although there are various variations of implementing this model, the case study in this paper presents the possibility of use in broadband access on the example of Cisco CSR1000v router with IOS XE operating system. The realization of the ZTP process in the emulated network has confirmed the assumption about its efficiency, which is primarily reflected in the saving of time, in our case of over 95% (depending on the number of device installations). Although ZTP automates most part of the configuration process of new devices in the network, its execution requires certain preparation, i.e. training of the necessary servers, creation of the script and configuration file and certain tests. Consequently, such a model has special advantages in somewhat larger network implementations where the savings of time, costs and reduced probability of error especially come to the fore.

In discussing the ZTP model it should be emphasized that all the major network equipment manufacturers are oriented to device configuration automation, but the way of implementing the ZTP model differs somewhat from manufacturer to manufacturer. Therefore, the implementation of the ZTP model in various scenarios of heterogeneous networks with several different manufacturers will be a little less efficient. Using the method of correlation and regression as well as the method of comparison (Checklist method, Before-and-after method, etc.) it is possible to define the deviations in the implementation of the ZTP model in various scenarios of heterogeneous networks with several different manufacturers. In order to solve this problem it will be necessary to perform additional research and develop an appropriate type of joint platform and the necessary components that would allow the performance of the ZTP model in the networks with devices from several manufacturers, which is at the same time the direction of the planned future research.

References

1. Bakshi, K.: Considerations for software defined networking (SDN): approaches and use cases. In: 2013 IEEE Aerospace Conference, pp. 1–4. IEEE, Big Sky (2013).
2. Prajapati, A., Sakadasariya, A., Patel, J.: Software defined network: Future of networking. In: 2018 2nd International Conference on Inventive Systems and Control (ICISC), pp. 1351–1354. IEEE, Coimbatore, India (2018)
3. Cisco Software-Defined Access. https://www.cisco.com/c/dam/en/us/products/se/2018/1/Collateral/nb-06-software-defined-access-ebook-en.pdf. Accessed 14 Oct 2020
4. Ahmed, K., Nafi, N.S., Blech, J.O., Gregory, M.A., Schmidt, H.: Software defined industry automation networks. In: 2017 27th International Telecommunication Networks and Applications Conference (ITNAC), pp. 1–3. IEEE, Melbourne, Australia (2017)
5. Kreutz, D., Ramos, F.M.V., Verissimo, P.E., Rothenberg, C.E., Azodolmolky, S., Uhlig, S.: Software-defined networking: a comprehensive survey. Proc. IEEE **103**(1), 14–76 (2015)
6. Yoshino, M., Astawa, I.G., Trinh, T., Suzuki, H., Koswara, M., Nguyen, B.: Zero-touch multi-service provisioning with pluggable module-type olt on access network virtualization testbed. In: 25th Opto-Electronics and Communications Conference OECC 2020, pp. 2020–2022 (2020)
7. Boskov, I., Yetgin, H., Vucnik, M., Fortuna, C., Mohorcic, M.: Time-to-provision evaluation of IoT devices using automated zero-touch provisioning. In: IEEE Global Communications Conference GLOBECOM 2020 - Proceedings, vol. 2020-Jan (2020)
8. Brockelsby, W., Dilda, S.: Tactical network automation with NetZTP and one shot. In: IEEE 40th Sarnoff Symposium, Newark, NJ, USA, pp. 1–3 (2019)
9. Demchenko, Y., et al.: ZeroTouch provisioning (ZTP) model and infrastructure components for multi-provider cloud services provisioning. In: IEEE International Conference on Cloud Engineering Workshop (IC2EW), Berlin, Germany, pp. 184–189 (2016)
10. Andrus, B.M., et al.: Zero-touch provisioning of distributed video analytics in a software-defined metro-haul network with P4 processing. Optics InfoBase Conference Paper, vol. Part F160, pp. 2019–2021 (2019)
11. Szigeti, T., Zacks, D., Falkner, M., Simone, A.: Cisco Digital Network Architecture: Intent-based Networking for the Enterprise. Cisco Press, Hoboken (2018)
12. Filiposka, S., et al.: Enabling high performance cloud computing using zero touch provisioning. In: 23rd Telecommun Forum (TELFOR), pp. 67–70. IEEE, Belgrade (2015)
13. Demchenko, Y., et al.: Enabling Automated Network Services Provisioning for Cloud Based Applications Using Zero Touch Provisioning. In: 8th International Conference on Utility and Cloud Computing (UCC), pp. 458–464. IEEE, Limassol (2015)
14. Programmability Configuration Guide, Cisco IOS XE Everest 16.6.x. https://www.cisco.com/c/en/us/td/docs/ios-xml/ios/prog/configuration/166/b_166_programmability_cg/zero_touch_provisioning.html. Accessed 20 Oct 2020
15. Mishra, R., Gijare, V., Malik, S.: Zero touch network: a comprehensive network design approach. Int. J. Eng. Res. Technol. (IJERT) **8**(9), 792–794 (2019)
16. Zero-Touch Provisioning. https://infocenter.nokia.com/public/7750SR1910R1A/index.jsp?topic=%2Fcom.sr.basic%2Fhtml%2Fztp.html. Accessed 22 Oct 2020
17. Deliverable D13.3 Proposed Network Architectures – White Paper. https://www.geant.org/Projects/GEANT_Project_GN4-1/Documents/D13-3_Proposed-Network-Architectures_White-Paper.pdf. Accessed 22 Oct 2020
18. Introduction to GuestShell. https://www.ciscolive.com/c/dam/r/ciscolive/us/docs/2018/pdf/DEVNET-1695.pdf. Accessed 23 Oct 2020

19. Programmability Configuration Guide, Cisco IOS XE Amsterdam 17.1.x. https://www.cisco.com/c/en/us/td/docs/ios-xml/ios/prog/configuration/171/b_171_programmability_cg.html. Accessed 23 Oct 2020

20. Kumar, A., Panda, S.P.: A survey: how python pitches in IT-world. In: 2019 International Conference on Machine Learning, Big Data, Cloud and Parallel Computing (COMITCon), pp. 248–251. IEEE, Faridabad, India (2019)

Multilayer Network Analysis:
The Identification of Key Actors
in a Sicilian Mafia Operation

Annamaria Ficara[1,2](✉) ⓘ, Giacomo Fiumara[2] ⓘ, Pasquale De Meo[3] ⓘ,
and Salvatore Catanese[2] ⓘ

[1] DMI Department, University of Palermo, Via Archirafi 34, 90123 Palermo, Italy
aficara@unime.it
[2] MIFT Department, University of Messina, V.le F. S. D'Alcontres 31,
98166 Messina, Italy
{gfiumara,scatanese}@unime.it
[3] DICAM Department, University of Messina, V.le G. Palatuci 13,
98168 Messina, Italy
pdemeo@unime.it

Abstract. Recently, Social Network Analysis studies have led to an improvement and to a generalization of existing tools to networks with multiple subsystems and layers of connectivity. These kind of networks are usually called multilayer networks. Multilayer networks in which each layer shares at least one node with some other layer in the network are called multiplex networks. Being a multiplex network does not require all nodes to exist on every layer. In this paper, we built a criminal multiplex network which concerns an anti-mafia operation called "Montagna" and it is based on the examination of a pre-trial detention order issued on March 14, 2007 by the judge for preliminary investigations of the Court of Messina (Sicily). "Montagna" focus on two Mafia families called "Mistretta" and "Batanesi" who infiltrated several economic activities including the public works in the north-eastern part of Sicily, through a cartel of entrepreneurs close to the Sicilian Mafia. Originally we derived two single-layer networks, the former capturing meetings between suspected individuals and the latter recording phone calls. But some networked systems can be better modeled by multilayer structures where the individual nodes develop relationships in multiple layers. For this reason we built a two-layer network from the single-layer ones. These two layers share 47 nodes. We followed three different approaches to measure the importance of nodes in multilayer networks using degree as descriptor. Our analysis can aid in the identification of key players in criminal networks.

Keywords: Social network analysis · Criminal networks · Multilayer networks

D. Perakovic and L. Knapcikova (Eds.): FABULOUS 2021, LNICST 382, pp. 120–134, 2021.
https://doi.org/10.1007/978-3-030-78459-1_9

1   Introduction

During his lifetime, each individual continuously deal with multiple social networks. He does it with no effort and this does not mean that it is a trivial activity which can be overlooked. The connections between people through multiple types of relational ties represent only one possible view of a problem already known long before the field of Social Network Analysis (SNA) was developed. Looking only at a single type of relational tie within a single social network risks either defining a world where different kinds of relationships are ontologically equivalent or overlooking the invisible relationships emerging from the interactions among different types of ties. For a long time, these interactions have largely been studied within a single-layer perspective and one of the most effective SNA tools to measure social interactions has been the simple graph. A simple graph is defined as a set of nodes, also called actors (*i.e.*, individuals or organizations) with edges between them, also called links or connections (*i.e.*, relational ties such as friendship relationships) and with no edges connecting a node to itself [1].

According to Wasserman and Faust [2], social networks contain at least three different dimensions: a structural dimension corresponding to the social graph (*e.g.*, actors and their relationships); a compositional dimension describing the actors (*e.g.*, their personal information); and an affiliation dimension (*e.g.*, members of the same family or organization). These three dimensions provide a minimal description needed to understand the full complexity of social structures. An alternative conceptual approach to dealing with the same set of problems is to think of multiple relationships as a set of connected levels, or layers, forming a single multidimensional social network [1]. In fact, a social network with nodes and/or edges can be organized into multiple layers, where each layer represents a different kind of node or edge, a different social context, a different community, a different online social network (OSN), and so on. The analysis of multiple layers can provide knowledge that is not present in each layer when layers are considered independently of each other.

Kivelä et al. [3] review and discuss many of the relevant works on the topic. Then they try to unify the literature by introducing a general framework for multilayer networks [4–7]. Such framework can represent the different notions of networks (*e.g.*, single-layer or monoplex networks [4,8], multiplex networks [9–11], interdependent networks, networks of networks) by simply introducing cumulative constraints on the general model [12].

Multilayer social networks appear in a number of different contexts, where data are characterized by different sizes, different natures (*e.g.*, online, offline, hybrid), and different layer semantics (*e.g.*, contact, communication, time, context, etc.). Many multirelational networks, that is actors connected by multiple types of ties, have been collected during SNA studies. These networks are often characterized by a small size, because they were often collected through offline questionnaires or interviews and they can be very useful in qualitatively checking the behavior and results of new methods [1].

An interesting multirelational network about criminal relationships is described by Bright et al. [13] who focused on eight types of edges related to the exchange of a particular resource (*e.g.*, drugs, money) in a criminal network with 128 actors.

We propose a new real multilayer criminal network derived from two simple graphs described in our earlier works [14–17], whose datasets are publicly available on Zenodo [18]. These simple graphs capture the physical meetings and phone calls among suspects in an anti-mafia operation called "Montagna", concluded in 2007 by the Public Prosecutor's Office of Messina (Sicily). Starting from these two simple graphs, we created an undirected and weighted multilayer network with two layers called Meetings and Phone Calls, 154 nodes and 439 edges.

The Sicilian Mafia [19–21] is one of the most renowned criminal organisations (*i.e.*, clans, families, gangs, syndicates) whose social structure analysis generated great scientific interest [22]. SNA has become an important tool for the study of criminal networks [23–25] and it can be used to describe the structure and functioning of a criminal organisation, to construct crime prevention systems [15, 26], to identify leaders within a criminal organisation [27] or to evaluate police interventions aimed at dismantling and disrupting criminal networks [16,28,29].

To identify leaders within a criminal network, we have to use a family of measures aimed at identifying the most important actors in a social network [2]. The family of centrality measures is probably the most widely applied set of SNA tools in practical contexts. Centrality [30] is an intrinsically relational concept, because to be central, an actor needs to have relations [1]. An actor might be important because he is connected to a large number of different nodes or because he is connected to other important nodes. An actor can also be considered important because his absence would result in a loosely connected social network made of many isolated components. Centrality is also often described in terms of the power that an actor could receive from it (*e.g.*, an actor strategically located within a network will have a high control over the information flowing through the network).

In this paper, we focus on the importance of nodes in multilayer networks. We used three different approaches (see details in Sect. 4) to compute the nodes' degree (*i.e.*, the number of edges adjacent to it) and to identify the 20 most important nodes (*i.e.*, the key actors) in our criminal multilayer network.

2   Background

2.1   Single-Layer Networks

A *single-layer network* is a simple graph [2] which can be defined as a tuple $G = (V, E)$ where $V = \{v_1, v_2, \ldots, v_N\}$ is the set composed by N nodes and $E = \{l_1, l_2, \ldots, l_L\}$, $E \subseteq V \times V$, is the set of edges, whose generic element l_k represents the edge existing between a pair of nodes (v_i, v_j). The graph edges sometimes have weights, which indicate the strength (or some other attribute) of each connection between the nodes.

From a purely mathematical point of view, the information contained in both sets V and E can be represented in an A matrix of dimension $N \times N$ called the *adjacency matrix* [2], whose generic element a_{ij} is defined as

$$a_{ij} = \begin{cases} 1 & \text{if } v_i \to v_j \qquad i, j = 1, 2, ..., N \\ 0 & \text{otherwise} \end{cases} \tag{1}$$

In undirected graphs, $a_{ij} = a_{ji}$ for all $i \neq j$ and therefore the adjacency matrix A will be symmetrical: $A = A^T$ (where T is the transpose representation).

It is possible to define some descriptive measures able to highlight particular characteristics of a network. For example, we define the *degree* of a node $d(v_i)$ as the number of nodes adjacent to it [2] or as the cardinality of the set of neighbors of that node:

$$d(v_i) = |\mathcal{N}(v_i)| = |\{v_j : \exists(v_i, v_j) \vee \exists(v_j, v_i), j \neq i\}| \tag{2}$$

The degree assumes a discrete value between a minimum of 0 when a node is isolated (*i.e.*, it is not connected to any other node) and a maximum of $N - 1$ if the node is connected to all other nodes in the network. The degree of a node can be calculated by adding the columns (or rows) of the adjacency matrix A [2]:

$$d(v_i) = \sum_{j=1}^{N} a_{ij} = \sum_{i=1}^{N} a_{ij} \tag{3}$$

The concepts presented so far can be expressed using an alternative notation, which makes use of tensors and Einstein's notation [4,8].

Given the canonical basis in the vector space $\mathbb{R}^N$, $\xi = \{e_1, e_2, \ldots, e_N\}$ where $e_i = (0, \ldots, 0, 1, 0, \ldots, 0)^T$ is 1 in the ith component, and 0 otherwise. Given a set of N nodes v_i (where $i = 1, 2, \ldots, N$ and $N \in \mathbb{N}$), we associate with each node a *state* that is represented by the canonical vector e_i in the vector space $\mathbb{R}^N$. A node v_i can be related with each other and the presence and the intensity of such relationships in the vector space is indicated using the tensor product [31] (*i.e.*, the *Kronecker product*) $\mathbb{R}^N \otimes \mathbb{R}^N = \mathbb{R}^{N \times N}$. Thus, second-order (*i.e.*, rank-2) canonical tensors are defined by $E_{ij} = e_i \otimes e_j^T$ (where $i, j = 1, 2, \ldots, N$). The *relationship tensor* can consequently be written as

$$W = \sum_{i=1}^{N} \sum_{j=1}^{N} w_{ij} E_{ij} = \sum_{i=1}^{N} \sum_{j=1}^{N} w_{ij} e_i \otimes e_j^T \tag{4}$$

where the intensity of the relationship from node v_i to node v_j is indicated by w_{ij}.

The matrix W is an example of an *adjacency tensor* and, in the context of single-layer networks, it is just a $N \times N$ matrix of a weighted graph with N nodes which is equivalent to the adjacency matrix A.

The covariant notation by Ricci and Levi-Civita [32] can be used to write an adjacency tensor. In this case, a row vector $a \in \mathbb{R}^N$ can be represented using its covariant and controvariant components which are the vector a_α (*i.e.*, $\alpha = 1, 2, \ldots, N$) and its dual vector a^α (*i.e.*, a column vector in the Euclidean space). A linear combination of tensors in the canonical basis can be used to represent the adjacency tensor W:

$$W_\beta^\alpha = \sum_{i=1}^{N}\sum_{j=1}^{N} w_{ij}e^\alpha(i)e_\beta(j) = \sum_{i=1}^{N}\sum_{j=1}^{N} w_{ij}E_\beta^\alpha(ij) \tag{5}$$

where $e^\alpha(i)$ and $e_\beta(j)$ are respectively the αth and the βth components of the ith contravariant and jth covariant canonical vectors in $\mathbb{R}^N$, $E_\beta^\alpha(ij) \in \mathbb{R}^{N \times N}$ is the tensor in the canonical basis which represents E_{ij} (*i.e.*, the tensor product of the canonical vectors assigned to nodes v_i and v_j).

Define the 1-vector $u^\alpha = (1, 1, \dots, 1)^T \in \mathbb{R}^N$ and let $U_\alpha^\beta = u_\alpha u^\beta$ be the second-order tensor whose elements are all equal to 1 (*i.e.*, a so-called *1-tensor*). The *degree vector* is calculated adding up all the columns of the adjacency tensor defined in Eq. 5:

$$k_\beta = W_\beta^\alpha u_\alpha \tag{6}$$

It is possible to calculate the degree of node v_i by projecting the degree vector onto the ith canonical vector:

$$k(i) = k_\beta e^\beta(i) \tag{7}$$

2.2 Multilayer Networks

Kivelä et al. [3] define a multilayer network as the most general structure which can be used to represent any kind of network. At the base of this structure, there is the elementary concept of graph, defined in Subsect. 2.1. The representation of networks at multiple levels or with multiple types of edges (or with other similar features) requires structures that have *layers* in addition to nodes and edges. Moreover, the concept of *aspect* can be defined as a feature of a layer representing one dimension of the layer structure (*e.g.*, the type of an edge or the time at which an edge is present) [12]. More specifically, an "elementary layer" is an element of one of the possible sets of layers from a specific aspect and the term "layer" refers to a combination of elementary layers from all aspects.

A *multilayer network* can be defined as a quadruplet $M = (V_M, E_M, V, L)$. $V_M \subseteq V \times L_1 \times \cdots \times L_d$ is the set of the node-layer combinations, that is the set of layers in which a node $v_i \in V$ is present. $E_M \subseteq V_M \times V_M$ is the edge set containing the set of pairs of possible combinations of nodes and elementary layers. V is the set of all nodes independently from the layer. $L = \{L_a\}_a^d = 1$ is the sequence of sets of elementary layers such that there is one set of elementary layers L_a for each aspect a. If $d = 0$, the multilayer network M reduces to a single-layer network. If $d = 1$, then M reduces to a multiplex network.

Using multiple layers, it is possible to represent different types of edges: those among nodes in the same layer, called *intralayer edges*, and those among nodes in different layers, called *interlayer edges*. For this reason, the concepts of intralayer and interlayer adiacency tensor are introduced [4]. The *intralayer adiacency tensor* $C_\beta^\alpha(\widetilde{kk})$ is defined as the relationships among nodes in the same layer $\widetilde{k}$ which is indicated by the second-order tensor $W_\beta^\alpha(\widetilde{k})$, where $\alpha, \beta = 1, 2, \ldots, N$ as defined in Eq. 5. Indices which refer to layers are distinguished from those which correspond to nodes using the tilde symbol. The second-order *interlayer adjacency tensor* $C_\beta^\alpha(\widetilde{h}\widetilde{k})$ is introduced instead to encode information about relationships between nodes on different layers (*e.g.*, a node v_i from layer $\widetilde{h}$ can be connected to a node v_j in an other layer $\widetilde{k}$). The interlayer adjacency tensor $C_\beta^\alpha(\widetilde{h}\widetilde{k})$ corresponds to the intralayer adjacency tensor $W_\beta^\alpha(\widetilde{k})$ when the same layer $\widetilde{k}$ is represented by a couple of layers.

Following a similar approach to the one used to define the adjacency tensor for single-layer networks (see Eq. 5), the vector $e^{\widetilde{\gamma}}(\widetilde{k})$ (where $\widetilde{\gamma}, \widetilde{k} = 1, 2, \ldots, L$) of the canonical basis in the space $\mathbb{R}^L$ is introduced. In this definition, the vector components are indicated by a greek index while the kth canonical vector is indicated by a latin index. Therefore the second-order tensors, which correspond to the canonical basis in the space $\mathbb{R}^{L \times L}$, are constructed as

$$E_{\widetilde{\delta}}^{\widetilde{\gamma}}(\widetilde{h}\widetilde{k}) = e^{\widetilde{\gamma}}(\widetilde{h})e_{\widetilde{\delta}}(\widetilde{k}) \tag{8}$$

The *multilayer adjacency tensor* [8] can be written from Eq. 8, using a tensor product between the adjacency tensors $C_{\widetilde{\beta}}^{\widetilde{\alpha}}(\widetilde{h}\widetilde{k})$ and the canonical tensors $E_{\widetilde{\delta}}^{\widetilde{\gamma}}(\widetilde{h}\widetilde{k})$. A fourth-order tensor is obtained as

$$M_{\beta\widetilde{\delta}}^{\alpha\widetilde{\gamma}} = \sum_{\widetilde{h}=1}^{L} \sum_{\widetilde{k}=1}^{L} C_\beta^\alpha(\widetilde{h}\widetilde{k}) E_{\widetilde{\delta}}^{\widetilde{\gamma}}(\widetilde{h}\widetilde{k}) \tag{9}$$

The second-order interlayer adjacency tensor $C_\beta^\alpha(\widetilde{h}\widetilde{k})$ can be written when $\widetilde{h} = \widetilde{k}$ as

$$C_\beta^\alpha(\widetilde{h}\widetilde{k}) = \sum_{i=1}^{N} \sum_{j=1}^{N} w_{ij}(\widetilde{h}\widetilde{k}) E_\beta^\alpha(ij) \tag{10}$$

where $w_{ij}(\widetilde{h}\widetilde{k})$ are just real numbers which specify the intensity of the relationship between a node v_i in layer $\widetilde{h}$ and a node v_j in an other layer $\widetilde{k}$. Then, the fourth-order tensor of the canonical basis of the space $\mathbb{R}^{N \times N \times L \times L}$ is defined as

$$\xi_{\beta\widetilde{\delta}}^{\alpha\widetilde{\gamma}}(ij\widetilde{h}\widetilde{k}) = E_\beta^\alpha(ij)E_{\widetilde{\delta}}^{\widetilde{\gamma}}(\widetilde{h}\widetilde{k}) = e^\alpha(i)e_\beta(j)e^{\widetilde{\gamma}}(\widetilde{h})e_{\widetilde{\delta}}(\widetilde{k}) \tag{11}$$

Replacing in Eq. 9 the expressions obtained in Eq. 10 and Eq. 11, the multilayer adjacency tensor can be written as

$$M_{\beta\widetilde{\delta}}^{\alpha\widetilde{\gamma}} = \sum_{\widetilde{h},\widetilde{k}=1}^{L} \sum_{i,j=1}^{N} w_{ij}(\widetilde{h}\widetilde{k}) \xi_{\beta\widetilde{\delta}}^{\alpha\widetilde{\gamma}}(ij\widetilde{h}\widetilde{k}) \tag{12}$$

In some cases, it is possible to aggregate multiple networks constructing a single-layer network. This aggregation can be useful in different kind of studies such as those on temporal or social networks. To change a multilayer network into a weighted single-layer network, the corresponding tensor is multiplied by the 1-tensor $U_{\alpha\tilde{\gamma}}^{\beta\tilde{\delta}}$. The obtained *projected single-layer network* P_{β}^{α} [4] is

$$P_{\beta}^{\alpha} = M_{\beta\tilde{\delta}}^{\alpha\tilde{\gamma}} U_{\tilde{\gamma}}^{\tilde{\delta}} = \sum_{\tilde{h}=1}^{L}\sum_{\tilde{k}=1}^{L} C_{\beta}^{\alpha}(\tilde{h}\tilde{k}) \qquad (13)$$

A structure similar to the projected single-layer network is the *aggregate* or *overlay single-layer network* [4]. It is obtained ignoring the interlayer edges and summing for each node the edges over all layers in the multilayer network. The multilayer adjacency tensor is used to define the aggregate network contracting the indices which correspond to the layer components as

$$O_{\beta}^{\alpha} = M_{\beta\tilde{\gamma}}^{\alpha\tilde{\gamma}} = \sum_{\tilde{r}=1}^{L} W_{\beta}^{\alpha}(\tilde{r}) \qquad (14)$$

In the case of an aggregate network, the degree computation is the same of a single-layer network and it is computed like in Eq. 6.

On the contrary, the *multidegree centrality vector* K^{α} [4] is defined using 1-tensors of the appropriate order as in the case of single-layer networks:

$$K^{\alpha} = \left[M_{\beta\tilde{\delta}}^{\alpha\tilde{\gamma}} U_{\tilde{\gamma}}^{\tilde{\delta}} \right] u^{\beta} = \left[P_{\beta}^{\alpha} \right] u^{\beta} = \left[\sum_{\tilde{h}=1}^{L}\sum_{\tilde{k}=1}^{L} C_{\beta}^{\alpha}(\tilde{h}\tilde{k}) \right] u^{\beta} = \sum_{\tilde{h}=1}^{L}\sum_{\tilde{k}=1}^{L} k^{\alpha}(\tilde{h}\tilde{k}) \qquad (15)$$

where $k^{\alpha}(\tilde{h}\tilde{k})$ is the degree vector defined in Eq. 6 computed on the interlayer adjacency tensor $C_{\beta}^{\alpha}(\tilde{h}\tilde{k})$.

3   Dataset

Our dataset (available on Zenodo [18]) derives from an anti-mafia operation called "Montagna" concluded in 2007 by the Public Prosecutor's Office of Messina (Sicily) and a specialized anti-mafia police unit of the Italian Carabinieri called R.O.S. (Special Operations Group). The investigation focused on two Mafia families known as "Mistretta" and "Batanesi". From 2003 to 2007, these families infiltrated several economic activities including the public works in the north-eastern part of Sicily, through a cartel of entrepreneurs close to the Mafia. The "Mistretta" family had also a role of mediator between other families in Palermo and Catania and other criminal organizations around Messina, such as the "Barcellona" and the "Caltagirone" families.

Our main data source is the pre-trial detention order issued on March 14, 2007 by the judge for preliminary investigations of the Court of Messina. The Court ordered the pre-trial detention for 38 individuals writing a document of more than two hundred pages with an lot of details about the suspects' crimes, activities, meetings, and calls.

From the analysis of this document, we initially built two graphs: Meetings and Phone Calls, in which nodes were uniquely associated with suspected criminals and edges specified meetings and phone calls respectively among individuals [14–17]. The Meetings graph had 101 nodes and 256 edges. The Phone Calls graph had 100 nodes and 124 edges. There were 47 individuals who jointly belonged to both graphs.

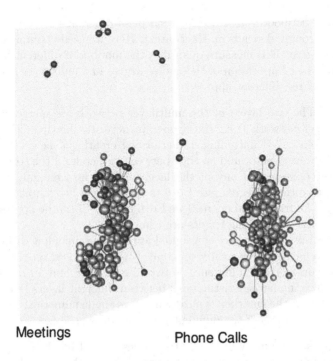

Meetings   **Phone Calls**

Fig. 1. Multilayer network. The layered visualization is obtained using Muxviz. The color of nodes is given by their community assignment (*i.e.,* how actors are clustered together) and the size by their degree. (Color figure online)

Starting from the Meetings and Phone Calls simple graphs, we created an undirected and weighted multilayer network with two layers called Meetings and Phone Calls, 154 nodes and 439 edges (see Fig. 1). The links within layer Meetings refer to the meetings among members of the criminal network while edges in the layer Phone Calls represent phone communications among distinct phone numbers they use. The weight encodes the number of meetings or phone calls. According to the definition of the different kind of multilayer networks in Subsect. 2.2, we can identify our network as an edge-colored multilayer (*i.e.,* a network with multiple types of edges) and more precisely a multiplex network which does not require all nodes to exist on every layer. Each layer have to share at least one node with some other layer in the network to be multiplex. In our case the two layers share 47 nodes. Moreover, interlayer edges are only those between nodes and their counterparts in another layers and no cost is associated to them.

4   Methodology and Results

In this paper, we perform an analysis of the nodes' importance in the multiplex network described in Sect. 3. The concept of centrality as "importance" is debated and strongly depends on the context. Here we used a simple descriptor which is the degree. This measure quantifies the number of different interaction of each node. The computation of the nodes' degree in a multilayer network can be done using three different approaches:

Approach 1 The two layers of the multilayer network are merged to obtain a single-layer network (*i.e.*, the aggregate network shown in Fig. 2). This process, often called flattening, is performed creating a new network with one node for every actor and an edge between two nodes if the corresponding actors are connected in any of the layers. Once the aggregate network is obtained, traditional degree (see Eq. 6 in Sect. 2) can be computed.

Approach 2 The traditional degree (see Eq. 6 in Sect. 2) can be applied to each layer separately. Then, the results are compared.

Approach 3 Multiple layers are considered at the same time, but without treating them as being ontologically different. Measures based on this approach explicitly consider the difference between interlayer and intralayer edges and also make numerical distinctions between different layers (*e.g.*, through weights), but at the end they typically produce single numerical values merging the contributions of the different types of edges [4,5] (see Eq. 15).

Table 1 gives a summary of the 20 top nodes ranked by their degree in the Aggregate network (*i.e.*, according to Approach 1), in the single layers Phone Calls and Meetings (*i.e.*, according to Approach 2) and in the Multilayer network (*i.e.*, according to Approach 3). The nodes' importance given by their degree is compared with the real roles these nodes had in the Sicilian Mafia families observed during the "Montagna" operation. These roles have been reconstructed by us while reading court documents of the "Montagna" operation and they are also available on Zenodo [18].

In particular, a Mafia Family has a typical structure which is shown in Fig. 3. On top of the pyramid hierarchical chart is the *Boss* who makes all the major decisions, controls the Mafia members and resolves any disputes. Usually the real boss keeps a low-profile and keeps his real identity hidden. Just below the boss is the *Underboss* who is the second in command. He can resolve disputes without involving the boss himself and replaces the boss if he is old or in danger of going to jail. In-between the boss and underboss is a role of the *Consigliere* who is an advisor to the boss and makes impartial decisions based upon fairness and for the good of the Mafia. Also in-between there is the *Messaggero* who is a messenger who functions as liaison between criminal families. He can reduce the need for sit-downs, or meetings, of the mob hierarchy, and thus limits the public exposure

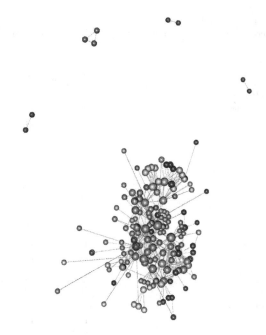

Fig. 2. Aggregate network. The edge-colored multigraph visualization is obtained using Muxviz. The color of nodes is given by their community assignment (*i.e.,* how actors are clustered together) and the size by their degree. (Color figure online)

of the bosses. Below the underboss is the *Caporegime* (also called *Captain* or *Capo*) who manages his own crew within the criminal family in a designated geographical location. A Capo's career relies heavily on how much money they can bring into the family. How many capos there are in a given family simply depends on how big that family is. Then, there are *soldiers* who report to their Caporegime. They are street level mobsters who essentially are no more than your average type criminals. Many soldiers can be assigned to one Capo. The final part of a family comes in the shape of *associates*, who are not actual members of the Mafia, but they work with Mafia soldiers and caporegimes on various criminal enterprises. An associate is simply someone who works with the mob, including anyone from a burglar or drug dealer to a pharmacist, entrepreneur, lawyer, investment banker, police officer or politician.

We performed the analysis of nodes' degree for each layer separately, the aggregate and the multilayer networks using Muxviz [33] and Python. The multilayer framework allows to quantify the importance of a node across all the layers. The top 20 nodes ranked by their degree are shown in Fig. 4. The results for each layer separately (*i.e.*, *Meetings* or *Phone Calls*), shown in the stacked histogram, reveal that the most important actors per layer are nodes 18 and 47. The result from the aggregate network, obtained by summing up all interactions across the whole network while neglecting the layered structure, also identify nodes 18 and 47 as the most central actors. The same result is obtained for

Table 1. The 20 top ranked nodes in the Multilayer, Aggregate, Phone Calls and Meetings networks compared with their roles in the "Montagna" Operation.

Node		Degree			
Name	Role	Multilayer	Aggregate	Phone calls	Meetings
18	Caporegime Mistretta Family	51	41	25	24
47	Deputy Caporegime Batanesi Family	42	29	21	19
27	Caporegime Batanesi Family	29	21	11	16
68	Caporegime Batanesi Family	27	19	10	15
29	Enterpreneur	24	16	9	13
61	Caporegime Mistretta Family	23	19	17	4
45	Associate Batanesi Family	20	14	6	12
12	Associate Mistretta Family	19	16	1	16
11	Mafia activity coordinator in Messina	18	15	4	12
22	Pharmacist	18	15	2	14
51	Associate Batanesi Family	17	11	4	11
25	Caporegime Mistretta Family	16	13	1	13
43	Messaggero	16	11	5	9
48	Associate Batanesi Family	15	12	1	12
19	External partnership	14	11	3	9
36	Aiding and abetting of a fugitive	14	11	4	8
75	Associate Mistretta Family	14	12	8	4
89	Associate Batanesi Family	14	12	Absent node	12
54	Enterpreneur	13	7	5	6
5	Sighted with nodes 11 and 12	12	10	Absent node	10

Fig. 3. The structure of a Mafia Family.

the multilayer network, *i.e.,* considering the layered structure. These two nodes are effectively important because they are respectively Caporegime of the Mistretta family and deputy Caporegime of the Batanesi family. Using the multilayer

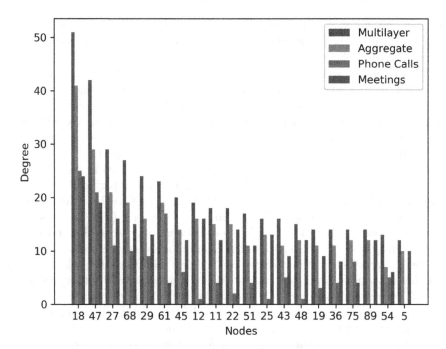

Fig. 4. The 20 top ranked nodes by degree in Multilayer (Blue), Aggregate (Orange), Phone Calls (Green) and Meetings (Red) networks. (Color figure online)

framework it was possible to identify two key Caporegimes of the Mistretta family (*i.e.*, Nodes 61 and 25). Node 61 was one of the twenty most important nodes in the Phone Calls layer but not in the Meetings layer. Node 25 was one of the twenty most important nodes in the Meetings layer but not in the Phone Calls layer. So, the importance of these nodes doesn't emerge from the analysis of the single layers but only from the analysis of the Aggregate network and even more of the Multilayer one. We can also identify the Messaggero (*i.e.*, Node 43) who didn't seem so important from the analysis of the single layers. Then, we can identify some key associates such us pharmacist or entrepreneurs needed in synthetic drug synthesis processes or to facilitate the award of public contracts to companies close to criminal organizations. The identification of these figures can be very useful to define attack strategies to disrupt criminal networks [16,28,29].

5   Conclusions

In this paper, we used a real criminal dataset obtained by parsing a two hundred pages pre-trial detection order by the Court of Messina during an anti-mafia operation called "Montagna" concluded in 2007. Starting from this dataset we initially built two social networks, one for meetings and one for phone calls among suspects. Since some suspects meet and also call each other, it was natural to identify meetings and phone calls with the layer of a multiplex network. First thing we did was to import the data as an undirected and weighted network where the weight encoded the number of meetings or phone calls.

We wanted to perform an analysis of suspects' importance for each layer separately, for the aggregate network and the multilayer one which allowed to quantify the importance across the whole series of layers. The concept of centrality as "importance" is debated and strongly depends on the context. Here we used a simple descriptor which is the degree. This measures just quantifies the number of different meetings or phone calls of each suspect.

We showed the top 20 characters ranked by their degree in each layer, in the aggregate network and in the multilayer network comparing the resulting importance with the role they had in the Sicilian Mafia families which were the protagonists of the "Montagna" operation.

As future works, we want to apply to our network other centrality descriptors such as multiplexity which quantifies the fraction of layers where a node appears and PageRank which was introduced by Google's founders and ranks nodes by assuming that more important ones are likely to interact with other important nodes. Then we want to compute the multiplex participation coefficient [9] which quantifies the participation of a node to the different communities of a network.

A further analysis of our dataset revealed the possibility to build a new multilayer network with three layers, one for meetings, one for phone calls and a third layer for the crimes committed by the suspects.

References

1. Dickison, M.E., Magnani, M., Rossi, L.: Multilayer Social Networks. Cambridge University Press (2016). https://doi.org/10.1017/CBO9781139941907
2. Wasserman, S., Faust, K.: Social Network Analysis: Methods and Applications. Cambridge University Press (1994). https://doi.org/10.1017/CBO9780511815478
3. Kivelä, M., Arenas, A., Barthelemy, M., Gleeson, J.P., Moreno, Y., Porter, M.A.: Multilayer networks. J. Complex Netw. **2**(3), 203–271 (2014). https://doi.org/10.1093/comnet/cnu016
4. De Domenico, M., et al.: Mathematical formulation of multilayer networks. Phys. Rev. X **3** (2013). https://doi.org/10.1103/PhysRevX.3.041022
5. De Domenico, M., Solé-Ribalta, A., Omodei, E., Gómez, S., Arenas, A.: Ranking in interconnected multilayer networks reveals versatile nodes. Nat. Commun. **6**(1), 6868 (2015). https://doi.org/10.1038/ncomms7868
6. Boccaletti, S., et al.: The structure and dynamics of multilayer networks. Phys. Rep. **544**(1), 1–122 (2014). https://doi.org/10.1016/j.physrep.2014.07.001
7. Catanese, S.A.: New perspectives in criminal network analysis: multilayer networks, time evolution, and visualization. Ph.D. thesis, University of Catania (2017)
8. Degani, E.: Monoplex to Multiplex networks analysis generalization: formalization, description and implementation of the commonest measures via a statistical package. B.Sc. thesis, University of Padua (2016)
9. Battiston, F., Nicosia, V., Latora, V.: Structural measures for multiplex networks. Phys. Rev. E **89** (2014). https://doi.org/10.1103/PhysRevE.89.032804

10. Solé-Ribalta, A., De Domenico, M., Gómez, S., Arenas, A.: Centrality rankings in multiplex networks. In: Proceedings of the 2014 ACM Conference on Web Science, WebSci 2014, pp. 149–155. Association for Computing Machinery, New York (2014). https://doi.org/10.1145/2615569.2615687
11. Nicosia, V., Latora, V.: Measuring and modeling correlations in multiplex networks. Phys. Rev. E **92** (2015). https://doi.org/10.1103/PhysRevE.92.032805
12. Tomasini, M.: An introduction to multilayer networks (2015). https://doi.org/10.13140/RG.2.2.16830.18243
13. Bright, D.A., Greenhill, C., Ritter, A., Morselli, C.: Networks within networks: using multiple link types to examine network structure and identify key actors in a drug trafficking operation. Glob. Crime **16**(3), 219–237 (2015). https://doi.org/10.1080/17440572.2015.1039164
14. Ficara, A., et al.: Social network analysis of Sicilian Mafia interconnections. In: Cherifi, H., Gaito, S., Mendes, J.F., Moro, E., Rocha, L.M. (eds.) COMPLEX NETWORKS 2019. SCI, vol. 882, pp. 440–450. Springer, Cham (2020). https://doi.org/10.1007/978-3-030-36683-4_36
15. Calderoni, F., Catanese, S., De Meo, P., Ficara, A., Fiumara, G.: Robust link prediction in criminal networks: a case study of the Sicilian Mafia. Exp. Syst. Appl. **161** (2020). https://doi.org/10.1016/j.eswa.2020.113666
16. Cavallaro, L., et al.: Disrupting resilient criminal networks through data analysis: the case of Sicilian Mafia. PLOS ONE **15**(8), 1–22 (2020). https://doi.org/10.1371/journal.pone.0236476
17. Cavallaro, L., et al.: Graph comparison and artificial models for simulating real criminal networks. In: Benito, R.M., Cherifi, C., Cherifi, H., Moro, E., Rocha, L.M., Sales-Pardo, M. (eds.) COMPLEX NETWORKS 2020. SCI, vol. 944, pp. 286–297. Springer, Cham (2021). https://doi.org/10.1007/978-3-030-65351-4_23
18. Cavallaro, L., et al.: Criminal Network: The Sicilian Mafia. "Montagna Operation". Zenodo (2020). https://doi.org/10.5281/zenodo.3938818
19. Gambetta, D.: The Sicilian Mafia: The Business of Private Protection. Harvard University Press, Cambridge (1996)
20. Paoli, L.: Italian organised crime: mafia associations and criminal enterprises. In: Global Crime Today: The Changing Face of Organised Crime, vol. 6, no. 1, pp. 19–32 (2004). https://doi.org/10.1080/1744057042000297954
21. Paoli, L.: Mafia Brotherhoods: Organized Crime, Italian Style. Oxford University Press, Oxford Scholarship Online (2008). https://doi.org/10.1093/acprof:oso/9780195157246.001.0001
22. Kleemans, E.R., de Poot, C.J.: Criminal careers in organized crime and social opportunity structure. Eur. J. Criminol. **5**(1), 69–98 (2008). https://doi.org/10.1177/1477370807084225
23. Ferrara, E., De Meo, P., Catanese, S., Fiumara, G.: Visualizing criminal networks reconstructed from mobile phone records. In: CEUR Workshop Proceedings, vol. 1210 (2014)
24. Ferrara, E., De Meo, P., Catanese, S., Fiumara, G.: Detecting criminal organizations in mobile phone networks. Exp. Syst. Appl. **41**(13), 5733–5750 (2014). https://doi.org/10.1016/j.eswa.2014.03.024
25. Agreste, S., Catanese, S., De Meo, P., Ferrara, E., Fiumara, G.: Network structure and resilience of Mafia syndicates. Inf. Sci. **351**, 30–47 (2016). https://doi.org/10.1016/j.ins.2016.02.027
26. Berlusconi, G., Calderoni, F., Parolini, N., Verani, M., Piccardi, C.: Link prediction in criminal networks: a tool for criminal intelligence analysis. PLOS ONE **11**(4), 1–21 (2016). https://doi.org/10.1371/journal.pone.0154244

27. Johnsen, J.W., Franke, K.: Identifying central individuals in organised criminal groups and underground marketplaces. In: Shi, Y., et al. (eds.) ICCS 2018. LNCS, vol. 10862, pp. 379–386. Springer, Cham (2018). https://doi.org/10.1007/978-3-319-93713-7_31

28. Duijn, P.A.C., Kashirin, V., Sloot, P.M.A.: The relative ineffectiveness of criminal network disruption. Sci. Rep. 4(1), 4238 (2014). https://doi.org/10.1038/srep04238

29. Villani, S., Mosca, M., Castiello, M.: A virtuous combination of structural and skill analysis to defeat organized crime. Socio-Econ. Plan. Sci. 65(C), 51–65 (2019). https://doi.org/10.1016/j.seps.2018.01.002

30. Ficara, A., Fiumara, G., De Meo, P., Liotta, A.: Correlations among game of thieves and other centrality measures in complex networks. In: Fortino, G., Liotta, A., Gravina, R., Longheu, A. (eds.) Data Science and Internet of Things. IT, pp. 43–62. Springer, Cham (2021). https://doi.org/10.1007/978-3-030-67197-6_3

31. Abraham, R., Marsden, J.E., Ratiu, T.: Manifolds, Tensor Analysis, and Applications, 2nd edn. Springer, Heidelberg (1988). https://doi.org/10.1007/978-1-4612-1029-0

32. Ricci, M.M.G., Levi-Civita, T.: Méthodes de calcul différentiel absolu et leurs applications. Math. Ann. 54(1), 125–201 (1900). https://doi.org/10.1007/BF01454201

33. De Domenico, M., Porter, M.A., Arenas, A.: MuxViz: a tool for multilayer analysis and visualization of networks. J. Complex Netw. 3(2), 159–176 (2014). https://doi.org/10.1093/comnet/cnu038

Internet of Things and Smart City/Smart Environment Applications

Enhanced European Internet of Things (IoT) Platform Assessment Key Performance Indicators (KPIs)

Okta Nurika[1]([⊠]) and Low Tan Jung[2]

[1] HELP University, No. 15, Sri Semantan 1 Street, Off Semantan Street, Damansara Heights,
50490 Kuala Lumpur, Malaysia
okta.nurika@help.edu.my
[2] Computer and Information Sciences Department, Universiti Teknologi PETRONAS, 32610
Perak, Seri Iskandar, Malaysia
lowtanjung@utp.edu.my

Abstract. The current most established IoT platform assessment standard called CREATE-IoT is missing essential KPIs that cover both technical and business aspects. These new KPIs would enhance this standard and improve the quality of assessment outcomes, which eventually would encourage more IoT platform deployments worldwide and open more technology-related jobs that will drive the global economy upward. Through experiences in studying IoT platform technical architecture and business model, this paper formulates and adds 22 unique new KPIs to this standard that initially consists of 198 KPIs. Or conclusively, 11.11% of distinct enhancement has been made. Thus, now this enhanced version of CREATE-IoT assessment standard may cover more IoT platform elements than before.

Keywords: IoT · Platform · Assessment · KPI · CREATE-IoT

1 Introduction

Currently, there is only one known standard to assess Internet of Things (IoT) platform, which is the one developed by CREATE-IoT [1]; it is a set of evaluation methodologies and Key Performance Indicators (KPIs) based on a set of verifications. This standard has gained reputation as the standard used to assess IoT Large-Scale-Pilot projects in European countries. However, the KPIs in this standard are missing other essential KPIs that we have formulated. Therefore, this paper suggests additions and consolidations of more KPIs to be included into the original CREATE-IoT standard. Furthermore, these newly formulated KPIs would be normalized according to the existing categorization groups.

The author of this paper aspires to enhance the current CREATE-IoT assessment standard, because he has worked as an IoT platform assessment consultant for an Asian major telecommunication company. In the process, he had formulated additional assessment

© ICST Institute for Computer Sciences, Social Informatics and Telecommunications Engineering 2021
Published by Springer Nature Switzerland AG 2021. All Rights Reserved
D. Perakovic and L. Knapcikova (Eds.): FABULOUS 2021, LNICST 382, pp. 137–153, 2021.
https://doi.org/10.1007/978-3-030-78459-1_10

items that can complement this existing standard. Therefore, the area of IoT platform assessment would get significant enhancement.

Reference [1] categorizes IoT assessment items into eight dimensions or groups, which are Technology Development, Technology Deployment and Infrastructure, Ecosystem Strategy and Engagement, Ecosystem Openness and External Collaboration, Marketplace and Business Impacts, Societal and Economic Impacts, Policy and Governance Impacts, and Community Support and Stakeholders' Inclusion.

The review of these existing assessment dimensions above would become the basis of analyzing the missing or lacking KPIs.

2 IoT Platform Comparative Analysis

IoT platform assessment KPIs are based on the business and technical aspects that construct an IoT platform. There have been brief and simpler IoT platform assessments practices, which only cover the high level features and services of the platform – We prefer to call these comparative analysis instead of full assessment. These may offer quick insight into the platform's capabilities, however deeper assessment is needed to conclude the level of readiness and establishment of the platform. An example of comparative analysis was done by Paper [2], which assessed major IoT platform providers based on their capabilities and shortcomings. The results are presented in the next table (Table 1).

Table 1. Generic Major IoT Platform Assessments

Platform	Strength	Limitation
IBM IoT	Augmented reality, cognitive data processing, blockchain, edge analytics, natural language processing, integrated data sources (weather, maps, social media), pre-built apps (e.g., prescriptive maintenance)	Utilizing private cloud with limited set of public, private, & on-premises delivery options
C3 IoT	Predictive maintenance, inventory optimization, energy management, sensor health, fraud detection, supply network, CRM, anti-money laundering	Lacking augmented & virtual reality, steep learning curve at model-driven type system, less user-friendly UI
Microsoft	Comprehensive dev tools, advanced analytics capabilities, end-to-end security, broad set of open source tools, rich platform deployment options	Less pre-built apps compared to others, limited augmented reality capabilities
SAP Leonardo	Machine Learning, blockchain, analytics, big data, comprehensive industrial protocols, various pre-built apps	Confusing portfolio terminologies, limited device management functionality
PTC	Comprehensive device connectivity, comprehensive industrial connectivity protocols, comprehensive augmented reality use cases	Less user-friendly UI for device connectivity, limited tools for developers

(continued)

Table 1. (*continued*)

Platform	Strength	Limitation
Software AG	Comprehensive device connectivity (a specialized device management platform)	Loose augmented reality solutions integration in the platform, limited pre-built support for business KPIs
Hitachi	Rich & intuitive management console, various use cases	Limited wireless connectivity options, less pre-built apps, less strategic partners & resellers
GE Digital	Various pre-built apps for data analysis from industrial machines	Weaker monitoring & alerting functions, weaker support & training
Atos	Strong solution development for industrial customers, rich partner ecosystem (AWS, Azure), provide development, hosting, and integration services to Siemens MindSphere customers	Lacking pre-built solutions
Oracle	Rich pre-integrated apps, rich Oracle native features (Java Cloud Suite; ElasticSearch, Oracle Big Data Cloud, Oracle DB Cloud, Oracle NoSQL, Oracle Storage Cloud)	Limited industry-specific interfaces, limited strategic partners, limited augmented reality solutions
Siemens	Rich pre-built apps, growing community of 3rd party developers & partners, wide range of hardware devices for deployment	Weak set of KPIs at the MindSphere OS, weaker device management capabilities
Bosch	Strong industrial device controls, use both AWS cloud and Bosch IOT cloud, open source platform key components, strategic partnership with Eclipse Foundation and OSGi Alliance	Weak analytics, less compelling 3rd party apps & services
Schneider Electric	Pre-built apps extendibility to local requirements, growing network of partners & developers, rich, integrated, and stable industrial equipment (Schneider products)	Lacking multi-vendor device support
AWS	Wide range of database, analytics, & storage services	Less pre-built apps, small in-house professional service team
Cisco	Vast global telecom partnership to connect, manage, & monitor SIM-based IIOT devices, user-friendly control center	Disjointed UI between Cisco Jasper (SIM card based monitoring) and Cisco Kinetic (gateway management, edge processing, data control functions), limited support for industrial IOT use cases

At the more granular level, author of [3] divides IoT platform comparative analysis into nine function domains, which are Application Development, Device Management, Heterogeneity Management, Data Management, Statistical Analysis, Deployment Management, Monitoring Management, Visualization, and Research. The outcomes are summarized in the tables below (Tables 2, 3, 4, 5, 6, 7, 8, 9 and 10).

Table 2. IoT application development domain: actuator vetted assessments

Platform	Strength	Limitation
KAA	NoSQL DBs (Cassandra, Hadoop, MongoDB), open source	Lesser hardware modules supported
Carriots	Trigger-based apps, custom alarms, NoSQL DBs	Less user-friendly interface
Temboo	Choreos based apps: Yahoo weather, Amazon cloud, Ebay shopping, Flockr photo management, Facebook Graph API, Google Analytics, Twitter, Twilio, Paypal, Youtube, etc.	Unsuitable for resource intensive application

Table 3. IoT device management domain assessments

Platform	Strength	Limitation
SeeControl	Open API based push/pull architecture to support wide range of devices	Poor visualization
SensorCloud	Ability to manage massive sensor devices from Lord Microstain's	Open source devices are harder to manage
Etherios	Specialized clouds for devices & 3rd party software are provided, 30-day trial for 5 devices	Developers are restricted by selected devices
Xively	Easy to integrate devices; flexible API	Notification services are minimal
Ayla's IOT Cloud Fabric	Easy mobile application development	Unsuitable for small scale developers
thethings.io	Various connection protocols are able to connect varieties of devices	Lacking self-sustainance, dependent on 3rd party web services
Exosite	Easy system development	Lacking big data provisioning

Table 4. IoT heterogeneity management domain assessments

Platform	Strength	Limitation
Arrayent Connect TM	Flexible to use	Lagging at trigger-based services
Open remote	Open cloud service is provided	Too costly for developers

Table 5. IoT data management domain assessments

Platform	Strength	Limitation
Arkessa	Enterprise enabled design facet	Poor visualization
Axeda	Machine-to-machine based data management	Lacking self-sustainance, dependent on 3rd party web services
Oracle IoT Cloud	Sophisticated database support	Lacking open source devices connectivity
Nimbits	Easy to adopt for developers	Insufficient real-time query processing
ThingWorx	Easy to build data intensive app	Limited number of devices that can be attached

Table 6. IoT statistical analysis domain assessments

Platform	Strength	Limitation
InfoBright	Knowledge Grid architecture	Incomplete statistical services
Jasper Control Center	Rule based behaviour patterns enabled	Insufficient for automation services

Table 7. IoT deployment management domain assessments

Platform	Strength	Limitation
Echelon	Providing complete set of industrial-grade modules; microchips, protocols, management software	Lacking development scenario for beginners

Table 8. IoT monitoring management domain assessments

Platform	Strength	Limitation
AerCloud	Scalable machine-to-machine services	Not suitable for developers
ThingSpeak	Public cloud enablement with triggering facility	Less simultaneous number of devices connectivity

Table 9. IoT visualization domain assessments

Platform	Strength	Limitation
Plotly	Comprehensive visualization tools	Limited amount of storage
GroveStreams	Seamless event monitoring	Lacking statistical services

Table 10. IoT research domain assessments

Platform	Strength	Limitation
Microsoft Research Lab of Things	Suitable for home automation	Lacking IoT supported APIs
IBM IoT	Device identity (identity as a service)	Difficult for application prototyping

The above presented IoT platform comparative analyses imply the high importance of IoT platform assessment area, even if done only at the high level without delving into technical and management details. Hence, this paper's significance is justified since it formulates and delivers deeper and more detailed IoT platform assessment KPIs.

3   IoT Platform Assessment Enhancement Method and Outcomes

The eight dimensions of CREATE-IoT assessment standard [1] are comprised of constituents and each constituent has its own Key Performance Indicators (KPIs) or identifiers - with every KPI examines different elements of IoT platform - be it technical, management, or business-related element. The next table's left column presents these dimensions and constituents, while the existing current KPIs are omitted for brevity purpose.

The workable method in order to enhance the CREATE-IoT assessment standard [1] is direct IoT platform assessment, which consists of studying the IoT platform's technical architecture and business model. These would help formulate the new KPIs, which are currently missing from the CREATE-IoT assessment standard [1].

After studying IoT platform's technical architecture and business model in his IoT consultancy career journey, the author of this paper finally formulates 22 new IoT platform assessment KPIs, which are subsequently merged into the existing CREATE-IoT assessment standard [1] that originally consists of 198 KPIs. Each of them is listed on the right column next to the constituent on the left column where it is categorized under. The table below concludes this newly enhanced standard (Table 11).

Table 11. Integration of existing CREATE-IoT constituents and the newly formulated KPIs

Existing dimension & constituent	Newly added KPI
1. **Dimension:** Technology development	
Constituents:	
IoT devices and modules	1. *Options for IoT Device Additions* Description: The current industrial methods for device additions are as follows: • Plug-in based (JSON-based and MQTT-based) for external components i.e., device connection, service integration • Software Development Kits (SDKs) e.g., SDKs for Arduino, ESP, Raspberry PI, etc. • HTTP-based or CoAP-based device integrations In addition, simulation prior to deployment is recommended for safety measure. An example of IoT platform, which provides sophisticated device integration options is PTC Kepware [4]. It features the following: • Centre of device connectivity standards to simplify the management of device drivers and plug-ins • Telemetry configurations with modem, scheduling, etc. • Quick project deployment using automatic tag generation and device discovery • One-click mapping from industrial tags to properties on the IoT platform • Ability to push full projects from the IoT platform to a remote connectivity server • Configuration API for 3rd-party server management • Simulation options for testing prior to deployment • Data conditioning and compression, in order to minimize bandwidth and resource utilization • Machine-to-Machine (M2M) connectivity between homogeneous and heterogeneous systems • Consistent UI to manage device connectivity 2. *Availability and Readiness of Device Facing APIs* Description: Some abilities of device-facing Application Programming Interfaces (APIs) include the following: • Receive events from devices • Receive filtered queries • Send events to devices • Video stream load and retrieve files • Update device configuration • Upgrade firmware • Synchronize with edge processing An IoT platform that is a leader in this area is Software AG Cumulocity IoT [5], which delivers the following features: • Same APIs and same interface technology for all use cases • Various interfacing technologies i.e., HTTP, HTTPS, REST • New user interface functionality can be developed using plug-in

(continued)

Table 11. (*continued*)

Existing dimension & constituent	Newly added KPI
	3. *Supported Varieties of Device Types* Description: The varieties of device types depend on the needs of the use cases. Nevertheless, common device types are RFID, acoustic, automotive, navigation, pressure, force and level, temperature, humidity, proximity, etc. PTC [4] and Software AG Cumulocity IoT [5] are the shared leader of varieties of device types as each of them supports more than 150 types of device. There are also generic sensor devices such as Raspberry Pi, Cinterion boards, and Tinkerforge sensors 4. *Long Term Cost Efficiency of IoT Platform's Compatible Devices* Description: In order for IoT platforms operations to sustain for long period, they need to be economical and legally compliant to local regulations, thus locally manufactured IoT devices should be prioritized, unless the required function can only be fulfilled by imported devices. This is due to local devices being built usually with local compliance in mind 5. *Device Security* Description: The activities for securing IoT devices may include the following: • Minimizing exposure of ports or services to the Internet • Individual device registration to anticipate emergency disconnection measure in case the compromised device needs to be isolated • Changing the device's default username and password • Ensuring devices have enough memory for firmware upgrades and to encrypt communications • Encrypting the device's database/storage • Encrypting data transmission from and to the device; use only secure protocols Special for devices exposed to the Internet, they better support the following key cryptographic capabilities: • Data encryption with minimum 128-bit AES symmetric-key encryption algorithm • Digital signature with minimum 128-bit symmetric-key signature algorithm • TCP connection with minimum encryption layer using TLS version 1.2 or DTLS version 1.2 encryption layer for datagram-based communication paths • Unique key identification for every device that is stored securely (encrypted) on the device; this key should be updateable regularly over the device's link interface, or immediately if an intrusion towards the platform is detected • The device's firmware should be updateable Also, physical manipulations of IoT devices could be prevented by the below precautions: • Equip microcontrollers/microprocessors/auxiliary hardware with secure storage and cryptographic keys such as Trusted Platform Module (TPM) integration • Equip TPM with a secure boot loader and software loading • Gate the surrounding of the IoT devices with security sensors e.g., CCTV with motion recognition to detect trespassers. Further mitigation may involve "digital self-destruction" when the device is compromised

(*continued*)

Table 11. (*continued*)

Existing dimension & constituent	Newly added KPI
IoT platforms	6. *Platform Security at the Device Border* Description: IoT platform security at the device border can be built by the following actions: • Device registration and whitelisting. Other whitelisting methods may also be used i.e., network-based, serial number-based, or SIM-based • Device spoofing prevention • If possible and necessary, map every device to single user for better track of usage • Encrypt the connection from the device to the platform's back-end
IoT system monitoring	
IoT architecture	7. *Size of Data Storage* Description: The data storage should be able to accommodate massive data economically (may be achieved through data summarization method), it should also be scalable without downtime (may be achieved by high availability architecture or redundant server), have long data retention period (years or even infinite), and have adjustable computing power subject to the load An IoT platform that provides industry leading data storage is Microsoft Azure IoT [6] – with their separate databases for warm and cold data, which are mentioned below: • Azure Cosmos DB for warm storage: holds recent data (within seconds since ingestion) that needs to be accessed with low latency • Azure Blob Storage for cold storage: holds historical data that may tolerate higher latency • Azure Time Series Insights (TSI): an analytics, storage and visualization service for time series data, providing capabilities such as SQL-like filtering and aggregation • Azure SQL DB: max. capacity: 4 TB, throughput limit: max 4000 DTUs/eDTUs per database/Elastic Pool • Azure Data Lake: unlimited distributed data store that can persist large amounts of relational and nonrelational data without transformation or schema definition
IoT system functional design	8. *Service Redundancy or High Availability (HA) Mechanism* Description: Service redundancy provides the following capabilities: • Service fail-over and cross-region fail-over • Scaling the solution on multiple sites • Multi-site with roaming (device is homed in one of the sites, but may connect to the closest datacenter location based on proximity estimation; the collected information is routed to the home site of the device) • Multisite-multihome (device may roam across sites, and captured data is stored across the various sites that the device connects to, and can be collected and consolidated as required) • Isolation of service interruption; upgrades do not affect service (separated by broker that provides buffer; multiple brokers exchange data)

(*continued*)

Table 11. (*continued*)

Existing dimension & constituent	Newly added KPI
IoT verification, validation, testing and certification	9. *IoT Platform Audit* Description: The IoT platform should be audited continuously to guarantee performance and ensure SLAs are met; monitoring tools should be deployed to supervise the following statuses in the IoT platform: • Whether devices or systems are in erroneous state • Whether devices or systems are correctly configured • Whether devices or systems are generating accurate data • Whether the IoT platform is achieving the expectations of both business and end customers according to Service Level Agreements (SLAs) • Security-wise, Vulnerability Analysis (VA) may be conducted every 4 or 6 months, while penetration testing may be done once a year. Code check should be done in every application deployment. And logs monitoring should be done daily • IoT specific AI-driven vulnerability scanner tailored for Smart House and IoT devices could also be utilized, such as the one offered by Cybersecurity Help [7] Both Software AG Cumulocity IoT [5] and Microsoft Azure IoT [6] provide visual tool for auditing/monitoring. Azure IoT has Azure Operations Management Suite (OMS), Application Map, and App Insights for operations monitoring, logging, and troubleshooting, while Software AG Cumulocity IoT gives an auditing interface to capture security-relevant events and enable applications and agents to write audit logs, which are persistently stored and cannot be externally modified after being written. Audit records related to login and device control operations are also included
2. **Dimension:** Technology deployment and infrastructure	
Constituents:	
Use of open technologies devices and platforms	
Use of supported standards	
Capacity to solve interoperability and connectivity issues	
Scalability	10. *Reporting Capability and Expandability* Description: Report generation should not hamper the IoT platform. The IoT platform should be capable to store all produced reports for long period or even for infinite duration. In order to achieve this, report generation may be done by a dedicated data analytics cluster. However, each reporting duration may be determined by the complexity of data analytics models 11. *Tenants' Share of Events* Description: In a multi-tenant IoT platform environment, where there are multiple verticals (fields of IoT implementation) handled by different offices in the same IoT platform provider, there may be a need to share data and events among tenants, for examples: sharing of device definitions, sharing of sensor data, etc.

(*continued*)

Table 11. (*continued*)

Existing dimension & constituent	Newly added KPI
Efficiency in the maintenance, deployment and life-cycle of services and software running	12. *Affordability of Service Performance* Description: The cost of service performance may be related to the time duration to execute a transaction flow or the fee for every unit of ingested transaction per unit time, or other possible metric Software AG Cumulocity IoT [5] has structured costing for the amount of ingested data into the platform - For every additional request (inbound data), it costs €3 per 100,000 API and this is billed monthly Performance cost could revolve around the following factors: • Number of users • Data ingested over time or transactions per second (TPS) • Number of rules • Complexity of rules • Number of service APIs A transaction is defined as a complete flow through the IoT platform; from Event message to the Message Bus, on to the Event Consumer Service, getting information from the Device admin service, sending information to the Scene Evaluation Engine, and then sending to the Device Interaction Engine to send the message to perform a resultant action. Since a transaction is event based, the number of rules is not linear to TPS. In order to cater to growing TPS, a capable and scalable message broker must be utilized. A scalable and affordable public cloud infrastructure is also desired for an economical yet significant performance improvement An example of a transaction is the one described by GE Predix Platform's [8] wind forecasting application. For its deployment of four wind farms, the application ingests data from edge/devices, runs analytics on the data, and then sends the analytics results to the edge. All this flow is accomplished in 18 s It is a general practice to reduce operation cost by migrating to Docker on AWS. Computing power is expandable via AWS settings. An enterprise-grade message broker such as RabbitMQ may also be deployed to cater more connections compared to entry level brokers like ActiveMQ. For even larger scaling, an MQTT-based message broker could be used 13. *Affordability of Data Storage* Description: The cost of data storage should be economical for future scalability and storage scaling should not require downtime (may be achieved by redundancy or HA architecture) - in order to preserve data service. Furthermore, data storage cost could be reduced by data summarization Moreover, the cost of data storage would be more affordable and scalable when data storage is outsourced to public cloud, such as AWS. Even so, there may be a need to make use of private data centre in case sensitive data needs to be stored locally, or when local data retention is enforced by the local authorities. On the downside, storing data in private data centre usually costs more than utilizing public cloud storage; this is due to development cost and infrastructure cost (electricity, premise building and maintenance, security cost, etc.)

(*continued*)

Table 11. (*continued*)

Existing dimension & constituent	Newly added KPI
	Both Software AG Cumulocity IoT [5] and Microsoft Azure IoT [6] offer structured data storage costing based on utilized storage and ingested request count. A detailed information on bundling of storage limit and request count for Standard Tenant packages is given by Software AG Cumulocity IoT [5] as follows: • Standard Tenant Bundle Pricing I: €500/month (€5/device/month), 12 months term, business support included, max. 100 devices supported, 2 millions inbound data transfers per month, 10 GB storage • Standard Tenant Bundle Pricing II: €1,500/month (€3/device/month), 12 months term, business support included, max. 500 devices supported, 10 millions inbound data transfers per month, 50 GB storage • Standard Tenant Bundle Pricing III: €2,500/month (€2.5/device/month), 12 months term, business support included, max. 1,000 devices supported, 20 millions inbound data transfers per month, 100 GB storage • Standard Tenant Bundle Pricing IV: €3,500/month (€0.35/device/month), 12 months term, business support included, max. 10,000 devices supported, 5 millions inbound data transfers per month, 10 GB storage • Additional storage costs €1 for every 100 MB per month
Integration with the existing and new infrastructure	
3. **Dimension:** Ecosystem strategy and engagement	
Constituents:	
Ecosystem awareness	
Stakeholders' engagement	
External partnerships and collaboration	
Public and government engagement	
4. **Dimension:** Ecosystem openness and external collaboration	
Constituents:	
Value chain openness	
Inclusiveness and participation for third parties	14. *Value-Adding Data from External Sources or 3rd Parties* Description: Freely available external data sources may be integrated to trigger specific actions, for example: external weather forecast data that triggers watering sensors and actuators in a smart greenhouse IoT implementation An established IoT platform that fulfils external data sources integration is IBM IoT [9], which integrates weather, maps, and social media data Typically, external data can be queried or integrated easily via APIs

(*continued*)

Table 11. (*continued*)

Existing dimension & constituent	Newly added KPI
Openness of business models	
Open source strategy	
5. **Dimension:** Marketplace and business impacts	
Constituents:	
Business models	
Market readiness and monetization mechanisms	15. *Sale Package* Description: IoT service sale bundling is subject to the state of supply and demand for the target market. An infant IoT market may start by bundling on cellular data package usage, which incorporates IoT platform service in its offer. While an IoT market in stable growth may offer independent IoT platform service package, this independent offer is related to the provided vertical solutions e.g., smart house, smart parking, etc. Sale package could also be designed based on the following factors: 1. Number of devices 2. Number of users 3. Subscription term 4. Data ingestion rate 5. Data storage 6. Services offered 7. Platform-to-platform (P2P) offered 8. Selections of device's link interfaces, whether it is Wi-Fi, NB-IoT, 5G, SigFox, ZigBee, or others 9. Data analytics methods 10. User customization options
Business benefits	
Market competitiveness	
Legal issues	
Privacy, security, trust and ethical issues	16. *Data Expiry* Description: Data expiry is also known as data aging or data deletion after certain period – usually subject to SLA, for example: GE Predix [8] defines a contract that mentions the responsibilities of parties in the life cycle of sensitive data, which includes data retention and data deletion; the longer the data retention the safer it is for data aging practice There is also a useful temporary data retention feature at the edge device called inbox-mode, which stores data and command for a device when it loses connection to the edge hub – and when the device regains its online connection, it will receive the cached data and command from the edge hub 17. *Tenants' Regulated Data Sharing* Description: This is the ability to conduct and regulate data sharing securely among tenants by enabling event subscription. It is useful to exchange data among different verticals of IoT implementation. Besides events, tenants may also share device definitions in case the same devices would be deployed by different tenant/s

(*continued*)

Table 11. (*continued*)

Existing dimension & constituent	Newly added KPI
	18. *Technically and Legally Compliant IoT Platform* Description: A technically and legally compliant IoT platform should comply to the following: • Secure Software Development Life Cycle (SDLC) • IT security guidelines e.g., OWASP, WASC, ISO 27001 • Privacy and data protection legislation by the local authority • Vertical, application layer, or software architecture standard: Domain Driven Design (DDD) • Architecture and documentation standard: TOGAF • Process-related activity standard: ISO 9001 Furthermore, support from the local government may also encourage the growth and compliance of IoT platform, for example: Sri Lankan and Malaysian government [10] give tax compensation/exemption for IoT-related infrastructure development An example of compliant practices is done by IBM IoT [9], which includes: • Certifications: ISO 27001, ISO 27017, ISO 27018, ISO 9001, ISO 22301, ISO 31000, SOC 1, SOC 2 and SOC 3, PCI, HITRUST, FedRAMP, IRAP (Australia), ISO 14001, ISO 50001, OHSAS 1800 • Global regulations: EU Model Clauses, FERPA, HIPAA, My Number Act (Japan), United States International Traffic in Arms Regulations (ITAR), Cloud Computing Compliance Controls Catalog (C5) (Germany) • Alignments and Frameworks: Criminal Justice Information Systems (CJIS), The Cloud Security Alliance CSA, EU-US Privacy Shield, Federal Financial Institutions Examination Council (FFIEC), The Center for Financial Industry Information Systems (FISC), The Federal Information Security Management Act of 2002 (FISMA)
Experience readiness level	19. *Rule Activity Management (Programmable Rule)* Description: An established IoT platform should be able to provide an interface to program IoT scenarios i.e., Stateless processors and static rules are preferable if analysis rules do not change and do not refer to dynamic external data. Furthermore, stateless processors and static rules are suitable when the following conditions exist: • Input data records are serialized in JSON format • There is only small number of rules • Data records can be analyzed one at a time i.e., there is no need to aggregate data over multiple data points (e.g., averaging) or data streams (e.g., merging data from multiple devices) On the other approach, stateful processors and dynamic rules are more appropriate for scenarios, where flexibility is desired to support variable load, frequent changes to stream processing logic, and mutable external reference data. In details, they are suitable for the following conditions: • Input data records demand advanced analysis, such as time windows, streams aggregation, or joining with external data sources - which is not possible with the stateless architecture • The processing logic has rules or logic units, which might grow significantly along the way • Input telemetry data is serialized in a binary format like Avro Moreover, safety measures for action rule can be implemented as follows: • Simulate the rule before it is deployed • Utilize rule versioning system, in order to provide rollback capability

(*continued*)

Table 11. (*continued*)

Existing dimension & constituent	Newly added KPI
	• Add a feature to control additional information points within a scene or action rule • Add scheduling feature to rules i.e., rule actions may depend on time of the day e.g., a rule may state that when Event A occurs and time is earlier than 10am, then execute Action X, or else do Action Y • Add nested rules feature to anticipate complex scenario • Embed safety-related Artificial Intelligence (AI) capability at edge processing An example of IoT platform that provides programmable rule is SAP Leonardo IoT [11], it utilizes insight of device data to trigger appropriate actions in the business systems. It also makes use of the IoT capabilities of the SAP Cloud Platform to offer more varieties of services 20. *Self Navigation for Reporting and Data Analytics* Description: Ideally, IoT platform users should be able to maneuver through data analytics and reporting features independently without the assistance of dedicated data scientists. User-friendliness in data analytics is a sign of readiness of an IoT platform; the more sophisticated the platform, the simpler the feature navigation Data analytics server or cluster may be made accessible via a set of APIs e.g., Apache Solar indexes or Power BI. In case each vertical's data is stored in separate tables in order to enforce privacy, on the downside, this might make it harder to conduct cross-vertical analytics when it needs to merge data from different verticals Based on Forrester 2018 IoT platforms comparative analysis report [2], Microsoft's advanced analytics that are based on open source technology makes them the best in analytics category [6]. Specifically, Microsoft Azure IoT's analytics capability includes HDInsight. Power BI, Apache Spark 21. *Comprehensive Reporting and Data Analytics* Description: At minimum, any IoT platform should fulfil common purposes of data analytics, which include the following: • Pattern recognition • Anomaly detection • Frequency finding • Parameter values over time distribution (behavior analysis) • Mapping or heat mapping • Event prediction • Behavior or action detection • Causality and correlation analysis In an IoT platform vertical, comprehensive reporting and analytics should be able to fulfil the objectives of the deployed use cases – within the reasonable time - even when under maximum load capacity In Feb 2017, Google conducted research about the average mobile web page load times across different industries [12] and discovered that the average load time duration was 8.66 s. They further recommended that a reasonable duration should be below 3 s. Therefore, if data analytics process is added to the duration, then analytics report generation within this duration or a little above it would be deemed acceptable

(continued)

Table 11. (*continued*)

Existing dimension & constituent	Newly added KPI
	In general, all IoT platforms are capable to do data analytics and reporting, however IBM IoT [9] and C3IoT [13] are considered leaders in this area with their varieties of pre-built applications and use cases. Specifically, for C3IoT, their analytics features provide the following: • C3 Data Science service: a complete AI/ML capabilities to generate an accurate prediction, and offers configurable visualization methods, including time-series, tables, charts, scatter plots, etc. • C3 Data Science service: a visual tool to build analytics process pipeline
Holistic innovation	
6. **Dimension:** Societal and economic impacts	
Constituents:	
Indirect revenue generation	
Employment macro-impact	
User worktime/life impact	
Targeted social groups	
7. **Dimension:** Policy and governance impacts	
Constituents:	
European IoT ecosystem promotion and competitiveness safeguard	
IoT standards promotion	
Trusted, safe, secure IoT environment promotion	22. *Multi-tenant IoT Platform* Description: In common practice, the IoT's hierarchical platform would allow the top boss or the super admin of the company to access all IoT verticals owned by the company, while a branch office head or branch manager would only be allowed to access their own vertical. This practice would enforce data privacy and legal compliance towards the SLAs and the local governmental regulations
Impact on SMEs, start-ups and young entrepreneurs	
8. **Dimension:** Community support and stakeholders' inclusion	
Constituents:	
Developers' community accessibility	
Education availability	
Accessibility levels	
Community engagement	

4   Conclusion

The existing CREATE-IoT IoT platform assessment standard [1] has been successfully enriched with sizeable 22 new essential KPIs. In other words, the overall enhancement is 11.11% from the original number of KPIs (198). This is considered significant as all additions are unique and necessary; they would significantly increase the quality of IoT platform assessment outcomes and may be used by IoT platforms all over the world. Nonetheless, this enhanced standard would also drive new IoT deployments worldwide as it gives confidence of the readiness state of the assessed IoT platform – as well as its legal compliance.

More IoT deployments mean more jobs would be created, thus it is beneficial for the global economy. This would also connect and modernize different nations in sophisticated ways through sharing permissible IoT events and data, which are fundamental for acceleration of national infrastructure automation purpose.

References

1. Micheletti, G., et al.: Common methodology and KPIs for design, testing and validation. In: Cross Fertilisation Through Alignment, Synchronisation and Exchanges for IoT, pp. 1–49 (2017)
2. Miller, P., Pelino, M.: Industrial IoT software platforms, Q3 2018: the 15 providers that matter most and how they stack up. In: The Forrester Wave (2018)
3. Ray, P.P.: A survey of IoT cloud platforms. Fut. Comput. Inform. J. 1(1–2), 35–46 (2016)
4. PTC IoT (2020). https://www.kepware.com/en-us/industries/internet-of-things/2020/11/6. Accessed 11 Jun 2020
5. Software AG Cumulocity IoT (2020). https://www.softwareag.com/en_corporate/platform/iot.html/2020/11/6. Accessed 11 Jun 2020
6. Azure IoT (2020). https://azure.microsoft.com/en-us/overview/iot/2020/11/6. Accessed 11 Jun 2020
7. SaaS Vulnerability Scanner (2020). https://www.cybersecurity-help.cz/security-services/saas-vulnerability-scanner.html/2020/11/6. Accessed 11 Jun 2020
8. GE Predix (2020). https://www.ge.com/digital/iiot-platform/2020/11/6. Accessed 11 Jun 2020
9. IBM IoT (2020). https://www.ibm.com/cloud/internet-of-things/2020/11/7. Accessed 11 Jul 2020
10. Halim, A.H.A., et al.: National Internet of Things (IoT) Strategic Roadmap. MIMOS Berhad (2014). https://www.mestecc.gov.my/web/wp-content/uploads/2017/02/IoT-Strategic-Roadmap-1.pdf
11. SAP Leonardo IoT (2020). https://help.sap.com/viewer/product/SAP_Leonardo_IoT/1904b/en-US/2020/11/11. Accessed 11 Nov 2020
12. Google Research. https://www.machmetrics.com/speed-blog/average-page-load-times-websites-2018/
13. C3IoT (2020). https://www.welcome.ai/tech/data-resources-management/c3-iot-c3-iot-platform/2020/11/11. Accessed 11 Nov 2020

Categorizing IoT Services According to Security Risks

Ostroški Dominik[✉], Mikuc Miljenko, and Vuković Marin

Faculty of Electrical Engineering and Computing,
University of Zagreb, Zagreb, Croatia
{dominik.ostroski,miljenko.mikuc,marin.vukovic}@fer.hr

Abstract. Internet of things has been a part of our lives, both at home and in workplace, for several years now. However, due to its popularity, numerous security issues are emerging related to devices, network communication or Internet of things (IoT) acquired data storage and processing in the cloud. This paper presents a model for categorization of existing and novel IoT services based on estimated security risks. The goal is to develop security requirements for each service category in such a way that service creators are able to classify their services and follow the requirements in order to harden the services in development. The paper proposes a categorization model based on DREAD (Damage potential, Reproducibility, Exploitability, affected users, and Discoverability) and gives examples of existing services classification. A set of simple questions is proposed at the end of the paper that should be answered by service creators in order to categorize its service into one of the proposed categories.

Keywords: Internet of Things · Security requirements · Service categorization · Security and privacy risks

1 Introduction

Internet of things (IoT) has been a part of our lives for several years now, while its beginnings date to more than several decades ago, in specific domains such as industry, logistics and retail [1]. With more and more integration of IoT in our lives, various devices began to gather more and more information about the environment, other systems and, perhaps most controversially, its users, resulting in possible exposure of users' private data. This risks became apparent with the first attacks targeted specifically on IoT devices, such as Mirai botnet [2], where a malware was used to gain control of web cameras and use them to perform further network DDoS attacks. When looking at the attacks in IoT domain nowadays, we conclude that there are three main parts of an IoT system from security point of view: (i) device with administration

D. Perakovic and L. Knapcikova (Eds.): FABULOUS 2021, LNICST 382, pp. 154–166, 2021.
https://doi.org/10.1007/978-3-030-78459-1_11

interface, (ii) network communication and (iii) cloud based platform for control, data acquisition and processing. Most of the attacks in the earlier years of IoT focused on administration interfaces (i) and network communication (ii) [3] and the devices typically became parts of a botnet used for further attacks. When looking at end-users and their privacy issues, there have been numerous examples of privacy breaches with or "around" IoT devices. Since IoT devices are typically low in processing and storage power, they gather data, possibly filter it, and then upload it to the cloud where the data storage, processing and knowledge discovery is performed (iii). As expected, most of the data breaches actually happened in the cloud, where malicious individuals or groups gained access to cloud-based platforms. Because of this, many researchers focused on privacy-preserving solutions in IoT over the years, with very interesting examples of how consumer data can be used for various malicious purposes. An interesting example of this is presented in [4] and [5] where it is shown how data acquired through wearable devices can even be used to outline maps of military bases. This examples show how the data acquired can be used in various malicious ways which were previously not possible, especially when data from more users is aggregated.

With regards to these issues from the domain of security and privacy, we find it necessary to create a model that will allow IoT service creators to try and assess security and privacy risks to their service and its users. The ultimate goal is to develop a framework that will allow the service creators to answer questions about their service and the model will estimate the risk and offer necessary security requirements to consider when developing and implementing the service. In this paper we propose a first step towards this goal - a model for categorization of IoT services based on security requirements. We use a DREAD model and apply it to common IoT services in order to establish a categorization of services with regards to security and privacy. In means of terminology, we use the notation of CVSS 3.0 vulnerability severity ratings [6] in order to describe the risk severity for IoT service category.

The rest of the paper is organised as follows. Next Section gives an overview of existing research on security issues in IoT, discusses recent IoT services with regards to security and notes most common attacks on IoT platforms and infrastructure. Section 3 attempts to group IoT services into categories according to potential security risks, using the DREAD model. In Sect. 4 we demonstrate the proposed service categorization on example IoT services. Finally, we conclude the paper in Sect. 5 and give guidelines for future work.

2 Previous Research

In this section, we examine state-of-the-art related to defining security requirements in IoT domain and give review of most well-known attacks on IoT systems categorized by area of application.

In [7] the authors present a systematic approach to understanding the security requirements for IoT. When developing these requirements, they offer various scenarios and outline potential threats and attacks in the IoT. Based on the characteristics of the IoT, they group possible threats and attacks into five areas: communication, devices/services, users, mobility, and resource integration. They then examine the existing IoT security requirements in the literature and describe in detail their approach to IoT security requirements.

Abomhara et al. [8] Examine the requirements of the IoT security architecture in relation to three main topics: data protection for individuals, confidentiality of business processes, and reliability of third parties. The article recommends the use of cryptographic techniques and light-weight security mechanisms for the things that are at the edge of the network.

The research by Sicari et al. [9] discusses contributions providing confidentiality, security, access control, and privacy for the IoT and security of middleware. The authors discuss trust management, authentication, privacy issues, data security, network security, and intrusion detection systems.

As stated in [10], the connection of each thing creates new problems with data security and data protection, such as the confidentiality, authenticity, and integrity of the data that things "feel and exchange". This author lists the standard security requirements resilience to attacks (the system must avoid individual points of failure and should adapt to node failures), data authentication(retrieved address and object information must be authenticated) and access control (information providers must be able to carry out access control for the transmitted data). When protecting the privacy of the customer, measures need to be taken that only the information provider is able to infer from observing the use of the lookup system.

In [11] the authors analyzed three forms of IoT security: communication, application interface, and data security. They reviewed the current IoT technologies, approaches, and models and found a security gap in existing communication technologies, application interfaces, and data security. They also gave an overview of related work in the IoT.

The authors in [12] conducted a comprehensive study of existing IoT technologies and their security problems. They focused on smart homes and the urban environment and discussed possible IoT security solutions to improve the latter. These security solutions focused not only on the security problems of today's endpoints but also on predicting future attacks on data protocols and connectivity.

In [13], the authors presented a classification of attacks from different networks related to IoT. The classification distinguished between common and specific attacks from each network and used certain criteria such as security attributes, congestion, and disturbances. In addition, some current security solutions are presented in detail that demonstrate the security requirements for IoT protection [14].

Alqassem [15] proposes a requirements engineering framework ensuring privacy and security. They identify the complexity of analyzing security in IoT systems and states that the key components in IoT are only two: RFID systems and networks of sensors. The framework proposed in this study was aimed at building an effective model that can handle the heterogeneity of the IoT network by tackling the privacy and security concerns at the earliest stage possible.

In [16] authors analyze the security aspects for each layer of the IoT architecture and on this basis propose a risk classification of the layers of the IoT architecture. The analysis of the security vulnerabilities revealed that the greatest security risk is the perception layer of the IoT architecture due to the specific limitations of the devices and transmission technologies used on this layer. The highest level of risk for the IoT application was determined for the finance, production and multimedia sectors due to the largest increase in its use.

Last, but definitely not the least, the OWASP Foundation began work on IoT Security Verification Standard (ISVS) [17], similar to the well-accepted and very useful Application Security Verification Standard (ASVS) [18] used for (web) applications. Although they state that ISVS is still in very early stages of development, we expect it to become a standard for security requirements once it is finished.

Based on the previous work, IoT services can be categorized into seven categories by area of application. These are: smart city, smart energy, intelligent transport systems, industry automation, smart health, public safety, and smart agriculture. In the rest of this chapter will be given a review of attacks on IoT systems based on proposed categories.

Some smart city applications are smart waste management, smart parking, smart street lighting, smart water grids, smart home, and smart HVAC. In 2011 the control system of the city water utility in Springfield, Illinois was hacked. Hackers gained remote access to the control system causing the system to turn on and off repeatedly leading to the burnout of a water pump Cybersecurity firm ForeScout Technologies has discovered that thousands of vulnerable IoT devices in heating, ventilation, and air conditioning (HVAC) systems are vulnerable to cyber-attacks. Their research showed that nearly 8,000 connected devices, mostly located in hospitals and schools, have security vulnerabilities that allow unauthorized access and are very vulnerable to cyber-attacks [19]. Changing the temperature setpoints or switching off devices used for heating, ventilation, and air conditioning can harm people in facilities where these devices are vital, such as tunnels or hospitals.

Most notable smart energy services are smart grids, remote monitoring and data collection for oil and gas production, and smart renewable energy. On December 23, 2015, hackers managed to successfully compromise the information systems of three energy companies in Ukraine and temporarily cut off electricity supply to consumers. It is thought to be the first known successful cyberattack on the power grid, resulting in several outages that caused some 225,000 customers to lose electricity in various areas [20]. The most significant, malicious software that targets remote monitoring and data collection systems is Stuxnet. It was launched solely to target a centrifuge at a uranium enrichment plant at a nuclear power plant in Iran. Although Iran has not released specific details about the effects of the attack, the Stuxnet worm has destroyed numerous uranium enrichment centrifuges [21]. A Utah renewable energy producer was hit by a cyberattack that briefly cut off contact with a dozen wind farms in the spring of 2019 [22]. Although this attack had no serious consequences, it was the first attack to cut off communication between the power grid operator and the power generation station.

Intelligent Transport Systems (ITS) are management and information systems that use integrated communication and data processing technologies to improve the mobility of people and goods, increase safety, reduce traffic congestion, manage incidents effectively and meet transport policy objectives [23]. They include smart cars, roadway reporting, and traffic flow controls, and communications applications and systems. In 2016, the San Francisco Municipal Transport Agency was hit by a cyberattack that displayed a hacker message on their systems[24]. The underground stations displayed the message "System not working". Unable to charge customers, free rides were allowed which led to a loss of profit. In 2017, 70% of storage devices that recorded data from police surveillance cameras were infected with ransomware [25]. Due to the attack, the local police could not record for 3 days, and the attack hit 120 of the 180 network video recorders. A group of university researchers devised how to hack autonomous cars by putting stickers on street signs [26]. The researchers analyzed image sorting algorithms used by autonomous vehicle vision systems and then visually manipulated street signs with stickers to deceive machine learning models. In one example, they used stickers to trick the autonomous car's visual system into reading the STOP sign as a 45-mile-per-hour sign. The consequences of such attacks can be devastating in the real world.

As industrial automation and process management systems become available to businesses they become increasingly digitally connected. Data collection, exchange, and analysis is a valuable practice of companies today, as it is often used to increase efficiency. The most notable services in industrial automation are smart logistics and Supervisory control and data acquisition (SCADA) systems. Smart logistics provide the ability to monitor not only the location of things but also the characteristics of things. For example, during the transport of some drugs or chemicals, temperature, object orientation, and pressure inside the tank are treated as sensitive data. SCADA systems for power substations and distribution networks or even nuclear power plants are potential targets for cyber attacks. In the attack on the German iron factory, the attackers accessed the iron plant's office network and used this approach to enter the production network, from where they could cause damage to the blast furnace [27]. There was an accumulation of failures of individual components of the control system. System failures resulted in an incident in which the furnace could not be closed properly, leading to enormous damage to the entire system. In 2019, 8 attacks by hacker groups on industrial companies were recorded [28]. Most of the attacks were aimed at stealing intellectual property and gaining control of control and management systems, which could have devastating effects on companies.

IoT technologies encourage the development of smart systems to support and improve health systems and are applied to interconnect available medical resources and provide reliable and efficient health services to the elderly and patients. The two most common use cases of IoT in healthcare are remote health monitoring systems and remote surgery. A team of researchers from the University of Washington in Seattle successfully discovered security holes in the Raven II surgical robot [29]. By attacking using the "man in the middle" technique, which changes the commands flowing between the operator and the robot, the team managed to maliciously disrupt a wide range of robot functions, making it difficult to capture objects with robotic hands, and even completely change the original commands. During denial-of-service attacks, in which attackers flooded the system with useless data, robots became slower and harder to use. In situations where precise movements can mean the difference between life and death, such as surgery or in search and rescue missions, these types of cyberattacks can have serious consequences. The most common form of attack on wearable devices and implanted medical devices is an acoustic attack that uses ultrasonic or other audio frequencies at the resonant frequencies of the device to attack the devices [30]. Acoustic attacks have been shown to work against implanted heart defibrillators and pacemakers, insulin pumps, and devices that monitor activity among other medical devices [31]. These attacks can acquire confidential medical data, alter data that cause system malfunctions and deliver inappropriate therapies, and cause devices to lose power to become unusable [32].

Internet of Things-based public safety applications offers a number of benefits, including greater situational awareness and improved decision-making, reduced response times and improved emergency response capabilities, improved citizen safety and infrastructure security, improved prevention and escalation of critical situations, and dissemination of information to citizens [33]. Some applications of IoT in public safety are critical communication systems and smart systems for emergency response. Successful attacks on these systems can result in the transmission of inaccurate messages, denial of service, data leakage, and changes in GPS coordinates used to calculate positioning [34]. Faults in the operation of these systems affect a large number of people. An attack can result in greater loss of life in emergencies because rescuers cannot coordinate effectively and the public is not alerted in a timely manner, or inaccurate information is transmitted.

While beneficial to industry productivity, the use of Internet-connected devices has revealed potential cyber-attacks and vulnerabilities in the agricultural sector. IoT systems in agriculture are usually used for purpose of smart irrigation and crop monitoring. One of the most common threats to smart farming is a malware injection attack [35]. Malware can steal data on agricultural material consumption, purchase information, data on agricultural machinery, etc. It can also recruit smart devices as part of a botnet used to commit malicious acts. Furthermore, malware can interfere with the functions of physical smart equipment which in turn can have a devastating effect on a particular crop or farm. Attacks on smart irrigation systems can have an even greater impact. An attack that consumes water and empties a city water tank can result in the inability to provide water to residents until the local water tank is filled, with an attack on smart irrigation systems increasing water consumption and causing financial loss, and by applying a distributed attack against smart irrigation systems on the same pipeline system as city water, an attacker can reduce the flow of water in all households connected to the pipeline. An attack targeting urban infrastructure is a very dangerous attack, as preventing people from accessing critical infrastructure resources can result in disaster, depending on the number of people affected [36].

3   IoT Service Categorization

In this section, a security analysis of all the aforementioned Internet of Things services using the DREAD model is made. We will use the DREAD model to evaluate the likelihood of an attack by exploiting a particular threat. It is worth noting that several literature reviews have adopted various methods for modelling threats, such as popular STRIDE model developed by Microsoft, which provides mnemonic for security threats in six categories [37–39], PASTA, which represents the Process for Attack Simulation and Threat Analysis and is a seven-step risk-centric methodology [40] and VAST (visual, agile and simple threat modelling) [41]. In addition to performing threat detection, most threat modelling attempts did not rate the identified threats, except in some reviewed papers that used the DREAD model to rate and calculate the device risk score. We chose DREAD over other models because it provides a categorization of vulnerabilities based on the threats and the aggregation of risk values to a single numerical value and is capable to determine the severity of a threat.

Using the DREAD model (Table 1), we obtain a risk assessment for a given service by asking the following questions [42]:

- Damage potential: How big is the damage if a successful attack occurs?
- Reproducibility: How easy is it to reproduce an attack?
- Exploitability: How easy is it to launch an attack?
- Affected users: How many users were affected by the attack?
- Discoverability: How easy is it to find a vulnerability?

The risk assessments in this chapter are based on actual attacks on existing systems and on the characteristics of these systems.

Based on previous research and risk assessment, we propose the following 4 safety categories:

- Low risk services - DREAD rating 5–6
- Medium risk services - DREAD rating 7–9
- High risk services - DREAD rating 10–12
- Critical services - DREAD rating 13–15

In Table 2 all previously mentioned IoT services have been rated using DREAD model. Variations in grades are possible depending on the expert conducting the research. We believe that, based on the data collected and previous work, we have given the most objective assessment.

Table 1. Thread rating table

Rating	High(3)	Medium(2)	Low(1)
Damage potential	The attacker can subvert the security system; get full trust authorization; run as administrator; upload content.	Leaking sensitive information	Leaking trivial information
Reproducibility	The attack can be reproduced every time and does not require a timing window	The attack can be reproduced, but only with a timing window and a particular race situation	The attack is very difficult to reproduce, even with knowledge of the security hole
Exploitability	A novice programmer could make the attack in a short time	A skilled programmer could make the attack, then repeat the steps	The attack requires an extremely skilled person and in-depth knowledge every time to exploit
Affected users	All users, default configuration, key customers	Some users, non-default configuration	Very small percentage of users, obscure feature; affects anonymous users
Discoverability	Published information explains the attack. The vulnerability is found in the most commonly used feature and is very noticeable	The vulnerability is in a seldom-used part of the product, and only a few users should come across it. It would take some thinking to see malicious use	The bug is obscure, and it is unlikely that users will work out damage potential

4   Example Service Categorization

In order for services that are not listed in this paper to be classified in one of the safety categories without conducting a risk assessment according to the DREAD model, we propose the following model of service evaluation. The service can be assigned a grade from 7 to 15 based on answering the following questions and adding up the received grades.

- How many people use the service?
  - Less than 10 (1)
  - 10 to 100 (2)
  - More than 100 (3)
- Does the system collect personal, financial or medical information about users or confidential company information?
  - No (1)
  - Yes (2)
- Are the devices in the system physically secured or easily accessible?
  - Physically insured (1)

Table 2. Threat rating using DREAD model

	Damage potential	Reproducibility	Exploitability	Affected users	Discoverability	Total	Rating
Smart city							
Smart parking	2	2	2	2	2	10	High
Smart waste management	1	2	1	1	1	6	Low
Smart street lighting	2	2	1	3	2	10	High
Smart water grid	3	2	1	3	1	10	High
Smart home	3	3	3	1	3	13	Critical
Smart HVAC	3	2	1	3	1	10	High
Smart energy							
Smart grid	3	2	2	3	2	12	High
Remote monitoring and data collection	3	2	1	2	1	10	High
Smart renewable energy	3	2	1	3	2	11	High
Intelligent transport systems							
Smart vehicles	3	2	2	1	2	10	High
Roadway reporting and traffic flow controls	2	3	2	2	2	11	High
Communications applications and systems	2	3	2	2	3	12	High
Industry automation							
Smart logistic	2	2	2	2	1	9	Medium
SCADA	3	2	2	2	1	10	High
Smart healthcare							
Remote health monitoring	2	3	2	1	2	10	High
Remote operation	3	2	2	1	1	9	Medium
Public safety							
Critical communication	2	2	2	2	2	10	High
Smart Emergency Response	3	2	2	3	2	12	High
Smart agriculture							
Smart irrigation	3	3	2	3	2	13	Critical
Corp monitoring	2	3	2	1	2	10	High

- • Easily accessible (2)
- – Is the system connected to a public or private network?
  - • Private network (1)
  - • Public Network (2)
- – Are the devices active (Active devices collect data and then generally do something based on the collected data, such as changing the colour of traffic lights or starting a machine) or are they passive (Passive devices collect data and send it somewhere)?
  - • Passive (1)
  - • Active (2)
- – Are devices upgradeable? Could new software versions be put on them?
  - • Yes (1)
  - • No (2)

– Is there authentication when accessing the device?
  • Yes (1)
  • No (2)

After receiving a rating based on Table 3, you can classify the service into one of the security categories.

Table 3. Security categories based on the rating obtained by the proposed model

Security category	Rating
Critical services	14–15
High risk services	11–13
Medium risk services	9–10
Low risk services	7–8

For example, we will take 3 real services and categorize them according to the proposed model into one of the security categories. The services we will categorize are an air quality system, a portable device for athletes, and smart greenhouses. The air quality system is used by a small number of people (1), it does not collect personal or confidential data (1). The devices are physically secured (1) and can be connected to the public network (2). The devices in the system are passive (1), not upgradeable (2) and there is authentication to access the device (1). Based on this assessment, we obtain a grade of 9, which classifies the air quality monitoring system into medium risk systems.

Only one person uses a sports carrying device (1). These devices collect personal and medical information about the people who use them (2), but they are passive devices (1). The devices are constantly located next to the person wearing them so that they are physically secured (1) and do not connect to the public internet (1). The devices are upgradeable (1) and there is authentication when accessing the device (1). Based on this assessment, we get a grade of 8 and we can classify wearable sports equipment as low risk services.

The system in smart greenhouses is used by more than 10 people (2). The devices collect sensitive information (2), are physically secured (1), and are not connected to the public network (1). The devices are active (2), upgradeable (1) and there is authentication to access the device (1). Based on this assessment, we get a score of 10 and we can classify smart greenhouse systems as medium risk services.

5   Conclusion

The paper proposes a model for categorizing IoT services based on security risks to the services and their users. The purpose of the proposed categorization is to allow IoT service creators to assess the security and privacy risks to services they are developing. Ultimately, the goal is to provide guidelines for hardening the services while in development, since one of great issues in security in general is lack of security considerations during design and implementation phases. In this paper we propose four service categories, corresponding to risk levels low, medium, high and critical, based on DREAD model. We give a simple set of questions that should be answered by service creators in order to get a total score for the service, thus categorizing it into one of the proposed categories. Finally, we demonstrate how existing services can be categorized into on of the proposed categories.

In future work, we plan to further examine existing IoT services, especially the services that were breached on any level (i.e. device, network or cloud platform) and determine the drawbacks that eventually lead to service compromise, and also expand the number of services that we look at so we can get more generalized solution. Based on the detected flaws and issues, the plan is to further tune the questions and categorization in order to get a better fit for possible new IoT services. Finally, guidelines for service creators should be implemented in form of security requirements to be used during service design and implementation. Each service category should have a list of security requirements that should be considered. It is our opinion that in this way service creators can be more aware of possible risks and take precautions when they really should; in the early phases of service development.

Acknowledgement. This work has been supported by Croatian Science Foundation under the project 1986 (IoT4us: Human-centric smart services in interoperable and decentralised IoT environments).

References

1. Suresh, P., Daniel, J.V., Parthasarathy, V., Aswathy, R.: A state of the art review on the Internet of Things (ToT) history, technology and fields of deployment. In: 2014 International Conference on Science Engineering and Management Research (ICSEMR), pp. 1–8. IEEE (2014)
2. Antonakakis, M., et al.: Understanding the Mirai botnet. In: 26th Security Symposium (Security 17), pp. 1093–1110 (2017)
3. Davis, D.B.: ISTR 2019: Internet of Things cyber attacks grow more diverse (2019)
4. Hassan, W.U., Hussain, S., Bates, A.: Analysis of privacy protections in fitness tracking social networks-or-you can run, but can you hide? In: 27th Security Symposium (Security 18), pp. 497–512 (2018)
5. Hern, A.: Fitness tracking app Strava gives away location of secret us army bases, January 2018
6. Common vulnerability scoring system v3.0: Specification document
7. Pal, S., Hitchens, M., Rabehaja, T., Mukhopadhyay, S.: Security requirements for the Internet of Things: a systematic approach. Sensors 20(20), 5897 (2020)
8. Abomhara, M., Køien, G.M.: Security and privacy in the Internet of Things: current status and open issues. In: 2014 International Conference on Privacy and Security in Mobile Systems (PRISMS), pp. 1–8. IEEE (2014)
9. Sicari, S., Rizzardi, A., Grieco, L.A., Coen-Porisini, A.: Security, privacy and trust in Internet of Things: the road ahead. Comput. Netw. 76, 146–164 (2015)

10. Babar, S., Mahalle, P., Stango, A., Prasad, N., Prasad, R.: Proposed security model and threat taxonomy for the Internet of Things (IoT). In: Meghanathan, N., Boumerdassi, S., Chaki, N., Nagamalai, D. (eds.) CNSA 2010. CCIS, vol. 89, pp. 420–429. Springer, Heidelberg (2010). https://doi.org/10.1007/978-3-642-14478-3_42

11. Sain, M., Kang, Y.J., Lee, H.J.: Survey on security in Internet of Things: state of the art and challenges. In: 2017 19th International Conference on Advanced Communication Technology (ICACT), pp. 699–704. IEEE (2017)

12. Bastos, D., Shackleton, M., El-Moussa, F.: Internet of Things: a survey of technologies and security risks in smart home and city environments (2018)

13. Davoli, L., Veltri, L., Ferrari, G., Amadei, U.: Internet of Things on power line communications: an experimental performance analysis. In: Kabalci, E., Kabalci, Y. (eds.) Smart Grids and Their Communication Systems. ESIEE, pp. 465–498. Springer, Singapore (2019). https://doi.org/10.1007/978-981-13-1768-2_13

14. Suryani, V., et al.: A survey on trust in Internet of Things. In: 2016 8th International Conference on Information Technology and Electrical Engineering (ICI-TEE), pp. 1–6. IEEE (2016)

15. Alqassem, I.: Privacy and security requirements framework for the Internet of Things (IoT). In: Companion Proceedings of the 36th International Conference on Software Engineering, pp. 739–741 (2014)

16. Cvitić, I., Vujić, M., et al.: Classification of security risks in the IoT environment. Ann. DAAAM Proc. **26**(1) (2015)

17. Owasp: IoT security verification standard (2020)

18. Owasp: Application security verification standard (2020)

19. Researcher at Forescout Technologies Inc.: Discovering and defending against vulnerabilities in building automation systems (BAS), June 2020

20. Case, D.U.: Analysis of the cyber attack on the Ukrainian power grid. Electr. Inf. Shar. Anal. Cent. (E-ISAC) **388** (2016)

21. Holloway, M

22. Cimpanu, C.: Cyber-attack hits Utah wind and solar energy provider, October 2019

23. Huq, N., Vosseler, R., Swimmer, M.: Cyberattacks against intelligent transportation systems. TrendLabs Research Paper (2017)

24. Rodriguez, J.F.: 'You hacked' appears at muni stations as fare payment system crashes, November 2016

25. Williams, C.: Hackers hit d.c. police closed-circuit camera network, city officials disclose, January 2017

26. Eykholt, K., et al.: Robust physical-world attacks on deep learning visual classification. In: Proceedings of the IEEE Conference on Computer Vision and Pattern Recognition, pp. 1625–1634 (2018)

27. Goldman, J.: Cyber attack causes physical damage at German iron plant (2014)

28. Kaspersky, I.: Threat landscape for industrial automation systems (2019)

29. Langston, J.: UW researchers hack a teleoperated surgical robot to reveal security flaws (2015)

30. Fu, K., Xu, W.: Risks of trusting the physics of sensors. Commun. ACM **61**(2), 20–23 (2018)

31. Li, C., Raghunathan, A., Jha, N.K.: Hijacking an insulin pump: security attacks and defenses for a diabetes therapy system. In: 2011 IEEE 13th International Conference on e-Health Networking, Applications and Services, pp. 150–156. IEEE (2011)

32. Halperin, D., et al.: Pacemakers and implantable cardiac defibrillators: software radio attacks and zero-power defenses. In: 2008 IEEE Symposium on Security and Privacy (sp 2008), pp. 129–142. IEEE (2008)
33. Zhang, Q., Fitzek, F.H.P.: Mission critical IoT communication in 5G. In: Atanasovski, V., Leon-Garcia, A. (eds.) FABULOUS 2015. LNICST, vol. 159, pp. 35–41. Springer, Cham (2015). https://doi.org/10.1007/978-3-319-27072-2_5
34. Loukas, G., Gan, D., Vuong, T.: A review of cyber threats and defence approaches in emergency management. Future Internet 5(2), 205–236 (2013)
35. Gupta, M., Abdelsalam, M., Khorsandroo, S., Mittal, S.: Security and privacy in smart farming: challenges and opportunities. IEEE Access 8, 34564–34584 (2020)
36. Bennett, C.: Russia tied to cyberattack on Ukrainian power grid, February 2016
37. Abomhara, M., Gerdes, M., Køien, G.M.: A stride-based threat model for telehealth systems. NISK J., 82–96 (2015)
38. Alhassan, J.K., Abba, E., Olaniyi, O., Waziri, V.O.: Threat modeling of electronic health systems and mitigating countermeasures. In: International Conference on Information and Communication Technology and Its Applications (ICTA 2016). Federal University of Technology, Minna, Nigeria (2016)
39. Amini, A., Jamil, N., Ahmad, A., Zaba, M.: Threat modeling approaches for securing cloud computin. JApSc 15(7), 953–967 (2015)
40. Lin, X., Zavarsky, P., Ruhl, R., Lindskog, D.: Threat modeling for CSRF attacks. In: 2009 International Conference on Computational Science and Engineering, vol. 3, pp. 486–491. IEEE (2009)
41. De Cock, D., Wouters, K., Schellekens, D., Singelee, D., Preneel, B.: Threat modelling for security tokens in web applications. In: Chadwick, D., Preneel, B. (eds.) CMS 2004. ITIFIP, vol. 175, pp. 183–193. Springer, Boston, MA (2005). https://doi.org/10.1007/0-387-24486-7_14
42. Meier, J., Mackman, A., Dunner, M., Vasireddy, S., Escamilla, R., Muruka, A.: Threat modeling (2003)

Analysis of IoT Concept Applications: Smart Home Perspective

Ivan Cvitić[1] ⓘ, Dragan Peraković[1(✉)] ⓘ, Marko Periša[1] ⓘ, Marko Krstić[2] ⓘ,
and Brij Gupta[3] ⓘ

[1] Faculty of Transport and Traffic Sciences, University of Zagreb, Vukelićeva 4,
10000 Zagreb, Croatia
{ivan.cvitic,dragan.perakovic,marko.perisa}@fpz.unizg.hr
[2] Regulatory Agency for Electronic Communications and Postal Services (RATEL),
Palmoticeva 2, Belgrade 11103, Republic of Serbia
marko.krstic@ratel.rs
[3] Department of Computer Engineering, National Institute of Technology, Thānesar,
Kurukshetra, India

Abstract. The concept of the Internet of Things (IoT) is a widely applicable set
of technologies and services. Therefore, it is essential to have a clear insight into
the trends of development and application of this concept in different vertical and
horizontal economic areas and follow future trends' predictions. In this way, it
is possible to direct future research into several problems in those areas where
the concept of IoT is most widespread. With this research, the analysis is focused
on the smart home environment as one of the most common and fastest-growing
applications of the IoT concept. The positive trends of current and future growth
of this area in various categories and functionalities of IoT devices such as comfort
and lighting, energy, security, monitoring, entertaining and home appliances have
been confirmed. Growth is seen in the number of devices used, the number of
homes using at least one IoT device, total revenue and market value. Therefore,
it is concluded that it is necessary to intensify efforts in researching problems
related to smart homes by optimizing access communication networks, the impact
of generated traffic on core network parameters, cybersecurity, identification and
classification of such devices in the network, development of innovative smart
services home and several other research challenges.

Keywords: Smart energy · Smart home security · Smart home entertainment ·
Smart home appliances · Smart home control · Smart lighting

1 Introduction

The concept of the Internet of Things (IoT) is a direction of technological development
that has found its application in almost all industries. This concept's benefits have resulted
in its implementation in a number of vertical and horizontal economic areas, processes,
and activities.

© ICST Institute for Computer Sciences, Social Informatics and Telecommunications Engineering 2021
Published by Springer Nature Switzerland AG 2021. All Rights Reserved
D. Perakovic and L. Knapcikova (Eds.): FABULOUS 2021, LNICST 382, pp. 167–180, 2021.
https://doi.org/10.1007/978-3-030-78459-1_12

Due to this concept's wide application, it is essential to have a clear insight into how it is represented in a particular area. This makes it possible to focus future research on various problems in the field of application where it is needed. An example of this is the strengthening of research efforts in the security problems of those IoT concept applications that are most widespread because thus the security challenges are more significant and their solution is crucial. To this end, it is important to analyze historical and current data on the application of the IoT concept and consider predictions of future trends.

This research is focused on the analysis of trends in the application of the IoT concept from the perspective of a smart home environment. Numerous indicators show that this type of application of the IoT concept is the most common. It can attract numerous investments, generate large profits, and introduce specific challenges such as cybersecurity challenges caused by various restrictions imposed through numerous requirements before applying this concept.

2 Previous Research

The IoT concept was first defined by Kevin Ashton, co-owner and CEO of Auto-ID Center in 1999. Auto-ID Center has researched and developed automatic identification technology. In doing so, they presented a concept in which all objects, regardless of whether they are physical or electronic, have an electronic identification mark assigned to them. Such a tag contains information about the object to which it is assigned. In doing so, each physical object with the assigned label becomes a node in the communication network, which enables remote, contactless access to information related to the observed object [1, 2]. With further development and increase in application, the concept of IoT has been defined by numerous professional standardization bodies, organizations and associations in the field of IC technologies, and numerous researchers. Therefore, the definition of the concept of IoT can be considered from the aspect of professional organizations in the field of IC technologies and the scientific-research aspect.

According to the European Internet Research Cluster, this concept is global and requires a generic definition. According to the IERC document, defining the IoT concept is a demanding task given the foundations of the concept and the technologies and technological processes used, from sensor devices, communication systems, data aggregation and preprocessing to the provision of services to the end-user [3]. Thus, IERC defines the concept of IoT as a dynamic global network infrastructure with the ability to configure independently and is based on standard and interoperable communication protocols where physical and virtual objects have identities, physical attributes and virtual personalities and use intelligent interfaces. They are integrated into the communication network.

Numerous professional bodies and organizations in the field of IC technologies recognize IoT as an important concept in the further development of IC technologies that can automate various processes, decision-making, provide new forms of services, and provide added value for the end-user. In addition to expert bodies, the concept of IoT has been the subject of research by several researchers who have provided different but overlapping definitions and explanations. The European Internet of Things Research Cluster is one of the most important associations in the field of IoT research [4].

The research [5] recognized the importance of the concept of IoT and was defined through three ways of mutual communication between man and object: man - man, man - object and object - object. According to the same research, objects can recognize and communicate, and built-in intelligence allows them to make decisions based on context and exchanged information. According to research [6], IoT addresses and potentially plays a key role in addressing the global societal challenges defined by the Horizon 2020 framework, relating to health, demographic change, sustainable agriculture, safe, clean and efficient energy, smart and integrated transport. and transport, climate change, environment and safe and innovative society.

Acceptance and prevalence of the IoT concept require an analysis of this concept's application and penetration in various industries that this research seeks to provide. In this way, the scientific community will have a clearer insight into the representation of this concept, which will enable better guidance of future research in various fields and fields of science. An example of this is seen in the potential of research and development of new services, encouraging the application of the IoT concept in less represented areas, discovering new areas of application to researching cyber threats in areas where this concept is most widespread, and intensify research on identification and classification of such devices in the network [7–11].

3   Vertical Areas of the IoT Concept Application

The concept of IoT can be observed by expanding the existing interaction between people and applications through a new dimension of integration and communication represented by objects. The IoT concept's potential enables its implementation and application in various areas covering society, environment and industry, the descriptions and indicative examples of which are shown in Table 1 [12].

Table 1. Areas of the IoT concept application [12]

Scope	Description	Indicative examples
Industry	Activities involving financial or commercial transactions between companies, organizations and other entities	Production, logistics, service sector banking, intermediation, etc.
Environment	Activities related to the protection, control or development of all natural resources	Agriculture and cultivation, recycling, environmental management services, energy management, etc.
Society	Activities/initiatives related to the development and involvement of societies, cities and people	Government services to citizens and other social structures, e-inclusion (seniors and people with disabilities), etc.

Depending on the area of application, objects can be perceived differently. For example, facilities in an industrial area can represent products, equipment, means of transportation, and anything involved in the product life cycle. In the environment, the object can represent construction objects, devices for measuring environmental conditions, etc. Finally, in the field of society, the object can refer to devices in public spaces, household devices, etc. In applying the IoT concept, it is almost impossible to isolate one sub-scope of application, but a single service is often applied at a level that covers more than one area. For example, the hazardous waste monitoring service is not applying only to the industry as an application area but also to the environment and society.

Numerous authors and researchers have identified different applications of the IoT concept. As part of the IoT-I project implemented in 2010, a total of 65 concrete applications of the IoT concept were identified, grouped into 14 vertical areas (smart cities, smart environment, smart water supply, smart metering, security, sales, logistics, industrial control, smart agriculture, smart livestock, home automation and smart health).

In contrast, research [13] classifies the application of the IoT concept to seven vertical areas, also called smart environments, i.e., smart city, smart home, smart energy grid, smart buildings, smart traffic, smart healthcare and the smart industry shown in Fig. 1. Mutual communication of devices in the environment, automation of individual processes and decision-making without human intervention has resulted in the frequent use of the term "smart" in a particular application area. Thus, a set of services based on the IoT concept in the city environment results in a concept called the smart city, the application of environmental management results in the concept of smart environment and the like.

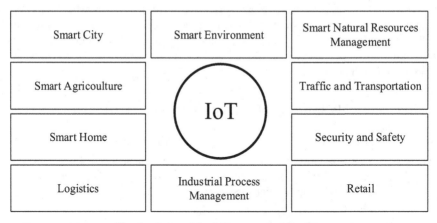

Fig. 1. Areas of the IoT concept application

Consequently, it is possible to conclude that a set of services based on the IoT concept, and applied in a specific environment, makes such an environment smart in the context of communication, data processing, decision making and activities.

Smart City is an environment where all city resources are virtually connected and remotely managed [14]. The IoT concept introduces new capabilities, such as the ability to remotely monitor and manage devices, analyze and take action based on information received from different real-time data streams. As a result, the IoT concept's application is changing cities by improving infrastructure, creating more efficient utilities, improving transportation services by reducing road congestion, and improving citizens' safety. According to [15], the smart city context services are shown in Table 2.

Table 2. IoT-based services within the smart city concept [15]

Service name	Service description
Smart parking	Monitoring the occupancy of parking spaces in the city
Structural correctness	Monitoring of vibrations and condition of materials of buildings, bridges, traffic infrastructure, etc.
City noise maps	Real-time noise monitoring
Traffic congestion management	Vehicle and pedestrian tracking to optimize the driving route or walk routes
Smart lighting	Intelligent and time-efficient street lighting control
Waste management	Container filling detection to optimize the removal route
Intelligent transport systems	Smart roads and highways with the application of dynamic warning and diversion signs depending on weather conditions and unexpected events such as accidents or congestion

According to the above, smart cities must meet two key goals. The first is to provide an advanced infrastructure that enables collecting and processing data using and interacting with IC technologies and services based on them listed in Table 2. The second goal is users' ability to interact with the environment using applications to positively impact the environment and reduce pollution and quality of life in cities.

Given the continuous growth of electricity consumption in private households and the growing number of electricity users and increasing environmental and regulatory constraints, the need to improve electricity networks' overall efficiency is one of today's fundamental problems [16]. Smart grid environment services have their application in the generation, transmission, distribution and consumption of electricity. The integration of advanced services based on the IoT concept increases the traditional energy network's efficiency by providing a higher level of automation, reliable power network load prediction, and safer operation of electrical devices, resulting in increased quality of energy delivery service and greater customer satisfaction. Lower load fluctuations and subsequent reductions in network dynamics, greater stability, lower line losses and lower operating costs are also expected in terms of matching energy demand with supply [17].

Over the years, residential buildings and structures have become more complex and dynamic with multiple systems and devices supporting a number of activities and processes. Complexity often leads to inefficiencies in managing such environments. A smart building environment has existed for many years, and examples of this can be seen in motion-activated lighting and a programmable heating, cooling and ventilation control system (Heating, Ventilation, Air-Condition, HVAC). The IoT concept application in a smart building environment allows managers better visibility of building components, greater control, and management efficiency [18, 19]. Figure 2 shows the architecture of a smart building environment using the IoT concept. The multiple application of various sensors to monitor numerous parameters (movement, air pressure, lighting, temperature, water flow) in different scenarios is visible to enable autonomous collection of relevant data, their transmission, analysis, and execution of activities based on the information obtained.

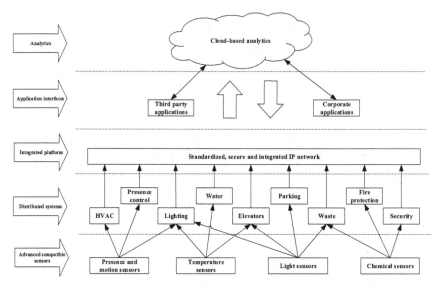

Fig. 2. The architecture of IoT concept application in smart building environment [20]

Building owners are enabled to manage costs and resources more clearly by addressing inefficiencies and improving space utilization. Building owners' problem is a holistic insight into all the processes that take place within a building. Smart building solutions enable stakeholders to identify problems faster, correct maintenance, improve processes, save resources and adapt to different stakeholder requirements [21].

4   Statistical Indicators of the IoT Concept Application

4.1   Trend Analysis for the Overall Application of the IoT Concept

The number of IoT devices has been steadily increasing over the last decade. The exact number of u-devices and growth rate varies depending on the research. According to [22], approximately 20.5 billion IoT devices are projected by the end of 2020, while research [23] predicts approximately 30.7 billion IoT devices by the end of the same year and 75 billion IoT devices by 2025, as shown in Fig. 3.

According to Ericsson's global statistics, which refer to the representation of a particular category of connected devices, IoT devices' dominance is observed in relation to the hitherto dominant mobile devices. Figure 4 shows the number of connected devices by categories for the period from 2015 to 2022. According to forecasts, IoT devices' annual growth rate (CAGR) is expected to be 23% from 2016 to 2022 [24].

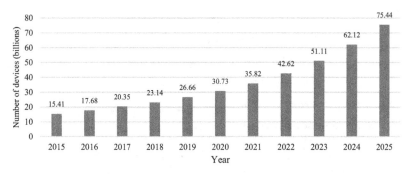

Fig. 3. Prediction of the total number of IoT devices by 2025 (globally) [23]

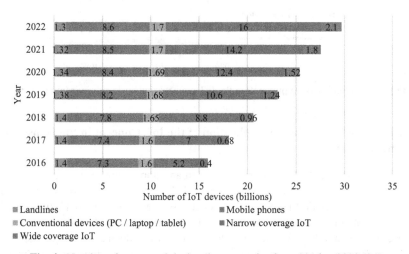

■ Landlines   ■ Mobile phones
■ Conventional devices (PC / laptop / tablet)   ■ Narrow coverage IoT
■ Wide coverage IoT

Fig. 4. Number of connected devices by categories from 2016 to 2022 [24]

The application of the IoT concept in different economic sectors is becoming a key factor for business improvement. According to [25], 92% of companies believe that the concept of IoT will be important for their business by 2020. Consequently, companies see security, privacy, cost, and regulatory issues as the biggest challenges in implementing and enforcing the IoT concept.

Research [26] conducted on 1430 companies (small, medium and large) indicates many advantages recognized by the vast majority (95%) of adopters of the IoT concept. At the same time, more than half (53%) of respondents confirm the significant advantages of implementing the IoT concept in business, while 79% of respondents believe that applying the IoT concept achieves positive results in various areas of work that would not otherwise be achieved. Some of the more prominent advantages are shown in Fig. 5.

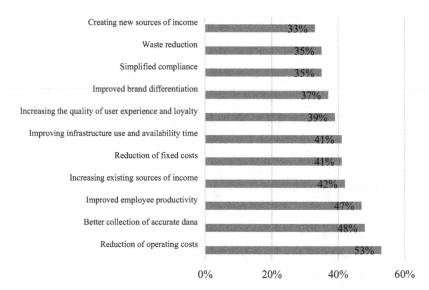

Fig. 5. Advantages of implementing the IoT concept in a business environment [26]

4.2 Analysis of Trends in the Application of the IoT Concept in the Household Environment

According to Gartner, the largest representation and application of the IoT concept in terms of the number of IoT devices used until 2017 was in the area of smart building environments. After 2017, the smart home concept is an environment that brings together the largest number of IoT devices [20]. The representation of IoT devices by application categories is shown in Fig. 6, where the dominance of IoT devices in the private sector, which includes the smart home environment, is observed in relation to the business sectors.

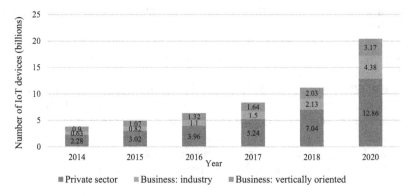

Fig. 6. Number of implemented devices by application category [22, 23]

More precise insight into the representation of IoT devices by individual areas of application is provided by the company IHS Markit's research [27]. Figure 7 shows that the smart home concept records the largest number of installed IoT devices (822.6 million) than other sub-areas of application. The annual growth rate (prediction by 2021) is 19.6%, which makes the concept of smart homes and the concept of industrial IoT (CAGR 23.4%), the fastest-growing area of IoT applications.

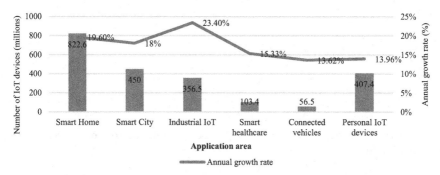

Fig. 7. Number of IoT devices and annual growth rate by area of application [27]

The number of smart homes that have implemented SHIoT devices from each group is shown in Fig. 8. The graph shows the prediction of continuous growth in devices' implementation from all these categories until 2023. According to [28], the largest increase is expected for homes with implemented SHIoT devices from the group "surveillance and connectivity," including devices such as smart sockets, switches and speakers. The statistical indicators presented in [29] indicate a continuous increase in revenues of this group of devices until 2023 by region. The prediction for the Asia area (refers to China) indicates an annual revenue growth rate of 35%, while for the US and Europe area it ranges from 17% to 25%.

The other fastest-growing smart homes implement SHIoT devices from the group "comfort and lighting", which includes devices such as lighting fixtures as the most common devices in this group and window and door sensors and control devices such as garage doors. Given the ease of implementation of devices in this category, which primarily refers to lighting fixtures, they often represent an entry point for users to implement the concept of a smart home. According to [30], this group's global market value in 2023 will be approximately $ 14.32 billion. China's expected annual revenue growth rate is 41%, and for Europe and the US, ranging from 19% to 27%.

The number of homes with implemented SHIoT devices from the category smart appliances is approximately equal to the number of homes with implemented devices from the previous group. This group includes appliances such as washing machines, refrigerators, coffee machines, etc. Figure 9 shows the market value for each group of appliances by years, expressed in billions of dollars. Comparing the values and trends of individual groups of devices in Graphs 8 and 9, the disproportion of market values concerning the number of smart homes that have or will have implemented this categories' device is noticeable. The observed disproportion results from the price of devices of this

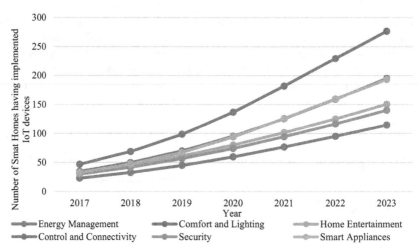

Fig. 8. Number of smart homes that have implemented SHIoT devices from one of the categories (2018–2023.) [28]

category, which is higher than the price of other categories' devices. Smart homes that implement SHIoT devices from the group "multimedia", "security", and "energy management" are represented to a lesser extent than the previous two groups. Nevertheless, continuous growth and significant market value are expected for these three categories as well.

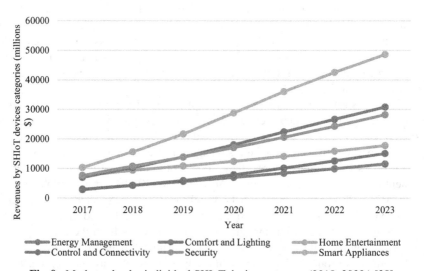

Fig. 9. Market value by individual SHIoT devices category (2018–2023.) [28]

An essential indicator of the smart home concept's growth and importance is the number of SHIoT devices per household. Predictions differ depending on the source, so Kaspersky states that currently, the average household has 6.3 connected devices, including all types of devices (conventional and SHIoT) that connect to the Internet [31].

Figure 10 shows Statista and Forrester's aggregate data, comparing the number of smart homes and other connected devices, including SHIoT devices. According to the picture shown, it is predicted that by the end of 2020, there will be 19.9 million smart homes and 130 million implemented SHIoT devices, which makes an average of 6.53 SHIoT devices per smart home.

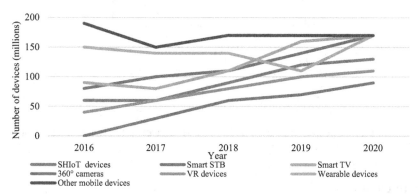

Fig. 10. The ratio of the prediction of the number of smart homes, SHIoT and other connected devices [32, 33]

A study by Telsyte in Australia indicates that the average household owns 13.7 connected devices and predicts that by the end of 2021, there will be 30.7, of which 14 will be SHIoT devices [34]. Given the limited number of statistical indicators that indicate the average number of SHIoT devices installed per smart home, impact indicators of such devices can be observed through the current number and prediction of the future trend in the number of connected devices (conventional + SHIoT) per user. Thus, Cisco research predicts that by the end of 2021, there will be four connected devices per user (globally), with the largest number of connected devices (13) being in North America, 6.5 in Europe (average value), while the lowest number of connected devices per user is foreseen for the Middle East and Africa (1) [35].

A comparison of the global market with that in the Republic of Croatia (RH) in terms of each category of SHIoT devices' penetration rate can be seen in Fig. 11. The penetration rate indicates the ratio of the number of smart homes and the total number of private homes. Despite the indicators that predict a lower penetration rate in the Republic of Croatia compared to the global market, continuous growth is predicted. According to [36], the total value of the smart home market in 2018 in the Republic of Croatia was $ 40 million, and by 2023, linear growth and a value of $ 151 million is projected. The current representation of smart homes in the Republic of Croatia is 0.14 million, with an average price of implemented SHIoT devices of $ 441.94 per smart home, and by 2023 0.36 million smart homes are projected with an average price of $ 419.27 per smart home.

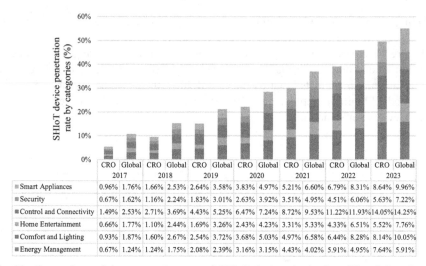

	CRO	Global	CRO	Global	CRO	Global	CRO	Global	CRO	Global	CRO	Global	CRO	Global
	2017		2018		2019		2020		2021		2022		2023	
■ Smart Appliances	0.96%	1.76%	1.66%	2.53%	2.64%	3.58%	3.83%	4.97%	5.21%	6.60%	6.79%	8.31%	8.64%	9.96%
■ Security	0.67%	1.62%	1.16%	2.24%	1.83%	3.01%	2.63%	3.92%	3.51%	4.95%	4.51%	6.06%	5.63%	7.22%
■ Control and Connectivity	1.49%	2.53%	2.71%	3.69%	4.43%	5.25%	6.47%	7.24%	8.72%	9.53%	11.22%	11.93%	14.05%	14.25%
■ Home Entertainment	0.66%	1.77%	1.10%	2.44%	1.69%	3.26%	2.43%	4.23%	3.31%	5.33%	4.33%	6.51%	5.52%	7.76%
■ Comfort and Lighting	0.93%	1.87%	1.60%	2.67%	2.54%	3.72%	3.68%	5.03%	4.97%	6.58%	6.44%	8.28%	8.14%	10.05%
■ Energy Management	0.67%	1.24%	1.24%	1.75%	2.08%	2.39%	3.16%	3.15%	4.43%	4.02%	5.91%	4.95%	7.64%	5.91%

Fig. 11. Comparison of the penetration rate of SHIoT devices in the Republic of Croatia and globally [28, 36]

5 Conclusion

The analysis of trends in applying the IoT concept presented in this paper indicates its strong growth in several economic and application areas. Globally, by 2025, the total number of IoT devices is projected to exceed 75 billion. This figure indicates the need to invest significant research efforts in many areas because the stated number of devices will have implications, i.e., resulting from or being a cause and driver of numerous needs. There is a need to increase cybersecurity, reorganize business and business processes, and need for new business models or improvement of existing ones, develop higher performance and capacity network equipment, optimize communication networks, and many others. The results of this research indicate a significant increase in the application of this concept in the private segment, which focuses primarily on environments such as smart homes, which shows one of the highest annual growth rates (with industrial IoT) and among the largest number of IoT devices in use.

An additional analysis of trends in applying the IoT concept in the smart home segment concludes the positive growth trend in smart homes that have installed IoT devices from different device categories, with those devices from the Control and Connectivity category standing out. Besides, all categories of IoT devices applicable in a smart home environment record significant revenue growth with the prediction of future growth, which indicates the business importance of this area of application of the IoT concept.

The positive trend of penetration of the IoT concept into households is also visible in the Republic of Croatia, which monitors global trends. The analyzed indicators precisely and unambiguously indicate that the concept of a smart home is currently the most common and fastest-growing area of application of the IoT concept.

According to the analyzed and presented indicators, the critical role in researching the application of the IoT concept in the smart home environment is exact. Numerous research problems and issues arise, such as cybersecurity, communication network optimization and adaptation to the smart home environment's requirements in the access and core segment, development and implementation of innovative services and applications of IoT devices in the household. The authors will try to address these research domains in future research.

References

1. Sarma, S., Brock, D.L., Ashton, K.: The Networked Physical World Proposals for Engineering the Next Generation of Computing, Commerce & Automatic-Identification [Internet] (2000). http://222.autoidlabs.org/uploads/media/MIT-AUTOID-WH-001.pdf
2. Farooq, M.U., Waseem, M., Mazhar, S., Khairi, A., Kamal, T.: A review on Internet of Things (IoT). Int. J. Comput. Appl. **113**(1), 1–7 (2015). http://research.ijcaonline.org/volume 113/number1/pxc3901571.pdf
3. European Research Cluster on the Internet of Things: Internet of Things - Position Paper on Standardization for IoT Technologies (2015)
4. De Saint-Exupery, A.: Internet of Things: Strategic Research Roadmap. European Research Cluster on Internet of Things, 50 (2009). http://www.internet-of-things-research.eu/
5. Patel, K., Patel, S.: Internet of Things-IOT: definition, characteristics, architecture, enabling technologies, application & future challenges. Int. J. Eng. Sci. Comput. **6**(5), 6122–6131 (2016)
6. Atzori, L., Iera, A., Morabito, G.: Understanding the Internet of Things: definition, potentials, and societal role of a fast evolving paradigm. Ad Hoc Netw. **56**, 122–140 (2017)
7. Cvitić, I., Peraković, D., Periša, M., Gupta, B.: Ensemble machine learning approach for classification of IoT devices in smart home. Int. J. Mach. Learn. Cybern (2021). http://link.springer.com/10.1007/s13042-020-01241-0
8. Adat, V., Gupta, B.B.: Security in Internet of Things: issues, challenges, taxonomy, and architecture. Telecommun. Syst. **67**(3), 423–441 (2018)
9. Cvitić, I., Periša, M., Vujić, M., Husnjak, S.: Classification of security risks in the IoT environment. Procedia Eng., 0731–0740 (2016)
10. Cvitić, I., Peraković, D., Periša, M., Husnjak, S.: An overview of distributed denial of service traffic detection approaches. Promet Traffic Transp. **31**(4), 453–64 (2019). https://traffic.fpz.hr/index.php/PROMTT/article/view/3082
11. Cvitić, I., Peraković, D., Periša, M., Botica, M.: Novel approach for detection of IoT generated DDoS traffic. Wireless Netw. **27**(3), 1573–1586 (2019)
12. Vermesan, O., Harrison, M., Vogt, H., Kalaboukas, K., Tomasella, M., Wouters, K., et al.: Vision and challenges for realising the Internet of Things. In: Sundmaeker, H., Guillemin, P., Friess, P., Woelfflé, S. (eds.) Cluster of European Research Projects on the Internet of Things. Publications Office of the European Union, Brussels (2010)
13. Ahmed, E., Yaqoob, I., Gani, A., Imran, M., Guizani, M.: Internet-of-things-based smart environments: state of the art, taxonomy, and open research challenges. IEEE Wireless Commun. **23**(5), 10–16 (2016)
14. Lin, J., Yu, W., Zhang, N., Yang, X., Zhang, H., Zhao, W.: A Survey on Internet of Things: architecture, enabling technologies, security and privacy, and applications. IEEE Internet Things J. **4**(5), 1125–1142 (2017)
15. Vermesan, B.O., Friess, P., Woysch, G., Guillemin, P., Gusmeroli, S., Sundmaeker, H., et al.: Europe's IoT Strategic Research Aagenda (2012)
16. Lobaccaro, G., Carlucci, S., Löfström, E.: A review of systems and technologies for smart homes and smart grids. Energies **9**(5), 1–33 (2016)

17. Khan, I., Mahmood, A., Javaid, N., Razzaq, S., Khan, R.D., Ilahi, M.: Home Energy Management Systems in Future Smart Grids [Internet] (2013). http://arxiv.org/abs/1306.1137. Accessed 2019 Nov 25
18. Electric, S.: Get Connected: smart buildings and the Internet of Things, USA (2019)
19. Plageras, A.P., Psannis, K.E., Stergiou, C., Wang, H., Gupta, B.B.: Efficient IoT-based sensor BIG data collection–processing and analysis in smart buildings. Future Gener. Comput. Syst. **82**, 349–357 (2018)
20. Kejriwal, S., Mahajan, S.: Smart buildings: how IoT technology aims to add value for real estate companies [Internet]. Deloitte University Press (2016). http://www2.deloitte.com/us/en/pages/technology-media-and-telecommunications/topics/the-internet-of-things.html
21. Microsoft: Transforming buildings with the Internet of Things (2016)
22. van der Meulen, R.: Gartner Says 8.4 Billion Connected "Things" Will Be in Use in 2017, Up 31 Percent From 2016 [Internet]. https://www.gartner.com/en/newsroom/press-releases/2017-02-07-gartner-says-8-billion-connected-things-will-be-in-use-in-2017-up-31-percent-from-2016. Accessed 12 Feb 2019
23. Statista: Internet of Things (IoT) connected devices installed base worldwide from 2015 to 2025 (in billions) [Internet] (2018). https://www.statista.com/statistics/471264/iot-number-of-connected-devices-worldwide/. Accessed 24 Jun 2018
24. Ericsson: Ericsson Mobility Report - November 2013, June 2013. https://www.ericsson.com/assets/local/news/2013/11/ericsson-mobility-report-november-2013.pdf
25. DigiCert Inc.: State of IoT Security Survey 2018 [Internet] (2018). https://www.digicert.com/wp-content/uploads/2018/11/StateOfIoTSecurity_Report_11_02_18_F_am.pdf
26. Vodafone Business: IoT Barometer 2019 (2019)
27. IHS: The Internet of Things: a movement, not a market Start revolutionizing the competitive landscape. IHS Markit (2017). https://ihsmarkit.com/Info/1017/internet-of-things.html
28. Smart Home - worldwide | Statista Market Forecast [Internet]. https://www.statista.com/outlook/279/100/smart-home/worldwide. Accessed 9 Mar 2019
29. Blumtritt, C.: Smart Home Report 2019 – Control and Connectivity (2019)
30. Blumtritt, C.: Smart Home Report 2019 – Comfort and Lighting (2019)
31. Kaspersky Lab: Press Releases & News | Kaspersky Lab [Internet]. https://www.kaspersky.com/about/press-releases/2017_63-connected-devices-24-people-and-03-pets-per-home-in-the-new-household-20-era. Accessed 11 Mar 2019
32. Meena, S., Gillett, F.E.: Forrester Data: Smart Home Devices Forecast, 2017 To 2022 (US) [Internet] (2017). https://www.forrester.com/report/Forrester+Data+Smart+Home+Devices+Forecast+2017+To+2022+US/-/E-RES140374. Accessed 14 Mar 14 2019
33. Statista: Unit sales of smart devices worldwide by category worldwide from 2013 to 2020 (in millions) [Internet] (2019). https://www.statista.com/statistics/671053/smart-devices-unit-sales-worldwide/. Accessed 14 Mar 2019
34. Telsyte: Internet of Things @ Home [Internet]. https://www.telsyte.com.au/research#/iot-home/. Accessed 11 Mar 2019
35. Cisco: Cisco Visual Networking Index (VNI): Forecast and Methodology [Internet] (2019). http://www.cisco.com/en/US/solutions/collateral/ns341/ns525/ns537/ns705/ns827/white_paper_c11-481360.pdf
36. Smart Home - Croatia | Statista Market Forecast [Internet]. https://www.statista.com/outlook/279/131/smart-home/croatia. Accessed 9 Mar 2019

SMART Production System with Full Digitalization for Assembly and Inspection in Concept of Industry 4.0

Kamil Žídek[✉], Vratislav Hladký, Ján Piteľ, Jakub Demčák, Alexander Hošovský, and Peter Lazorík

Faculty of Manufacturing Technologies with a Seat in Presov, Department of Industrial Engineering and Informatics, Technical University of Kosice, Bayerova 1, 08001 Presov, Slovakia
`kamil.zidek@tuke.sk`

Abstract. The paper describes design of smart production system with full digitalization for requirements of Industry 4.0. The system consists of three level of technologies: production technologies, inspection subsystem and digitalization software system. Production technologies creates parts for assembly: small CNC, Rapid prototyping device and standardized parts storage with assisted assembly process by collaborative robot combined with mixed reality device. This system provides assisted assembly work cell. Inspection subsystems consist of RFID readers with passive tags, vision system with basic 3D inspection, multi-spectrum light for error detection and 3D profilometer precise measuring. Digitalization software is represented as Digital Twin model implemented to server, which uses OPC communication for data transfer from production system to Cloud Platform with additional data from IoT devices.

Keywords: SMART manufacturing · Inspection · Digitalization · RFID · Vision systems · Cloud platforms

1 Introduction to Smart Production Systems

SMART production system automatizes operation with some level of adaptability during whole manufacturing and assembly process. The additional task is data digitalization from every operation, production, inspection, and assembly. The other research in area of smart production was published in these articles [1–8]. The current technology trend is implementation of contactless technologies for inspection especially vision systems and RFID devices. Some research published in area of vision systems aimed to object recognition by artificial neural networks [9–12]. All acquired data during digitalization are used for creating digital twin and some paper solving problems in this area [13]. Extra data after production can be acquired during product lifecycle from customer by IoT devices combined with MEMS sensors. Some articles published in area of IoT and MEMS are [14, 15]. Principle scheme of experimental SMART production system with

© ICST Institute for Computer Sciences, Social Informatics and Telecommunications Engineering 2021
Published by Springer Nature Switzerland AG 2021. All Rights Reserved
D. Perakovic and L. Knapcikova (Eds.): FABULOUS 2021, LNICST 382, pp. 181–192, 2021.
https://doi.org/10.1007/978-3-030-78459-1_13

connection to digital data processing developed in our department for research and teach activities is shown on the Fig. 1.

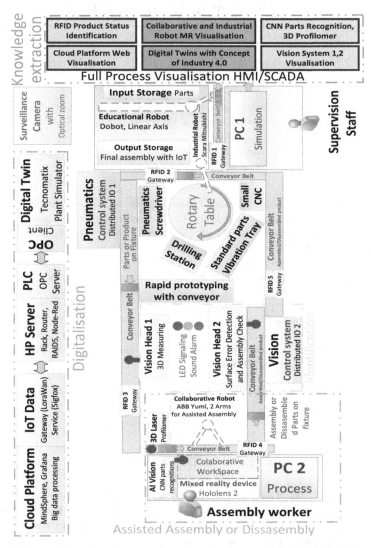

Fig. 1. Proposal flowchart diagram of smart production system with full digitalization.

All used technologies need some digital feedback to ensure self-diagnostics with some level of adaptability and automatized prediction of future status for operation as SMART production system. It can be defined three groups of technologies, which need digitalization. The first group is manufacturing technologies and second group inspection devices and last third group are control systems and Data processing. All data must be accumulated in one place (Cloud Platform) for knowledge extraction and complex decision plan. Detailed description of production technologies and its parameters with possibilities of data digitalization are shown the list of technologies used for inspection of experimental product in production system is shown in Table 1.

Table 1. Table of used technologies in production parts of system.

Production system	Used product	Digitalization possibilities
Pneumatics screwdriver	*Schneider DRS 1000*	Only position sensors
Vibratory feeder bowl	*DOXX*	Binary/speed control
Small CNC	-	Ehternet
Rapid prototyping	*Conveyor*	Ethernet
Industrial SCARA robot	*Mitsubishi RH6-FRH*	Profinet
Collaborative robot	*ABB Yumi*	Profinet

The list of technologies used for part production, manipulation and assembly process is shown in the list of technologies used for inspection of experimental product in production system is shown in Table 1.

The list of technologies used for inspection of experimental product in production system is shown in Table 2.

Table 2. Table of used technologies for inspection process.

Inspection technology	Used product	Digitalized data
Vision system 1	*Keyence CV-X 3D Measurements*	Parts shape errors
Vision system 2	*Keyence CV-X Multispectral*	Assembly check
3D profilometer	*Keyence LJ-X 3D Measurements*	Dimension check
RFID low frequency	*Siemens RF200*	Standard parts ID
RFID high frequency	*Siemens RF300*	Manufactured parts ID
RFID ultra high frequency	*Siemens RF600*	Fixture ID

Table 3. Table of used technologies for system control and data storage.

Control systems and data processing	Used product	Digitalized data
PLC	*Siemens S7-1500*	OPC Server/Profinet
SCADA	*Siemens TP-1500*	Profinet
Server	*HP Primergy*	OPC client

The list of technologies used as control system for all parts of production system and data backup is shown in The list of technologies used for inspection of experimental product in production system is shown in Table 3.

2 Prototype of SMART System

The design of experimental SMART production system consists of three stages. The first preparation of 3D models of all physical devices (manufacturing devices, inspection technologies and control and data collection system) connected to communication chain. The second is realisation of protype SMART manufacturing system and last transformation all 3D models to digital twin and real time connection to all real processes.

2.1 3D Design Model and Experimental Prototype

The production system was designed in 3D software Autodesk Inventor before establishment to laboratory, the first idea is shown on the Fig. 2.

Fig. 2. Autodesk Inventor 3D model of production system before real installation.

Realized experimental prototype of SMART production system established in laboratory is shown on the Fig. 3.

2.2 Cooperative Assembly Robot and Experimental Product

The main workplace is montage cell with assisted assembly of the product on the fixture. Collaboration with robot is realized by mixed reality device Hololens 2, which can detect worker hand and part position in assembled assembly. Collaborative robot detect parts by integrated camera and for positioning uses separate grippers and vacuums.

The collaborative robot and disassembled product are shown on the Fig. 4.

The used mixed reality device Microsoft Hololens 2 and the simulation of assembly process with help of mixed reality device is shown on the Fig. 5.

Fig. 3. Current prototype status of experimental production system installed in our department.

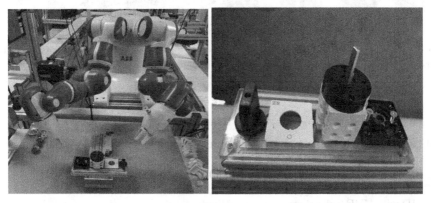

Fig. 4. Collaborative robot from ABB Yumi (left), fixture with assembled product (right).

Fig. 5. Mixed reality device Microsoft Hololens 2 (left), Simulation of assembly process with assisted assembly by collaborative robot (right).

2.3 Inspection Technologies Vision Systems and 3D Profilometer

Inspection technologies consists of vision system and RFID readers. Vision systems check input parts quality and output assembly surface errors. 3D profilometer check dimension of the parts before assembly process. RFID systems localize assembly and parts during production process by RFID tags placed on parts, assembly, and fixture.

Inspection devices integrated to smart production system are shown on the Fig. 6.

Fig. 6. 3D vision camera system with basic parts check (left), Multispectral vision system for surface error detection (middle), 3D profilometer for parts dimension check (right).

2.4 Inspection Technologies by RFID Readers and Tags

SMART manufacturing system integrates three different types of RFID technologies:

- RFID with LF technology, Siemens RF200
- RFID with HF technology, Siemens RF300
- RFID with UHF technology, Siemens RF600

RFID with UHF frequencies is used for fixture identification in conveyor belt. It was used two RFID readers with two external antennas. The fixtures can be identified in four places before every production operation during movement in conveyor belt.

LF and HF RFID technologies are used for part identification for bigger parts manufactured parts (plastic parts) and for small, standardized parts.

The example of implementation UHF RFID tag in production system is shown on the Fig. 7.

2.5 Control System and Control Software

Electric distribution box with control system based on PLC have separate converter for motor for each conveyor to independent speed control. Two types of PLC are used: Industrial PLC and Software PLC as backup system. Inside structure of distribution box is shown on the Fig. 8.

Schematics of all control and inspection technologies connected to one Profinet networks is show on the Fig. 9.

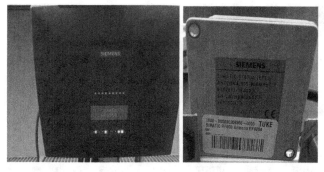

Fig. 7. Example of RFID system based on UHF technology

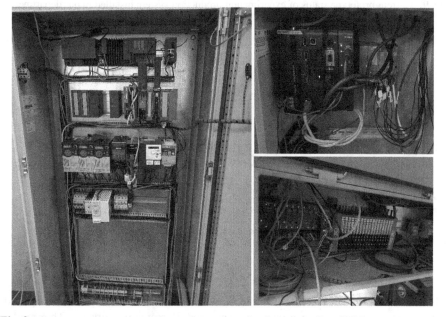

Fig. 8. Current prototype status of experimental production system installed in our department.

2.6 Networking and Communication Systems

To arrange reliable communication which is necessary for real-time data synchronisation to digital twin it must be designed networking structure with optimal bandwidth.

Design of networking structure for SMART production system with optimal backbone is shown on the Fig. 10.

The main system for data storage in Clouds is based on rack server Fujitsu Primergy. The data backup is realized by server HP Proliant. Data are visualized by six LCD panels for monitoring production process and error localization.

The computing section for data storage, backup and knowledge extraction is shown in the Fig. 11.

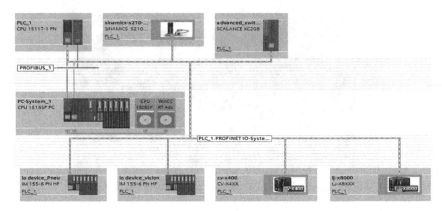

Fig. 9. Current prototype status of experimental production system installed in our department.

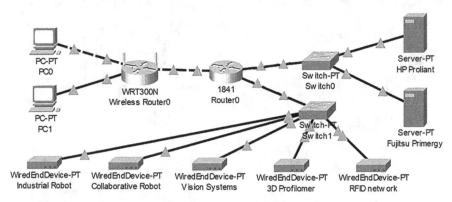

Fig. 10. Design of network backbone for SMART production system.

3 Digital Twin Model

All used technologies were included to simulation software to evaluate timing and optimalisation of production process. It was used Tecnomatix software. This model can be connected to real control system by OPC communication to visualize real-time production process.

2D design of technologies placement from top is shown on the Fig. 12.

Better visualization for operator inspection is possibility of switch 2D model to 3D representation to show error placement or production process delay and is shown on the Fig. 13.

4 Example of Acquired Data

4.1 Inspection System

Inspection systems consist of two industrial vision systems the first with 3D feature acquisition by structural light for product error detection in 2D and 3D and second with

Fig. 11. Rack servers HP Proliant and Fijitsu Primergy (Left), Visualisation of data for monitoring and error localisation (Right).

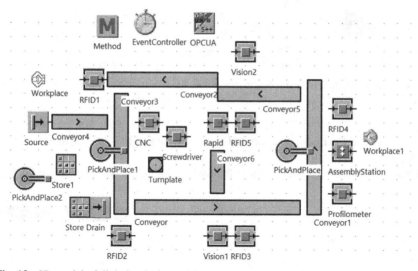

Fig. 12. 2D model of digital twin for realtime optimalisation of SMART production system.

multispectral light system RGB IF and UV for final assembly check as output product inspection. 3D profilometer check dimension of manufactured part in real-time in fixture during movements.

All inspection devices are shown in the Fig. 14.

4.2 Cloud Platform and IoT Devices

Experimental SMART production systems use two different Cloud Platforms for data collection: commercial Mind Sphere with OPC data and open source Grafana with influx

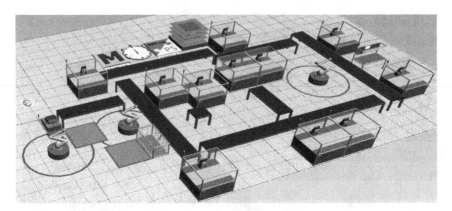

Fig. 13. 3D representation of SMAT production system as digital twin model.

Fig. 14. Graphical output from inspection process: multispectral (left), 3D (middle), profilometer (right).

DB for IoT data collection. The Thinger IO was used for graphical output from simulated IoT device.

Example of data from Mind Sphere Platform and Grafana is shown on the Fig. 15.

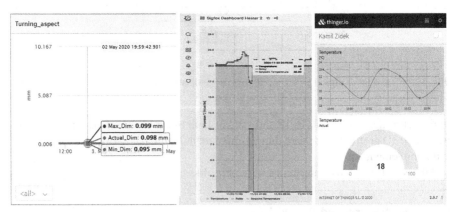

Fig. 15. Mind Sphere Cloud Platform (Left), Grafana with Influx (Middle), Thinger IO output from IoT device (Right).

5 Conclusions and Discussion

The paper present concept of SMART production system with full digitalization based on cutting edge technologies from inspection system and data knowledge extraction by Cloud platform. This concept will be used later for research in maximalization of autonomous tasks and learning activities thru remote access during distance teaching course from web technologies, information and control systems and digital engineering.

Operation staff for whole SMART production system can be minimalized to two people, the first for maintenance, monitoring and engineering and second for manual work like input/output storage service and assisted assembly tasks.

The future works will be implementation of web interface for product customization by user and automated activation of manufacturing, assembly and inspection with personalized data digitalization for each product.

Acknowledgments. This work was supported by the Slovak Research and Development Agency project VEGA 1/0700/20 Identification of Product Defects using Advanced Object Recognition Techniques with Convolutional Neural Networks, KEGA 055TUKE-4/2020 granted by the Ministry of Education, Science, Research and Sport of the Slovak Republic, Slovak Research and Development Agency under the contracts No. APVV-19-0590.

References

1. Gorecki, S., Possik, J., Zacharewicz, G., Ducq, Y., Perry, N.: A multicomponent distributed framework for smart production system modeling and simulation. Sustainability **12**, 6969 (2020)
2. Fu, W., Chien, C.F., Tang, L.: Bayesian network for integrated circuit testing probe card fault diagnosis and troubleshooting to empower Industry 3.5 smart production and an empirical study. J. Intell. Manuf. (2020)
3. Oluyisola, O.E., Sgarbossa, F., Strandhagen, J.O.: Smart production planning and control: concept, use-cases and sustainability implications. Sustainability **12**, 3791 (2020)
4. Dey, B.K., Pareek, S., Tayyab, M., Sarkar, B.: Autonomation policy to control work-in-process inventory in a smart production system. Int. J. Prod. Res. **59**(4), 1258–1280 (2020)
5. Fragapane, G., Ivanov, D., Peron, M., Sgarbossa, F., Strandhagen, J.O.: Increasing flexibility and productivity in Industry 4.0 production networks with autonomous mobile robots and smart intralogistics. Ann. Oper. Res. (2020)
6. Balog, M., Sokhatska, H., Iakovets, A.: Intelligent systems in the railway freight management. In: Trojanowska, J., Ciszak, O., Machado, J.M., Pavlenko, I. (eds.) MANUFACTURING 2019. LNME, pp. 390–405. Springer, Cham (2019). https://doi.org/10.1007/978-3-030-18715-6_33
7. Lazár, Ivan, Husár, J.: Validation of the serviceability of the manufacturing system using simulation. J. Effi. Responsib. Educ. Sci. **5**, 252–261 (2012)
8. Hrehova, S.: Predictive model to evaluation quality of the manufacturing process using Matlab tools. In: Procedia Engineering, pp. 149–154. Elsevier Ltd. (2016)
9. Žídek, K., Maxim, V., Sadecký, R.: Diagnostics of errors at component surface by vision recognition in production systems. Appl. Mech. Mater. **616**, 227–235 (2014)

10. Židek, K., Hosovsky, A., Piteľ, J., Bednár, S.: Recognition of assembly parts by convolutional neural networks. In: Hloch, S., Klichová, D., Krolczyk, G.M., Chattopadhyaya, S., Ruppenthalová, L. (eds.) Advances in Manufacturing Engineering and Materials. LNME, pp. 281–289. Springer, Cham (2019). https://doi.org/10.1007/978-3-319-99353-9_30
11. Židek, K., Lazorík, P., Pitel', J., Hošovský, A.: An automated training of deep learning networks by 3D virtual models for object recognition. Symmetry 11, 496 (2019)
12. Zidek, K., Maxim, V., Pitel, J., Hosovsky, A.: Embedded vision equipment of industrial robot for inline detection of product errors by clustering-classification algorithms. Int. J. Adv. Rob. Syst. 13, 1–10 (2016)
13. Židek, K., Pitel', J., Adámek, M., Lazorík, P., Hošovský, A.: Digital twin of experimental smart manufacturing assembly system for industry 4.0 concept. Sustainability 12, 3658 (2020)
14. Clark, J.: Self-calibration and performance control of MEMS with applications for IoT. Sensors 18, 4411 (2018)
15. Židek, K., Pitel, J.: Smart 3D pointing device based on MEMS sensor and bluetooth low energy. In: Proceedings of the 2013 IEEE Symposium on Computational Intelligence in Control and Automation, CICA 2013 - 2013 IEEE Symposium Series on Computational Intelligence, SSCI 2013, pp. 207–211 (2013)

Production Quality Control Using the Industry 4.0 Concept

Stella Hrehova[✉], Jozef Husár, and Lucia Knapčíková

Faculty of Manufacturing Technologies, Technical University of Kosice, Presov, Slovakia
{stella.hrehova,jozef.husar,lucia.knapcikova}@tuke.sk

Abstract. Industry 4.0 is an application of the network concept of digital objects interconnection and the collection, exchange, analysis and distribution of data among them in industrial enterprises. For this purpose, other technologies belonging to the Industry 4.0 concept are also used. By appropriate application of these technologies, companies can obtain relevant information about the ongoing level of quality of the production process. Improving quality will significantly increase the profitability of the product and will act as a key strategic factor in the market. Many manufacturing companies use traditional manual techniques to assess product quality control. They take a sample from one batch at random and check the quality of the product at different points on the line. However, such an approach has its limitations and does not allow active intervention in the production process. A possible solution is to use the Internet of Things approach, which allows manufacturers to analyse product data that is generated from devices and thus they are informed about the quality of the production process in real time. Product data can be further used to remotely diagnose of the product and reduce the time it takes to process customer service requests.

It this paper will be described some technologies, which can help to achieve these aims and there will be also designed a possible information flow to get appropriate data.

Keywords: Information flow · Industry 4.0 · Data

1 Introduction

Achieving the required quality of production in the long run is currently one of the most important factors for the customer in deciding on the choice of supplier organization. Costumer selects companies which are able to declare the quality of production based on their long-term activities through historical and current data. In this context, data is becoming an important factor for companies of their position in the market. One of the prerequisites is the implementation of technologies and methods of the Industry 4.0 concept, which can significantly help companies succeed in the market. The most important in this context is the collection and subsequent analysis of data, where means and tools belonging to the category of Internet of Things (IoT) can be used. The basis is the interconnection of large number of heterogeneous terminals and the provision of

© ICST Institute for Computer Sciences, Social Informatics and Telecommunications Engineering 2021
Published by Springer Nature Switzerland AG 2021. All Rights Reserved
D. Perakovic and L. Knapcikova (Eds.): FABULOUS 2021, LNICST 382, pp. 193–202, 2021.
https://doi.org/10.1007/978-3-030-78459-1_14

acquired data for all kinds of different digital services. The role of IoT is to connect to the Internet, provide computing power, and enable the ability to scan, count, communicate, and control the environment. These capabilities are applied in many applications due to their potential impact. IoT offers a new perspective on what kind of data should be collected and how often and from where it should be collected in order to make available information that was not previously available [1].

The presented paper will analyse the proposed information flow in obtaining the necessary information about the quality achieved. Several technologies and procedures will be used in order to obtain as much relevant data as possible that can be further processed. The proposed information flow should also ensure the control of the operation activities to eliminate the possibility of poor quality production.

2   Tools and Methods

In the proposed information flow, we assume the use of several technologies and methods. According that, there will be introduce their brief description in the following subchapters.

2.1   IoT

Industry is increasingly focused on using resources more efficiently, increasing labour productivity, reducing operating costs, ensuring worker safety, and all this, it is brought about by the revolutionary Internet of Things (IoT). According to one of many definitions, it is a network of interconnected objects that are uniquely addressable, the network being based on standardized communication protocols for exchanging or sharing data and information in order to achieve higher added value. IoT is thus a concept for physical and virtual objects (things) that can share data through the Internet [2]. It is already possible to see that the Internet of Things is one of the main sources of big data [3]. The application of this technology to production creates a new concept - the Industrial Internet of Things (IIoT) (Fig. 1).

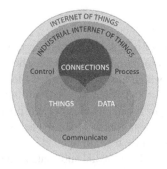

Fig. 1. Internet of things in manufacturing [4].

2.2 Vision System

These systems are used in all industry areas and are an essential part of achieving efficiency and high quality standards. They have also found application in the field of product
quality control. Industrial machine vision systems are typically implemented in automated lines with manipulators or industrial robots to inspect, identify, diagnose, measure,
count and track products. In most cases, industrial automation systems are designed to
inspect known objects in fixed positions, characterize faults on items, and take steps to
report and correct these faults and replace or remove faulty parts from the production
line [5]. One such system is industrial vision systems, which are described as computer
systems where the software performs tasks for acquiring, processing, analysing and
understanding digital images. They are usually focused on industrial quality assurance,
defect detection, part recognition, etc. [6]. They form "eyes" that capture the process
and recover the analysed digital image using image special processing software (Fig. 2).

Fig. 2. A view of camera vision.

The basic principle of the machine vision system is that the camera captures images
that are sent to the computer via one type of the serial communication protocol standard.
Obtained images are subsequently evaluated in computer according set of rules. For
assumed system it is the very important part because of its ability to detect wrong parts
of objects. This aim can be fulfil using various methods. Nowadays there are used various
methods of artificial intelligence to recognize the object [7, 8].

This system has advantages over other techniques in that the integration of a vision-
based inspection system reduces production time, increases the efficiency and quality of
inspection activity by eliminating human interaction in the inspection process [9].

2.3 Radio Frequency Identification

Radio Frequency Identification (RFID) is a technology that has gained popularity in many business sectors thanks to the relatively wide area of its applications [10] in many industries. RFID is a technology used to identify objects and transmit information from a distance via radio waves. Different types of RFID tags are used for different applications [11]. The advantage of RFID systems is that many objects can be detected automatically and almost simultaneously without visual contact [12]. Some of the reported benefits of RFID applications include flawless machining, reduced cycle times leading to shorter lead times, smaller inventory reductions, and more accurate inventory (lower inventory and out-of-warehouse opportunities). RFID systems consisting of one or more readers and several tags also play a key role in the IoT attitude. These technologies help automatically identify everything to which they are connected and allow objects to assign unique digital identities, integrate them into a network, and associate them with digital information and services (Fig. 3).

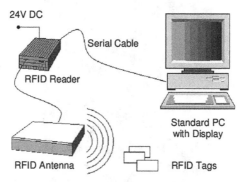

Fig. 3. Principle of RFID technology [13].

RFID technology, as the core of IoT, acts as a link between process flow data and physical asset data. All physical asset data can be assigned to process nodes based on RFID [14].

In the prosed information flow, we assume using the programmable logic controllers (PLC). They are described as reliable control system that can continuously monitor the status of devices connected to the inputs. A PLC is a controller with functions for performing timing, counting, arithmetic manipulations, control logic, and sequencing. PLCs are basically very similar to an industrial computer, which has a built-in memory, I/O interface, central processing unit (CPU) and programming device. 3 The central processing unit (CPU) of a PLC consists of a microprocessor, memory chips and control logic circuits for communication and monitoring. The CPU can be operated in programming mode to download logic from the device and in operating mode to execute the program and start the process [15] (Fig. 4).

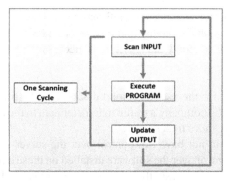

Fig. 4. Principle of PLC [16].

2.4 Software Tools

When a company obtains data from a number of sensors, each of these sensors is loaded with a large amount of computing power. In this case, it is more advantageous if the data is transferred to the cloud and processed there. Cloud computing capabilities are used to manage and store such data. By storing data in the cloud, companies can access large amounts of data. Cloud computing and IoT work to increase the efficiency of everyday tasks, and the two complement each other. IoT generates a lot of data, while cloud computing provides a way to process that data. It can be said that the cloud is the "brain" for most IoTs, because most of the collected data is finally processed and analysed in the cloud [17].

2.4.1 Cloud Technology

Cloud computing has changed the way technologies can be accessed, managed and delivered [17]. Cloud storage is a computer data storage model in which digital data is stored in logical files that are said to be located in a "cloud." Physical storage is spread across multiple servers (sometimes multiple locations), and the physical environment is usually owned and managed by the host company. These cloud storage providers are responsible for maintaining the availability and accessibility of data and the protection and operation of the physical environment. People and organizations purchase or rent storage capacity from providers to store data about users, organizations, or applications.

Cloud and IoT is a platform that enables intelligent use of applications, information and infrastructure in a cost-effective way. Although IoT and cloud computing are different, their properties are almost complementary [3].

2.4.2 Cloud Database Possibilities

In the presented proposal of information flow, we assume the storage of obtained data in a database, which should serve as a tool for various outputs based on individual queries, as well as a source of basic information about the product.

There are currently many different cloud database service providers that provide database as a service, DBaaS such as Amazon RDS, Microsoft SQL Azure, Google

AppEngine Datastore and Amazon SimpleDB and more. Each service provider differs from the other depending on the quality and type of provided services.

When implementing a cloud database, it is necessary to consider some of its disadvantages:

- Companies must pay for the use of a cloud database every time data is transferred from the database. If the company's traffic to transfer data to the database is high, then the company may pay more than expected.
- Security issues - we do not have full control over the server where our database is stored. We have no control over the software installed on these computers. To increase the security of the cloud database, the client must rely only on the provider.
- Internet speed. Because a large amount of data is stored in a cloud database, it is very difficult to transfer this data to a personal computer. For this reason, the speed of the Internet must be high.
- Change of provider. If a client wants to change the database from one service provider to a new one, they may encounter problems. This is because each service provides its own methods and techniques for storing data.
- Data from the database is retrieved over the Internet, so if the server is down, it may make it impossible to access the data from the server. This causes huge losses when information is not available when needed.

The advantage, however, is that the cloud database is a very powerful technology and companies prefer it because they can get information from anywhere and at any time.

3 Design of Information Flow

For the proposed information flow, we assume the storage of individual parameters, using database software. An already created database schema with clear items is assumed, into which information will be written through individual supporting technologies.

The following scheme shows the expected information flow of the workplace (Fig. 5).

3.1 Description of the Assumed Events

In position "1", the initial product information (eg information from the drawing documentation, ID numbers, etc.) is read using RFID technology and sent to the PLC.

RFID tags can be attached to the pallet and RFID readers and antennas are placed at fixed workstations to monitor the entry or exit of these pallets. Through wireless identification, these tags can communicate with RFID readers to obtain real-time data and possibly decide on further material flow.

The information continues through the server to the database on the cloud storage. The product continues with further production operations and in a certain state of development it is necessary to check the current quality "2" (e.g. to assess the key dimension of the product, whether it meets the requirements, or to find out the correct location during assembly, etc.) (Fig. 6).

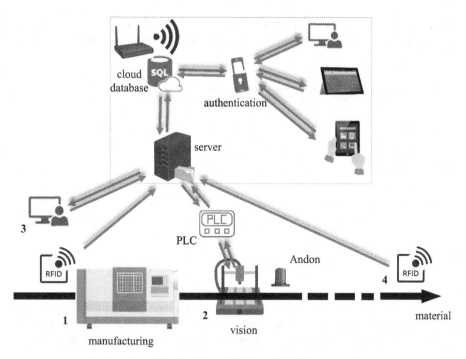

Fig. 5. Assumed information flow

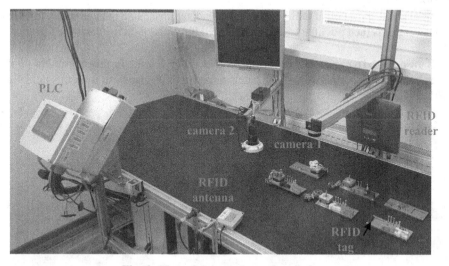

Fig. 6. View of the experimental workplace.

At this point, a camera system can be used, which evaluates the set parameters and sends the information via PLC again to the database, where the added information will be paired based on the agreed rules.

The course of individual products is displayed at the control station "3". The following figure represents a desktop showing a possible software environment (Fig. 7).

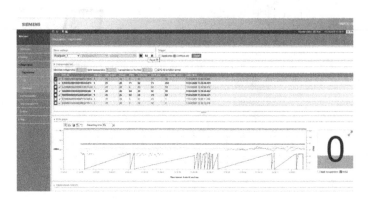

Fig. 7. Settings SIMATIC web controler.

As part of the quality assessment at this point, LEAN tools and methods can be used, where a warning system (e.g. andon) can be applied, which in case of non-compliance will signal an error. In this case, different approaches can be used to solve the problem:

– stop of operation and determination of the causes of non-compliance with the set parameters
– automated disposal of an individual product and its subsequent manual inspection. In this case, it is then possible to add the required information to the database off-line.

If the required parameters are met, the product proceeds with further operations until it reaches the last required item "4". Data is reloaded to the database from this item via RFID.

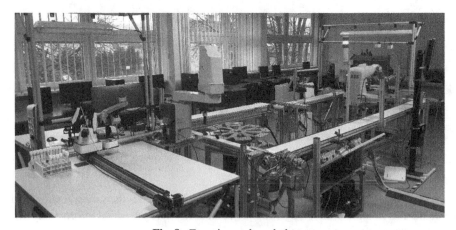

Fig. 8. Experimental workplace.

In the near future, the goal is to expand the experimental workplace with other objects (e.g. robots) and create an experimental automated line where the possible use and interconnection of the described technologies and tools would be tested. The next figure shows experimental workplace (Fig. 8).

The area of research will be mainly the area of production quality control, data collection and its analysis to ensure the automatize quality control and to create relevant database, which can serve as a possible tool for customers decision..

Conclusion

Today, data is one of the most important areas of interest in any business. By using the latest trends and technologies, companies try to obtain and analyse as many relevant data as possible, which would allow them to assert themselves, respectively. Remaining in the market. In the present paper, the anticipated information flow is proposed, with the application of various current high-performance technologies and tools. All the described technologies have great potential to bring the required data in shape with the right configuration, regardless of place and time. Companies thus gain important information for their presentation to potential new customers and can strengthen their position with existing customers.

Acknowledgments. This work was supported by the Slovak Research and Development Agency under the contracts No. APVV-19-0590 and also by the projects VEGA 1/0700/20, KEGA 055TUKE-4/2020 granted by the Ministry of Education of the Slovak Republic.

References

1. Mocnej, J., Pekar, A., Seah, W.K.G., Papcun, P., Kajati, E., et al.: Quality-enabled decentralized IoT architecture with efficient resources utilization. Robot. Comput. Integr. Manuf. **67**, 1–17 (2020)
2. Botta, A., De Donato, W., Persico, V., Pescapé, A.: Integration of cloud computing and internet of things: a survey. Future Gener. Comput. Syst. **56**, 684–700 (2016)
3. AlShehri, W.: Cloud database database as a service. Int. J. Database Manag. Syst. **5**(2), 1–12 (2013)
4. What is IoT & What Role Does It Play in Manufacturing (2017). https://getfreepoint.com/iiot-role-play-manufacturing/. Accessed 22 Nov 2020
5. Atlam, H. F., Alenezi, A., Alharthi, A., Walters, R.J.: Integration of cloud computing with internet of things: challenges and open issues. In: IEEE International Conference on Internet of Things (iThings) and IEEE Green Computing and Communications (GreenCom) (2017)
6. Zidek, K., Modrak, V., Piteľ, J., Šoltysová, Z.: The digitization of quality control operations with cloud platform computing technologies. In: Industry 4.0 for SMEs (2019)
7. Kuric, I., Kandera, M., Klarák, J., Ivanov, V., Wiecek, D.: Visual product inspection based on deep learning methods. In: Advanced Manufacturing Processes, pp. 148–156 (2020)
8. Zakaria, M.F., Choon, H.S., Suandi, S.A.: Object shape recognition in image for machine vision application. Int. J. Comput. Theory Eng. **4**(1) (2012)
9. Kiran, R., Amarendra, H.J., Lingappa, S.: Vision system in quality control automation. In: MATEC Web of Conferences, vol. 144 (2018)
10. Gladysz, B., Ejsmont, K., Kluczek, A., Corti, D., Marciniak, S.: A method for an integrated sustainability assessment of RFID technology. Resources **9**(9), 1–24 (2020)

11. Fescioglu-Unver, N., Choi, S.H., Sheen, D., Kumara, S.: RFID in production and service systems: technology, applications and issues. Inform. Syst. Front. **17**, 1369–1380 (2015)

12. Kaur, C.: The cloud computing and internet of things (IoT). Int. J. Sci. Res. Sci. Eng. Technol. 19–22 (2020)

13. Wang, K.-S.: Intelligent and integrated RFID (II-RFID) system for improving traceability in manufacturing. Adv. Manuf. **2**(2), 106–120 (2014). https://doi.org/10.1007/s40436-014-0053-6

14. Langheinrich, M., Mattern, F., Rmer, K., Vogt, H. First steps towards an event-based infrastructure for smart things (2004). https://www.researchgate.net/publication/2885099_First_Steps_Towards_an_Event-Based_Infrastructure_for_Smart_Things. Accessed 22 Apr 2016

15. Farrukh, M., Halepoto, I.A., Chowdhry, B.S., Kazi, H.: Design and implementation of PLC based automatic liquid distillation system. Indian J. Sci. Technol. **10**(29), 1–6 (2017)

16. Ykanchanam: PLC Introduction (2019). https://medium.com/@ykanchanam/plc-troduction-bb037a447d58. Accessed 22 Nov 2020

17. Kai, D., Pingyu, J.: RFID-based production data analysis in an IoT-enabled smart job-shop. J. Automatica Sinica **5**(1), 128–138 (2018)

Smart Factory Environment: Review of Security Threats and Risks

Petra Zorić[1]([✉]) [iD], Mario Musa[2], and Tibor Mijo Kuljanić[3]

[1] Faculty of Transport and Traffic Sciences, University of Zagreb, Vukelićeva 4,
10000 Zagreb, Croatia
petra.zoric@fpz.unizg.hr
[2] Hrvatska Lutrija D.O.O., Ulica grada Vukovara 72, 10000 Zagreb, Croatia
mario.musa@lutrija.hr
[3] HEP ODS D.O.O., Ulica grada Vukovara 37, 10000 Zagreb, Croatia

Abstract. The Industry 4.0 concept represents a new way of managing production processes. With its application, connections between people, systems, and objects become more complex, creating a dynamic and real-time optimized network. With the establishment of such a network, a smart factory is created. In a smart factory environment, each process must be precisely planned into a connected functional unit in order for the production process to run smoothly. A factory designed in this way has a complex information and communication infrastructure, and thus potentially more significant security threats and risks that it faces than a factory that operates traditionally. The technologies found in the smart factory environment have been evolving for some time. However, their integration with industrial systems poses new security challenges. The smart factory environment's rapid development imposes the need to ensure safe interaction between the production system elements. This paper provides an insight into the environment of a smart factory and the information and communication technologies that enable its operation. The paper provides an overview of security threats and risks that such an environment faces based on the acquired knowledge.

Keywords: Industry 4.0 · Information and communication technology · Manufacturing system

1 Introduction

The fourth industrial revolution era represents an era of the enormous potential for the development of innovation and companies' growth in the market. Production is becoming increasingly digital as the industry adopts automation. The digital transformation of the production process and the creation of added value of the services that manufacturing companies provide to end users are the Industry 4.0 environment's main features. With the Industry 4.0 concept introduction, there are changes in company strategies, business models, value chains, production processes, services, and relationships with stakeholders who participate in one production process.

© ICST Institute for Computer Sciences, Social Informatics and Telecommunications Engineering 2021
Published by Springer Nature Switzerland AG 2021. All Rights Reserved
D. Perakovic and L. Knapcikova (Eds.): FABULOUS 2021, LNICST 382, pp. 203–214, 2021.
https://doi.org/10.1007/978-3-030-78459-1_15

One of the crucial components of Industry 4.0 development is a smart factory created by establishing a real-time dynamic, and optimized network. As part of this network, smart sensors, implemented in factories and workplaces, are the drivers of Industry 4.0 and the Internet of Things (IoT). It is possible to achieve new ways of data analysis, which results in adaptable production processes that ensure and improve performance in the industrial sector using sensors.

Failure of certain parts of the industrial facility can endanger the safety and quality of the product and lead to serious personal injuries and cause material damage. The combination of smart sensors with specific technology implemented in a smart factory environment, such as artificial intelligence, leads to self-testing, monitoring, and improving the sensor's performance, thus reducing the number of damaged data.

Despite the many opportunities provided to all stakeholders in the smart factory environment, new vulnerabilities have been created that must be managed to have a positive impact on both business and society as a whole. Complex and precise systems, such as a smart factory, bring with them certain risks and challenges in security.

Terms such as Industry 4.0 or smart factory have seen an exponential increase in the number of published scientific and professional papers in recent years. The topic of security in such an environment is still insufficiently researched and represented in the currently available scientific and professional literature. For this reason, this paper deals with the presentation of security threats and challenges that are possible in a smart factory environment. This paper aims to provide insight into the most critical information and communication technologies in a smart factory environment and present the security risks and threats possible in a smart factory environment.

2 Smart Factory Environment

Smart factories (Fig. 1) are production systems that respond in real-time to meet the changing requirements and needs of end-users and the factory's conditions and supply network. The goal of such a system is to optimize production processes fully. In one highly digitized production plant like a smart factory, all systems are interconnected and participate in the exchange of data of every aspect of production in real-time. The communication between different systems in such an environment takes place without significant interference and completely imperceptibly, and the entire production process takes place automatically without human interference.

Data is a crucial aspect of smart factories. When transferring data through systems to connect all production operations, the entire facility in which the smart factory environment is implemented can learn and adapt to the business's changing needs. This concludes that smart factories are intelligent production systems that can dynamically adapt to changes that occur due to their ability to learn on the go.

This achievement of a high level of automation of production processes and efficiency is enabled by using many currently available technologies, some of the most critical IoT, artificial intelligence (AI), and Machine-to-Machine communication (M2M). Above mentioned creates specific products ordered by end-users and creates entire related value chains [2]. Increasing productivity and reducing labor costs by adopting smart factories

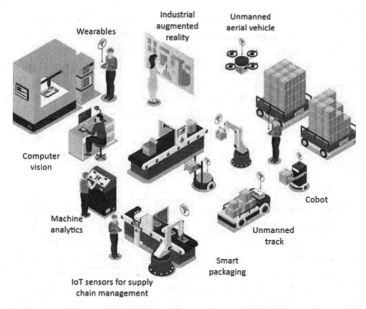

Fig. 1. Smart factory concept [1]

powered by innovative technologies can be significant. For example, by 2025, the adoption of smart factories launched by AI could increase productivity by 30%, while labor costs would decrease by 18–33% [3].

New business models are accelerating the manufacturing industry's transformation, changing the current business methods and market structure, and establishing digital supply networks (Fig. 2) [4].

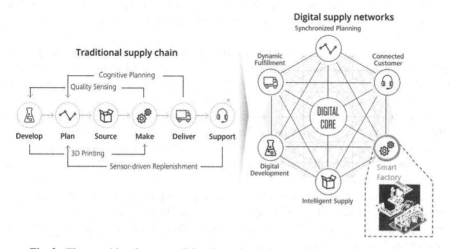

Fig. 2. The transition from a traditional supply chain to a digital supply network [4]

In the model shown in Fig. 2, it can be seen that traditional supply chains are linear. Today's supply chains are transformed into a dynamic system in which all the links are interconnected - the digital supply network. This network integrates information from many different sources and from various locations to initiate the physical act of production and distribution of the service, i.e., the end product of a smart factory. This method allows for a greater connection between areas that did not even exist before. Communication between different network parts is multidirectional, creating a link between traditionally unconnected links in the supply chain.

2.1 The Main Features of a Smart Factory

Smart factories can significantly help the manufacturing industry mostly because the development and application of digital technology can offer greater efficiency at all manufacturing processes, better quality products with fewer errors, and greater flexibility of the manufacturing processes themselves. There are five main features through which a smart factory can be described: connectivity, optimization, transparency, proactivity, and agility [5]. All of these features individually can play a significant role in enabling more informed decisions and improving the production process. Given that each production process is specific and that for this reason, the two smart factories are unlikely to look the same, manufacturers decide which of the features are relevant to meet their production needs.

Connectivity is one of the most crucial features of any smart factory. Linking core processes and materials to create data crucial for real-time decision making is one of the main requirements of a smart factory environment. Smart sensors equipped with the asset allow the systems to update the data continuously. Together with information coming from the market, they provide insight into supply chain processes, thus ensuring the supply network's greater efficiency.

Optimization enables the execution of operations in the production process with minimal manual interventions and high reliability. Optimized energy consumption with workflow automation leads to increased revenue and quality of work and decreased costs and waste.

The transparency of data collected in a smart factory environment allows for greater visibility of production processes based on the cloud's available data. The transparent network enables more excellent monitoring of the facility in monitoring the execution of the process in real-time.

As a smart factory feature, proactivity provides the system with anticipation and action before specific challenges arise. This feature may include identifying anomalies, identifying and predicting the resolution of quality problems, and monitoring safety and maintenance concerns. This can improve the time frame of a process, quality but also prevent security problems.

Agility allows smart factories to adapt to changes in production with minimal intervention. Independent configuration of equipment and material flow depending on the type of product and the impact of changes on the product in real-time reduces downtime and increases profits.

These features allow manufacturers greater visibility of their assets and system and cope with some of the challenges faced by more traditional factory structures. This improves productivity in the production process itself and more significant responses to fluctuations in suppliers and customers' conditions.

2.2 Advantages of a Smart Factory

Asset efficiency is one of the most prominent advantages of a smart factory. Continuous analysis of large amounts of data reveals asset performance issues that may require some corrective optimization. This kind of self-correction distinguishes a smart factory from traditional automation leading to greater overall asset efficiency. Smart factories optimize different assets and help the organization get the most out of them. It also helps an organization take advantage of all these resources' synergy to gain a significant advantage in productivity and revenue.

The maintenance problems characteristic of traditional factories does not occur in smart factories that overcome this problem with proactive, predictive maintenance capabilities. In this way, downtime or losses in business are eliminated. The scalable infrastructure of a smart factory environment is cost-effective because it can be easily expanded to meet the manufacturing process's growing needs [6].

A smart factory's self-optimization characteristic can predict and detect trends in machine quality failures in the manufacturing process. A more optimized quality process could lead to a higher quality product with fewer defects and recalls in production. Such a process has traditionally led to more cost-effective processes. A better process could also mean an integrated view of the supply network with fast, non-delayed responses.

It is also important to note a smart factory's self-sustainability that can replace specific roles that require repetitive and tedious activities. However, the human worker's role in a smart factory environment can take on a higher level of judgment and discretion on the spot, which can lead to greater job satisfaction and reduced traffic. Also, in terms of safety, greater process autonomy may provide less human error potential, including industrial accidents that cause injuries [4].

It is also important to emphasize that governments worldwide have recognized the importance of the new generation of production and have become active in investment in infrastructure, sponsorships, tax breaks, and the like to facilitate its implementation in companies [7].

3 The Most Crucial Information and Communication Technologies in a Smart Factory Environment

Equipment located in a smart factory environment generates a large amount of data during the execution of specific actions in the production process. Such data are not structured and are usually unused. However, with the advent of IoT and Big Data technologies, such data analysis takes place with ease. Equipment should be ready to collect data and transfer it to a platform that can analyze it. To be able to do this, it must be equipped with sensors. It can support industry-standard protocols such as TCP/IP, SECS (SEMI Equipment Communications Standard)/GEM (Generic Equipment Model) or OPC (Open Platform Communications) [8].

Smart sensors have become devices with detection and self-awareness capabilities. They are designed as IoT components that convert real-time information into digital data transmitted to the gateway. They can predict and monitor scenarios in real-time and take corrective action in an instant [1].

Nowadays, millions of such embedded devices are used in security-critical applications such as critical infrastructure or industrial control systems. Examples include necessary technology such as RFID (Radio-Frequency Identification) to identify and track products in supply chain scenarios to smartphones and wearable equipment that have significant computing capabilities and Internet connections. Such a network enables new services in the industrial sector and is known as IoT [9].

Industrial IoT (Fig. 3) is a collective name for automation, intelligent computer systems, and classical manufacturing engineering [10]. It consists of vertical and horizontal connections of people, object machines, and information and communication technology systems in real-time, enabling dynamic control of complex systems [11].

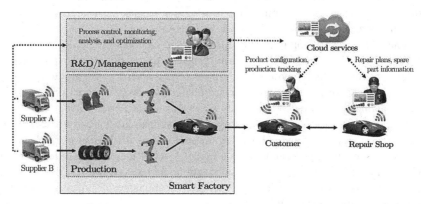

Fig. 3. Industrial IoT in smart factory environment [10]

Programmable logic controllers characteristic of classic factories have been replaced by more advanced cyber physical systems (CPS) whose prominent roles are to meet agile and dynamic production requirements and improve the industry's efficiency as a whole. CPS is the foundation of industrial IoT and represents computer platforms that monitor and control production's physical processes. Such systems typically communicate via closed industrial communication networks via IoT but are often connected to the Internet [12–15]. CPS can be facilities, products, devices, buildings, production facilities, or logistics components that contain embedded systems [16].

In addition to the above, Fig. 4 shows the various technologies present in the smart factory environment needed to achieve innovation and improve production processes' capacity. M2M communication in such an environment is direct and intensive and refers to a technology that facilitates direct communication between devices in a network without human assistance. Advanced industrial robots are designed for complex tasks and can learn from their mistakes and improve their performance.

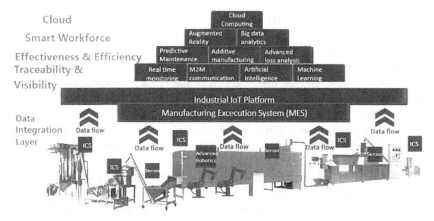

Fig. 4. Technologies within smart factory environment [18]

The evolution of big data presents challenges for data management itself. Traditional data tools, procedures, and infrastructures are not designed to manage diverse and large amounts of data. For this reason, a new immense data management discipline has been developed. Techniques have been developed to address storage, contextualization, integration, and access to extensive data to support data processing and learning. In a smart factory environment, big data analytics is necessary to test vast amounts of different types of data sets generated by smart sensors or devices in real-time [17].

AI and Machine Learning (ML) have revolutionized numerous industries in recent years. AI algorithms allow computers and digital machines to perform tasks accurately related to intelligent human beings. ML algorithms, on the other hand, allow computers to operate and improve their prediction capabilities without explicit programming. The most significant difference is visible in the requirement of human action with these technologies. In AI, the human aspect is useless, while in ML, a minimal level of human involvement in the production process is required [3].

Predictive solutions in a smart factory environment monitor the equipment's condition and predict the time of occurrence of a particular equipment failure with the aim of efficient maintenance. Real-time monitoring includes technologies that serve to collect and aggregate security data from system components and monitor and analyze events taking place online. Advanced loss analysis includes methods of analysis of different types of losses to eliminate and/or reduce them.

Additive manufacturing technologies, such as 3D printing, allow creating objects of different geometric shapes by adding materials. Augmented Reality in a smart factory environment is used to improve the efficiency of manual assembly tasks. Cloud Computing solutions provide access to shared sets of resources, such as networks, servers, and applications [18].

The 5G network has the potential to revolutionize IoT and industrial IoT. From a security perspective, 5G adds an essential new functionality to EAP-TLS (Extensible Authentication Protocol Transport Layer Security) authentication that allows non-SIM-based credentials such as certificates [19].

4 Security Threats and Risks

In the traditional production process, the security of production was achieved with physical isolation carried out based on strict access rights management. The smart factory is connected by nature, and the essential part of the factory networks is connected to wireless networks and more expansive corporate systems. Devices involved in the manufacturing process become accessible to unauthorized attacks. For this reason, the risk of cybersecurity poses more significant concern in such an environment than in a traditional manufacturing facility environment. Such concerns need to be addressed within the overall smart factory architecture [4].

Each information and communication system is most often defined through three fundamental principles, known as the CIA triad: confidentiality, accessibility, and integrity [20]. Confidentiality is related to ensuring the protection of property inspections from unauthorized entities. Integrity is focused on protecting assets from unauthorized alterations, while availability is a feature related to allowing access to assets to authorized entities at any time allowed. Availability and integrity are of paramount importance in the production system because data gaps and false data can lead to significant changes in the processes themselves or production [21].

Many attacks are motivated by political reasons, but they can also be motivated by financial reasons [22]. Cyber-attacks on a smart factory often pursue one of the following three goals [23]:

- Theft of personal data of end customers - criminals use a unique integrated CRM (Customer Relationship Management) system, for example, access to the operating system through heating and air conditioning suppliers,
- Interruption of the entire system - can cause dramatic losses associated with hacker attacks,
- Industrial espionage and sabotage - technology vulnerabilities can be exploited to steal intellectual property and gain a significant competitive advantage over competitors.

Although production systems in a smart factory environment are designed and set up in such a way as to be isolated, and there is great confidence in such systems, minimal integrity checks are performed to prevent malicious activity. Systems and machines that are potentially weak links in the security chain and can be maliciously used to damage manufactured goods or cause failures are MES (Manufacturing Execution System), HMI (Human Machine Interfaces), and industrial IoT devices. An experiment [24] was also conducted to check how and to what extent malicious attacks can affect the insufficiently protected information and communication system of the production environment. The feasibility of several attacks was tested under different assumptions of the attacker model, and five attacks were analyzed (Fig. 5).

Due to the high level of interconnection of production and IT components and integration based on information technology, the physical production process's operation depends on the smooth operation of information and communication services that lead to them. For this reason, smart factory networks face new threats to information and

Vectors   Entry points   Targets

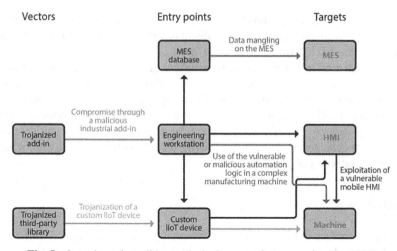

Fig. 5. Overview of possible attacks in the smart factory environment [24]

communication security concerning four dimensions: availability, access, accuracy, and accountability. Consequently, smart factory security threats arise from four channels [25]:

- Software errors and hardware malfunctions,
- Open Internet protocols used in such an environment and standard networks,
- Numerous parties involved in the execution of the production process and
- A large number of devices that can be accessed.

Technologies that are located within a smart factory environment enable its operation to carry with them specific safety requirements. Due to the different requirements that such technologies have and are essential for their proper implementation, new risk categories are generated because vulnerabilities and threats increase throughout the smart factory environment. All components found in such a dynamic system become security-critical as industrial surveillance systems become the target of malicious cyber-attacks [26, 27]. The protection of personal data is also an essential aspect of the smart factory environment's security. The BYOD (Bring Your Own Device) approach carries with it many threats [28]. Confidential data stored on connected devices, which can be accessed in more ways than ever before, offers a way for infiltrators to infiltrate the network, increasing industrial espionage risk.

Threats can come from various sources, such as worker activity in such an environment or hacker attacks. They can cause various damages in the business process itself and even interrupt the business [29]. One of the most critical threats in the smart factory environment is the unusability of the on-demand service. Given the growing dependence of production infrastructure on the reliable functioning of information and communication services, data and access to them are crucial.

DDoS (Distributed Denial of Service) attacks are among the most significant threats in the modern production environment [30]. This attack seeks to prohibit legitimate users from accessing a property in a production environment. They use multiple vulnerable systems infected with malware, and such a threat is difficult to protect for any externally accessible interface [21, 28].

It is imperative to invest in preventive measures and active defense against attacks to ensure connected production systems. These include cryptographic countermeasures, intrusion detection systems, proactive staff training, and good incident management. However, there is still insufficient awareness of the importance of cybersecurity in the manufacturing industry. Given the investments in digital technology significant every year, 34% of manufacturers do not include cybersecurity in their risk register, which is a devastating and worrying statistic [31].

5   Conclusion

The constant progress of information and communication technologies applied in the manufacturing industry promises excellent potential for developing production processes, which leads to a paradigm shift in production. Emerging production systems enable automated and flexible production facilities and can economically create personalized products.

However, such systems' interconnectedness in a smart factory environment causes its vulnerability to increase and makes it risky. Today's production systems are still not sufficiently sophisticated in terms of defense against malicious threats. This applies to attacks on CPS that can cause physical damage and endanger human life. Given the many threats to which the smart factory environment is exposed, companies are forced to implement extensive security and protection measures for information and communication systems that allow a large flow of data to optimize the entire production process.

This paper is a platform to develop security tools that can be used to protect the smart factory environment maximally. Future work will also address a proposal to design security mechanisms to protect the CPS in this environment.

References

1. Kalsoom, T., Ramzan, N., Ahmed, S., Ur-Rehman, M.: Advances in sensor technologies in the era of smart factory and industry 4.0. Sensors **20**, 6783 (2020). https://doi.org/10.3390/s20236783
2. Grabowska, S.: Smart factories in the age of industry 4.0. Manag. Syst. Prod. Eng. **28**, 90–96 (2020). https://doi.org/10.2478/mspe-2020-0014
3. Gisler, A.: Smart factories (2019). https://digital-library.theiet.org/content/journals/10.1049/et.2012.0610
4. Burke, R., Mussomeli, A., Stephen, L., Marty, H., Brenna, S.: The smart factory (2017)
5. Ilanković, N., Zelić, A., Gubán, M., Szabó, L.: Smart factories – the product of Industry 4.0. Prosperitas **7**, 19–31 (2020). https://doi.org/10.31570/Prosp_2020_01_2
6. Rathnam, L.: Industry 4.0: building the 'smart factory' of tomorrow—today. http://techgenix.com/smart-factory/. Accessed 09 Nov 2020
7. Büchi, G., Cugno, M., Castagnoli, R.: Smart factory performance and industry 4.0. Technol. Forecast. Soc. Change **150**, 119790 (2020). https://doi.org/10.1016/j.techfore.2019.119790

8. Illa, P.K., Padhi, N.: Practical guide to smart factory transition using IoT, big data and edge analytics. IEEE Access **6**, 55162–55170 (2018). https://doi.org/10.1109/ACCESS.2018.287 2799
9. Peraković, D., Periša, M., Cvitić, I., Zorić, P.: Information and communication technologies for the society 5.0 environment. In: Zbornik radova trideset osmog simpozijuma o novim tehnologijama u poštanskom i telekomunikacionom saobraćaju – POSTEL 2020, pp. 203–212. University of Belgrade, Faculty of Transport and Traffic Engineering, Belgrade (2020). https://doi.org/10.37528/FTTE/9788673954318/POSTEL.2020.020
10. Virat, M.S., Bindu, S.M., Aishwarya, B., Dhanush, B.N., Kounte, M.R.: Security and privacy challenges in internet of things. In: Proceedings of the 2nd International Conference on Trends in Electronics and Informatics, ICOEI 2018, pp. 454–460. Institute of Electrical and Electronics Engineers Inc. (2018). https://doi.org/10.1109/ICOEI.2018.8553919
11. Arnold, C., Kiel, D., Voigt, K.I.: Innovative business models for the industrial internet of things. In: 26th International Association for Management of Technology Conference, IAMOT 2017, pp. 1379–1396 (2020). https://doi.org/10.1007/s00501-017-0667-7
12. Lu, Y.: Industry 4.0: a survey on technologies, applications and open research issues (2017). https://doi.org/10.1016/j.jii.2017.04.005
13. Zheng, P., et al.: Smart manufacturing systems for industry 4.0: conceptual framework, scenarios, and future perspectives. Front. Mech. Eng. **13**(2), 137–150 (2018). https://doi.org/10.1007/s11465-018-0499-5
14. Rao, S.K., Prasad, R.: Impact of 5G technologies on industry 4.0. Wirel. Pers. Commun. **100**(1), 145–159 (2018). https://doi.org/10.1007/s11277-018-5615-7
15. Alcácer, V., Cruz-Machado, V.: Scanning the industry 4.0: a literature review on technologies for manufacturing systems (2019). https://doi.org/10.1016/j.jestch.2019.01.006
16. Mabkhot, M., Al-Ahmari, A., Salah, B., Alkhalefah, H.: Requirements of the smart factory system: a survey and perspective. Machines **6**, 23 (2018). https://doi.org/10.3390/machines6 020023
17. Gao, R.X., Wang, L., Helu, M., Teti, R.: Big data analytics for smart factories of the future. CIRP Ann. **69**, 668–692 (2020). https://doi.org/10.1016/j.cirp.2020.05.002
18. ENISA: Good practices for security of internet of things in the context of smart manufacturing. In: European Union Agency for Network and Information Security (ENISA), Attiki, Greece (2018)
19. Small, M.: 5G and identity. https://www.kuppingercole.com/blog/small/5g-and-identity. Accessed 15 Oct 2020
20. Ahmad, A., Bosua, R., Scheepers, R.: Protecting organizational competitive advantage: a knowledge leakage perspective. Comput. Secur. **42**, 27–39 (2014). https://doi.org/10.1016/j. cose.2014.01.001
21. Tuptuk, N., Hailes, S.: Security of smart manufacturing systems. J. Manuf. Syst. **47**, 93–106 (2018). https://doi.org/10.1016/j.jmsy.2018.04.007
22. Walker-Roberts, S., Hammoudeh, M., Aldabbas, O., Aydin, M., Dehghantanha, A.: Threats on the horizon: understanding security threats in the era of cyber-physical systems. J. Supercomput. **76**(4), 2643–2664 (2019). https://doi.org/10.1007/s11227-019-03028-9
23. FPT Software: 5 Ways to Mitigate Cybersecurity Risks in Smart Manufacturing. https://www.fpt-software.com/5-ways-to-mitigate-cybersecurity-risks-in-smart-manufa cturing/. Accessed 10 Dec 2020
24. Trend Micro: Threats and Consequences A Security Analysis of Smart Manufacturing Systems. https://www.trendmicro.com/vinfo/us/security/news/internet-of-things/threats-and-consequences-a-security-analysis-of-smart-manufacturing-systems. Accessed 11 Oct 2020
25. Häckel, B., Hänsch, F., Hertel, M., Übelhör, J.: Assessing IT availability risks in smart factory networks. Bus. Res. **12**(2), 523–558 (2018). https://doi.org/10.1007/s40685-018-0071-5

26. Tupa, J., Simota, J., Steiner, F.: Aspects of risk management implementation for industry 4.0. Procedia Manuf. **11**, 1223–1230 (2017). https://doi.org/10.1016/j.promfg.2017.07.248

27. Ervural, B.C., Ervural, B.: Overview of cyber security in the industry 4.0 era. In: Ervural, B.C., Ervural, B. (eds.) Industry 4.0: Managing the Digital Transformation. SSAM, pp. 267–284. Springer, Cham (2018). https://doi.org/10.1007/978-3-319-57870-5_16

28. Herrmann, F.: The smart factory and its risks. Systems **6**, 38 (2018). https://doi.org/10.3390/systems6040038

29. Cavusoglu, H., Cavusoglu, H., Son, J.Y., Benbasat, I.: Institutional pressures in security management: direct and indirect influences on organizational investment in information security control resources. Inf. Manag. **52**, 385–400 (2015). https://doi.org/10.1016/j.im.2014.12.004

30. Cvitić, I., Peraković, D., Periša, M., Botica, M.: Novel approach for detection of IoT generated DDoS traffic. Wirel. Netw. **27**(3), 1573–1586 (2019). https://doi.org/10.1007/s11276-019-020 43-1

31. Swivel Secure: Industry 4.0 and the cybersecurity risks to the future of manufacturing. https://swivelsecure.com/solutions/manufacturing/manufacturing-is-at-risk-from-cyb ercrime/. Accessed 15 Nov 2020

Information and Communications
Technology

Embedded Machine Learning for Machine Condition Monitoring

Michael Grethler[1]([✉]), Marin B. Marinov[2] [iD], and Vesa Klumpp[3]

[1] Institute for Information Management in Engineering (IMI), Karlsruhe Institute of Technology (KIT), Karlsruhe, Germany
michael.grethler@kit.edu

[2] Department of Electronics, Technical University of Sofia, 8, Kliment Ohridski Blvd., 1756 Sofia, Bulgaria

[3] Knowtion GmbH, An der RaumFabrik 33c, 76227 Karlsruhe, Germany

Abstract. With the application of a new generation of information technology in the field of manufacturing and the deep integration of computer technology and manufacturing, industrial production is moving towards intellectualization and networking . Because the current production system cannot fully exploit the value of industrial data and the existence of information islands in the production process, this paper presents a study on the development, testing, and evaluation of a machine learning process that can be run on low-cost standard microcontrollers with limited computing and memory resources. This paper first analyzes the basic idea of whether it is possible to develop software for intelligent sensors whose algorithms run on microcontrollers. At the same time, it is considered whether the training and the adaptation of the model parameters can be done on the microcontroller to enable an online adaptation of the machine to be monitored. The goal is a closed system that does not need a backend and the storage of large amounts of data is not necessary.

Keywords: Embedded machine learning · Microcontroller · Intelligent sensor · Industrie40 · IoT · AI

1 Introduction

1.1 Motivation

Modern sensor technologies are at the basis of many applications, such as monitoring the state of structures [1, 2] Internet-of-Things (IoT), diagnostics of machines [3, 4], human body monitoring [5], health [6, 7], localization of sites [8, 9], ecological monitoring [10], electronic circuits analysis [11], etc. The application of sensor technologies is often related to the processing of large volumes of data, which creates problems with storage, transmission, and security [12, 13].

Modern research shows that by the end of 2020, embedded systems provide more than 10% of all digital data [14]. Sharing sensor systems and using cloud and edge computing

D. Perakovic and L. Knapcikova (Eds.): FABULOUS 2021, LNICST 382, pp. 217–228, 2021.
https://doi.org/10.1007/978-3-030-78459-1_16

technologies is an alternative for achieving efficient processing of large volumes of data and high transmission speeds.

This paper discusses the capabilities of embedded sensor systems of limited resources to undertake machine learning tasks.

The design, implementation, and integration of a machine learning algorithm based on a conventional sensor development kit of the Bosch company are also presented [15]. The algorithm that is implemented uses sensor data obtained in real-time. To apply the machine learning algorithms to the sensor board, an appropriate data structuring is made and the calculation sequence is optimized.

The process of machine learning and classification is demonstrated by real-time experiments.

The chosen hardware platform and machine learning software offer many advantages, such as:

a)   enabling the sensor system to be continuously trained;
b)   providing an opportunity for real-time analysis of the condition of the machine;
c)   scalability so that the algorithms also work with additionally mounted sensors;
d)   reduction of the data volume from the sensors and improved security through the communication of parameters instead of large volumes of raw data.

1.2   Artificial Intelligence in Embedded Systems

Until now, implementing artificial intelligence (AI) in embedded systems has been a lengthy process requiring the expertise of data scientists, months or years of development time, complex, large datasets, lots of computing power, and often expensive specialized hardware. The study was concerned with the development, testing, and evaluation of a machine learning procedure that can be executed on low-cost standard microcontrollers with limited computing and memory resources. The entire learning process was thus to be executed directly on the microcontroller. The task here was to implement data compression directly on the sensor for automated condition monitoring of machines with low communication bandwidths. The idea here was to develop software for intelligent sensors that output (only) the status of the machine and not the raw data. The respective algorithms for this are to run on a microcontroller. The solution approach here goes further than the calculation of a Fourier transform, as it is often used in vibration analysis, special machine learning methods are used. The training and adaptation of the model parameters are also to be performed at runtime on the microcontroller, thus enabling online adaptation to the particular machine to be monitored.

The learning itself is to be done completely locally on the microcontroller. This provides a closed system that does not require a backend for learning. The learning process is done online, iteratively in a kind of streaming pipeline. A short data vector of a few 100 to 1000 data points is ingested and after pre-processing and feature extraction (consisting of whitening, pooling, principal component analysis, and frequency analysis), a model update is performed based on the features. This is performed iteratively several times, each time with new data, so there is no need to store large amounts of data.

The study was conducted as part of the funding measure "Industrie 4.0 test environments - mobilizing SMEs for Industrie 4.0". The unique selling point of the funding measure was the short-term and focused collaboration between SMEs and Industrie 4.0 test environments at research institutions. The project focused on the development, testing, and further development of digitized processes and products as well as networked business models.

The Industrie 4.0 Collaboration Lab of the Institute for Information Management in Engineering (IMI) at the Karlsruhe Institute of Technology was selected as the test environment. The selection was based primarily on the following:

- The availability of machines and qualified personnel to operate them,
- The main focus of the Institute IMI on automation and data management,
- The equipment of the laboratories.

2 Materials and Methods

2.1 Embedded Machine Learning

Machine learning (ML) is a category of artificial intelligence that uses algorithms and statistical methods to efficiently perform a variety of tasks on embedded processors without the need for precise instructions [16, 17].

Deep learning is a common name for a family of ML methods based on neural networks. Examples are Convolutional Neural Networks, Recurrent Neural Networks, Deep Neural Networks (DNN). These methods are currently widely used in areas such as computer vision, speech recognition, and natural language processing [18, 19].

To be able to solve various tasks through machine learning, it is necessary to obtain results from a trained ML model of the embedded system. There are two main approaches for solving this problem: cloud computing and edge/distributed computing. With the cloud approach, all data collected from embedded devices are sent to the cloud over the Internet so that remote servers can execute ML algorithms, and then the results are sent back. With the second approach - edge computing, ML models are pushed to the periphery of the network [20].

Embedded machine learning refers to the second approach, i.e. placement of the ML model in the embedded device and local execution of calculations. The training phase can be done locally or externally. Besides, the main focus of Embedded ML is the use of deep learning training methods. Therefore, for the successful implementation of Embedded ML, it is necessary to choose the optimal configuration of hardware architecture and algorithms to achieve a balance between performance, accuracy, and cost. When designing a built-in solution for ML, a number of questions should be carefully answered, the most important of which are [20]:

- What type of neural network model provides the best trade-off for the accuracy and performance of that particular application?
- What type of processor should be used? (e.g. with a reduced instruction set (RISC) or with a complete instruction set (CISC)?
- How much RAM is needed?

2.2 Machine Learning on Any M-Cortex-Based MCU

"Twenty-five billion objects will be AI-smart by 2025 - that's 25 percent of all edge devices sold by then," Rubino quotes from a recent IDC study. To reach this enormous number, he says, it will be necessary to make the development of integrated AI algorithms much easier, faster, and more affordable than it is today. The problem: Until now, ML, or creating and training neural networks (NNs), has required a lot of computing power. A lot of computing power. That's why these tasks typically run on specialized, power-hungry processors in large data centers, such as in a cloud environment. Outsourcing precisely such tasks to microcontrollers in edge devices, which are trimmed for cost and energy efficiency and therefore have only (very) limited computing power, seems daring at first glance, to say the least. During the study, research on the state of the art was conducted at regular intervals. The product "Bob Assistant" of the French manufacturer Cartesiam became known. It is a solution in the area of anomaly detection using IoT sensors, which are directly attached to devices to be monitored. But Cartesiam promises exactly that with the recently introduced NanoEdge AI Studio integrated development environment (IDE) for AI and ML applications. However, the company approaches the problem from a different angle. Instead of developing and optimizing an NN model from scratch for each new task, embedded developers will be able to select one from a huge library of pre-built models that best fit their application. But that's not all: According to Rubino, the models are capable of adapting themselves to the application better and better.

2.3 Mounting the Sensors

This section describes the work carried out and the results obtained. (Each subchapter corresponds to a work package.) Deviations from the planned implementation are shown. Selection of sensors. Two potential candidates were investigated as IoT sensors: Bosch XDK 110 (XDK) and the Analog Devices Evaluation Board EV-COG-AD4050LZ with the sensor extension board EV-GEAR- MEMS1Z (ADI). The selection of the sensor technology was based on different criteria. ADI was less suitable because it is a development board primarily for hardware manufacturers and does not have its power supply using an accumulator. Furthermore, ADI does not have a gyroscope, which is especially important for the detection of dynamic movements, and protective housing, which would have to be designed and manufactured. ADI has a slightly more powerful microcontroller with a floating-point unit (Cortex M4F, compared to Cortex M3 in XDK), but the main memory configuration is identical for both sensors. XDK has an accumulator as well as these accelerometers and gyroscope and also provides wireless communication technologies such as WLAN and Bluetooth Low Energy (BLE), which allows the wireless installation of the sensors. Furthermore, XDK offers a slot for micro SD cards, which can be used for recording raw data.

For these reasons, XDK was chosen.

Machine selection and sensor installation. The following machines were selected for testing:

- Milling machine consisting of CNC portal machine EAS(Y) 300 and spindle set Jäger 42-2 W38 FS.

- AUBO i5 robot arm.

From preliminary work by Knowtion and IMI, a mounting location for the XDK on the milling machine had already been selected and evaluated from several possibilities. Furthermore, a mounting point for an XDK was available here on the underside of the spindle. This allows the sensor to be mounted as close as possible to the location of the chip removal, see Fig. 1. It has been found that fine chips are deposited on the housing of the sensor. However, these did not influence the functionality of the XDK.

Fig. 1. Bosch XDK on the milling machine. Deposits on the sensor caused by the machining process can be seen here.

Based on the 6 axes of the robot arm, investigations were carried out into the possible mountability of the XDK. After an initial attachment of the XDK to the flange, the configuration was changed. To increase the observability of the joint and to use the flange for tools, two brackets were produced which allow XDKs to be attached to the rigid ends of joint 6 and joint 3. The brackets are shown in Fig. 2. All joints of the robot arm are shown in Fig. 3.

2.4   Recording of Sensor Data

This was due to the changed configuration of the attachment of the XDKs to the robot arm and the subsequent recording of data for the milling machine.

First, the existing software was adapted for XDK to store raw data on an SD card. The raw data was displayed in CSV format.

When recording the data for the robot arm, acceleration data, and rotation rate data of several different trajectories were recorded. Three trajectories were defined (Trajectory A, Trajectory B, and Trajectory C), which differed slightly in individual motion sections. Trajectory A was defined as "normal case", trajectories B and C were created as copies

Fig. 2. Bosch XDK sensor on joint 3 of the AUBO i5.

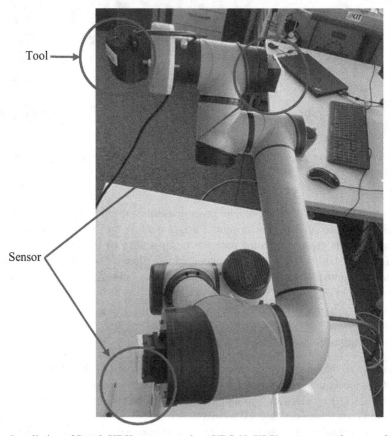

Fig. 3. Installation of Bosch XDK sensors on the AUBO i5. XDKs are mounted on axes 3 and 6.

and slightly modified (either single points of the trajectory or the speed of movement) to be used as an anomaly. The recording of the data to an SD card was done in three steps with several repetitions of each trajectory.

For the data recording of the milling machine, a CNC program was first designed, which performs a simple trajectory as a milling movement. For comparability, the same program was always used. For the selection of the tools different tools were used in each case:

- 6 mm ball cutter
- 14 mm end mill
- 6 mm end mill new
- 6 mm end mill used (slight defect on the cutting edge).

The spindle was operated at speeds of 15,000 rpm and 35,000 rpm. Data sets with several repetitions of the tool and speed combinations were recorded.

2.5 Algorithm and Software Development

The development of the algorithms was done in Python to solve the mathematical and algorithmic problem sufficiently well and to extend the existing algorithms. Algorithmic approaches were developed and evaluated based on the acquired measurement data in a rapid prototyping environment.

The procedure was iterative, first, the algorithms were revised or developed and then the performance of the algorithms is checked with the measured data.

Contrary to the plan, it turned out relatively early on that differentiating between different machine states is less helpful. Thus, the approach was taken to have only one "normal state" and mark deviations from it as an anomaly.

The processing chain was extended to be able to process the acceleration and gyroscope data with as little memory consumption as possible. Here, an approach was chosen that uses as little memory as possible and does not require multiple data.

As a result, several processing stages with the following functionalities have been developed:

In preprocessing, multidimensional sensor data are processed to a feature vector. This vector still contains the same necessary information but is more memory efficient. First, the sensor data are normalized and scaled appropriately. Furthermore, eigenvectors are calculated and frequency analysis is performed.

In training, the sensor data are converted into feature vectors by preprocessing. Subsequently, a recursive calculation of further quantities is performed to unify several feature vectors by smoothing. The result is processed into a clustering algorithm and leads to a model update. Here, adjustments of the algorithms could lead to a significantly faster convergence rate. This is necessary to be able to perform a model adjustment as easy and time-saving as possible in case of misclassification. For this purpose, approaches were developed and investigated that allow an iterative update of the model.

Anomaly detection was implemented by deriving feature vectors from the raw data and comparing them to the clusters. A challenge here was the delimitation of the affiliation of a data point to a cluster. Here, different approaches to the distance measure were developed and evaluated.

In contrast to the planned procedure, the processing effort was not reduced. The focus of the optimizations was to achieve the highest possible accuracy in classification and the most efficient use of memory.

To determine the quality of results and performance, an evaluation of each development iteration was carried out. For this purpose, a Python script was developed, which applies the procedures to the existing data sets and allows a systematic comparison of the results. The algorithms were trained with a part of the measured data and the result was checked against the non-training data.

Implementation. Following the algorithm development, the implementation was done in C. Several requirements were of special interest:

The portability of the developed source code should be kept as high as possible. This was achieved by using standard C language constructs without external libraries. This should make the source code as compatible as possible with different development platforms and it should be easy to make the algorithm executable on other microcontrollers and their build environments.

The optimization of the memory consumption was of great interest, because with lower memory consumption per unit of information more information can be stored in the main memory of the microcontroller and thus the trained model can capture more complex relationships. For this purpose, a representation of real numbers reduced to 16 bits was used, which still achieves useful results for the application despite the loss of accuracy. Thus feature vectors and cluster parameters could be represented more memory efficient.

To be as close as possible to the Python source code from the process step of algorithm development, comparisons of the results of both implementations were carried out. This was done as an automated test to easily perform regression tests during implementation and optimization.

It was not necessary to optimize the program code concerning computing resources, since all program parts could be processed within fractions of a second.

The result of the implementation was software running on the XDK, which processes acceleration and gyroscope data and can train and process a model for anomaly detection with low memory requirements.

2.6   Integration in a Test Environment

The software for XDK has been extended so that the calculated data can be made available via Bluetooth Low Energy (BLE). BLE has the advantage that no additional infrastructure is required and does not need to be integrated into a local network. This allows a higher flexibility in use. The data was provided via a Generic Attribute Profile (GATT) as a separate Bluetooth profile, which includes the anomaly indicator and a measure of model complexity.

As a user interface, an Android app was developed. This app communicates via BLE with the XDKs and allows the user to view the status of the learned models. Furthermore, the app allows the user to continue the training of the model. This updates the model in case of misclassification.

The app essentially consists of an activity, which graphically displays the anomaly indicator and the model complexity as time series.

3 Experimental Results

The operation and evaluation of the system were carried out under testbed conditions and feedback on the system was obtained.

3.1 Test Operation

The test operation showed the following essential results:

- During operation, users had difficulties mapping the anonymous machine states reported by the software to the actual process in the machine. Therefore, the consideration was limited to anomaly detection only without considering individual machines or operating states.
- There had been program errors that caused invalid results due to an incorrect numerical calculation. As a result, either no results or wrong results were displayed.
- Outliers in the measured data and not considered disturbances, such as impacts, had a significant influence on the calculated result. However, these short-term disturbances did not affect the machine.
- A faulty classification had to be reported immediately by the user as long as the faulty classification was still displayed and the behavior of the machine and sensor data did not change. Here the wish was to be able to consider history to be able to make corrections on the model afterward.
- The transferability of the model from one XDK to another XDK was also a listed wish. This was especially relevant when replacing a sensor.
- Depending on the application scenario, the developed procedure requires an independent orientation or alignment of the XDK during installation. This occurred when the XDK was reinstalled in reverse orientation.
- It was possible to train a model relatively well with one run. However, two to three runs are advantageous in training to take into account the dispersion of data.
- In addition, raw data were recorded to investigate certain misclassifications, e.g. the correct differentiation of tools in the milling machine. An evaluation is shown in Fig. 4.

3.2 Adjustments

The adjustments were mainly related to the algorithmic part of the system to increase the accuracy and robustness of the results. Here, programming errors in the prototypical

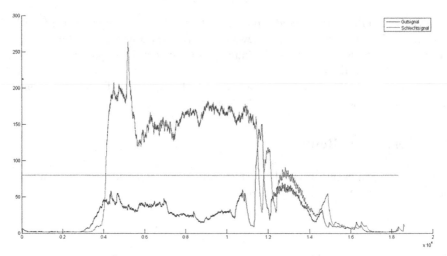

Fig. 4. Differentiation between good signal (blue; no error) and bad signal (green; error present) (Color figure online).

implementation were fixed and an adaptation of the quantification of internal quantities in a 16-bit format was performed. Furthermore, parameters and the measure of quality regarding cluster membership were adjusted. Here, the sensitivity or the question of whether a measurement series can be assigned to a state or not was investigated further. The result of the adaptation of the algorithms was that the selectivity could be improved with an increasing number of existing training data.

4 Conclusions and Future Work

Embedded machine learning involves several limitations and the need to compromise. There is no common best practice and the best way to successfully implement it is to make optimal use of available resources. The present work presents some challenges in the implementation of machine learning on embedded devices.

In general, most of the challenges associated with the use of machine learning in embedded devices can be overcome through appropriate software and hardware optimizations. That is why this approach is increasingly used.

Today, there are a variety of software solutions for machine learning, but these are usually only available for the PC and use Python as the programming language [21]. A solution that allows neural networks to be executed and trained on embedded systems, such as microcontrollers, is not currently available. However, it may be helpful to perform training directly on the embedded system - for example, if an implanted sensor is to calibrate itself. The vision is for sensor-related AI that can be integrated directly into a sensor system. The artificial neural network also for deep learning.

With "Artificial Intelligence for Embedded Systems", the development team has realized this idea and developed a machine learning library in the C programming language that can be run on micro-controllers, but other platforms such as PC, Raspberry PI, or Android are also considered. The technology library currently includes a fully configurable artificial neural network (KNN) that can generate deep networks for deep learning if the interest is there. The use case used here was optimized specifically for embedded systems. The use case was optimized specifically for embedded systems. "We kept the source code to a minimum so that the KNN can be learned directly on the microcontroller or sensor, i.e. the embedded system. In addition, the source code is universal; it can be compiled for almost any platform. Since the same algorithms are always used, a KNN created on a PC, for example, is easily portable to a microcontroller . This was previously not possible with commercially available software solutions.

Acknowledgments. This research is partly supported by the Bulgarian National Science Fund in the scope of the project "Exploration the application of statistics and machine learning in electronics" under contract number КП-06-Н42/1.

References

1. Lynch, J.P.: A summary review of wireless sensors and sensor networks for structural health monitoring. Shock Vibr. Digest **38**(2), 91–128 (2006)
2. Yick, J., Mukherjee, B., Ghosal, D.: Wireless sensor network survey. Comput. Netw. **52**(12), 2292–2330 (2008)
3. Jardine, A.K.S., Lin, D., Banjevic, D.: A review on machinery diagnostics and prognostics implementing condition-based maintenance. Mech. Syst. Sig. Process. **20**(7), 1483–1510 (2006)
4. Aldrich, C., Auret, L.: Unsupervised Process Monitoring and Fault Diagnosis with Machine Learning Methods. In: Advances in Computer Vision and Pattern Recognition. Springer, Berlin (2013). https://doi.org/10.1007/978-1-4471-5185-2
5. Liang, M., Zhuang, Y., Cai, C.: Face classification using sparse reconstruction embedding. In: Proceedings of International Conference on Computational Intelligence and Software Engineering (CiSE), Wuhan, China, December 2010
6. Patel, S., et al.: A review of wearable sensors and systems in rehabilitation. J. Neuroeng. Rehab. 1–17 (2012)
7. Rajan, D., Spanias, A., Ranganath, S., Banavar, M., Spanias, P.: Health monitoring laboratories by interfacing physiological sensors to mobile android devices. In: Proceedings of IEEE FIE (2013)
8. Zhang, X., et al.: Performance comparison of localization techniques for sequential WSN discovery. In: Proceeding of IEEE SSPD, September 2012
9. Zhang, X., Tepedelenlioglu, C., Banavar, M., Spanias, A.: Distributed location detection in wireless sensor networks. In: Proceedings of IEEE Asilomar Conference on Signals, Systems and Computers, November 2013
10. Hino, M., Benami, E., Brooks, N.: Machine learning for environmental monitoring. Nat. Sustain. **1**, 583–588 (2018). https://doi.org/10.1038/s41893-018-0142-9
11. Ivanova, M.: Methodology for analysis of gm-c filters based on statistical, fuzzy logic, and machine learning approach. In: EEET 2020: Proceedings of the 2020 3rd International Conference on Electronics and Electrical Engineering Technology, September 2020
12. Hu, H., Wen, Y., Chua, T.-S., Li, X.: Toward scalable systems for big data analytics: a technology tutorial. IEEE Access, 652–687 (2014)
13. Xia, W., Mita, Y., Shibata, T.: A nearest neighbor classifier employing critical boundary vectors for efficient on-chip template reduction. IEEE Trans. Neural Netw. Learn. Syst. **27**(5), 1094–1107 (2016)

14. A'râbi, M.-A., Schwarz, V.: General constraints in embedded machine learning. In: SCA, Freiburg, July 2019
15. Cross-Domain Development Kit XDK110 Platform for Application Development. Bosch Connected Devices and GmbH (2016)
16. Bishop, C.M.: Pattern Recognition and Machine Learning. Information Science and Statistics, Springer, Heidelberg (2006)
17. Andrade, L., Prost-Boucle, A., Pétrot, F.: Overview of the state of the art in embedded machine learning. In: 2018 Design, Automation & Test in Europe Conference & Exhibition (DATE), Dresden (2018)
18. LeCun, Y., Bengio, Y., Hinton, G.: Deep learning. Nature **521**, 436–444 (2015)
19. Krizhevsky, A., Sutskever, I., Hinton, G.E.: ImageNet classification with deep convolutional neural networks. In: Proceedings of the 25th International Conference on Neural Information Processing Systems (NIPS 2012) (2012)
20. Arm, E.M.: Learning Design for Dummies. Wiley, Hoboken (2019)
21. Lowhead, J.: Learning GeoSpatial Analysis with Python, 2nd edn. Packt, Birmingham (2015)
22. Zekveld, M., Hancke, G.P.: Vibration condition monitoring using machine learning. In: IECON 2018 - 44th Annual Conference of the IEEE Industrial Electronics Society, Washington, DC, pp. 4742–4747 (2018). https://doi.org/10.1109/IECON.2018.8591167
23. Paolanti, M., Romeo, L., Felicetti, A., Mancini, A., Frontoni, E., Loncarski, J.: Machine learning approach for predictive maintenance in industry 4.0. In: 2018 14th IEEE/ASME International Conference on Mechatronic and Embedded Systems and Applications (MESA), Oulu, pp. 1–6 (2018). https://doi.org/10.1109/MESA.2018.8449150
24. Alsheikh, M.A., Lin, S., Niyato, D., Tan, H.: Machine learning in wireless sensor networks: algorithms, strategies, and applications. IEEE Commun. Surv. Tutor. **16**(4), 1996–2018 (2014). Fourth quarter. https://doi.org/10.1109/COMST.2014.2320099
25. Wilkinson, M., Darnell, B., Delft, T.V., Harman, K.: Comparison of methods for wind turbine condition monitoring with SCADA data. IET Renew. Pow. Gener. **8**(4), 390–397 (2014). https://doi.org/10.1049/iet-rpg.2013.0318
26. Hodge, V.J., O'Keefe, S., Weeks, M., Moulds, A.: Wireless sensor networks for condition monitoring in the railway industry: a survey. IEEE Trans. Intell. Transp. Syst. **16**(3), 1088–1106 (2015). https://doi.org/10.1109/TITS.2014.2366512

Analysis of Aviation Pollution in the Selected Regions of the World

Samer Abdo Saleh Al-Rabeei[✉], Peter Korba, Michal Hovanec, Patrik Šváb, Branislav Rácek, and Miroslav Spodniak

Faculty of Aeronautics, Department of Aerospace Engineering, Technical University of Kosice, 7041 21 Kosice, Slovakia
{Samer.abdo,Peter.korba,Michal.hovanec,patrik.svab, branislav.racek,miroslav.spodniak}@tuke.sk

Abstract. The focus of this paper is to find out the impact made by aircraft on the environment of Europe. In this paper, we will focus on how far aircraft are influencing and contaminating the environment. The paper cover-up the various case studies conducted by different authors to estimate the impact by various universal indicators and to ascertain the level of the impact made by the particular factors on the environment and comparing the EU facts and figures with that of policies put forward by the various governments which are U.S and Australia. Paper evaluates the facts and figures to identify the ascertain the environmental hazards caused by aircraft across the globe. The aviation industry is presently responsible for 12% of worldwide CO_2 dis-charges. Aviation could represent up to 24% of worldwide outflows by 2050 except if there is a critical innovative move. Surveys hydrogen's potential as a greener method of impetus and talks about the significant difficulties for its appropriation.

Some studies find several broad ways in which the aviation industry's emissions could be decreased. The main advantage of using hydrogen technology is zero emissions. In addition, the hydrogen needed for operation is generated from renewable sources. Another advantageous hydrogen fuel cell vehicle and the growing interest is that it has comparable properties to conventional vehicles.

Keywords: Emission · Influencing and contaminating · Aircraft and environment

1 Introduction

Aviation sector had an important role in world over a decade due to its peculiarities. It is the fastest, safest and most reliable transportation mode due its high mobility. This acts as one of the main catalysts for the growth of world economy. The ability to move people and products all over the globe quickly and safely. At present, nearly half the global population are dependent on the world's airlines for mobility. Aviation contributes to quality of life by allowing us to visit friends and relatives, to travel, to experience new places, to explore the world.

© ICST Institute for Computer Sciences, Social Informatics and Telecommunications Engineering 2021
Published by Springer Nature Switzerland AG 2021. All Rights Reserved
D. Perakovic and L. Knapcikova (Eds.): FABULOUS 2021, LNICST 382, pp. 229–239, 2021.
https://doi.org/10.1007/978-3-030-78459-1_17

As we look from the Economic perspectives, aviation industry is one of the fast means of transport and contributing a large share in terms of global trade, tourism, cultural exchanges, employment opportunities and so on. By the arrival of aircrafts, the mobility of trade got much easier than before. Aviation was a revolution and still the industry is undergoing huge innovational changes. In this paper we aim to find the Impact made by the aircrafts across the globe regarding climate changes. Even though the share of toxic gases from aircraft are comparatively very low comparing with the other factors. Aviation affects the environment in many ways. People living near airports are exposed to noise from aircraft and aircraft engines emit pollutants to the atmosphere.

In this paper we are mainly considering the impact made by these aircrafts in the environment. This paper describes the emission associated with commercial aviation and the health and welfare impacts that can result from those aviation emissions that degrade air quality which can in turn can cause environmental problems.

2 Methodology

The methodology part consists of details describing the purpose of the study and the related research questions and the various methods used in order to acquire the data needed for the research paper. In this part we will fix our aim to find the rate of impact made by aircrafts to the environment and the environmental hazards caused by the aircrafts apart from other factors. This paper aims to find out the various research questions such as:

What is the level of impact made by the aircrafts to the environment?

Do the regulatory policies set by different regions reduce the impact of air pollution caused by the aircrafts?

To measure the environmental impact made by aircraft, we will observe Air Quality, impacts on the Ozone layer, contributions to Climate Change, Waste Generation and reports general wellbeing made by the WHO.

To measure the environmental impact of aircraft we will be using a history of case studies and reports. We will first focus on literal emission figures, after that on various specific case studies which include other different parameters which we can take into consideration. Then we will look at existing solutions and regulations that various institutions have applied and measure their effectivity.

3 Theoretical Part

In this section it will be followed the analysis of emissions their impacts on the environment and mention some studies which they deal with survey how to decease CO_2 emissions.

3.1 Case Studies and Findings

Emissions from the aviation industry are steadily increasing since the year 1990 [1]. Since then they have doubled and are projected to continue rising at an even faster pace.

Even reductions in average fuel burn did not help decrease total emissions. This fact illustrates the upwards trend of increasingly more people using airlines as they become more accessible and crucial to many people's lives.

Apart from air pollutants emitted by aircraft travel, we also have to take into consideration the noise pollution created by the aircrafts. There are not yet any universal international regulations for aircraft emissions [2]. They are being created by specialized U.N. bodies which have faced criticism for being too slow which in turn has caused a slower adaptation to the necessary regulations all over the world with some countries pushing their own in the meantime creating a chain of chaos in the atmosphere causing climate changes and other destructive environmental calamities.

Until recently, airlines and water transport were excluded from the Paris agreement, Kyoto Protocol and similar efforts [3]. This has led to a worldwide delay in deciding and applying universal standards. International standards were first proposed in 2017 and are projected to come into full effect by 2028 [4].

3.2 Hydrogen Alternative Propulsion

Comparing to conventional fuels and SAFs, hydrogen is better because it eliminates carbon dioxide emissions quit but also has the eventual to reduce other GHG emissions. Comparative with batteries, hydrogen has a high energy thickness, both in gravimetric and volumetric measures. Moreover, hydrogen is probably going to enter into different businesses, which could accelerate the advancement of power devices and capacity frameworks, advance downstream foundation and push down inventory network costs. Two principle choices for hydrogen-energized aircraft exist. In a hydrogen ignition airplane, the push is created through the burning of hydrogen in an adjusted stream motor, which kills most yet not all GHG emanations. Generally, the progress would require less airplane and motor upgrade than hydrogen energy component drive, making it to some degree less troublesome to the current arrangement of the aeronautic trade Hydrogen fuel cell (HFC) aircraft could offer a "true zero" solution for GHG emanations as the lone yield of power devices is water fume, the effect of which can be limited through cautious airplane activity. Studies show that hydrogen power device aircraft would be 20–40% more effective than hydrogen ignition plans. Although more than a dozen companies are involved in the development of electric aircraft, the relatively low energy density of batteries limits the range of action of such machines. In the near future, therefore, only smaller battery-powered electric aircraft can be expected, which can be used for short-haul flights - in the order of several hundred kilometers. The reason is the mentioned energy density, which is currently around 300 Wh/kg for high-end Li-ion batteries. Although hydrogen does not reach the energy (mainly volume) density of gasoline, compared to batteries, its energy density is significantly higher. From one kg of hydrogen we can obtain 120 to 142 MJ of energy by combustion, which corresponds to an energy density of about 33 to 39 kWh/kg. That's 100x more than Li-ion batteries allow. When obtaining electricity from hydrogen in fuel cells, although part of the energy is lost or released in the form of heat, it is still an energy-efficient source. And that is essential in air transport. The environmental aspects of air transport are becoming increasingly important. Already today, aviation emissions account for 12% of CO_2 production in the entire transport segment, and this share is growing rapidly. By 2050, it should be doubled.

Electric aircraft and especially hydrogen-electric aircraft will therefore be a welcome benefit. In principle, there should be nothing to prevent the production of large-capacity hydrogen fuel cell aircraft in the future. It will not be supersonic machines, but the environment will deviate from major polluters (Fig. 1).

Hydrogen Fuel Cells

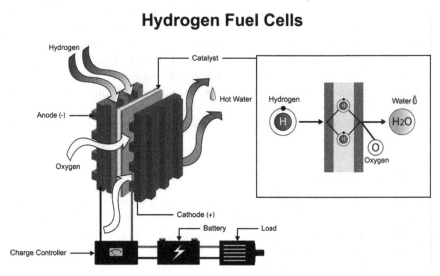

Fig. 1. Hydrogen fuel cells [14].

The aviation industry is presently responsible for 12% of worldwide CO_2 discharges. Aviation could represent up to 24% of worldwide outflows by 2050 except if there is a critical innovative move. Surveys hydrogen's potential as a greener method of impetus and talks about the significant difficulties for its appropriation. Some studies find several broad ways in which the aviation industry's emissions could be decreased. These range from incremental evolutionary improvements, to net-zero solutions, to "true zero" solutions, which have no impact on the environment at all [14, 18]. Unsurprisingly, the methods that offer the greatest emissions reductions also present the most complex challenges. The main advantage of using hydrogen technology is zero emissions. A truck or bus produces only water. In addition, the hydrogen needed for operation is generated from renewable sources. Another advantageous hydrogen fuel cell vehicle and the growing interest is that it has comparable properties to conventional vehicles. However, as with any new technology, there are many challenges. The technology is not yet fully developed. A big step needs to be taken in the short term. Solve fuel cell degradation and life (Fig. 2).

To make hydrogen technology seems to be the solution for the aerospace industry. However, this technology requires extensive innovation. Modification and reworking of the aircraft, from the engine unit to the tanks and refueling itself. Improvements in light storage tanks and cryogenic refrigeration systems to take advantage of high hydrogen energy density. Significant improvements have been made in "green" hydrogen and/or

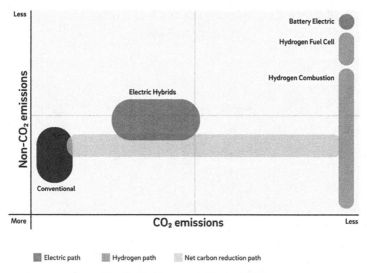

Fig. 2. Environmental impact [14].

carbon capture and storage (CCS) to increase the share of anhydrous hydrogen production. The infrastructure for hydrogen fuel supply to airports and refueling at airports would need to be redesigned. Due to the still complex production, cheaper hydrogen production needs to be transported in order to compete with fossil fuels. If we compare the advantages and disadvantages of hydrogen compared to other sustainable aviation technologies, it will probably be a very important sector of the narrow body/middle market, where hydrogen will be a strong candidate for future propulsion. Manufacturers will need to demonstrate that the introduction of hydrogen as an alternative fuel is a competitive fuel and better than hybrid propulsion solutions such as a hybrid or mild hybrid where operation requires a battery [15, 18].

In addition to electric propulsion, the authors of Roland Berger's study have a clear role for hydrogen in solving sustainable aviation problems and recommend that managers allocate resources to ensure that its potential is realized [13, 14].

3.3 Facts and Figures

In total the aviation industry contributes about 2% to the total amount of all CO2 emissions produced across the globe [5].

It has a share of 12% in CO2 emissions from when we are taking in concern regarding the total of emission rate out of all transport mediums. [6].

From "Fig. 3," when we closely examine graph, we can identify that from the year 1990 till 2020 the emission rate was nearly a doubled figure when comparing with the figures from 1990. From that we can identify the impact of aircraft industry across the globe and the increased mobility through air. As we closely look into the figure, we can find that there is a uniformity in the emission rate from the year 2005 till the year 2017. As a result of technological revolution and huge innovational changes occurred to the aircraft industries at this period of time, the emission rate was controlled or regulated

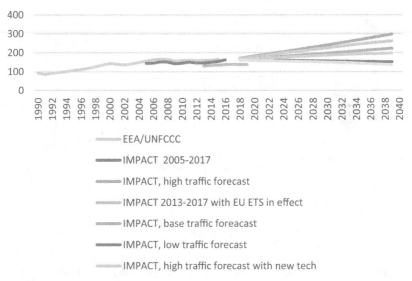

Fig. 3. Emissions in the EU over time (EU aviation report 2019).

with the necessary set of standards which reflected in a moderate rate of emission rate when compared to the other factors causing emission.

4 Analysis and Comparison

Comparing between 3 content EU, US and AU show the difference of CO2 percentage for each content and the universal indicators.

4.1 Comparison Between EU and US

Comparing emission data from the U.S and E.U, the U.S has 10% more emissions (180MT vs 200MT). The US also has the biggest aviation industry. Since U.S aviation policies are more favorable to the aviation parameters there are no particular set of standards as we are comparing with the E.U

The E.U has been working on limiting emissions by implementing the Emissions Trading System (ETS) [7]. Each airline operator receives a set amount of free, tradeable emission allowances in addition to which they can buy more at an auction. This allows airlines to operate at maximum capacity without negatively affecting the environment too much and making compromises possible in special cases.

The U.S has stated in 2019 that it has been implementing regulations for aircrafts too, but at a slower pace [8].

4.2 Comparison Between EU and Australia

Compared to the E.U, Australia has a relatively small aviation market which emits about 24MT (vs 180MT (**metric tons**) EU).

Similar to the E.U, Australia has been making efforts for regulation since the year 2012 with the release of their Action Plan. They are also partaking in the Carbon Offsetting and Reduction Scheme for International Aviation (CORSIA) proposed by the International Civil Aviation Organization (ICAO) similarly to the E.U. Start of the phased implementation is projected to 2021 [9].

There also have been efforts to make airports carbon-neutral which has already seen success in some places.

4.3 Universal Indicators Followed in the US

Until recently, the U.S government didn't make any steps in regulating Aircraft emissions. Until mid-2020, the market was completely unregulated. Because of that, airlines have seen an increase in fuel consumption paired with diminishing increases in fuel efficiency. It took several years and lawsuits for the U.S government to finally start taking action.

4.4 Universal Indicators Followed in Australia

The Australian government has been implementing measures since the introduction of the 2012 Action Plan. They are also partaking in the CORSIA plan with planned implementation starting in 2021. They plan to gradually improve all parts of the aviation industry including Air Traffic Management and Airports [10–12]. They already have deployed some measures such as renewing their fleet to use the latest advances in technologies or investing into research and market development of sustainable biofuels 16.

5 Proposal Part

In this part its fuscous in some conclusion from the survey and analysis for future. The aircraft traffic tries keep increasing of emissions,

5.1 Findings and Observations

From our research and analysis, we have come to a few conclusions and projections for the future. Totally aircraft contribute only very small percentage to the total amount of human-induced emissions, 2% from recent observations. It has a share of 12% in emissions from all transport (Fig. 4).

Aircraft traffic is projected to keep increasing in volume, following the trend of over a 40% increase compared to the 2005 levels. The trend also keeps accelerating, projected to an additional 60% or more increase in traffic and emissions going into the year 2032.

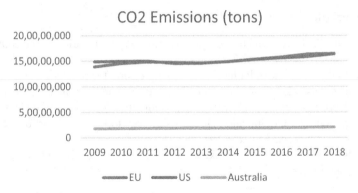

Fig. 4. Comparison on the basis of CO2 emissions (own elaboration).

Up until recently, there was little work done to implement an international standard. Many countries, including the US, did not have any regulations regarding aircraft emissions up until now. It is crucial that countries collaborate and make an effort to unify the industry and its regulations for healthy grow.

The CORSIA scheme proposed by the ICAO is set to begin its gradual implementation in the year 2021 following complete implementation by the year 2028. Their proposals, which aims to reduce emissions and other environmental hazards from aircraft, is deemed dated by some. That is mainly because today's aircrafts are already meeting their limits which they proposed a few years by default. Their main aim is to keep aircraft emissions at 2020 levels while still allowing for growth of the industry. The main areas of optimization are novel fuels, modern aircraft, carbon-neutral airports and carbon offset schemes.

Currently more than 70 countries are participating including Australia, all EU member countries and recently the US.

The initiative to increase fuel efficiency won't be enough to offset the continuously accelerating grow of the industry. Alternative methods such as biofuels from sustainable sources or significant advances in technologies are needed to make the industry carbon-neutral.

The E.U has been probably the most efficient in controlling emissions and other environmental factors. It is already using its ETS to regulate emissions. It's also closely working together with international organizations to help create a plan.

Australia is also already efficient in regulating its aircraft emissions by starting implementation of the system back in the year 2012. They also have multiple voluntary running initiatives to make their airports carbon-neutral and are actively investing into research and development of alternative biofuels together with the facilities and infrastructure needed for it [17, 19].

The US has not up until recently, despite having the biggest aviation market, been working together with the U.N. on its regulations plan for aircraft and shipping markets. That resulted in an uncontrolled market for a considerable amount of time which will take some effort to clean up.

5.2 Discussions and Proposals

Despite long periods of no action, in the recent year's efforts to regulate the aircraft industry have been put forward with some countries taking the lead and some falling behind.

Currently there are no universal standards and also no global ETS. Standards are being worked on and their implementation already started in some countries. A global ETS is not yet implemented.

The focus currently is on the implementation of the existing CORSIA program with many (over 90% of the market) countries participating. Some countries which for example have a small aviation industry can be excluded from this program).

Another area of optimization is a global ETS. This system is already applied in some countries and regions. At the moment the biggest market is the EU.

To reduce other negative factors (such as noise pollution), regulations should be developed and applied. There are also no regulations except general noise regulations. These are likely not suited for a situation like an airport, where the noise is very frequent.

5.3 Results

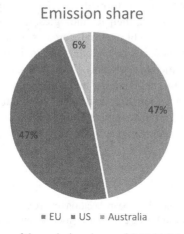

Fig. 5. Graphic representation of the emission shares of E.U, U.S & Australia (own elaboration).

As from the results obtained from our research indicates the emission share of Australia is lower (6%) when comparing with the other two regions such as E.U and U.S. Which clearly indicates that from the "Fig. 5", Australian aircraft authority implemented strong measures to regulate the traffic and closely kept monitoring the factors like emission rate, sound pollution and other factors caused by the aircrafts which resulting in there growth in aircraft industries. Similarly, E.U had set up various schemes and regulations to control the air traffic and to put a control over the factors causing environmental damages. As far as concerned, U.S has recently agreed to draw some attention regarding the aircraft emissions and the tremendous increase in their air traffic as a result we can expect that in near future U.S will come up with an authority to govern the air traffic and environmental hazards caused by aircrafts.

Recent developments and discoveries in engine and biofuel technology coupled together with a global ETS alongside improvements in places such as airports, production facilities e.g. have shown that the targets set by the CORSIA project are achievable and being worked on. These achievements can make a huge impact in terms reducing the level of pollution and to restore the environment.

Other factors (such as noise) are not being effectively regulated (except general regulations) in most places yet but are also being taken into account in the recent years with research showing them being significant factors in general wellbeing and therefore health.

6 Conclusion

Our conclusion is that the authorities should focus on the implementation of global systems for ease of tracking and trading emissions. From the above study we understood that the world is already moving on a faster pace on terms of technology advancement and the aircraft industry across the globe is experiencing strong innovational changes. In addition, innovation in technology and approaches are essential to redefining mobility. Across the world, consensus is being formed and countries are gradually implementing new regulations and innovating their technologies. Cutting-edge technology, such as autonomous devices and ultralight materials, creates opportunities to transform the mobility system by enabling new business models and mobility services. Innovations in aviation industry such as artificial intelligence, biometrics, robotics, block chain, alternative fuels and electric aircraft are booming in the market. Aviation is therefore ideally positioned to support the innovation discourse and its potential impacts on new mobility. After that all focus should be shifted to implementing and enforcing so-called regulations using data from the global systems to reach the projected milestones.

References

1. European Environment Agency, European Aviation Environmental Report 2019. https://ec.eur opa.eu/transport/sites/transport/files/2019-aviation-environmental-report.pdf. ISBN: 978–92-9210-214-2
2. EDF.org (Environmental defense fund). Reducing aviation's climate impact. https://www.edf.org/climate/aviation
3. Australian Government- Department of Infrastructure, Transport, Regional Development and Communications
4. Jakubiak, M.: Environmental impact of air transport - case study of Krakow Airport-2015
5. ICAO – Uniting Aviation a United Nations Specialized Agency
6. European Union, European Aviation Environment Report
7. EIA – U.S. Energy Information Administration
8. Russell, G.: Air services .Environment_Strategy_2011–16
9. Commonwealth of Australia, Managing the Carbon Footprint of Australian Aviation 2017
10. Vajdová, I.: Environmental Impact of Burning Composite Materials Used in Aircraft Construction on the Air - 2019

11. Pačaiová, H., Oravec, M., Šmelko, M., Lipovský, P., Forrai, F.: Extra low frequency magnetic fields of welding machines and personal safety - 2018. J. Electr. Eng. Roč. **69**(6), 493–496 (2018). ISSN: 1335-3632

12. Hovanec, M., Pačaiová, H., Hrozek, F., Varga, M.: Proactive ergonomics based on digitalization using 3D scanning and workplace modeling in texnomatix jack with augmented reality - 2014. Our Sea Int. J. Marit. Sci. Technol. **61**(1–2), 22–26 (2014). ISSN: 0469–6255, Spôsob prístupu: http://hrcak.srce.hr/index.php?show=toc&id_broj=9924&lang=en

13. Al-Rabeei, S.A.S., et al.: Enhancing the Aircraft maintenance management process for increasing safety. In: EAI MMS 2020: 5th EAI International Conference on Management of Manufacturing Systems, pp. 1–13. Springer Nature, Cham (Švajčiarsko) (2020)

14. Procházka, J.: ZeroAvia chce vodíkom zmazať ekologický dlh lietania. https://techbox.dennikn.sk/zeroavia-chce-vodikovymi-lietadlami-prekonat-ekologicky-dlh-lietania/ (2019). Techobox 15

15. Thomson, R.: Hydrogen: a future fuel for aviation? https://www.rolandberger.com/en/Insights/Publications/Hydrogen-A-future-fuel-for-aviation.html (2020)

16. Macintosh, A., Wallace, L.: International aviation emissions to2025: Can emissions be stabilised without restricting demand? Energy Policy 37(1) (2009). ISSN: 264–273 0301 4215

17. Blakey, S., Rye, L., Wilson, C.W.: Aviation gas turbine alternative fuels: a review. Combust. Inst. **33**(2), 2863–2885 (2011). ISSN: 1540–7489

18. Wangai, A., Kale, U., Kinzhikeyev, S.: An application of impact calculation method in transport **35**(4), 435–44 (2020) https://doi.org/10.3846/transport.2020.13909. ISSN: 1648–4142/eISSN: 1648–3480

19. Ekici, S., Sohret, Y., Karakoc, T.H.: Performance evaluation parameters for turbojet engines, J. Aviation **1**(1) (2017). ISSN: 2564–8004

Smart UAV Monitoring System for Parking Supervision

Goran Jausevac[1] ⓘ, Dalibor Dobrilovic[2] ⓘ, Vladimir Brtka[2] ⓘ,
Gordana Jotanovic[1] ⓘ, Dragan Perakovic[3](✉) ⓘ, and Zeljko Stojanov[2] ⓘ

[1] Faculty of Transport and Traffic Engineering, University of East Sarajevo,
Doboj, Bosnia and Herzegovina
{goran.jausevac,gordana.jotanovic}@sf.ues.rs.ba
[2] Technical Faculty "Mihajlo Pupin" Zrenjanin, University of Novi Sad, Zrenjanin, Serbia
{dalibor.dobrilovic,zeljko.stojanov}@uns.ac.rs,
vbrtka@tfzr.uns.ac.rs
[3] Faculty of Transport and Traffic Sciences, University of Zagreb, Zagreb, Croatia
dperakovic@fpz.unizg.hr

Abstract. Unmanned Aerial Vehicles (UAVs), or drones, are used in the field of remote collection of images at the time of flight. They can also detect irregularities in vehicle parking and issue fines in case of parking violations. The parking monitoring system uses real-time visual information. In this paper, the proposed solution is for real-time monitoring of areas and detecting irregularities in-vehicle parking using a fleet of drones. In this study, a camera mounted on UAVs applies for taking pictures of public areas at predetermined points. For monitoring of area will be used Observer UAVs while for detection will be used, Inspector UAVs. Visual information collected with UAVs is used to detect irregularities in vehicle parking, while the processing of collected data is performed by an artificial neural network.

Keywords: Unmanned Aerial Vehicles (UAV) · Fleet of UAVs · Surveillance · Observer UAVs · Inspector UAVs · Convolutional neural networks · Deep learning · Tensorflow · Keras

1 Introduction

The increase in the number of vehicles in urban areas is one of the biggest problems that city administrations face today. The increase in the number of vehicles causes a problem of parking space. Very often, the public areas are used for parking the vehicles. One of the possible solutions is to monitor public areas with a fleet of Unmanned Aerial Vehicles to prevent this.

Unmanned Aerial Vehicles (UAVs) or drones have numerous applications in the urban world today. They can be used in various human life areas, for example, for delivery, surveillance, professional photography, traffic regulation, disaster relief, safety, and the list is growing daily. The term unmanned aerial vehicle has a broad meaning; it

© ICST Institute for Computer Sciences, Social Informatics and Telecommunications Engineering 2021
Published by Springer Nature Switzerland AG 2021. All Rights Reserved
D. Perakovic and L. Knapcikova (Eds.): FABULOUS 2021, LNICST 382, pp. 240–253, 2021.
https://doi.org/10.1007/978-3-030-78459-1_18

includes all UAVs, regardless of whether they are controlled remotely - RPAS (system of remotely piloted aircraft) or aircraft with a certain level of autonomy. The word unmanned aerial vehicle has the same meaning as the abbreviation UAS (Unmanned Aircraft System), which means combining an unmanned aerial vehicle and the system required to operate it [1–3]. Earlier, UAVs were mostly used only for military purposes until the advent of quadcopters, when they became increasingly popular and easily accessible to the civilian community. The drone industry began to develop rapidly, and there was room for many innovations and adaptations of UAVs to the common man. Today, UAVs are becoming increasingly popular. In the United States, the Federal Aviation Administration (FAA) has projected that the number of small hobby UAVs will increase from an estimated 1.1 million in 2017 to 2.4 million by 2022 [4]. UAVs can be classified into different types based on their design, size, cost, and flying mechanism. Among the existing types, quadrotors or quadrocopters are especially popular because of their simple design, small size, low cost, greater agility, and the ability to hover in place [5]. Low-cost quadrotors are increasingly used in various applications such as surveillance and monitoring, search and rescue operations, geographic mapping, photography and imaging, wildlife exploration and management, media coverage of public events, remote reading for agricultural applications, and air package delivery [6–9].

The potential application of UAVs is to address the problem of illegal parking in public areas. UAVs can monitor public areas, identify and locate objects (vehicles) parked in a public area. For the mentioned application of UAVs to become operational, it is necessary to create a system with UAVs that use Artificial Intelligence and Machine Learning algorithms. On that basis, we perform continuous monitoring of the public area. Designing a system architecture in which UAVs would fly predefined trajectories and coordinating a network of UAVs to cover urban areas is not an easy task.

This paper proposes a prototype model that solves the problem of observing and supervising UAVs' predefined trajectories and communication between UAVs in urban environments where there are static and dynamic obstacles. Finally, the paper presents a prototype system model with the application of the offered solution. We proceed as follows. Section 2 provides an overview of related works. The architecture of a proposed system for monitoring and identifying illegally parked vehicles in public areas is present in Sect. 3. Section 4 presents the implementation of the proposed system in a specific environment. The study was partially carried out in terms of recognizing the situation from images taken with UAVs. Finally, we present our conclusions and reference to future research in Sect. 5.

2 Related Work

The possible use of UAVs is to solve traffic problems in urban areas. Urban areas often consist of several square kilometers. To be able to monitor these areas, as well as due to the flight duration of commercial UAVs, it is necessary to use more UAVs for this task. Working in groups to perform tasks is often found in nature, such as swarms of bees, flocks of birds, herds of cattle, packs of wolves, and fish flocks. Each of the mentioned groups performs group work to perform tasks as efficiently as possible. By applying this analogy to UAVs, we can perform multiple chores in the shortest time [10–12]. However, using a fleet of UAVs to perform a task is only part of the problem. Secure coordination of many UAVs with their autonomy in performing tasks is a topic that has interested many researchers [11–13]. There are several algorithms in use for the automatic guidance of UAVs. The application of these algorithms allows UAVs autonomy [14–17].

To use UAVs in area detection and monitoring, we must first create a secure and reliable network in which drones can flyundisturbed and send images to base. The most often used networks for the communication of drones with the base are WiFi and LTE networks, whose security in data transfer is described in [18]. The application of homogeneous networks in drone communication is presented in papers [9, 19]. In addition to homogeneous networks, there is also a interest in heterogeneous networks, where papers [20–22] present the problems and advantages of using both networks to obtain the most reliable communication between UAVs and infrastructure, and UAVs with UAVs.

According to the research at Barry University [23], parking vehicles becomes a big problem because there is often a shortage of free parking spaces. The lack of parking lots often is caused by people's improper parking of their vehicles and unregistered vehicles parked in reserved places. The study explains how automated drone surveillance applies to detect unauthorized parking at Barry University.

A real-time motion coordination and collision system for the drone fleet is presented in [5]. The system uses UAV geographic locations to successfully detect static and moving obstacles as well as to predict and avoid them: (1) UAV-UAV collisions, (2) UAV-static-obstacle collisions, and (3) UAV-obstacle collisions in a walk. The proposed system's characteristic is the ability to predict the risk of collisions in real-time and find the best ways to avoid predicted collisions to ensure the entire fleet's safety. The presented system generates efficient UAV routes and is suitable for densely populated, i.e., flying zones in urban areas.

A scientific research data model for detecting empty street parking spaces in city road networks based on data provided by cameras located on the vehicle is presented in [24]. The convolutional neural network was trained and evaluated using images from a moving camera. After processing, the images are converted into appropriate matrices to save only useful information for detecting an empty parking space on the street. In terms of structural parameters and learning parameters, the optimized convolutional network gave predictions for detecting empty parking spaces on the street with an average accuracy of about 90%.

According to [25], the proposed system describes an unmanned aerial vehicle that detects a free parking space to guide car parking and to reduce parking attendants' workload. These experiments show that UAVs can detect free parking lots, but the software used in these experiments still needs improvement.

3   System Architecture

In the Smart UAV Monitoring system for Parking Supervision (SmartUAV-PS), UAVs operate to monitor an urban region to prevent illegal parking in public areas. The system is based on a centralized architecture. Due to the use of many UAVs in the system, their price will play a significant role in the complete system's value. We transferred all data processing to the Control Center, which we equipped with a high-performance server, to minimize the necessary equipment for UAVs. Furthermore, with commercial UAVs, the equipment on it plays a significant role in forming their price. Based on the fact that we have centralized data processing and the management of UAVs, we can call this system centralized.

Architecture of SmartUAV-PS consists of (see Fig. 1):

1 Fleet of UAV's
2 Communication system

    2a Gateways
    2b Network Infrastructure
    2c UAV docking stations

3 Control Center

    3a Control server
    3b Application server
    3c Datastorage

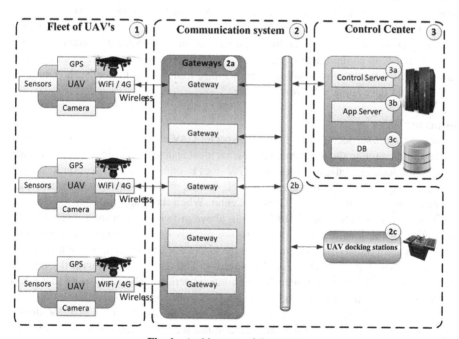

Fig. 1. Architecture of the system.

An explanation of Fig. 1 in more detail follows in the next sections.

3.1   Key Components of the System

A fleet of UAV's (1) refers to a group of three or more UAV's working together to achieve the same goal. The SmartUAV-PS consists of a fleet of UAV's that communicate with the Control Center to detect and identify improperly parked vehicles. The system is automated and operates with the help of Observer UAVs and Inspector UAVs. The Observer UAVs allow vehicle detection, while vehicle identification executes with the Inspector UAVs.

Observer UAVs

The purpose of Observer UAVs is an observation of public areas. A take-off of Observers performs according to a predetermined schedule. Observer UAVs move along defined paths, at altitudes of 30 to 70 m above the ground. On the one route, can be deployed several Observer UAVs. Those UAVs take in turns, one by one, and the time difference in starting the UAV depends on the number of UAVs deployed in a specific route. A higher altitude is necessary to avoid UAV detection and reduce the number of static obstacles while designing the UAV trajectory. Avoiding the detection of Observer UAVs is essential so that the vehicle owner would not drive the vehicle from the location when he sees the UAV. Observer UAVs take images of the monitored area's current state at the defined locations. After capturing images, the Observer UAV sends them via a wireless network to the Control Center. The Observer UAV continues its route to the next defined location, or if it is the end of the route, it flies to the UAV docking station where it has the battery recharge and flight report upload to the Control server (4). The Observer UAVs have the following configuration: GPS module, optional sensors for obstacle avoidance, Wi-Fi, LTE (4G) or both communication modules (depending on network infrastructure), and camera for image capturing and low latency image transfer. Additionally, the Observer UAVs should have support for route tracing.

Inspector UAVs

In the case of the suspect traffic situation, Inspector UAV is activated. Inspector UAV has the task of examining the location where the incident is detected. Using the location and route to the location data, the Inspector UAV goes to one or more inspection locations, where it takes video and image captures. He arrives at the position in a dynamically defined trajectory formed in the Control Center. When the Inspector UAV reaches the position, it descends to a height of 3 to 5 m above ground to perform a more detailed inspection of the location. Location snapshot records on SD storage. After finishing inspection at all defined areas, it returns to the UAVs docking station, where he uploads the data, repost logs, and recharge the batteries. The data collected with the help of Inspector UAV are used to initiate further forensic actions. The analysis of these data is proposed in the paper [26]. The Inspector UAV configuration is similar to Observer UAVs. Besides GPS, communication modules, and sensors, this type of UAV should support route tracing and camera (high resolution) for image and video capturing and SD storage for captured images.

Control Center

The Control Center (3) is the brain of the SmartUAV-PS. The elements of the Control

Center are: the Control server (3a), the Application server (3b), and Datastorage (3c). Besides UAVs' coordination, the Control server receives data from the UAVs, stores data in a database, performs analyses with machine learning algorithms, and performs further processing. It should have high data processing abilities to process images and process algorithms for defining UAV's routes.

The Control server should be with a high-performance data processing capability to process images in a reasonable time. The Control server, located in the Control Center, receives the Observer UAV data stores and processes it. If a situation is detected, it gives the instructions to the Inspector UAV to check the location. Based on the recording from the Inspector UAVs, the vehicle is identified in the Control Center based on registration plates to perform further processing.

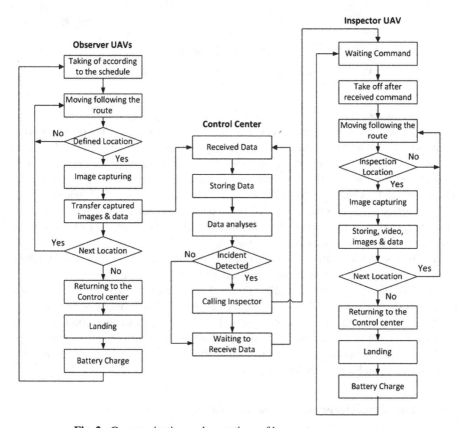

Fig. 2. Communication and operations of key system components.

Communication, relationships, and operations of the critical components of SmartUAV-PS through the algorithm are presented at Fig. 2.

3.2 Communication Components of the System

Generally, in multi UAV networks, there are two types of communication. These two networking modes are UAV-to-UAV (U2U) and UAV-to-Infrastructure (U2I). The design of the public areas monitoring and surveillance system is oriented as a UAV-to-Infrastructure (U2I) because communication between the UAVs manages with the assistance of a Control Server (3a) located in the Control Center (3) (see Fig. 3).

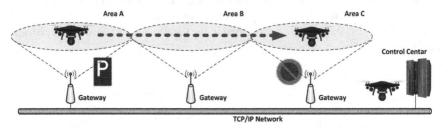

Fig. 3. The network infrastructure with the roaming UAVs.

The gateways (2a) have an essential role in maintaining UAVs' connection with the Control Center. Considering the UAVs' mobility, their aerial path in the urban environments with the numerous obstacles, the real image transfer from the Observer UAVs' to the Control Center is challenging. Also, considering the location of the system deployment and terrain configuration, the network infrastructure should have support for roaming in homogenous networks (only Wi-Fi, only LTE) presented in [22] or heterogeneous (hybrid) networks as presented in [20, 27]. To ensure as much reliable transfer of captured images as possible, support for MPTCP (MultiPath TCP), primarily on UAVs but in the rest of the system, should be considered.

The UAVs docking station (2c) is the place that is used for UAVs take-off and landing, battery charging, and communication with the Control Center (see Fig. 4).

The UAV docking station is a fully automated system that serves UAVs. The station is a precisely specified place for safe vertical take-off and landing of UAVs. In addition to this function, it should allow fast recharge of UAVs batteries, establish communication between the Control Center and the UAV, and maintain their airworthiness. It would be desirable for the proposed system to use static stations with a wired connection to the Control Center and electricity infrastructure.

3.3 Artificial Intelligence Components of Control Center

The image sent from UAVs to the Control Center is analyzed using the Convolutional Neural Network (CNN) to detect the suspect traffic situation in public areas. Role of CNN is to classify the traffic situation. The research described in this paper relies on previous research results[29, 30], as well as on a specific original case of classifying the traffic situations [31]. Compared to the previous research, the difference reflects the application of CNN in the context of a broader system that should provide Situational Awareness (SA) in the traffic environment. The broad definition of SA implies the case when an

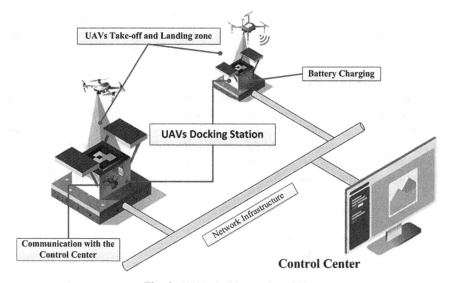

Fig. 4. UAVs docking station [28].

entity, whether human or machine, develops and maintains an understanding of events in the environment and the possible implications of those events. As in [32], SA has explored many operational contexts, including military settings, surface transportation, aviation, maritime, sport, healthcare/medicine, and process control. A generally accepted definition of SA comes from [33]: "perception of elements in the environment within a volume of time and space, the comprehension of their meaning, and the projection of their status soon".

The same author also introduced a three-level model of SA [34]:

- L1, perception of the elements in the environment,
- L2, comprehension of their meaning,
- L3, projection of future system states.

Figure 5 shows a simplified three-level SA model, which includes only the elements relevant to this research.

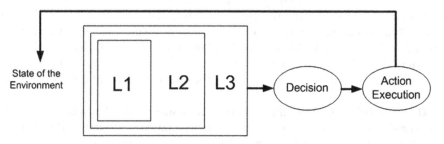

Fig. 5. Simplified three-level model of SA.

CNN application performs in L1, which is part of L2, and consequently L3, so it is primarily about the perception of objects in environment and less about the comprehension of their meaning. Projection of the future system states will be tackled in further investigations.

The initial results of the UAV application project in traffic control are presented in [31], specifically in the monitoring of particularly hazardous intersections in urban areas with properly or non-properly parked vehicles. Data were collected by recording a real situation using a camera mounted on UAVs. The experiments were conducted on a Tensorflow/Keras platform. The data sample was formed by image augmentation and was small in size: 40 images, classified into two classes: traffic situation OK/notOK. After multiple experiments, initial results were achieved by following CNN architecture:

1. Convolution2D (kernel = 64, kernel_size = (3, 3), activation = 'relu')
2. MaxPooling2D (pool_size = (2, 2))
3. Dense (164, activation = 'relu')
4. Dense (1, activation = 'sigmoid')

In previous experiments, images were down-scaled to 255-Gy 400p by 225p, but the learning process was pretty time-consuming. Given the high consumption of resources, we have conducted several case studies, and one of them is presented in the text that follows.

4 Case Study

The case study was conducted in the city of Doboj (Bosnia and Herzegovina). Doboj is a city under 100,000 inhabitants with many public areas. These areas usually are used as parking spaces. These irregularities in public areas are legally punishable and execute by the Communal Police department, which functions within the city administration. The area of the city of Doboj is 648 km^2, of which about 10 km^2 is the area of the city settlement of Doboj [35]. Because it is a large space, surveillance area needs to be separated into sectors. Separation into the sectors is defined considering UAVs' characteristics (max range, max flight speed, max flight length, battery capacity, etc.). In sectors, air corridors for UAVs based on precisely defined critical points would be formed. For our experiment, we chose Vojvode Mišića street in Doboj, where we defined five critical points to record for a case study. The image-taking points are determined based on the observed irregularities in public areas within this street and the Faculty of Transport and Traffic Engineering proximity, where Gateway's location is to achieve wireless communication with UAVs. For the recording, we used three DJI Mavic Air 2 commercial UAVs. Two UAVs were used as Observer UAVs, while one UAV uses as Inspector UAVs. UAVs trajectory was defined from the Control Center's to the observed street and back (see Fig. 6). Figure 6 was processed using the tools of the Google Earth application.

The chosen place for the Control Center is the building of the Directorate for Development and Construction of the City. That location is chosen for Control Center because it is in the center of the city zone and has all necessary infrastructure. This location of the Control Center is optimal for the implementation of SmartUAV-PS in the city of Doboj.

Fig. 6. Defined UAVs trajectory.

For the case study, we performed four flights according to a defined trajectory. Recording of images in defined points on this trajectory performs from a height of 5 to 30 m above the ground.

4.1 Results and Discussion

A previous case study showed significant problems with the use of UAVs, such as the impact of weather conditions, the problem of obstacles, the technical limitations of UAVs, and battery life. Nevertheless, the proposed concept is acceptable from the point of view of UAV operation and communication with the Control Center. Wireless communication using gateways and TCP/IP network infrastructure proved to be successful.

A special problem is collecting images because their number should be sufficient for the neural network's successful training. This is a significant problem because it is impossible to use at least three UAVs in a more extended period due to financial and safety reasons and legal regulations.

However, the previously proposed CNN architecture requires excessive resources: the accuracy on the training set was 0.90625, while the accuracy on the test set was 0.875. High time/memory consumption is not acceptable in applying the SA model, so the research presented in this paper refers to additional down-scaling of images. The system's rapid response is necessary because the UAVs' fleet on the circular path shown in the previous part of the paper will transfer the data to the server, where further training of CNN is performed. It is estimated that the system needs to react within a maximum of a few tens of minutes, so CNN training must be fast, given that drone cameras will collect a large number of images.

In previous applications, image sizes used for CNN training range from the recommended 32 by 32p, 96 by 96p, or 128 by 128p, to 512 by 512p. Of course, higher resolutions are possible, but these cases are rare. Also, it is possible to use more channels (e.g., 3 for RGB components), which further increases the training time. In this case, experiments were performed on grayscale images for the following resolutions: 32 by 32p, 96 by 96p, 128 by 128p, and 256 by 256p. Also, the number of epochs was varied, and the validation of the achieved result was performed using accuracy. Results are summarized in the following table (Table 1).

Table 1. Experiments summary

Id	Resolution/Epochs	Training set accuracy	Test set accuracy
1	32 by 32p 10 epochs	0.90625	0.625
2	32 by 32p 20 epochs	0.9375	0.75
3	32 by 32p 100 epochs	0.9375	0.875
4	32 by 32p 1000 epochs	0.96875	0.875
5	32 by 32p 2000 epochs	0.96875	0.875
6	96 by 96p 10 epochs	0.5	0.5
7	128 by 128p 10 epochs	0.9375	0.75
8	128 by 128p 2000 epochs	Out of resources	Out of resources
9	128 by 128p 500 epochs	Out of resources	Out of resources
10	128 by 128p 50 epochs	0.96875	0.875
11	256 by 256p 2000 epochs	Out of resources	Out of resources

Based on the result from the previous table, it can be concluded that the image resolutions from the training set higher than 128 by 128p are not suitable because the training time is too long (measured in hours/days) on the average/advanced hardware configuration. Lower resolutions remain, but it is evident that the maximum accuracy is 0.875. This clearly points us to the case of 32 by 32p and 100 epoch of training, although it remains to check the time of training in the case of a more extensive training set, which is one of the tasks of future research. Also, the accuracy of 0.875 is not so high. So there is an additional adjustment of CNN and a better selection of elements of the training set.

5   Conclusion

The paper presents the results of the experimental application and partial implementation of a new system concept for SmartUAV-PS. The aim was to propose a basic concept of a system that ensures scalability. The proposed system's scalability reflects in the centralization of UAVs control and the application of SmartUAV-PS in image processing and machine learning application.

It has been shown that it is possible to handle a fleet of UAVs on an experimental example. Several case studies have been undertaken, one of which is described in this paper and relates to UAVs use to identify illegally parked vehicles from images collected by UAVs. The recognition task is performed using the Convolutional Neural Network

(Tensorflow/Keras). It was concluded that the image's low resolution allows successful recognition on a small dataset: Training set accuracy was 0.9375 while test set accuracy was 0.875. It is clear that the achieved accuracy is not enough, so the system must be scalable.

The presented case study confirms the applicability of the proposed concept from the point of view of network infrastructure and UAVs' role. Namely, there are two roles that drones can play. Observers are in charge of recording situations, usually from a height. If an irregularity is noticed (using CNN), the Inspector drone will be sent to the location to take further action from a lower height. This concept allows saving resources in terms of minimizing the duration of the flight, the equipment needed (batteries, cameras, network equipment), but the main contribution relates to the possibility of centralized management of the entire process and scalability.

Centralization, in this case, has several advantages: it is possible to manage multiple fleets of drones operating simultaneously in different parts of the city, even in different cities, it is possible to share resources, as well as easy upgrades of hardware components. This also impacts further upgrading the system in terms of the number of UAVs, trajectories, and resources required to implement CNN.

From all the above, it is clear that it is necessary to improve the system and perform additional research and experiments in real conditions. Further research in this area will result in additional improvements based on various experimental scenarios of possible application. Regarding the system's software architecture, further work will be directed towards implementing a layered service-oriented architecture that will provide services for different devices, systems, and users. Improvement of the system's architecture could be a module for detecting irregular situations, in-vehicle parking, and traffic. Also, algorithms for routing UAVs may be the subject of further research. In future research, business models and new value chains for the offer of services based on the application of this system's results, on the principle of offering services on the principles of the IaaS paradigm, for smaller cities up to 100,000 inhabitants will be explored. Special attention will be on researching the security challenges of applying UAVs in urban areas.

References

1. Austin, R.: Unmanned Aircraft Systems: UAVS Design, Development and Deployment. Wiley, New York (2011)
2. Rothstein, A.: Drone. Bloomsbury Publishing USA (2015)
3. Granshaw, S.I.: RPV, UAV, UAS, RPAS… or just drone? Photogram. Rec. **33**, 160–170 (2018)
4. FAA: Federal Aviation Administration: https://www.faa.gov/news/updates/. Accessed 18 Sep 2020
5. Ashraf, A., Majd, A., Troubitsyna, E.: Online path generation and navigation for swarms of UAVs. Sci. Program. **2020**, 14 (2020)
6. Ashraf, A., Majd, A., Troubitsyna, E.: Towards a realtime, collision-free motion coordination and navigation system for a UAV fleet. In: Presented at the Proceedings of the Fifth European Conference on the Engineering of Computer-Based Systems (2017)
7. Dong, X., Chen, B.M., Cai, G., Lin, H., Lee, T.H.: Development of a comprehensive software system for implementing cooperative control of multiple unmanned aerial vehicles. In: Presented at the 2009 IEEE International Conference on Control and Automation (2009)

8. Ivanovas, A., Ostreika, A., Maskeliūnas, R., Damaševičius, R., Połap, D., Woźniak, M.: Block matching based obstacle avoidance for unmanned aerial vehicle. In: Presented at the International Conference on Artificial Intelligence and Soft Computing (2018)

9. Boccadoro, P., Striccoli, D., Grieco, L.A.: Internet of Drones: a Survey on Communications, Technologies, Protocols, Architectures and Services (2020). arXiv:2007.12611

10. Pajares, G.: Overview and current status of remote sensing applications based on unmanned aerial vehicles (UAVs). Photogramm. Eng. Remote. Sens. **81**, 281–330 (2015)

11. Bürkle, A., Segor, F., Kollmann, M.: Towards autonomous micro UAV swarms. J. Intell. Robot. Syst. **61**, 339–353 (2011)

12. Shim, D.H., Sastry, S.: A dynamic path generation method for a UAV swarm in the urban environment. In: Presented at the AIAA Guidance, Navigation and Control Conference and Exhibit (2008)

13. Cvitić, I., Peraković, D., Kuljanić, T.M.: Availability factors in delivery of information and communication resources to traffic system users. In: Mikulski, J. (ed.) TST 2017. CCIS, vol. 715, pp. 28–41. Springer, Cham (2017). https://doi.org/10.1007/978-3-319-66251-0_3

14. Wu, X., Xu, L., Zhen, R., Wu, X.: Biased sampling potentially guided intelligent bidirectional RRT* algorithm for UAV path planning in 3D environment. Math. Prob. Eng. **2019**, 12 (2019)

15. Majd, A., Ashraf, A., Troubitsyna, E., Daneshtalab, M.: Integrating learning, optimization, and prediction for efficient navigation of swarms of drones. In: Presented at the 2018 26th Euromicro International Conference on Parallel, Distributed and Network-based Processing (PDP) (2018)

16. Lamont, G.B., Slear, J.N., Melendez, K.: UAV swarm mission planning and routing using multi-objective evolutionary algorithms. In: Presented at the 2007 IEEE Symposium on Computational Intelligence in Multi-Criteria Decision-Making (2007)

17. de Melo, V.V., Banzhaf, W.: Drone Squadron Optimization: a novel self-adaptive algorithm for global numerical optimization. Neural Comput. Appl. **30**(10), 3117–3144 (2017). https://doi.org/10.1007/s00521-017-2881-3

18. Peraković, D., Cvitić, I., Kuljanić, T.M., Brletić, L.: Analysis of wireless routers vulnerabilities applied in the contemporary networks. In: Presented at the Proceedings of The 6th International Virtual Research Conference in Technical Disciplines (RCITD-2018) (2018)

19. Naveed, M., Qazi, S., Khawaja, B.A., Mustaqim, M.: Evaluation of video streaming capacity of UAVs with respect to channel variation in 4G-LTE Surveillance Architecture. In: Presented at the 2019 8th International Conference on Information and Communication Technologies (ICICT) (2019)

20. Mukhopadhyay, A., Hegde, R.R., Thomas, A.S.: Handover mechanisms in wireless heterogeneous telemedicine networks. In: Presented at the 2019 3rd International Conference on Computing Methodologies and Communication (ICCMC) (2019)

21. Husnjak, S., Peraković, D., Forenbacher, I.: Data traffic offload from mobile to wi-fi networks: behavioural patterns of smartphone users. Wireless Commun. Mob. Comput. **2018**, 13 (2018)

22. Jung, W.-S., Yim, J., Ko, Y.-B.: Adaptive offloading with MPTCP for unmanned aerial vehicle surveillance system. Ann. Telecommun. **73**(9–10), 613–626 (2018). https://doi.org/10.1007/s12243-018-0660-5

23. Dasilva, J., Jimenez, R., Schiller, R., Gonzalez, S.Z.: Unmanned aerial vehicle-based automobile license plate recognition system for institutional parking lots. In: Presented at the The 21st World Multi-Conference on Systemics, Cybernetics and Informatics (WMSCI 2017) Proceedings (2017)

24. Gkolias, K., Vlahogianni, E.I.: Convolutional neural networks for on-street parking space detection in urban networks. IEEE Trans. Intell. Transp. Syst. **20**, 4318–4327(2018)

25. Yuske, T., Mbaitiga, Z.: Development of drone detecting free parking space for car parking guidance. In: Presented at the 2019 International Conference on Intelligent Informatics and Biomedical Sciences (ICIIBMS) (2019)

26. Husnjak, S., Forenbacher, I., Peraković, D., Cvitić, I.: UAV forensics: DJI Mavic air non-invasive data extraction and analysis. In: EAI MMS 2020. Springer International Publishing, N/A, Cyberspace (2020). https://doi.org/10.1007/978-3-030-67241-6

27. Sharma, V., Song, F., You, I., Chao, H.-C.: Efficient management and fast handovers in software defined wireless networks using UAVs. IEEE Netw. **31**, 78–85 (2017)

28. FlytBase: FlytBase: Enterprise Drone Automation Platform. https://flytbase.com/. Accessed 10 Nov 2020

29. Wani, M.A., Bhat, F.A., Afzal, S., Khan, A.I.: Advances in Deep Learning. Springer (2020)

30. Singh, P., Manure, A.: Learn TensorFlow 2.0: Implement Machine Learning and Deep Learning Models with Python (2019)

31. Brtka, V., Jauševac, G., Jotanović, G., Stjepanović, A., Stojičić, M.: Identification of potentially hazardous traffic situations using deep learning. In: 10th International conference on Applied Internet and Information Technologies, pp. 137–140. University of Novi Sad, Technical Faculty "Mihajlo Pupin", Zrenjanin (2020)

32. Salmon, P.M., Read, G.J.M., Walker, G.H., Lenné, M.G., Stanton, N.A.: Distributed Situation Awareness in Road Transport: Theory, Measurement, and Application to Intersection Design. Routledge (2018)

33. Endsley, M.R.: Situation awareness global assessment technique (SAGAT). In: Presented at the Proceedings of the IEEE 1988 National Aerospace and Electronics Conference (1988)

34. Endsley, M.R.: Toward a theory of situation awareness in dynamic systems. Hum. Factors **37**, 32–64 (1995)

35. Doboj, G.: Odjeljenje za poslovekomunalnepolicije. https://doboj.gov.ba/bs/grad/uprava/odj eljenja/odjeljenje-za-poslove-komunalne-policije/. Accessed 05 Dec 2020

Object Detection and Mapping with Unmanned Aerial Vehicles Using Convolutional Neural Networks

Stefan Hensel[1], Marin B. Marinov[2]($\boxtimes$) (iD), and Max Schmitt[1]

[1] Department for Electrical Engineering, University of Applied Sciences Offenburg,
Badstraße 24, 77652 Offenburg, Germany
[2] Department of Electronics, Technical University of Sofia, 8, Kliment Ohridski Blvd.,
1756 Sofia, Bulgaria
mbm@tu-sofia.bg

Abstract. Significant progress has been made in the field of deep learning through intensive research over the last decade. So-called convolutional neural networks are an essential component of this research. In this type of neural network, the mathematical convolution operator is used to extract characteristics or anomalies. The purpose of this work is to investigate the extent to which it is possible in certain initial settings to input aerial recordings and flight data of Unmanned Aerial Vehicles (UAVs) in the architecture of a neural network and to detect and map an object. Using the calculated contours or dimensions of the so-called bounding boxes, the position of the objects can be determined relative to the current UAV location.

Keywords: Computer vision · Object detection · Deep learning · Convolutional neural network

1 Introduction

1.1 Motivation

A significant advancement in development due to scientific research has taken place in the field of deep learning over the past decade. The so-called convolutional neural networks (CNN) are an essential component. In this type of neural network, the mathematical convolution operator is used to extract features or abnormalities. Above all, very positive results can be found in the field of object detection using these networks. The research results in completely new, different application possibilities, all of which require analysis, whereby each application case must be based on an adapted selection of data for the training process [1].

Closely related to neural networks and their advantages for object detection is the associated mapping of objects to enable ongoing data analysis [2, 3]. Any device capable of recording, paired with an option for determining the position, can be able to carry out such a task and to put the detected objects on a local or global map.

© ICST Institute for Computer Sciences, Social Informatics and Telecommunications Engineering 2021
Published by Springer Nature Switzerland AG 2021. All Rights Reserved
D. Perakovic and L. Knapcikova (Eds.): FABULOUS 2021, LNICST 382, pp. 254–267, 2021.
https://doi.org/10.1007/978-3-030-78459-1_19

1.2 Task

This work aims to investigate to what extent it is possible, under certain starting points, to introduce aerial recordings and flight data of a UAV into the architecture of a neural network and to carry out object detection. With the help of the calculated contours, respectively dimensions of the so-called *Bounding Boxes*, the position of the objects relative to the current UAV location should be determined.

Vehicles in public parking lots should serve as objects for object detection. Despite changes in the direction of orientation and the flight altitude of the UAV, these objects should be stored with a high degree of accuracy in a global map [4].

1.3 Approach

To solve the task of detecting and mapping objects, the constant, secure flight operations of the UAV, for whose control option a separate controller is available, must first be enabled and guaranteed. A Python script must therefore be developed which is responsible for receiving the recorded image data and the associated measured values of flight parameters (e.g. positioning data, flight altitude, etc.). These should then be made accessible via the middleware ROS (Robot Operating System) for further components to solve the task.

The CNN YOLO was chosen for the detection of vehicles from aerial photographs. To make this network-aware of this type of data, an efficient training procedure is crucial. To enable this process, sufficient data for this process must be collected in advance with a successful implementation of the UAV script to enable the most robust detection possible with a high probability of detection. With the use of the measurement parameters of the UAV and the YOLO neural network, operated in the background, vehicles are ultimate to be positioned relative to the current UAV position. To solve this, the global positioning data, combined with the results of the object detection, must be included in mathematical calculations. Additional requirements (e.g. independence of the UAV's direction of orientation) are to be implemented.

2 Materials and Methods

2.1 Convolutional Neural Network

The most widespread algorithm among the deep learning algorithms is CNN, a class of artificial neural networks. Due to their impressive results in a competition for object recognition, known as the Image Net Large Scale Visual Recognition Competition in 2012, the performance of the convolution networks is steadily increasing [5].

2.1.1 Building Blocks of the CNN Architecture

The architecture of a CNN essentially consists of three types of layers:

- Convolutional Layer,
- Pooling Layer,
- Fully Connected Layer.

A typical network architecture consists of several repetitions of these types of layers. Different architectures can be created, each of which is advantageous for certain detection tasks. The convolution used in these networks is a linear operator that is used to extract features from an input image. Using a filter core and an element-wise product and summation with a tensor, which is derived from an array of the individual pixel values of the input image, an output tensor is created for each position. The entirety of all output tensors results in a so-called feature map [5].

Figure 1 shows an example of the process of convolution of an input tensor with a filter kernel, from which the feature map is created. The pooling layer represents a method for reducing the dimension of the feature maps to obtain translation independence from small displacements and distortions. Furthermore, the number of parameters to be learned is reduced below this layer. It should be noted that there are no parameters to be learned in the pooling layers [5].

The pooling layer is used to modify the output value of the next layer. This function replaces the output of the network at a certain position with a value that depends on the surrounding value neighborhood. Examples of pooling functions are [6]:

1) Max Pooling: Return of the maximum from a square region.
2) Average Pooling1: Returns the mean value from a square region.
3) L2 pooling: L2 norm from a square region.
4) Weighted Average Pooling: Returns the weighted average based on the distance from the center.

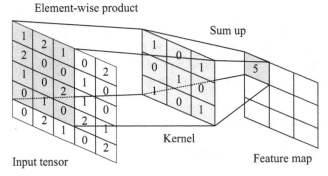

Fig. 1. Example of the process of convolution of an input tensor with a filter kernel of size 3 × 3 [5].

The fully connected layer is applied to the last, final, convolution, or pooling layer. Usually, a one-dimensional array or a one-dimensional vector is connected to form one or more fully networked layers. Each input value with a learnable weight is connected to an output. These outputs are then passed through a specific activation function, which assigns the outputs of the last fully connected layer to a probability of specific class affiliation [5].

2.1.2 CNN – Training

Training a neural network is the process of finding optimal filter cores in convolution layers and the weights that are used within the fully connected layers. For this purpose, training data sets are used which contain the so-called ground truth labels.

These ground truth labels are manually created data sets that contain the exact position of the objects in an image with the corresponding class affiliation. The training is intended to minimize the differences between the predictions and the given Ground Truth Labels [7]. There are essentially two steps that have to be carried out for this [5].

1) Forward Propagation: Calculation of the model performance using initial filter kernels and weights using the calculation of a Loss Function with the help of a training data set.
2) Backpropagation: Optimization algorithm that updates the learnable parameters (filter kernels and weights or hyperparameters) based on the values of the loss function and the gradient descent

The gradient descent is used to change the learnable parameters so that the value of the loss function is minimal. The gradient is the direction of the loss function in which it has the steepest rise. Each learnable parameter is changed so that it points in the opposite direction of the gradient [5]. The gradient results from

$$w := w - \alpha \cdot \frac{\partial L}{\partial w}, \tag{1}$$

where w stands for a trainable parameter, α for the learning rate, and L for the loss function. Since the calculation effort for the gradient of the loss function is very high, concerning the learnable parameters, a reduction is achieved using a subset of data records, the so-called mini-batches. This method is called Stochastic Gradient Descent [8].

The following Fig. 2 is intended to clarify the sequence of the gradient descent.

2.2 YOLO - You Only Look Once

The neural convolution network YOLO, which is used in this work, is a real-time capable object detector. The so-called mean average precision (mAP for short) is a standardized metric that provides information about the detection capability concerning all object categories of a neural network. Intersection over Union (IoU) is used to determine the accuracy of the object localization. If IoU is greater than a threshold value of 0.54, the object is declared as successfully detected [7, 9]. In addition to the performance of YOLO, Table 1 shows other common neuronal convolution networks. It can be seen that YOLO still achieves an mAP of 28.2%, mainly due to its short computing time of 22 ms. Although mAPs of up to 37.8% can be achieved with other networks, these require a duration of $\approx$200 ms for object detection.

YOLO is also available in the fourth version. However, since this version was only published in the course of this work, YOLOv3 will continue to be used in this work. In the following Subsect. 2.2.1, therefore, only the current structure of the neural convolution network is explained, as it is also used in this scientific work

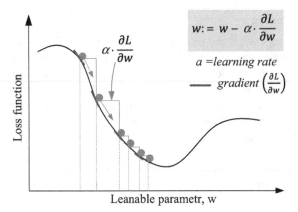

Fig. 2. Illustration of the gradient descent: The gradient of the loss function points in the direction of the steepest rise, the learnable parameters are updated in the negative direction of the gradient (adapted from [5]).

Table 1. mAP and computing time in selected neural convolutional networks [10].

Method	mAP	Time, ms
SSD321	28.0	61
DSSD321	28.0	85
R-FCN	29.9	85
SSD513	31.2	125
DSSD513	33.2	156
FPN FRCN	36.2	172
RetinaNet-50-500	32.5	73
RetinaNet-101-500	34.4	90
YOLOv3-320	28.2	22
YOLOv3-416	31.0	29

2.2.1 Network Structure

Due to a high number of localization errors as well as a low reproducibility of the detections, which the convolution network YOLO has in version 1, various changes have been made. These are mainly intended to remedy both of the problems mentioned, but maintain the classification accuracy of version 1 [11]. To increase the detection capability, various approaches are introduced in version 2, which, due to their success, will continue to be found in version 3 that follows. The neural network consists of 106 convolution layers in total. It is based solely on feature detection on its network, the so-called Darknet-53. Darknet-53 is responsible for extracting features. The entire YOLO convolution network is presented in detail in [12]. The process of detecting features of the entire YOLO network can be divided into 7 successive steps [13].

A special feature of the network is the prediction of bounding boxes on three different scale levels. This should ensure that even small objects can be detected and predicted. The center point of each feature map is responsible for predicting the object. There are three different scale entries in each feature map [10].

$$B(C + 5), \tag{2}$$

B is the number of Bounding Boxes each cell can predict. The value C, in turn, defines the attributes that each grid cell can have [14]:

- Bounding Box coordinates,
- Objectness Score: the probability that an object can be found within the bounding box,
- Class Score: Probability that the object belongs to a certain, predefined object class (e.g. car, bus).

2.3 ROS - Robot Operating System

The Robot Operating System, which uses the publisher-subscriber communication model, is available for communication and data exchange between the UAV and the computer or to enable data transfer in isolation on the latter. Due to their widespread use and frequent use in robot applications, there is a large collection of software tools and libraries available [15]. The platform offers the option of either creating complete software applications for computers, robots, or sensors yourself or using algorithms that have already been implemented. The data exchange between two nodes or users takes place via topics. The data is published via a topic, which can then be subscribed to by one or more nodes [16].

2.3.1 YOLO ROS: Real-Time Object Detection for ROS

The neural network responsible for the detection is a ROS package [17], which is made available on the GitHub development platform. This GitHub repository offers the core structure for the detection of objects in image or video data as well as the possibility to use the corresponding information of the neural network (e.g. coordinates of the bounding box) via ROS for further data processing. For complete implementation or the detection of cars, it is necessary to make changes within the corresponding directories. For this purpose, in addition to the topic of the video file, the launch file must also be supplied with the weights and the network structure of the neural network for the task of detection from a bird's eye view.

2.3.2 YOLO v4, v3, and v2 for Windows and Linux [18]

A separate GitHub repository is used for training the YOLO convolution network, which in addition to the ones for the neural network from Subsect. 2.3.1 necessary weights also provide information about the mAP. In Sect. 3.2 it is explained in more detail which settings or adaptations must be made to YOLO to obtain a solution to the task of the project [10].

2.4 Parrot Anafi

The UAV used in this work is a quadrocopter from the company "Parrot". Due to the multitude of possible uses and the additional software applications that are necessary for the operation of the UAV "Anafi", the manufacturer provides the independent application Olympe. Olympe is an interface based on the programming language Python, which offers the possibility of transmitting simulated or real UAV data to the computer [19]. To get a better overview of the UAV used, some key figures are listed below:

- Size of the ready-to-fly UAV: $175 \times 240 \times 65$ mm
- Weight: 0.320 kg
- Maximum transmission range: 4000 m
- Maximum altitude: 4500 m above sea level
- Maximum horizontal flight speed: 15 m/s
- Maximum vertical flight speed: 4 m/s
- Satellite positioning systems: GPS, GLONASS

An excerpt from the data-sheet is given to clarify the image processing sensor built into the UAV:

- Sensor: $1/24''$ CMOS
- Video resolution: optionally 4096×2160 with 24 fps, 3840×2160 with 24/25/30 fps, 1920×1080 with 24/25/30/48/50/60 fps

A controller is available to control the UAV, which, in addition to controlling it, also shows the possibility of making changes to the flight characteristics and camera settings in conjunction with a smartphone. This flight controller is characterized as follows:

- Weight: 0.386 kg
- Transmission system: Wi-Fi 802.11a/b/g/n
- Operating frequencies: 2.4–5.8 GHz
- Live stream resolution: 720p
- USB connection: USB-C (charging connection), USB-A (for connection to smartphone)

The UAV has a mechanical-electrical 3-axis image stabilizer to obtain the most stable aerial recording possible by a camera. Further technical data of the UAV or the controller can be found in the technical data sheet [20].

3 Implementation

To achieve a solution to the task, it is first necessary to transmit the flight and image data of the UAV to the computer. Only the image data is passed on to the YOLO neural network to carry out object detection. The position information, as well as the flight altitude of the UAV, are fed into an exclusively prepared Python script, which merges this data with the detected objects or the bounding box coordinates. The following Fig. 3

should clarify the flow of information, starting with the UAV. It also explains which sub-processes are processed online and offline, whereby these two terms are intended to mean a current or subsequent evaluation of the data.

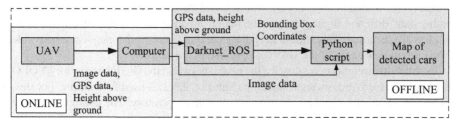

Fig. 3. Clarification of the data flow.

The following subsections go deeper into the sub-processes and are intended to clarify the respective solution approaches.

3.1   UAV Data Acquisition

To receive the flight data of the UAV, which is essentially composed of the image and position data, it is necessary to adhere to a specified flow of information. For this purpose, the data of the UAV are transmitted to the Skycontroller and then are forwarded to the computer. The flight information can be read out with the appropriate script via the bus connection (from USB Type C to USB A). It should be mentioned here that the UAV can only establish a single connection to a single software development kit (SDK for short). For this reason, it is not possible to establish a direct connection from a computer to the UAV and to maneuver it simultaneously with the Skycontroller. As in Sect. 2.4, the sample algorithms to be found online are used to create this Python script, whereby these must be significantly adapted and expanded to include the required functionalities.

3.2   YOLO Neural Network Training

To prepare the YOLO convolutional network as best as possible for the application problem at hand, a data record with ground truth labels of the cars must be created. Since no publicly accessible data sets with cars from a bird's eye view are available during the implementation of this project, these are recorded after successful implementation of the Python script from the previous Sect. 3.1 using the public parking lot of the Offenburg University of Applied Sciences.

The Visual Object Tagging Tool, or VoTT for short, from Microsoft, is used to create the Ground Truth Boxes and the corresponding Ground Truth Labels. This offers the possibility of extracting individual images from a video and drawing the cars contained therein with the appropriate label for each image. If you do this for all recorded videos, the following distributions result for the training, test, and validation data set1 is available:

- Number of training data: 350,
- Number of validation data: 100,
- Number of test data: 50.

Due to the limited number of cars available and the associated insufficient amount of training data, different flight patterns, and data from an altitude in the interval between 10–15 m are recorded. This should keep the neural network as independent as possible of the current yaw angle of the UAV and the size of the objects.

To obtain the weights necessary for the neural network, the GitHub repository YOLO v4, v3, and v2 for Windows and Linux (see Subsect. 2.3.2) is used for training. For this, it is necessary to adjust some parameters within this repository. The configuration file from

```
yolov3.cfg
```
as well as the pre-trained weights of
```
darknet53.conv.74
```

The changes that exist within the configuration file for the training step are shown below. These are carried out according to the specifications of the repository [18]:

```
batch = 64
subdivisions = 64
width = 608
height = 608
max_batches = 6000
steps = 4800, 5400
```

Since this project deals with the detection of only one single class "car", this fact must also be taken into account in all YOLO layers.

```
classes = 1
```

Furthermore, the size of the filters is adjusted before each last YOLO layer. As already in Subsect. 2.2.1 with Eq. (2), the size should be set to the value 18 due to a single class, because:

$$B(C + 5) = 3(1 + 5) = 18. \tag{3}$$

```
filters = 18
```

To indicate to the neural network, the paths in which the training and validation data are stored, a file must be created as follows. This also contains the path to a file in which the names of the classes are created. For this, the row index stands for the corresponding class that the neural network detects. The different weights that can be found every 1000 iterations are saved in the backup path.

```
classes = 1
train = data_Schmitt/train.txt
test = data_Schmitt/valid.txt
names = obj.names
backup = backup/
```

The images and the .txt files of the same name are stored in the two training and test paths. Furthermore, the following format is to be found in every .txt file, in which each bounding box is assigned a class and the coordinates of this box:

```
<object-class> <x_center> <y_center> <width> <height>
```

To start the training, the following code must be entered and confirmed in a terminal in the relevant management:

```
./darknet detector train data_Schmitt/obj.data ...
cfg/yolov3_MODIFIED.cfg darknet53.conv.74 -map
```

To avoid the problem of overfitting to the specified training data, it is possible, using the validation data, to output the mAP for the stored weights of different iteration steps. If you do this, the following values result:

Table 2. mAP after different iteration steps.

Test run	4000.weights	5000.weights	6000.weights	best.weights	final.weights
1	90.45%	87.84%	90.24%	91.86%	90.24%
2	94.05%	91.35%	93.93%	90.85%	93.93%

It can thus be seen that the mAP with the highest value is present in test run 2. Therefore, these weights are used for the detection of the vehicles.

4 Experimental Results

To achieve the best possible quality of the evaluation and to have a guideline for the implementation, this work adheres to the basic structures of the Standard for Evaluation of the Society for Evaluation e.V. [21].

During the investigations and evaluations of the results, the following questions, among others, should be answered:

- Is the amount of training data sufficient so that sufficient vehicles can be detected?
- Is the precision of the bounding boxes of the neural network sufficient to enable the position of the vehicles to be determined?
- Is the mathematical calculation process for obtaining the positions correctly?

- How precisely are the vehicle positions determined?
- Which optimization potential can be seen?
- Can this project be the basis for further research projects that deal with the detection and mapping of objects?

Since the parking lot of the Offenburg University of Applied Sciences serves as the object for the evaluation, the dimensions of the parking bays are presented in advance. (These apply to all selected scenarios):

- Width: 2.5 m,
- Length: 3.95 m,
- Distance between two parking strips: 5.45 m.

4.1 Mapping of a Section of a Parking Lot with a Stationary UAV

To investigate the mapping accuracy of the underlying mathematical algorithms, an aerial photograph of a car park section at the Offenburg University of Applied Sciences should first be carried out in this section. The UAV remains in the so-called hovering mode during the entire recording, i.e. without or with minimal movement in the x, y, or z components. The following Fig. 4 shows an aerial photograph of this situation, which has already experienced the process of object detection using the YOLO neural network. If you look at Fig. 4, a first insight must be made clear here. Due to variances in the detection and the associated entry of the bounding boxes in the image, it is the case that the horizontal and vertical lines of these boxes do not completely coincide with the vehicle contours.

Fig. 4. Presentation of the vehicle positions with the associated bounding boxes drawn by YOLO.

This results in inaccuracies in determining the vehicle. Analogously to this, Fig. 5 shows the result of entering the positions using the self-created Python script which uses mathematical algorithms from [22].

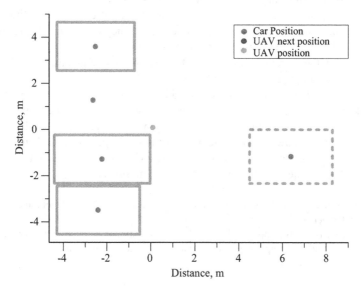

Fig. 5. Result of the vehicle identification with an entry of the drone position.

If one looks at Fig. 5 and the associated dimensions of the Bounding Boxes of the detected cars, an initial plausibility of the dimensions of these boxes can be confirmed. The motor vehicle is used at position $(x, y) = (6, 5 - 1, 3)$ to confirm the correct calculation of the coordinates of the position and the dimensions of the bounding boxes. Due to the selected starting point of the UAV directly on the parking lot marking, it is possible to determine the center of the vehicle with the coordinates just mentioned and thus to calculate $(x_{real}, y_{real}) = (7, 425, 1, 25)$, with tolerances in the determination of the car position, must be taken into account by the dimensions of the parking bay. However, since this is only an estimate, (x_{real}, y_{real}) are assumed to be actual values. This results in an uncertainty of $\left(1 - \left|\frac{6,5}{7,425}\right|\right) \cdot 100\% = 12, 45\%$ for the x component and $\left(1 - \left|\frac{-1,3}{1,25}\right|\right) \cdot 100\% = -4\%$ for the y component. Since the centers of the bounding boxes are used to determine the deviations and there is thus a dependency on the accuracy of the detection of the neural network, an increased inconsistency for the x component can be explained.

To answer all the evaluation questions dealt with at the beginning, the performance of the YOLO neural network must finally be addressed. It has been shown that the detection capability, especially (as already mentioned) with slow flight maneuvers, provides considerably more stable and robust results. To generally improve the performance of YOLO, it would be necessary to create a larger amount of training data (training, validation, and test data set as a whole) and to obtain an increase in robustness. Although the mAP is high at 94.05% (see Table 2), this value is calculated using static image data.

5 Conclusions and Future Work

The ready-to-fly drone provided the opportunity to prepare training data for the YOLO neural network. For this purpose, aerial photos of parked cars were taken, which should show the vehicles from as varied as possible angles and different flight altitudes. This procedure is intended to counteract a possible dependency on certain arrangements of the objects and to develop robust detection of the network.

Furthermore, the current behavior of YOLO was discussed and the need for a larger data set for the training process was explained.

If the results of the evaluation are included in the outlook of this work, the potential of the task can be assessed. It turns out that the question of the performance of the detection of the vehicles and the subsequent mapping works precisely within the framework of tolerances. There would be the option of not only performing all mathematical calculations offline afterward but also performing all of these filterings of the redundant results directly after the detection with a powerful, mobile computer.

Acknowledgments. The authors would like to thank the Research and Development Sector at the Technical University of Sofia for the financial support.

This research is partly supported by the Bulgarian National Science Fund in the scope of the project "Exploration the application of statistics and machine learning in electronics" under contract number КП-06-H42/1.

References

1. Al-Saffar, A.A.M., Tao, H., Talab, M.A.: Review of deep convolution neural network in image classification. In: 2017 International Conference on Radar, Antenna, Microwave, Electronics, and Telecommunications (ICRAMET), Jakarta (2017)
2. Saetchnikov, I., Tcherniavskaia, E.A., Skakun, V.V.: Object detection for unmanned aerial vehicle camera via convolutional neural networks. IEEE J. Miniaturizat. Air Space Syst. (2020)
3. Hensel, S., Marinov, M., Schmitt, M.: Experimental setup for investigation and evaluation of a mapping and localization system. In: Proceedings of the 9th FDIBA Conference - Challenges of the Digital World, Sofia, Bulgaria, 28–29 November 2019
4. Wu, Q., Zhou, Y.: Real-time object detection based on unmanned aerial vehicle. In: 2019 IEEE 8th Data-Driven Control and Learning Systems Conference (DDCLS), Dali, China (2019)
5. Yamashita, R., Nishio, M., Do, R., Togashi, K.: Convolutional neural networks: an overview and application in radiology. Insights Imaging **9**, 611–629 (2018)
6. Goodfellow, I., Bengio, Y., Courville, A.: Deep Learning. The MIT Press, Cambridge (2016)
7. Zou, Z., Shi, Z., Guo, Y., Ye, J.: Object detection in 20 years: a survey. ArXiv, p. abs/1905.05055 (2019)
8. Ioffe, S., Szegedy, C.: Batch normalization: accelerating deep network training by reducing internal covariate shift. In: ICML'15: Proceedings of the 32nd International Conference on Machine Learning, July 2015
9. Tao, J., Wang, H., Zhang, X., Li, X., Yang, H.: An object detection system based on YOLO in traffic scene. In: 2017 6th International Conference on Computer Science and Network Technology (ICCSNT), Dalian (2017)
10. Redmon, J., Farhadi, A.: YOLOv3: an incremental improvement (2018)

11. Redmon, J., Farhadi, A.: YOLO9000: better, faster, stronger. In: 2017 IEEE Conference on Computer Vision and Pattern Recognition (CVPR), Honolulu, HI (2017)
12. Zoev, I.V., Beresnev, A.P., Markov, N.G.: Convolutional neural networks of the YOLO class in computer vision systems for mobile robotic complexes. In: 2019 International Siberian Conference on Control and Communications (SIBCON), Tomsk, Russia (2019)
13. Mao, Q., Sun, H., Liu, Y., Jia, R.: Mini-YOLOv3: real-time object detector for embedded applications. IEEE Access **7**, 133529–133538 (2019)
14. Redmon, J., Divvala, S., Girshick, R., Farhadi, A.: You only look once: unified, real-time object detection. In: 2016 IEEE Conference on Computer Vision and Pattern Recognition (CVPR), Las Vegas, NV (2016)
15. Blasdel, et al.: About ROS.Version: 2020. https://www.ros.org/about-ros/
16. Quigley, M., et al.: ROS: an open-source robot operating system. In: ICRA Workshop on Open Source Software (2009)
17. Bjelonic, M.: YOLO ROS: Real-Time Object Detection for ROS, 2016–2020. https://github.com/leggedrobotics/darknet_ros
18. Redmon, B.A.: Darknet: YOLO v3 - neural network for object detection (2020). https://github.com/AlexeyAB/darknet
19. Parrot Drone SAS: Olympe - Overview (2019). https://developer.parrot.com/docs/olympe/overview.html
20. Anafi: The flying 4 K HDR camera that you can take (2020). https://www.parrot.com/assets/s3fs-public/2020-07/bd_anafi_productsheet_en_210x297_2018-06-04.pdf
21. Deutsche Gesellschaft für Evaluation e.V., Standards für Evaluationen, Köln: Redaktion: Dr. Wolfgang Beywl, Zimmermann-Medien (2002)
22. Lowhead, J.: Learning GeoSpatial Analysis with Python, 2nd edn. Packt, Birmingham (2015)

Information and Communication Architecture of the Passenger Information System on the Railway Network of the Republic of Croatia

Dragan Peraković⬤, Marko Periša⬤, Marjana Petrović⬤, Ivan Cvitić⬤,
and Petra Zorić(✉)⬤

Faculty of Transport and Traffic Sciences, University of Zagreb, Vukelićeva 4,
10000 Zagreb, Croatia
{dragan.perakovic,marko.perisa,marjana.petrovic,ivan.cvitic,
petra.zoric}@fpz.unizg.hr

Abstract. HŽ Infrastructure Ltd is a company in charge of management, maintenance, and building of railway infrastructure which is obliged to provide the user with all relevant information on the departure and arrival of trains and possible delays. There are currently 545 official places (stops and stations) on the Republic of Croatia's railway network. To implementing modern communication solutions in the function of informing passengers, it is essential to make a systematic analysis of the technical-technological ecosystem to connect all the elements and deliver information to passengers. In this paper, an analysis of the current state of telecommunication infrastructure and equipment of all official places on the Republic of Croatia's railway network is made. Based on the analyzed data, the central system's functions, the passenger information system's conceptual architecture, and the way the system communicates with the vehicle are defined. The technical-technological requirements that end users must obtain accurate and real-time information can be implemented according to the phased introduction and upgrade of the system, which is visible in the passenger information system's proposed conceptual architecture in this paper.

Keywords: Informing passengers · Telecommunication infrastructure · Internet of Things · Sensor networks

1 Introduction

List of railways lines in the Republic of Croatia is an integral part of the *Odluke Vlade Republike Hrvatske o razvrstavanju željezničkih pruga* (OG no. 03/14) [1]. According to this, the length of railway network in Republic of Croatia is 2,617 km and the lines are classified into: lines for international transport, lines for regional transport and lines for local transport.

© ICST Institute for Computer Sciences, Social Informatics and Telecommunications Engineering 2021
Published by Springer Nature Switzerland AG 2021. All Rights Reserved
D. Perakovic and L. Knapcikova (Eds.): FABULOUS 2021, LNICST 382, pp. 268–283, 2021.
https://doi.org/10.1007/978-3-030-78459-1_20

The infrastructure manager in the Republic of Croatia is HŽ Infrastructure Ltd (HŽI). According to the *Zakonu o sigurnosti i interoperabilnosti željezničkog sustava*, telematics applications for passenger traffic are a functional subsystem of the railway infrastructure, therefor they must ensure the minimum quality of service to passengers [2, 3]. Following the *Commission Regulation (EU) on the technical specification for interoperability* (No 454/2011, 1273/2013), the station manager is obliged to provide the user with train departure data at railway stations [4, 5]. In Croatia infrastructure manager acts as station manager, therefor it is the infrastructure manager responsibility to provide mentioned data.

Passenger information systems implemented on the EU railway network are based on modern information and communication (IC) solutions. The passenger information system's architecture is possible to perceive through the elements located at the station, stop or platform, and in the vehicle. The architecture is presented through four levels:

- application center,
- digital solution at the station,
- communication between train and track equipment and
- digital on-board solution.

The application center consists of applications and tools in the dispatch center, control center, ticket sales system, and information center. The digital solution at the station consists of a core network that is the network infrastructure's backbone. At that level, there is a passenger information system and other displayed elements (dispatch station, video surveillance station, ticket sales system, customer service center, and other communication equipment). Communication between the train and the track equipment consists of connection technologies (railway and distribution network) to the train by the track equipment (infrastructure). The train's digital solution consists of communication technologies for connection (LAN and Wi-Fi) of the train to the distribution network and in-vehicle technology (video surveillance and monitoring, passenger counting via sensor technology, Internet access, and other IC services).

Current research in this field represents solutions based on modern IC technologies in a smart city environment [6]. This research aims to design a system based on the concept of the Internet of Things (IoT) to provide real-time and accurate information to the system's user. Mobile applications are increasingly used in the field of providing information to system users [7]. The analysis of mobile applications' use in this study provided data on user expectations according to finding information in the user information system and the functions of the passenger information system. In the field of high-speed rail, system services bring more significant customer satisfaction and help create a socio-economic and balanced society as a whole. The development and application of newer communication networks such as 4G and 5G in the railway system enable networks with higher data and information capacities, leading to the system's more reliable operation [8].

The development and application of the LTE-R network and its introduction into railway systems in the world are shown in Fig. 1. Analysis of the application of different communication networks such as mobile communication system - railway (GSM-R), LTE-R, fifth-generation (5G), IEEE 802.11, and wireless sensor networks (WSN) have shown their capability in the operation of the Industrial IoT network [9]. In the environment of stations and stops, there is increasing use of WSN networks that can be used in object identification and applications in the environment of artificial intelligence, machine learning, and more [10]. The context of data modeling is essential from the point of view of creating and delivering real-time data to users. Forms of providing information to users are through web and mobile application services that have been increasingly used recently. In this context, it is possible to apply semantic web solutions and ontology [11].

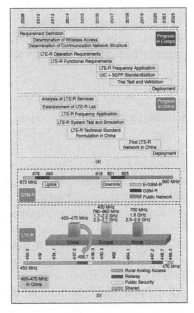

Fig. 1. Communication networks and their application in the railway system [8]

2   Analysis of the Current State of Telecommunication Infrastructure on the Railway Network in the Republic of Croatia

According to official data, there are 545 passenger stations for reception and departure of passengers on the Republic of Croatia's railway network. Each official place also contains specific technical characteristics: area for reception and departure of passengers, station/stop buildings with or without waiting rooms, the lighting of official places, number and type of tracks, the purpose of tracks, type of safety and signaling system at the railway stations, and communication infrastructure. Type of safety and signaling system are shown in Fig. 2. The figure's markings are RC – remote control, AB - Automatic block, TWT - two-way traffic, and SI - station interdependence. The communication infrastructure consists of the following elements:

- telecommunications and electronic devices,
- telephone devices and method of registration,
- radio devices,
- teleprinter and fax machines,
- types and manner of use of telecommunication lines
- receipt and dispatch of telegrams
- intercom and public address devices,
- IT devices,
- railway automatic telephone switching office and ways of intermediation, and
- telecommunication and information devices and lines.

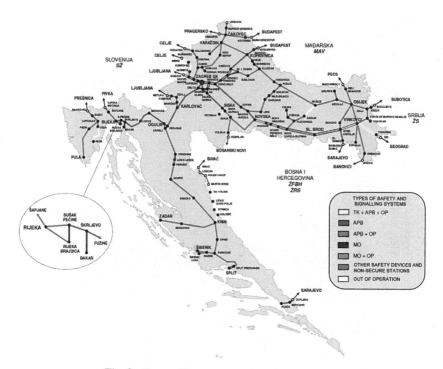

Fig. 2. Types of insurance on the railway network

The research analyzes the state of communication infrastructure for each official place: type of telephone use, type of radio, fax, teleprinter, type and method of using telecommunication lines, method of receiving and sending telegrams, intercom and public address devices, telecommunications devices, IT devices. Part of the analysis is shown in Table 1.

Train traffic, which includes signaling, regulation, reception, and dispatch of trains, and communication related to train traffic on the railway network, is managed by signal-safety devices and telecommunication devices. An overview of the types of telecommunication devices on railways network is shown in Fig. 3.

Table 1. The state of the communication infrastructure [12]

Stations	Telephone devices	Radio devices	Tele.[a] device	Types and method of use telecommunication lines	Receipt of telegram	Interphone and spiker device	IT devices	Telecommunication and information devices
Andrijevci	TT, T, R	RDV	Yes	Business line (PV) - 40-200, 41-200 Guideline - ČV 1, ČV 2 EV, SV, NEV, CDU and disp. line	e-mail	Yes	IST terminal	ŽAT-35961, ŽAT-35960, ŽAT-35969, ŽAT-35965, ŽAT-35966 (035)277-100 do 277-999
Bakar	T, R	UHF	No	PV-vod 40212 ČV-vod SV-vod	Telephone	No	IST terminal	ŽAT-54 470-478

(continued)

Table 1. (*continued*)

Stations	Telephone devices	Radio devices	Tele.[a] device	Types and method of use telecommunication lines	Receipt of telegram	Interphone and spiker device	IT devices	Telecommunication and information devices
Banova jaruga	T, inductor	Motorola Radio GP 300	No	DV - Zagreb - Novska 300-200 PV - Novska - Zagreb, 40-200,41-200,42-200 PV - Banova Jaruga - Virovitica 40-270 APB vod Lipovljani – Banova Jaruga – Kutina 60-200 SV Lipovljani – Banova Jaruga–Kutina 90-200 SV Banova Jaruga – Lipik 90-270 KV line	e-mail	Yes	IST terminal	Inductor 30–200, 40–200, 41–200, 42–200, 40–270, 60–200, 90–200, 90–270 Inductor (second) 40–200, 41–200, 42–200, 40–270 and 90–270 Inductor (signal) 90–200 Automatic ŽAT tel. 44611 Automatic HT tel. 044/892 611 Automatic ŽAT tel. 44601 Loudspeaker PC HP Compaq Pro 6305, monitor AOC LED E 2360P PC HP Compaq Pro 6305, monitor AOC LED E 2260P

Tele.[a] device – Teleprinter and telefax devices, TT - Telecommunication table, T – Telephone, R - Registrophone

The radio dispatching (RD) system represents a radio dispatching system, while some of the stations use the UHF - radio network. On lines where station staff have visual control of the condition of station spatial sections, permits (approvals) and deregistrations are given to signaling and safety devices operated by station staff. In contrast, on lines without visual control of station spatial sections' condition, station staff give permits and deregistrations by telecommunications devices (usually by telephone) in a proven manner. There is currently no automatic train protection system on the railway network. Auto-stop device (AS) - INDUSI (I60) is in use. The AS device is used to control the movement of trains on the track. According to the way it works, it belongs to the group of devices for controlling the movement of trains at one point, the so-called punctual system. The purpose of the AS device is to increase safety in railway traffic when the driver does not notice or does not take appropriate measures to reduce speed in front of the signal sign "Limited speed" or stop the train in front of the signal sign "Stop".

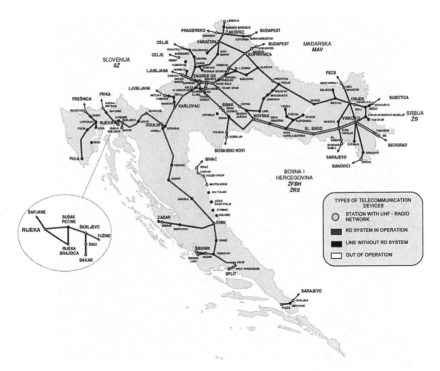

Fig. 3. Types of the telecommunication devices on railways network

According to official data, 124 stations and 132 stops are equipped with systems to provide visual information to users. Dynamic passenger information is provided via a screen at six stations. The current systems for providing information to passengers on the railway network managed by HŽI are EXOR and EK GIP-1.

IC infrastructure equipment analysis for each official position was made according to the assessment of the condition and existence of:

- passenger information systems with info boards, loudspeakers, clocks, and the manufacturer,
- cable sewers,
- concentration and connection of the official place with the railway cable,
- on-site electricity connection,
- possible components of the passenger information system.

Part of the conducted analysis is shown in Table 2. The analysis was made for all official positions (545 of them).

Table 2. Analysis of the current state of telecommunication infrastructure [12]

OP	Official place name	Status	Main stations	KM	Existing PIS	Cable canalization	Connection with official places (railway cable)	Rail cable available	Electro energetic cable
M101	DG- Savski Marof - Zagreb GK								
	Savski Marof	Main. station		446+116	no	no	yes/ STKA	1971/ good/ 5	yes
	Brdovec	Station	Savski Marof	443+800	no	no	no	nd	yes
	Zaprešić-Savska	Station	Zaprešić	441+500	no	no	no	nd	yes
	Zaprešić	Main. station		439+549	no	no	yes/ STKA	1971/ good/ 5	yes
	Podsused Stajalište	Station	Zaprešić	435+800	no	no	yes/ STKA	1971 /bed/ 1	yes
	Podsused Tvornica	Main. station		433+021	no	no	yes/ STKA	1971/ good/ 5	yes
	Gajnice	Station	Zagreb Zap.Kol	432+879	no	no	no	nd	yes
	Vrapče	Station	Zagreb Zap.Kol	431+061	no	no	yes/ STKA	1971/ bad/ 1	yes
	Kustošija	Station	Zagreb Zap.Kol	428+840	no	no	no	nd	yes
	Zagreb Zapadni Kol.	Main. station		427+584	no	yes	yes/ STKA	1971/ good/ 5	yes
	Zagreb Glavni Kol.	Main. station		424+500	EXOR/ 2002	yes	yes/ STKA	1971/ good/ 5	yes

PIS – passenger information systems, nd – No data available

3   Analysis of Transport Demand on the Railway Network of the Republic of Croatia

The analysis of transport demand on the Republic of Croatia's railway network includes passengers dispatched by long-distance, local and suburban trains based on available data (2019). An analysis of dispatched passengers by train traffic routes was made, separately for long-distance trains and local and suburban trains. The analysis showed that passengers from 498 stations and stops were dispatched in long-distance, local and suburban trains. The total number of dispatched passengers in these types of trains is 19,799,362 passengers during the 2018/2019 timetable period (TP). In the Republic of Croatia, most passengers depart from Zagreb GK station, which is expected given that most passenger trains start or end their journey at Zagreb GK station. Apart from Zagreb GK, among the first ten stations with the largest number of dispatched passengers are the stations and stops that are part of the Zagreb city-suburban traffic shown in Graph 1.

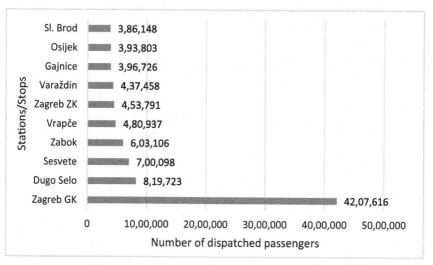

Graph 1. Stations with the highest number of dispatched passengers during 2018/2019 TP [12]

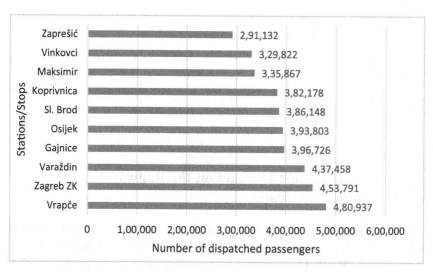

Graph 2. Top 10 stations with between 100,000 and 500,000 dispatched passengers [12]

On the Republic of Croatia's railway network, 355 passenger station dispatched between 1,000 and 100,000 passengers (Graph 2), while 66 official places dispatched less than 1,000 passengers during the 2018/2019 TP.

It is a devastating fact that 41 official places did not dispatch a single passenger based on the conducted analysis. Twenty-nine official places dispatched between 50,000 and 100,000 passengers, meaning 326 stations and stops dispatched between 1,000 and 50,000 passengers. 404 official places dispatched 4.2 million passengers, approximately equal to the number of dispatched passengers from Zagreb GK station in 2019.

A total of 1,813,083 passengers were dispatched in long-distance transport during 2018/2019 TP (Table 3).

Table 3. Passengers dispatched in long-distance transport [12]

Traffic relation	Trains per day		Number of passengers per year
Zagreb – Koprivnica GR	2		56,127
Tovarnik – Zagreb GK	4		169,290
Rijeka – Šapjane	4		31,466
Split – Zagreb GK	8		125,185
Osijek – Zagreb	4		298,569
Rijeka – Zagreb	1		4,130
Osijek – Rijeka	2		216,356
Vinkovci – Zagreb	10		696,109
Požega – Zagreb	2		8,561
Zagreb – Varaždin	2		131,778
Virovitica – Zagreb	1		37,790
Križevci – Virovitica	1		9,219
Zagreb – Bjelovar	1		24,993
Pula – Rakitovec	4		3,510
		Total:	1,813,083

The smallest number of trains was sent between Pula and Rakitovac, where trains do not run all year round. The average occupancy of long-distance trains for TP 2018/2019 is 52%, depending on the time of the year.

4 Proposal of the Conceptual Architecture of the Passenger Information System

For the passenger information system's reliable and efficient operation, the following subsystems are needed: automatic train control (ATC), automatic resolution of incident situations, timetable monitoring, ticket sales, and maintenance. According to the current

Network Status Report 2021, it can be seen that there is no ATC system [13]. The passenger information system needs to be integrated as a subsystem or module of the future operational management and traffic control center, which is a prerequisite for developing a system that will enable fully automatic traffic management.

The operational management center's goal is to achieve organization and greater efficiency of executive staff, regular traffic, reduction of train delays, more straightforward elimination of traffic disruptions, and providing information to system users. The operations center scheme is shown in Fig. 4, and the possible interaction with the passenger information system.

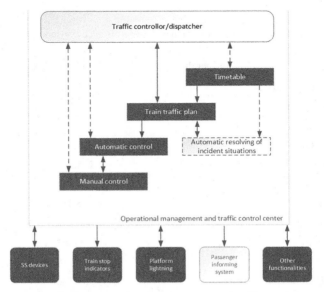

Fig. 4. Scheme of the operational management and traffic control center

Operational management and traffic control center consist of:

- system server (communication server, web server) and
- computer programs and applications to inform users.

According to the above, this includes and implies hardware equipment and devices (servers, personal computers, active and passive network equipment, etc.) and software components necessary for the passenger information system's operation. The system's operation's primary platforms include the most common operating systems such as Microsoft Windows, Linux, and operating systems for mobile devices Android, iOS, and Internet browsers for web-based applications (Google Chrome, Mozilla Firefox, etc.).

Modern solutions in this area are based on IoT technologies and sensor networks. The current state of the communication infrastructure on the railway network in the Republic of Croatia can lead to high initial costs of implementation and the complexity of integrating new systems. The advantages and opportunities that technologies, such as Cloud Computing and IoT, and modern communication and sensor networks can provide in the environment of railway infrastructure management are shown in Fig. 5. Such an approach creates a smart infrastructure within the railway system.

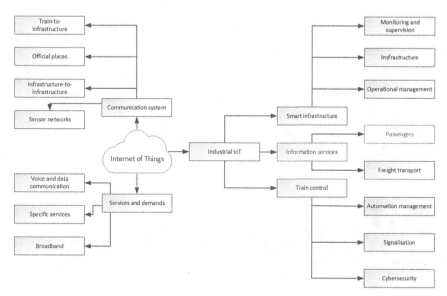

Fig. 5. Possibilities of IoT technology in the process of railway infrastructure management

The application of communication systems in railways can be divided into three functional groups: safety, management and user-oriented networks. The most common communication technologies [14]:

- train to infrastructure - GSM-R ili IEEE 802.11, LTE-R,
- Trans European Trunked RAdio (TETRA),
- Dedicated Short-Range Communications (DSRC),
- Ultra-wideband (UWB) - IEEE 802.15.4a,
- IEEE 802.11p,
- Machine-to-Machine (M2M),
- Human-Machine Interface (HMI),
- WSN,
- Ultra-High Frequency (UHF) RFID,
- Visible Light Communication (VLC),
- 3G, LTE, 5G,
- GPS.

The passenger information system is an integral part of the operational management and traffic control center. All data necessary for users' real-time information and the possibility of pre-trip information must be part of a central database. Based on the collected and analyzed all relevant data needed to define the central passenger information system's functions and elements, the conceptual architecture of the system was proposed. The conceptual architecture of the system is based on the concept of Cloud Computing and IoT sensor technology. It is an integral part of the system's central units (servers) in the operational management and traffic control center (Fig. 6).

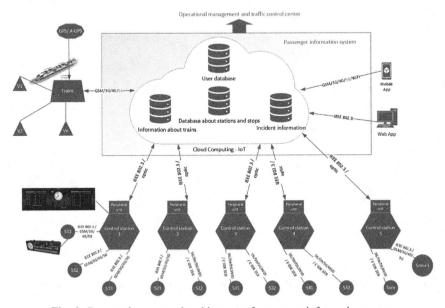

Fig. 6. Proposed conceptual architecture of passenger information system

All the data needed to inform users is in the Cloud Computing environment. Services provided via screens on official sites, web and mobile solutions can be tailored to user requirements. This option applies to people with disabilities who require adaptation of the content depending on the degree and type of damage.

Databases that are an integral part of the architecture contain data on trains, official places, and incident information. All relevant data are processed and included in appropriate applications depending on the purpose for:

- trip computers,
- information screens,
- computer applications for traffic monitoring and management,
- various web interfaces and mobile applications as well
- web servers.

Communication modes can be performed in several ways:

- as continuous real-time communication between trains and central system units (servers) during which information on the train's current status (position, status, occupancy, etc.) or other peripheral units of the system is continuously exchanged,
- as a continuous communication between information screens at stops/stations and central units of the system which exchanges all necessary data that will be displayed on information screens at stops (time until the arrival of an individual vehicle at the stop, deviations, etc.), but also the status of the information screen itself at the stop (automatic fault reporting, etc.),
- as occasional communication between the central units of the system, and trains and information screens at stations, which send various textual and/or voice notices and information on the traffic situation, intended for traffic staff or passengers,
- as an occasional communication between the central and peripheral units of the system which sends all the necessary data for the operation of the peripheral units (timetable, etc.).

In this way, the following functionalities would be enabled:

- supplying trains with all the necessary information in the shortest possible time, regardless of their current location,
- timely sending of changes in the timetables of trains in traffic, i.e., changes in the mode of traffic on the routes of individual lines (shortening, rerouting, etc.) and
- timely informing passengers on trains and at railway stations and stops about the current traffic situation or other events necessary for railway services.

Communication servers serve as a mediator in exchanging data between central and peripheral units of the system in real-time, using different protocols. Data communication should be based on mobile 3G/4G/LTE and 5G technology and wireless and wired technology (IEEE 802.11 and 802.3) in the access segment of the communication network, depending on the capabilities and technical performance of the communication infrastructure.

Web servers allow users to access web-based applications on the local network. Access via the public Internet network is possible if the servers are located in a network segment (demilitarized zone, DMZ), protected by a firewall and appropriate methods of protecting the internal communication network, and connected to an adequate connection to the Internet network.

Traffic controllors' workstations are computers through which traffic controllor in the operational management and traffic control center carry out supervision and management of overall traffic entities for which they are responsible. Workstations consist of computers, screens, and voice communication equipment and contain all the necessary computer applications to monitor and manage traffic.

The functions of the central passenger information system can be divided according to the presented architecture:

- user profile management
- activities and measures in case of incident situations
- management of train information and possible delays,
- information management of all official places.

A user database is used to manage user profiles, where all data about the user (passenger) are stored. It consists of information on special user requirements, the possibility of defining pre-trip information, reservation and purchase of tickets, and other facilities. Activities and measures in case of incident situations are related to the operational management and traffic control center. In an incident, the passenger is informed about the possible evacuation and emergency services, police, or fire brigade. The management of information on trains and possible delays of the function connected to the operational manager and traffic control center influences possible routes in traffic accidents or other forms of traffic jams.

It is also possible to integrate with other forms of passenger transport if it is integrated passenger transport. All official places' information comprises information on the monitoring station and all stations under its supervision and management. These places can also be adapted to people with disabilities, so this information needs to be stored. Information on additional facilities and the possibility of connecting with other forms of transport can also be part of this functionality.

5   Conclusion

The development and application of 4G and 5G communication networks in the railway system lead to more reliable system operation. In contrast, WSN networks can be used in object identification in the station and stops environment. There are 545 official places for the reception and departure of passengers on the Republic of Croatia's railway network, while out of that number, 124 stations and 132 stops are equipped with systems for providing visual information to users. Each official place also contains specific technical-technological characteristics, such as communication infrastructure or type of safety and signaling system at the station. The research also analyzed transport demand, which established the devastating fact that 41 official places did not dispatch a single passenger in the observed period.

The condition of the communication infrastructure on the railway network in the Republic of Croatia is not satisfactory. Thus, based on collected and analyzed all relevant data necessary for defining the functions of the elements of the central passenger information system, the conceptual architecture of the system was proposed. This system is an integral part of the operational management and traffic control center and is based on the concept of Cloud Computing and IoT sensor technology. In such a solution, end-users' requests to obtain real-time and accurate information would be considered. Future research will focus on the types of information needed for the transfer and information of passengers and the phases of the introduction of this system of passenger information in the Republic of Croatia.

References

1. Odluka o razvrstavanju željezničkih pruga. Official Gazette, Republic of Croatia (2014)
2. Croatian Parliament: Zakon o sigurnosti i interoperabilnosti željezničkog sustava (2020)
3. Croatian Parliament: Zakon o izmjenama i dopunama Zakona o sigurnosti i interoperabilnosti željezničkog sustava. Official Gazette (2015)
4. European Commission: Commission Regulation (EU) No 454/2011. Official Journal of the European Union (2011)
5. European Commission: Commission Regulation (EU) No 1273/2013. Official Journal of the European Union (2013)
6. Anudeep, P., Krishna Prakash, N.: Intelligent passenger information system using IoT for smart cities. In: Tiwari, S., Trivedi, M.C., Mishra, K.K., Misra, A.K., Kumar, K.K. (eds.) Smart Innovations in Communication and Computational Sciences. AISC, vol. 851, pp. 67–76. Springer, Singapore (2019). https://doi.org/10.1007/978-981-13-2414-7_7
7. Beul-Leusmann, S., Samsel, C., Wiederhold, M., Krempels, K.-H., Jakobs, E.-M., Ziefle, M.: Usability evaluation of mobile passenger information systems. In: Marcus, A. (ed.) DUXU 2014. LNCS, vol. 8517, pp. 217–228. Springer, Cham (2014). https://doi.org/10.1007/978-3-319-07668-3_22
8. He, R., et al.: High-speed railway communications: from GSM-R to LTE-R. IEEE Veh. Technol. Mag. 11, 49–58 (2016). https://doi.org/10.1109/MVT.2016.2564446
9. Mallikarjuna, B., Arunkumar Reddy, D., Sailaja, G.: Enhancement of railway reservation system using Internet of Things. SSRN Electron. J., 1–6 (2018). https://doi.org/10.2139/ssrn.3169034
10. Alawad, H., Kaewunruen, S.: Wireless sensor networks: toward smarter railway stations. Infrastructures 3, 24 (2018). https://doi.org/10.3390/infrastructures3030024
11. Morris, C., Easton, J., Roberts, C.: From data to information: provision of railway data to passengers in the information age. In: 11th World Congress on Railway Research, Milan, Italy (2016)
12. Peraković, D., Periša, M., Petrović, M., Cvitić, I., Zorić, P.: Studija implementacije sustava informiranja putnika na željezničkoj mreži, Zagreb, Croatia (2020)
13. HŽ Infrastruktura: Izvješće o mreži 2021, Zagreb, Croatia (2021)
14. Fraga-Lamas, P., Fernández-Caramés, T.M., Castedo, L.: Towards the internet of smart trains: a review on industrial IoT-connected railways. Sensors 17, 1457 (2017). https://doi.org/10.3390/s17061457

Application of Gaussian Process Estimation for Magnetic Field Mapping

Stefan Hensel[1], Marin B. Marinov[2]($\boxtimes$) (iD), Tino Schwilk[1], and Dimitar Nikolov[2]

[1] Department for Electrical Engineering, University of Applied Sciences Offenburg, Badstraße 24, 77652 Offenburg, Germany
[2] Department of Electronics, Technical University of Sofia, 8, Kliment Ohridski Blvd., 1756 Sofia, Bulgaria
mbm@tu-sofia.bg

Abstract. The applicability of characteristics of local magnetic fields for more precise determination of localization of subjects and/or objects in indoor environments, such as railway stations, airports, exhibition halls, showrooms, or shopping centers, is considered. An investigation has been carried out to find out whether and how low-cost magnetic field sensors and mobile robot platforms can be used to create maps that improve the accuracy and robustness of later navigation with smartphones or other devices.

Keywords: Autonomous navigation · Gaussian processes · Localization and mapping · Machine learning · Magnetic field sensors · ROS · SLAM

1 Introduction

While the outdoor location of objects has been determined a long ago by a combination of satellite navigation and inertial sensors, precise positioning inside buildings remains a subject of active research. In laboratories for measurement and sensor technologies, cost-effective sensors are being studied to reduce or prevent the inevitable drift of inertial navigation.

The naturally occurring geomagnetic field is partly massive distorted in buildings [1]. The distortion is caused by the construction materials and furnishing used [2, 3]. These disturbances of the magnetic flux density $\vec{B}$ are locally clearly expressed and largely stationary. They can, therefore, be used as a characteristic for position determination [4, 5]. Pre-calibrated magnetic field sensors measure these characteristics and use them in the navigation process [6, 7].

The data provided by the sensors is made available to the user in the form of a map [8]. The described project examines how these maps can be produced using mobile robots. Special attention is paid to bringing together several separately created maps so that either a swarm of robots can be deployed or a single robot can create the maps in multiple runs.

© ICST Institute for Computer Sciences, Social Informatics and Telecommunications Engineering 2021
Published by Springer Nature Switzerland AG 2021. All Rights Reserved
D. Perakovic and L. Knapcikova (Eds.): FABULOUS 2021, LNICST 382, pp. 284–298, 2021.
https://doi.org/10.1007/978-3-030-78459-1_21

2   Methodology

For the given problem, map creation was split into two parallel sub-processes. The position of the robot is determined by the fusion of inertial sensors, i.e. acceleration and rotation rate sensors, with odometry data and the distance data from a depth-sensing camera. The algorithm used is a particle filter that enables simultaneous localization and mapping (SLAM), providing as output data the position and a two-dimensional raster map of the environment. The magnetic field map is calculated using this position and the measurements from commercially available magnetic field sensors.

The map generation process must take into account the uncertainty of the position due to environmental influences and noisy sensors. The magnetic field sensors are susceptible to interferences which can cause a high degree of uncertainty. Since the data from the sensor are discrete and are on trajectory traveled by the robot, interpolation, and extrapolation of these data must be performed. The task of mapping with limited amounts of data is represented in Fig. 1 as an example of the considered two-dimensional case.

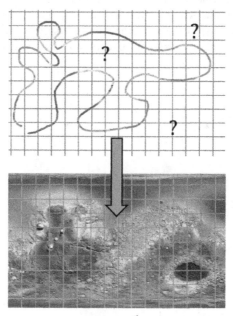

Fig. 1. Prediction of the magnetic flux density $\vec{B}$ in unknown areas based on distributed measurements.

For the prediction of these values for the map generation and the processing of the associated uncertainty in the form of covariance, the appropriateness of the Gaussian processes was investigated.

2.1 Gaussian Processes Regression and Interpolation

We use a Gaussian process (GP) to describe distribution over functions. A Gaussian process is a collection of random variables, any finite number of which have a joint Gaussian distribution.

Gaussian processes [9, 10] are considered as a generalization of the multivariate Gaussian distribution. They can be applied for the estimation of continuous and smooth functions that describe measured data.

Let m(x) and $\kappa(\boldsymbol{x}, \boldsymbol{x}')$ be the mean function and covariance function $\kappa(\boldsymbol{x}, \boldsymbol{x}')$ of a real process $f(x)$. A Gaussian process is completely specified by these two functions and it can be written as

$$f(\boldsymbol{x}) \sim GP\big(m(\boldsymbol{x}), \kappa(\boldsymbol{x}, \boldsymbol{x}')\big). \tag{1}$$

The mean function can be taken zero for notational simplicity. In our case, the random variables represent the value of the function $f(x)$ at location x.

A special case of the Gaussian Process Regression (GPR), used in the present work, is known in geostatistics as Kriging. Besides, Gaussian processes can be applied to a variety of machine learning problems, interpolation with splines, classification problems, or data prediction. An illustrative example of regression in the case of one, two, and three measurements are shown in Fig. 2.

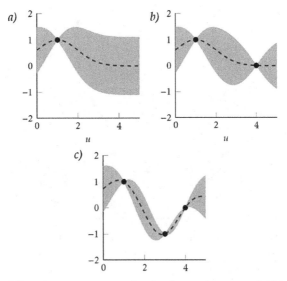

Fig. 2. Principle of Gaussian process regression for a) one measurement, b) two measurements and c) three measurements (adopted from [9])

Measurement points are shown in black, while the grey shaded area gives an interpretation of the so-called 95% confidence interval (twice the standard uncertainty of the estimated function) based on the measured values $y_1, y_2, \ldots, y_n$.

In the GPR applied here, the model functions $f(x)$ are considered/assumed to describe the realizations of a stochastic process whose covariance function $\kappa(x, x')$ is given a priori. They are determined by n given uncertain measurements $y_1, y_2, \ldots, y_n$, observed at the points $x_1, x_2, \ldots, x_n$. So, the model of the stochastic process can be represented as follows:

$$f(x) \sim GP(0, \kappa(x, x')),$$

$$y_i = f(x_i) + \varepsilon_i, i = 1, 2, \ldots, n.$$

(2)

The error $\varepsilon(\varepsilon_1, \varepsilon_2, \ldots, \varepsilon_n)$ corresponds to white noise. As the measurement- and the a priori models are normally distributed, the estimated a posteriori model will be also normally distributed.

2.2 Selection of the Covariance Function

The selection of a specific covariance function depends on the domain of available knowledge about the underlying process: in the considered case it is related to the behavior of the magnetic field in closed spaces. The problem of the inference requires estimating the parameters of this covariance function using the measurements. Here the parameters are referred to as the so-called hyperparameters; the type of the covariance function is defined a priori in the form of model knowledge. One of the most popular

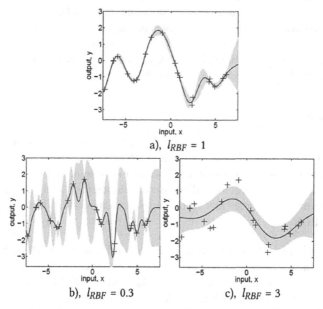

Fig. 3. Influence of the hyperparameters l_{RBF} on the estimation of the covariance function (adapted from [9])

covariance functions is a stationary exponential distribution (the so-called radial basis function RBF) of the form

$$\kappa_{RBF}(x, x') = \sigma_{RBF}^2 \cdot \exp\left(-\frac{\|x - x'\|^2}{2l_{RBF}^2}\right) \qquad (3)$$

where the hyperparameters σ_{RBF}^2 and l_{RBF} express the scale and granularity (bandwidth) of the function.

In Fig. 3 an example of the influence of the hyperparameter l_{RBF}, on the estimated function together with the confidence interval is represented.

The estimation of the hyperparameters on a database is done in the optimal sense by determining the maximum a posteriori probability.

The use of Gaussian processes not only allows the integration of all uncertainties occurring in the mapping but allows the subsequent merging of the created maps based on the estimated accuracy. This is possible by recalculating the map with all measurements or by merging several interpolated maps with weighted arithmetic mean based on covariance recorded at arbitrary times and with any sensors.

3   Experimental Set-up

The basic structure for recording the measurement runs consists of a central host PC on which a ROS kernel runs. Usually, a small Linux netbook is used for this, which sets up a W-LAN network. The individual ROS applications can now be started and monitored from a separate stationary PC. Since it is not necessary to use two separate PCs for this, only one PC was used in the setup pursued here. The magnetic field sensor is connected to the host PC via USB and a breakout board. Both the Turtelbot used and the gamepad required for control are connected to the host PC via USB.

3.1   Hardware

Turtelbot. A mobile robot system of the type Turtlebot was used for the testing. The middleware was the Robot Operating System (ROS) [11], which allows easy driver connection. The ROS is an open-source software environment that provides developers with various libraries and tools to facilitate the development of applications in robotics. Thus, manufacturers distributed numerous hardware elements for which there are device drivers under ROS.

A Turtlebot is a small robot platform in the low price segment. The robot is mostly used for feasibility studies and research purposes because of its flexibility and easy access. It consists of a flat mobile carrying platform, the Kobuki of Yujin Robot, a Kinect of Microsoft as well as a structure that provides space for laptops, other sensors, or constructions.

Inertial Measurement Unit (IMU). The localization of the system was implemented using a g-mapping SLAM algorithm [12]. The three-axis-MEMS magnetic field sensor

HMC5883L is used to record the magnetic field; it can be found, for instance, in smart-phones. Besides, a complete IMU consisting of a three-axis rotation rate sensor and three-axis acceleration sensor is integrated into the chip. By the calculated position of the system, the IMU allows to obtain the projection of the three-dimensional magnetic field measurement into a global coordinate system and thus, to determine the flux density components $\vec{B} = (B_X, B_Y, B_Z)^T$.

There is another advantage of the IMU: depending on the application, part of the data processing, and the signal processing can be transferred from the IMU to an ATmega328 microcontroller. The resolution of the magnetic field sensor is 0.5 μT with a measurement range of ±800 μT and a deviation of 0.2 μT.

Figure 4 shows the robot used and the experimental setup with a computer and magnetic field IMU sensor.

Fig. 4. Mobile robot platform (left) and experimental setup combined with magnetic field sensor IMU (right).

For later tests, additional floor markings were made in order to have clues for assessing the position recognition of the turtle bot in the event of multiple measurement runs. Since it was necessary to start measurements from an identical starting point for some series of measurements, a starting field that could be attached to the ground was designed.

3.2 Software

To estimate the parameters of a Gaussian process, complex optimization methods are needed, which usually require $O(n^3)$ operations. As there are hundreds to thousands of measured values at disposal, approximate methods were used to interpolate the magnetic field; the constructed function is known as a measurement function of the magnetic field. Gaussian noise was a priori assumed in the measurement function, the covariance was fixed a priori by the Matérn-function; the latter is a generalized version of RBF and contains an additional hyperparameter for determination of smoothness [13, 14]. The calculation was performed offline in the batch process, i.e. for the entire data set after the measured values were recorded. The input data are magnetometer measurements $\vec{B}$

along with the position, orientation, and covariance matrix determined by the SLAM algorithm.

Data Preprocessing. The magnetic flux density $\vec{B} = (B_X, B_Y, B_Z)^T$ was measured in x, y, and z direction. To clean up the signal of measurement noise and single outliers, for the time being, it was smoothed by a median filter of 5th order. Since the magnetic field cannot change very quickly due to the limited speed of the Turtlebot, the measurements were subsequently smoothed by moving average filter after rejecting outliers with a median filter of 5th order.

The size of the kernel varies between measurements and must be periodically adjusted. For a large part of the experimental measurements, in case the investigated magnetic field is very irregular, a kernel of size $n \approx 100$ was chosen. In areas where there is a homogeneous magnetic field and there are only separate regions in which the magnetic field strongly fluctuates, the filter kernel has to be reduced in size, so as not to completely remove the measurements.

The IMU and the odometry of the Turtelbot use different sampling frequencies, and the measurements have to be put into correspondence, i.e. to be synchronized, even though they already have a common timestamp by ROS [15].

A magnetic flux density $\vec{B}$ and a time t should be assigned to a point in the x, y plane:

$$\vec{B} = \vec{B}(x_m, y_m, t_m),\tag{4}$$

where x_m, y_m represent the points where the Turtlebot was at the time t_m.

For the assignment and adaptation to the different sampling times, the measurements of the individual topics with a common new sampling time are linearly interpolated. Then they are shifted so that all the measurements are completely synchronous. However, since the position of the magnetic field sensor was centered in the Turtlebot and thus, shifted to the IMU, the position had to be additionally corrected.

A layout regarding the positioning of the magnetic field sensor on the Turtlebot can be found in Fig. 5. In this case

$$\varphi_{sens} = \arctan\left(\frac{x_{dist}}{y_{dist}}\right), d_{sens} = \sqrt{x_{dist}^2 + y_{dist}^2},\tag{5}$$

The corrected pair of values $\tilde{x}$ and $\tilde{y}$ is calculated using the relationships

$$\tilde{x} = x + \cos(\varphi + \varphi_{sens})d_{sens}$$
$$\tilde{y} = y + \sin(\varphi + \varphi_{sens})d_{sens}, \Box\tag{6}$$

where φ represents the current orientation of the Turtlebot.

To determine the angle φ for each position of the Turtlebot, the orientation of the latter is evaluated using quaternions. For the computation of the three Euler angles (*Roll* Φ, *Pitch* Θ, *Yaw* Ψ) from the quaternions (q_1, q_2, q_3, q_4) the following relationships are used:

$$\begin{bmatrix} \Phi \\ \Theta \\ \Psi \end{bmatrix} = \begin{bmatrix} \text{atan} 2\, (2(q_0q_1 + q_2q_3),\, 1 - 2(q_1^2 + q_2^2)) \\ \text{asin}(2(q_0q_2 - q_1q_3)) \\ \text{atan} 2\, (2(q_0q_3 + q_1q_2),\, 1 - 2(q_2^2 + q_3^2)) \end{bmatrix}\tag{7}$$

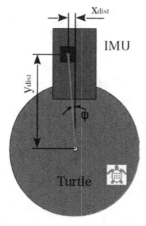

Fig. 5. The distance of the magnetic field sensor to the center of the Turtlebots

The angle φ corresponds to the pitch angle Θ. For greater clarity further on in this work, the coordinates of the magnetic field sensor are denoted by x and y instead $\tilde{x}$ and $\tilde{y}$.

With these transformations, it is possible to map the magnetic field measurements in the localization frame of the robot. These data are fused with the robot localization based on laser scan data and odometry. To get the robot trajectory we employ a classical particle filter-based localization and mapping algorithm (SLAM), based on [12]. This not only results in a trajectory driven by the robot but also in an uncertainty estimation of the actual position, which is expressed with the covariance matrix

$$\sigma_{max}^2 = \max\left(\begin{bmatrix} \sigma_{x,x}^2 & \sigma_{x,y}^2 \\ \sigma_{y,x}^2 & \sigma_{y,y}^2 \end{bmatrix}\right) \tag{8}$$

An exemplary result for the trajectory is shown in Fig. 6. The associated uncertainty is visualized with an ellipse based on the actual covariance.

Mapping. To create a magnetic field map from the driven path, different interpolation methods exist. Matlab offers the function *griddata* for the interpolation of functions $f(x, y)$ via a previously defined grid. The method used here is based on Delaunay triangulation, i.e. triangles are formed between pairs of points in space. These triangles are chosen to avoid long thin triangles. Since the triangles cover the entire grid and do not overlap, a value can be assigned to each point on the grid.

Multimap Data Fusion. To generate a map from several series of measurements, a fusion of the measured values is necessary. These can be performed either by running an environment multiple times with a single robot only or by running simultaneously more robots in the environment In the case of interpolation with Gaussian processes this fusion is easily realized. All measurements with an associated uncertainty can be added to the Gaussian process as training data. The resulting interpolation is already weighted and based on a distribution function. It makes no difference whether the same

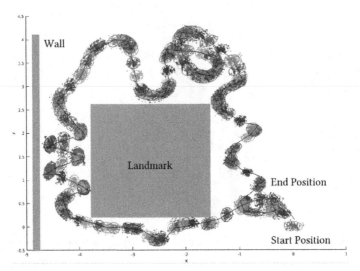

Fig. 6. Base data for data fusion of several maps, showing coordinates and associated magnetic field measurements and their estimated uncertainty.

point is traversed several times during measurement, or whether several measurements are fused. The consequence in both cases is that inaccuracies or measurement errors are less weighted in the resulting map.

In the case of classical interpolation, such an approach would not lead to the correct result, since each value enters the result with the same weight.

To fuse several maps according to their uncertainty, an uncertainty value σ is assigned to each geometric point $\tilde{P}$, in addition to a value z_{mag} which expresses the magnetic field strength at the positions x and y. This is depicted in Fig. 7 and follows the equation

$$\tilde{P}_{map} = \tilde{P}_{map}(x, y, z_{mag}, \sigma). \tag{9}$$

To associate appropriate weights to the individual measured values, an engineering approach is used.

It is assumed that the measurement of the magnetic field at the location $\tilde{P}$ is highly uncertain especially when the positional covariance is particularly great. A measured value has, therefore, a large influence on the result, only in case, the Turtlebot was there with a high degree of certainty.

For this purpose, the maximum value

$$\sigma_{max}^2 = \max\left(\begin{bmatrix} \sigma_{x,x}^2 & \sigma_{x,y}^2 \\ \sigma_{y,x}^2 & \sigma_{y,y}^2 \end{bmatrix}\right) \tag{10}$$

of the already known covariance matrix from the SLAM algorithm of the localization, a module is used.

Thus, a very small σ_{max} stands for very good position detection, i.e. for very accurate measurement of the magnetic field. Several N maps $P_{map,i}$ with i from 1 to N are now

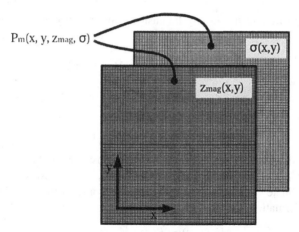

$P_m(x, y, z_{mag}, \sigma)$

$\sigma(x,y)$

$z_{mag}(x,y)$

Fig. 7. Base data for data fusion of several maps, showing coordinates and associated magnetic field measurements and their estimated uncertainty.

calculated to form a map P_{map}, using the following equation:

$$P_{map}(x, y) = \sum_{i=1}^{N} \left(\frac{z_i(x, y)}{\sigma_i^2(x, y)} \right) / \left(\frac{1}{\sigma_{max}^2(x, y)} \right). \tag{11}$$

It shows that a value of 0 is not permitted for the uncertainties. In a real process this indeed never occurs. Nevertheless, such a measurement can be skipped, so that at this point the map is showing a gap in the measurements.

If measurements that tightly cover the entire area in space are available, the map fusion can be performed using a weighted average. The advantage of this map fusion compared to the Gaussian processes is the lower computational load. However, the acquisition of the measured data with sufficient density is a fundamental problem: for this purpose, an intelligent interpolation and extrapolation of the measured values cannot be ruled out [16].

4 Experimental Results

In this section, selected experiments are presented and the results obtained from them are briefly discussed.

4.1 Mapping Procedure - Approach

Since the magnetic flux density $\vec{B}$ is a vector field $\vec{B}(x, y) = \left(B_x, B_y, B_z \right)^T$, but only one scalar can be interpolated over x and y, some considerations have to be made.

It is conceivable to interpolate every one of the measured components of $\vec{B}$. In the further course the measured values of B_x are described with $M_{B_x}(x, y)$. Similarly, the description of B_y and B_z. A two-dimensional interpolation of $M_{B_x}(x, y)$ results in $M_{I,B_x}(x, y)$

$$M_{B_x}(x, y) \xrightarrow{\text{interpoliert}} M_{I,B_x}(x, y),$$

$$M_{B_y}(x, y) \xrightarrow{\text{interpoliert}} M_{I,B_y}(x, y), \qquad (12)$$

$$M_{B_z}(x, y) \xrightarrow{\text{interpoliert}} M_{I,B_z}(x, y).$$

From these three interpolated maps, it is now possible to generate a map of the absolute value $M_{I,abs(B_x,B_y,B_z)}(x, y)$. For this, however, it is necessary to refer the values to a global coordinate system. Since the Turtlebot can only rotate around the z-axis, the necessary transformation results

$$M_{B_y}(x, y) = R(\varphi) \cdot \bar{M}_{B_x}(x, y). \qquad (13)$$

Here, R is the rotation matrix as a function of the orientation angle φ of the Turtlebot:

$$R = \begin{bmatrix} \cos(\varphi) & -sin(\varphi) & 0 \\ sin(\varphi) & cos(\varphi) & 0 \\ 0 & 0 & 1 \end{bmatrix} \qquad (14)$$

The absolute value for B_x, B_y and B_z is given by

$$M_{I,abs(B_x,B_y,B_z)}(x, y) = \sqrt{M_{I,B_x}(x, y)^2 + M_{I,B_y}(x, y)^2 + M_{I,B_z}(x, y)^2} \qquad (15)$$

4.2 Experimental Runs

Experimental runs in several environments have proven small to little influence of the magnetic field vector B_z for the sensitivity of the overall field strength. This is due to the considered scenarios, where the robot is mainly operating in industrial or home environments, where the ceiling is too far away to have any influence, and commonplace objects rather extend to the floor and thus permit to drive under. Therefore, the vertical magnetic component can be omitted, which significantly speeds up the interpolation and combination of the measured data. The overall field strength for B_x and B_y is given by

$$M_{I,abs(B_x,B_y)}(x, y) = \sqrt{M_{I,B_x}(x, y)^2 + M_{I,B_y}(x, y)^2} \qquad (16)$$

In an initial study, the suitability of Gaussian processes for interpolating measured data was examined. For comparison, we applied the classical two-dimensional linear interpolation. Although the latter cannot be used for covariance indication and evaluation, the computation time is several orders of magnitude smaller.

However, it quickly becomes clear what qualitative advantage can be achieved by interpolation and prediction with Gaussian processes. Figure 8(a) shows the linear interpolation based on the trajectory traveled, which is plotted in black. The result of the GP for the same record is shown in Fig. 8(b).

Magnetic maps were recorded based on several test runs in different areas of the university. Figure 9 illustrates the qualitative results for a small area of a laboratory.

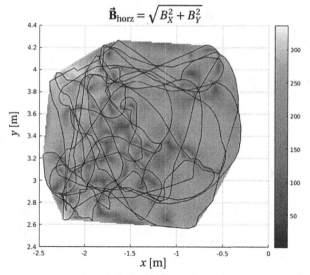

$$\vec{\mathbf{B}}_{\text{horz}} = \sqrt{B_X^2 + B_Y^2}$$

a) result obtained by linear interpolation

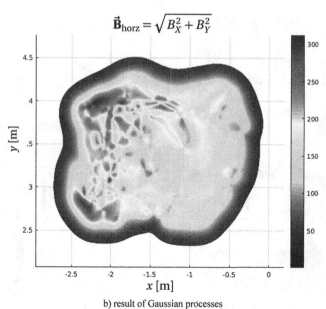

$$\vec{\mathbf{B}}_{\text{horz}} = \sqrt{B_X^2 + B_Y^2}$$

b) result of Gaussian processes

Fig. 8. Created map of the horizontal flow density

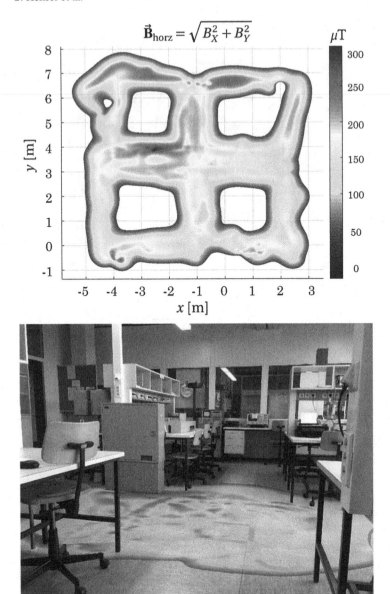

Fig. 9. Illustrative map of the horizontal flow of the laboratory for measuring and sensor technology

5   Conclusions

The investigation shows that the Gaussian regression is fundamentally suitable for producing a complete and usable map (of continuous features) from individual measurements. The maps created have a good degree of detail. The advantages compared to less expensive methods lie in the simple integration of new measurements, the availability of a quality measure in the form of a covariance matrix, and, based thereon, natural integration into stochastic localization methods. The modeling also allows the introduction of boundary conditions and model knowledge. However, all this is at the expense of extensive calculations.

The maps were created with a resolution of 5 cm, the potential for a positioning accuracy is within a few decimeters to meters, which is already sufficient for the continuous improvement and drift correction of inertial sensors.

Acknowledgments. This research is supported by the Bulgarian National Science Fund in the scope of the project "Exploration the application of statistics and machine learning in electronics" under contract number КП-06-Н42/1.

References

1. Saxena, A., Zawodniok, M.: Indoor positioning system using geomagnetic field. In: IEEE International Instrumentation and Measurement Technology Conference (I2MTC) Proceedings, Montevideo, Uruguay (2014)
2. Iatcheva, I.I., Andreev, A.D., Stancheva, R.D., Lilyanova, I.T.: Electromagnetic flow meter field distribution maximizing device sensitivity. Mater. Sci. Forum **856**, 157–162 (2016)
3. Shockley, J.A., Raquet, J.F.: Navigation of Ground vehicles using magnetic field variations. Navigation **61**, 237–252 (2014)
4. Li, B., Gallagher, T., Dempster, A., Rizos, C.: How feasible is the use of magnetic field alone for indoor positioning? In: Proceedings of the International Conference on Indoor Positioning and Indoor Navigation (IPIN), Sydney, Australia (2012)
5. Hensel, S., Marinov, M.B., Schmitt, M.: System setup for synchronized visual-inertial localization and mapping. In: 2020 XXIX International Scientific Conference Electronics (ET), Sozopol, Bulgaria (2020)
6. Frassl, M., Angermann, M., Lichtenstern, M., Robertson, P., Julian, B., Doniec, M.: Magnetic maps of indoor environments for precise localization of legged and non-legged locomotion. In: Proceedings of the IEEE/RSJ International Conference on Intelligent Robots and Systems (IROS), Tokyo, Japan (2013)
7. Filipov, F.: Forschung und Implementierung von Technologien für die Navigation in Innenräumen, Sofia: Dissertation, Technische Universität Sofia (2016)
8. Kim, H.S., Seo, W., Baek, K.R.: Indoor positioning system us-ing magnetic field map navigation and an encoder system. Sensors **17**(3), 651 (2017)
9. Rasmussen, C.E., Williams, C.K.I.: Gaussian Processes for Machine Learning. MIT Press, Cambridge (2006)
10. Jain, A., Nghiem, T., Morari, M., Mangharam, R.: Learning and control using gaussian processes. In: 2018 ACM/IEEE 9th International Conference on Cyber-Physical Systems (ICCPS), Porto, Portugal (2018)
11. Quigley, M., Gerkey, B., Smart, W.: Programming Robots with ROS. O'Reilly Media, Sebastopol (2015)
12. Grisetti, G., Stachniss, C., Burgard, W.: Improved techniques for grid mapping with rao-blackwellized particle filters. IEEE Trans. Rob. **23**, 34–46 (2007)
13. Minasny, B., McBradley, B.: Spatial prediction of soil properties using EBLUP with the Matérn covariance function. Geoderma **140**, 323–456 (2007)
14. Hensel, S., Marinov, M.B.: Estimation of magnetic field maps with mobile platforms. In: Proceedings of the 7th FDIBA Conference, Sofia, 30 November–1 December 2017

15. Kokolanski, Z.: Hardware techniques for improving the calibration performance of direct resistive sensor-to-microcontroller interface. Metrol. Meas. Syst. **20**(1), 529–542 (2013)
16. Klein, L.: Sensor and Data Fusion. SPIE-International Society for Optical Engineering, Washington (2004)

User Quality of Experience Comparison Between Skype, Microsoft Teams and Zoom Videoconferencing Tools

Marko Matulin[1]($\boxtimes$) , Štefica Mrvelj[1] , Borna Abramović[1] , Tomislav Šoštarić[1], and Marko Čejvan[2]

[1] Faculty of Transport and Traffic Sciences, University of Zagreb, Vukeliceva 4, 10000 Zagreb, Croatia
{mmatulin,smrvelj,babramovic}@fpz.hr
[2] Ericsson Nikola Tesla d.d, Krapinska 45, 10000 Zagreb, Croatia
marko.cejvan@ericsson.com

Abstract. In 2020, we investigated the quality of online meetings to find out whether various video and audio degradations can affect end-users' perception and experience. We collected a total of 542 questionnaires that were suitable for analysis. This paper uses the results to compare the Quality of Experience for three popular videoconferencing applications: Skype, Microsoft Teams, and Zoom. Due to the COVID-19 (Coronavirus disease 2019) and anti-epidemic measures, survey participants were all faced with using these applications daily, whether for work, attending lectures, or keeping in touch with friends and family. They rated their frustration level for specific quality degradations (e.g., blocking of the image or echo in the audio). The paper shows how the three applications compare to each other when different network performance degradation situations occur and how they affect the end user's perception.

Keywords: Videoconference · Application · Online meetings · Telecommuting · Quality of experience · Survey

1 Introduction

The unique circumstances created by the coronavirus disease forced humanity to accept different living and working ways that were rather unthinkable in the past. Probably the most significant change took place in our work environments when lockdown measures led to various videoconferencing applications coming to the fore. It is safe to say that there is no industry that does not use the above tools (often referred to as telecommuting) to at least some extent, and certain sectors, such as education, rely on them. According to [1, 2], usage of these tools began to rise significantly in 2010, and since then it has more than doubled. It is expected that by 2030, about 50% of the working population will participate in videoconferencing.

T. Šoštarić—Graduated with a masters' degree.

© ICST Institute for Computer Sciences, Social Informatics and Telecommunications Engineering 2021
Published by Springer Nature Switzerland AG 2021. All Rights Reserved
D. Perakovic and L. Knapcikova (Eds.): FABULOUS 2021, LNICST 382, pp. 299–307, 2021.
https://doi.org/10.1007/978-3-030-78459-1_22

Telecommuting has great potential to reduce costs, mainly for transportation to and from work/school/faculty (up to 30% according to [3]), as well as business operating costs. Zoom, a videoconferencing platform, currently holds the largest share in this market. At the end of 2019, Zoom was averaging 10 million users/month. In April 2020, the number peaked at 300 million daily meeting participants. Dozens of other videoconferencing applications on the market make it a competitive market with high growth expected in the coming years. Therefore, it was interesting to compare how the three most popular applications (according to our data) behave when various degradations in video and audio quality occur during online meeting sessions.

As the name suggests, video is the essential component of videoconferencing service. Nevertheless, there are crucial differences when comparing this service with, e.g., video streaming. During the conferencing session, video is not stored before playback; it is encoded and streamed live from a conference to a group of participants located at different network sites, often with limited upload/download capabilities. The limitations can affect the quality of the video transmission and thus the Quality of Experience (QoE) for all conference peers. Therefore, it is important to understand how users react in situations where network performance declines, leading to various video and audio quality degradations on the end-user side.

To this end, researchers focus their energy on understanding both objective and subjective aspects of videoconferencing services. This is in line with the QoE concept of service evaluation, which puts end-users into the focus and investigates how quantifiable (objective) and qualitative (subjective) parameters impact their perception. Network performances that can meet a specific application's demands are still an integral part of successful service provision, but they are not the only ones; users' subjective opinions come to the fore in the QoE paradigm of service evaluation.

The available research on the objective characteristics of the service includes a) video coding techniques for videoconferencing [4, 5], b) the development of adaptive video streaming methods [4, 6, 7], or c) the analysis of mobile audiovisual telemeetings with multiple participants [8–10]. However, our focus in this paper is on subjective aspects of user QoE, i.e., their perception of different quality degradations when using popular videoconferencing applications. Note that this follows up on our earlier work from [11], where we presented descriptive statistics of our survey results.

Belmudez in [12] presented the QoE model for videoconferencing services, which uses objective parameters to derive subjective user opinions about the service. Similar work but for a video streaming service is done in [13]. Another attempt to discover the interplay between network performance and user QoE for videoconferencing is done in [14], where Perceived Video Quality (PVQ) was used to evaluate the user experience. The results on how different coding strategies in video communication scenes affect subjective perception were published in [15] by Li et al. The authors investigated the applicability of varying encoding strategies to different video classes.

In [16], the authors investigate how varying network conditions affect four subjects' ability to collaborate and build a Lego model using a videoconferencing platform. Rao et al. [17] developed different scenarios to perturb network performance on the sender side. They quantified the perceived video quality at the receiver side but without performing subjective tests with actual test subjects.

Before moving on to the study design and presenting the results, we are obliged to highlight a crucial aspect of our research that distinguishes it from other research efforts reviewed here. We could not measure network performance during online meetings or the audiovisual quality of our survey participants' incoming videos as we approached them through social networks and personal channels. The survey was conducted outside of laboratory conditions without actual physical contact with respondents. Therefore, we did not focus on examining the quality of a particular session or inbound video stream. Instead, we revealed respondents' opinions about the quality of their typical videoconferencing session when using different applications.

As mentioned earlier, we are continuing our previous work [11], where we revealed and discussed how frequent various quality degradations are and how they affect end-users (e.g., different audio and video artifacts and meeting disconnections). In this paper, we are focused on discovering if the user perception is in interplay with the videoconferencing platform type, i.e., how different platforms perform in the network performance deprivation scenarios (from an end-user perspective).

This paper is organized as follows. Section 2 describes the questionnaire used in the survey and general statistics about the sample. The results obtained and discussions can be found in Sect. 3. Section 4 concludes and offers new research paths.

2 Subjective Study

A detailed description of the survey, the questionnaire used to collect the data, and the survey participants can be found in [11]; therefore, we aim to provide a more summary report in this paper.

We used the LimeSurvey platform and designed a questionnaire with 31 questions that took about 15 min to complete. In addition to demographic data, we collected responses on a) respondents' network environment from which they typically access meetings (device and network types, experiences with, e.g., long buffering times when viewing the video stream and other audiovisual quality degradations), b) typical meeting scenarios (meeting purposes, what videoconferencing applications they typically use, etc.) and meeting roles respondents were involved in, and c) respondents' opinions on meeting quality. The survey lasted three weeks and was anonymous.

After excluding uncompleted questionnaires and those where respondents indicated that they had not attended meetings, we finally obtained 542 questionnaires that were suitable for analysis. For this paper, we further filtered the data as follows: a) only respondents who attended more than five meetings in the last month were included (measured from the time they participated in the survey); b) respondents ranked over 100 applications based on how frequently they used them. We filtered the three top-ranked applications and performed data analysis based on those responses.

The results showed that the top three most frequently ranked applications were Zoom, Microsoft Teams[1], and Skype[2] (ranked as the number one choice by 104, 96, and 49 respondents, respectively).

---

[1] Hereinafter refered as Teams.

[2] Note that the distinction was made between Skype and Skype for Business.

As seen from Table 1, the sample is sufficiently diversified (given the gender and age group distributions). For each application studied here, over 60% of respondents participated in more than ten meetings in a month, making them experienced users. We also learned that the responders' devices are usually connected to a home network (DSL or WiFi) during the meetings. Based on the responses related to how long it takes for a typical video streaming playback to start, how often it re-buffers, and how

Table 1. Sample characteristics.

Sample data	Skype	Teams	Zoom
A number of responses:	49	96	104
Gender:			
Female	63.3%	38.5%	59.6%
Male	36.7%	61.5%	40.4%
Age group:			
19–30	6.1%	24%	7.7%
31–40	36.7%	16.7%	30.8%
41–50	40.8%	35.4%	37.5%
51–60	12.2%	16.7%	19.2%
61–70	4.1%	6.3%	3.8%
71 or older	0%	1%	1%
The number of attended meetings:			
Between 6 and 10	38.8%	27.1%	22.1%
Between 11 and 20	28.6%	26.0%	37.5%
Between 21 and 40	20.4%	27.1%	27.9%
41 or more	12.2%	19.8%	12.5%
Most frequently used device for meetings:			
Laptop	73.5%	80.2%	67.3%
Smartphone	8.2%	9.4%	15.4%
Desktop computer	16.3%	8.3%	14.4%
Tablet	2%	2.1%	2.9%
Common meeting purposes:			
Work-related	42.9%	67.7%	50.0%
To attend or give lectures	34.7%	29.2%	38.5%
To see friends and relatives	12.2%	3.1%	6.7%
Other	10.2%	0%	4.8%
Typical meeting role:			
Meeting leader and presenter	42.9%	35.4%	45.2%
Participant, sometimes a presenter	38.8%	37.5%	30.8%
Participant	12.2%	17.7%	14.4%
Presenter	2%	4.2%	6.7%
Guest	0%	1%	1.9%
Meeting leader but others present	4.1%	4.2%	1%

often the resolution changes, we conclude that the respondents' network was sufficiently capacitated in most cases for the videoconferencing service.

3   Results and Discussion

This section presents the results on three figures that follow the same structure and have six subplots, two for every application we analyze. Figure 1 and 2 show respondents' frustration levels for audio and video degradations, respectively, while Fig. 3 compares these frustrations to the most adversely perceived quality distortion – a meeting disconnections. The cumulative distribution function (CDF) was used to present the results. Five-point discrete scales were used to quantify the distortion frequency during one typical conference and describe the respondents' frustration levels.

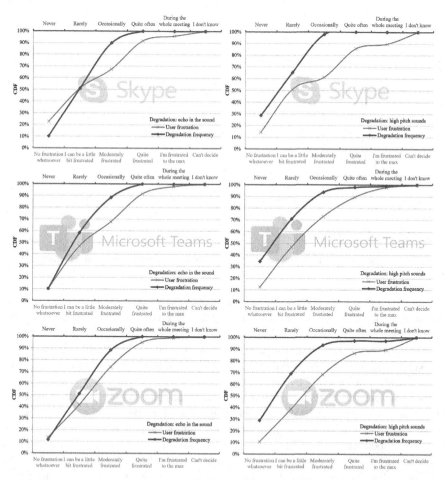

Fig. 1. Responders' frustration for a specific type of audio degradation and its' frequency.

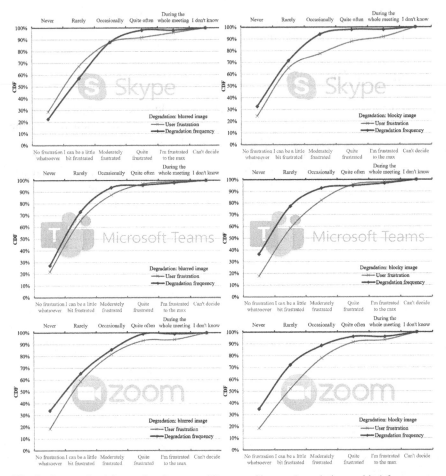

Fig. 2. Responders' frustration for a specific type of image degradation and its' frequency.

Note that in [11], the results showed that users value audio more than image quality. The same conclusion can be drawn here, for this filtered sample, if we compare the results shown in Fig. 1 and Fig. 2. For example, the value of CDF for *moderate* levels of frustration on Skype is 67.4% (for echo in the sound) and 61.2% (for high pitch sound) compared to 87.8% (for image blurriness) and 77.6% (for image blockiness). The same trends are seen for the other two applications.

The relationship between the frequency of degradation and user frustration is somewhat different for Skype. We can see that a higher level of frustration was recorded for this particular population. It is arguably most evident for *high pitch sound* (Fig. 1), where 61.2% of respondents indicated that this degradation was *not frustrating*, or could be a *little frustrating*, or was *moderately frustrating*. Conversely, the CDF values for Teams and Zoom, for the same *moderate* frustration level, are higher, i.e., there are fewer respondents who indicated higher levels of frustration (*quite frustrated* and *maximally frustrated*).

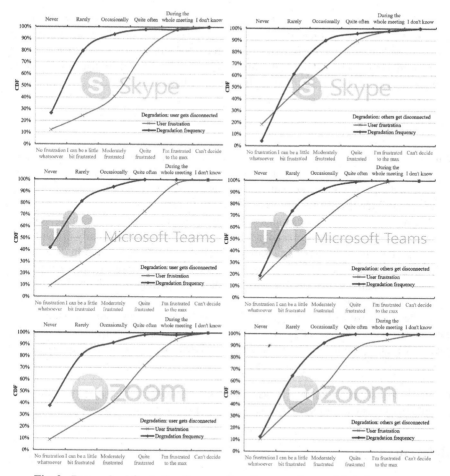

Fig. 3. Responders' frustration for a meeting disconnections and their frequency.

Respondents' attitudes towards the meeting disconnections is the last set of results to be presented here. Figure 3 shows the values of CDF for two types of degradations, namely when a user (a respondent) is disconnected from a conference (three subplots on the left) and when other conference peers are disconnected (the subplots on the right).

It is clear that the frustration values visualized in Fig. 3 are significantly higher than those we have previously reported for audio or video degradations. Of the three applications studied, Teams users were the least frustrated by this degradation, which is probably because the frequency of this degradation is slightly lower for Teams than Skype and Zoom. On the other hand, this result can be interpreted to mean that Zoom users are more accustomed to holding high-quality meetings, so these types of meeting interruptions are more likely to be perceived negatively. It can also be seen that in all three applications, more frustration is elicited when the responders were disconnected than when their conference peers were disconnected.

To test the differences between multiple sample proportions, we used the Chi-square test. We recorded a statistically significant difference between CDF values for *occasional* degradation frequency only for image related degradations. In contrast, the CDF values were statistically significantly different for *moderate* levels of frustrations for all degradations and between all three applications we have analyzed.

4   Conclusion

This paper tried to reveal correlations between different levels of user dissatisfaction and frequency of specific quality degradations for specific videoconferencing applications. We detected the three most frequently used applications and conducted the data analysis only for that filtered sample based on the survey results.

The results showed that disconnections during the meetings are most adversely perceived quality degradation, especially for Skype and Zoom users. Nearly 60% of these users reported higher levels of frustration with this type of degradation in cases where they were disconnected. It shows that even though various applications may provide similar functionalities, they can create different user experiences, which tells us that this research effort is worthwhile.

In the future, we will focus on performing more sophisticated statistical analyses that can uncover a deeper understanding of user perception and experience for videoconferencing. We also plan to explore the interplay between various objective and subjective factors of user QoE for this type of service.

Conflicts of Interest. The authors declare that there is no conflict of interest. The results were not influenced in any way by any organization mentioned in the manuscript.

References

1. GrandViewResearch.   https://www.grandviewresearch.com/industry-analysis/video-conferencing-market. Accessed 05 June 2020
2. Gminsights.   https://www.gminsights.com/industry-analysis/video-conferencing-market. Accessed 05 June 2020
3. Skillscouter. https://skillscouter.com/video-conferencing-statistics. Accessed 06 June 2020
4. Bakar, G., Kirmizioglu, R.A., Tekalp, A.M.: Motion-based rate adaptation in WebRTC video-conferencing using scalable video coding. IEEE Trans. Multimedia **21**(2), 429–441 (2019). https://doi.org/10.1109/TMM.2018.2856629
5. Boyce, J.M., Ye, Y., Chen, J.L., Ramasubramonian, A.K.: Overview of SHVC: scalable extensions of the high efficiency video coding standard. IEEE Trans. Circ. Syst. Video Technol. **26**(1), 20–34 (2016). https://doi.org/10.1109/TCSVT.2015.2461951
6. Hu, H., Zhu, X.Q., Wang, Y., Pan, R., Zhu, J., Bonomi, F.: Proxy-based multi-stream scalable video adaptation over wireless networks using subjective quality and rate models. IEEE Trans. Multimedia **15**(7), 1638–1652 (2013). https://doi.org/10.1109/TMM.2013.2266092
7. Hosking, B., Agrafiotis, D., Bull, D., Easton, N.: An adaptive resolution rate control method for intra coding in HEVC. In: IEEE International Conference on Acoustics, Speech and Signal Processing (ICASSP), Shanghai, China, pp. 1486–1490. IEEE (2016)

8. Li, CL., Xiong, HK., Zou, JN., Wu, DPO.: Joint dynamic rate control and transmission scheduling for scalable video multirate multicast over wireless networks. IEEE Trans. Multimedia **20**(2), 361–378 (2018). https://doi.org/10.1109/TMM.2017.2745709
9. Al Hasrouty, C., Lamali, M.L., Autefage, V., Olariu, C., Magoni, D., Murphy, J.: Adaptive multicast streaming for videoconferences on software-defined networks. Comput. Commun. **132**, 42–55 (2018). https://doi.org/10.1016/j.comcom.2018.09.009
10. Vučić, D., Skorin-Kapov, L.: QoE assessment of mobile multiparty audiovisual telemeetings. IEEE Access **8**, 107669–107684 (2020). https://doi.org/10.1109/ACCESS.2020.3000467
11. Matulin, M., Mrvelj, Š., Abramović, B.: How frustrated are you? User perception about different videoconference quality degradations. In: 5th EAI International Conference on Management of Manufacturing Systems (EAI MMS 2020), EAI, Online (2020)
12. Belmudez, B.: Audiovisual Quality Assessment and Prediction for Videotelephony. Springer, Berlin (2015). https://doi.org/10.1007/978-3-319-14166-4
13. Matulin, M., Mrvelj, Š.: Modelling user quality of experience from objective and subjective data sets using fuzzy logic. Multimedia Syst. **24**(6), 645–667 (2018). https://doi.org/10.1007/s00530-018-0590-0
14. ur Rehman Laghari, K., Issa, O., Speranza, F., Falk, T.H.: Quality-of-experience perception for video streaming services: preliminary subjective and objective results. In: Proceedings of The 2012 Asia Pacific Signal and Information Processing Association Annual Summit and Conference, Los Angeles, USA, pp. 1–9 (2012)
15. Li, Y., Zhou, Z.: Subjective video quality assessment and the analysis of coding strategies in video communication scene. In: Proceedings of The 13th International Congress on Image and Signal Processing, BioMedical Engineering and Informatics (CISP-BMEI), Chengdu, China, pp. 52–55 (2020). https://doi.org/10.1109/CISP-BMEI51763.2020.9263575
16. Schmitt, M., Redi, J., Bulterman, D., Cesar, P.S.: Towards individual QoE for multiparty videoconferencing. IEEE Trans. Multimedia **20**(7), 1781–1795 (2018). https://doi.org/10.1109/TMM.2017.2777466
17. Rao, N., Maleki, A., Chen, F., Chen, W., Zhang, C., Kaur, K., Haque, A.: Analysis of the effect of QoS on video conferencing QoE. In: 15th International Wireless Communications & Mobile Computing Conference (IWCMC), Tangier, Morocco, pp. 1267–1272 (2019). https://doi.org/10.1109/IWCMC.2019.8766591

Smart Health Applications

Investigating Protected Health Information Leakage from Android Medical Applications

George Grispos[1]([⊠]) [iD], Talon Flynn[1] [iD], William Bradley Glisson[2] [iD],
and Kim-Kwang Raymond Choo[3] [iD]

[1] University of Nebraska-Omaha, Omaha, NE 68182, USA
{ggrispos,tflynn}@unomaha.edu
[2] Sam Houston State University, Huntsville, TX 77340, USA
glisson@shsu.edu
[3] University of Texas at San Antonio, San Antonio, TX 78249, USA
raymond.choo@fulbrightmail.org

Abstract. As smartphones and smartphone applications are widely used in a healthcare context (e.g., remote healthcare), these devices and applications may need to comply with the Health Insurance Portability and Accountability Act (HIPAA) of 1996. In other words, adequate safeguards to protect the user's sensitive information (e.g., personally identifiable information and/or medical history) are required to be enforced on such devices and applications. In this study, we forensically focus on the potential of recovering residual data from Android medical applications, with the objective of providing an initial risk assessment of such applications. Our findings (e.g., documentation of the artifacts) also contribute to a better understanding of the types and location of evidential artifacts that can, potentially, be recovered from these applications in a digital forensic investigation.

Keywords: Information leakage · Protected Health Information · Privacy · Security · Medical device · Mobile phone

1 Introduction

Smartphone devices are becoming increasingly pervasive in today's medical environments. According to a survey conducted in the United States (US), just over 58% of surveyed individuals have downloaded a health-related mobile application on their smartphone [1]. Similarly, industrial surveys have estimated that more than 50% of physicians in the US encourage their patients to use smartphone medical applications [2, 3], particularly during medical emergencies (e.g., due to COVID-19 lockdowns [4, 5]). There is even evidence of increased usage of medical smartphone applications among healthcare professionals [6]. These smartphone applications can be used for a variety of different purposes, including disease self-management, remote monitoring of patients, as well as collecting and integrating patient data into Electronic Health Records (EHRs). However, the information collected and stored by these smartphone applications can also make them an attractive proposition for cybercriminals.

© ICST Institute for Computer Sciences, Social Informatics and Telecommunications Engineering 2021
Published by Springer Nature Switzerland AG 2021. All Rights Reserved
D. Perakovic and L. Knapcikova (Eds.): FABULOUS 2021, LNICST 382, pp. 311–322, 2021.
https://doi.org/10.1007/978-3-030-78459-1_23

The 2020 Healthcare Information and Management Systems Society survey, for example, reports that 70% of healthcare organizations experienced a "significant security incident" in the past twelve months [7]. Further complicating matters, the US Food and Drug Administration (FDA) and the US Government Accountability Office (GAO) have both warned that Internet-connected medical devices and their applications are likely to be susceptible to cyberattacks [8, 9]. These concerns were validated by the 2017 attacks on British hospitals when cybercriminals exploited unpatched and vulnerable Internet systems [10].

Hence, the security and privacy of patient information is an ongoing concern for the medical community [11, 12]. In 1996, the Health Insurance Portability and Accountability Act (HIPAA) became law in the US [13]. According to HIPAA, medical providers are required to implement administrative, technical, and physical safeguards in order to protect electronic Patient Health Information (ePHI) [14, 15]. More specifically, medical providers are expected to guarantee the confidentiality, integrity, and availability of ePHI, in order to protect this information. Patient and therapy data collected and stored by medical smartphone applications is likely to be considered as ePHI and, medical smartphone applications are likely to require additional security and privacy measures, as compared to typical smartphone applications.

Similar to other industries (e.g., banking, finance, and governments), the number of medical and healthcare applications that provide an Internet interface for medical devices is increasing [12, 16]. A number of these devices, and their accompanying smartphone applications, are FDA-approved for use in medical settings [17, 18]. However, mobile forensic researchers have demonstrated that many smartphone applications produce residual data, which introduces a variety of security and privacy challenges [19–21]. It has also been demonstrated that data stored within certain smartphone applications can be used by malicious actors to develop behavior profiles of the device user [22].

The increased usage of medical smartphone applications, in conjunction with continued healthcare system attacks, prompts the idea that these applications present security and privacy risks. It is also realistic to speculate that the residual data produced by medical smartphone applications is protected ePHI. This idea prompted the hypothesis that Android medical applications, which have interacted with medical devices, are putting user data at risk from a HIPAA security and privacy perspective. The contribution of this paper is twofold. Specifically, our findings support the idea that Android smartphone medical applications, which interact with medical devices, collect and store residual data that potentially violate HIPAA Security and Privacy regulations. The findings also contribute to the documentation of forensic artifacts recovered from specific Android medical smartphone applications.

The remainder of this paper is structured as follows. Section two presents related work, while section three describes the experimental design used to investigate the hypothesis. Section four presents the experiment results and an analysis of the findings, and section five concludes the paper and presents avenues for future work.

2 Related Literature

The widespread adoption of different consumer and operational technologies (e.g., mobile devices, and medical Internet of Things (MIoT) devices) into the healthcare domain has introduced a variety of security challenges and concerns [23]. Malasri and Wang [24] scrutinized implantable medical devices and describe how these type of devices are susceptible to various type of security attacks, which includes tracking patient information from the devices. Li et al. [25] reported that patient and device information is often transmitted in plaintext by medical devices, allowing an attacker to potentially recover device passwords and dosage information. Glisson et al. [26] explain that hospital teaching environments are also vulnerable to cyber-attacks by demonstrating brute force and denial-of-service attacks against a medical mannequin.

The past few years has seen the emergence of MIoT devices [27]. However, data collected and transmitted by such devices (e.g., patient and therapy details) could potentially be targeted by malicious actors [12, 28]. Securing such data is particularly difficult when MIoT devices are deployed in environments that make it challenging to protect the underlying network, e.g., public Wi-Fi hotspots [27]. Data collected and compiled from different devices and sources could be cross-linked and subsequently be used to draw conclusions about a patient [28]. Hence, researchers have attempted to identify the challenges associated with the deployment of MIoT devices in settings such as hospitals and homes [29–31]. For example, Classen et al. [29] used a variety of techniques, including protocol analysis, software decompiling, and reverse engineering to extract private information from Fitbit fitness trackers. Similarly, Fereidooni et al. [30] reported that many of the fitness trackers included in their study did not include data integrity checks and implemented weak digital signatures. Wood et al. [31] demonstrated how an attacker can intercept unencrypted MIoT data transmissions, and use such information to profile the device owner.

Recent research also focuses on the integration of smartphone applications in the medical community. Miller et al. [32] scrutinized three telehealth smartphone applications and reported that two out of the three evaluated applications store information in plaintext. Similarly, Kharrazi et al. [33] reported that seven out of the nineteen mHealth applications evaluated in their study did not implement basic security features including password protection and user authentication mechanisms. Azfar et al. [34] put forth a forensic taxonomy which is based on a study of forty Android mHealth applications. This taxonomy consists of a variety of artifacts including databases, user credentials, and user activities.

Smartphone devices enhance the capabilities of traditional mobile phones and as a result, can provide forensic investigators with a wealth of potential evidence including web-browsing history, GPS coordinates, and third-party application-related data [35–37]. As a result, researchers have investigated how smartphone devices have been used to interact with social networks, cloud storage providers, and instant messaging services. Levinson et al. [38] demonstrated how it was possible to recover forensic artifacts from an iPhone device including device user information, GPS location information, and audio/video files. Al-Mutawa et al. [39] focused their research efforts on examining the forensic artifacts generated by smartphone social network applications and reported that Android devices produce detailed artifacts that describe social network activities.

Anglano [40] investigated WhatsApp and reported that information recovered from its database artifacts can be used to reconstruct a timeline of the messages that have been exchanged between respondents. Grispos et al. [41, 42] analyzed smartphone cloud storage applications including Dropbox and Box, and reported data and metadata generated by these applications along with their storage paths. While previous research has investigated the recovery of digital artifacts from a variety of services and applications, minimal research has examined the artifacts that can be recovered from a medical device smartphone application, and how the storage of these artifacts, could potentially, violate HIPAA Security and Privacy regulations.

3 Experiment Design

A controlled experiment [43] was devised to investigate the extent to which residual data generated by Android medical applications, could potentially, violate Security and Privacy regulations within HIPAA. The experiment consists of five stages: 1) setup an Android smartphone and install the Android medical applications; 2) create test profiles on the medical applications and synchronize the associated medical devices with the applications; 3) use the medical applications and their associated medical devices; 4) process the smartphone device using a mobile phone forensic toolkit to create forensic images; 5) examine the resulting forensic image in order to recover artifacts related to the medical applications.

Six medical devices (hereafter referred to as the 'devices') from two manufacturers were evaluated in this experiment. These devices are described in Table 1 - Medical Devices. The devices were selected because they include an accompanying Android smartphone application and were available to the authors. The Android smartphone applications (hereafter referred to as the 'medical device applications') included in this experiment are iHealth MyVitals (version 3.7.1), iHealth Gluco-Smart (version 4.5.3), and Withings Health Mate (version 3.5.4).

Table 1. Medical devices.

Manufacturer	Device name	Model	Mobile application name
iHealth	Core scale	HS6	iHealth MyVitals
iHealth	Feel Blood pressure monitor	BP5	iHealth MyVitals
iHealth	Air pulse oximeter	PO3M	iHealth MyVitals
iHealth	Gluco-monitoring system	BG5	iHealth Gluco-Smart
Nokia	Cardio scale	03700546702341	Health Mate
Nokia	BPM+	04719873310050	Health Mate

The smartphone used in this experiment is a Samsung Galaxy S4. This smartphone was selected for two reasons. First, the mobile forensic toolkit used in this experiment supports the smartphone and allows the extraction of a forensic image of the smartphone.

Second, the smartphone executes Android as its operating system, which represents the most prevalent smartphone operating system at the time of the research [44]. While many smartphones could fulfill these criteria, the decision to use this specific device was based on availability and compatibility with the mobile forensic toolkit.

Two iterations of the experiment were executed. The first iteration involved the iHealth devices and applications, while the second iteration involved the Nokia devices along with their associated applications. The following steps were performed to prepare the smartphone, the devices, and medical device applications for the experiment.

1. The smartphone was restored to its factory settings. The smartphone was then powered-on, a Google account was created, and the initial setup process was completed.
2. The smartphone was connected to the Internet in order to download and install the medical device application via the Google Application store. The application was installed using the default setup options. A test profile was created along with a common password, for the experiment.
3. The medical device application was then used to 'pair' the medical device with the smartphone, using the instructions provided in the device user manuals. In the case of the iHealth Gluco-Monitoring System, additional steps were required before it can be paired with the smartphone. This device requires that a QR code is scanned, in addition to following the steps provided within its manual.
4. The medical devices and their accompanying medical device applications were then used by one of the authors for five days. In the case of the iHealth Gluco-Monitoring System, diluted sugared water was used instead of blood to measure glucose levels. In addition to the date and time of the recording, the following was also recorded for each medical device by observing the result on the device interface:

   - iHealth Core Scale: weight, body mass index, body fat, lean mass, body water, muscle mass, daily calorie intake, and bone mass.
   - iHealth Feel Blood Pressure Monitor: pulse, systolic, and diastolic values.
   - iHealth Air Pulse Oximeter: pulse, oxygen level, and perfusion index
   - iHealth Gluco-Monitoring System: blood sugar level.
   - Nokia Cardio Scale: weight, body fat, body water, pulse, bone mass, muscle mass, and body mass index.
   - Nokia BPM+ Device: pulse, systolic, and diastolic values.

   It must be noted that test information was used for the above measurements.

5. After the five-day period, a forensic image of the smartphone's internal memory was created using MSAB XRY (version 7.7). The instructions provided by XRY were completed and the smartphone's internal memory was read. The resulting forensic image was then saved to a desktop computer.
6. The forensic image, created in Step 5, was then examined using MSAB's accompanying analysis software, XAMN (version 3.2). This analysis involved locating files and artifacts related to the medical device application. Certain files and artifacts were exported from XAMN and examined further using FTK (version 6.3)

These steps were executed for each medical smartphone application on the smartphone. It must be noted that this research is limited in the following ways. The smartphone used in the experiment was purchased in the United States (US). Therefore, the smartphone contains software for US mobile phone carriers. Due to time constraints, the experiment was executed only once for each medical device and its accompanying smartphone application. Specific versions of the Android operating system and medical device smartphone applications were used in this experiment. Due to tool limitations, the version of the Android operating system was limited to Android version 5.0, in order to execute a Physical Extraction for the Android device. Furthermore, the experiment was limited to the application versions available at the time of the experiment. Finally, for this investigation, this experiment implemented replicated test data versus using real-world patient data.

4   Results and Analysis

The analysis of the files and artifacts generated by the medical device applications revealed information about the test patient and their use of the medical devices evaluated in the experiment. Within the Android operating system, application data and metadata are stored under the path /data/data. Applications installed on an Android device create folders under this location. The following subsections summarize the data retrieved from this analysis. These results only include the artifacts readily identifiable as associated with the medical device applications of interest and do not include all artifacts retrieved from the smartphone.

4.1   iHealth Applications

The iHealth MyVitals application generates a folder called iHealthMyVitals.V2. Artifacts related to the iHealth Core scale, the Feel Blood pressure monitor, and the Air pulse oximeter were recovered from this folder location. Within this folder is a subfolder called Databases, which contains a SQLite database called android-Nin.db. Plaintext data parameters related to the iHealth devices can be retrieved from tables within this database. The first table of interest is called TB_BPResult. This table includes data related to the blood pressure monitor, including timestamps of the user's measurements, the systolic and diastolic values, the user's pulse rate, the device identifier, any text notes the user has entered as part of a reading, as well as the name of the user account associated with a particular reading.

Data parameters concerning the pulse oximeter can be retrieved from the database table called TB_SPo2Result. The data retrieved from this table (Fig. 1) includes the user's pulse rate ('PR'), perfusion index ('PI') and oxygen level ('Result'), along with the username ('HealthID') and timestamp ('MeasureTime') of each reading. Two tables called TB_TemperatureHumidity and TB_WeightOnlineResult contain data related to the Core scale. The TB_TemperatureHumidity table contains the humidity, temperature, and level of lighting as recorded by the scale. The TB_WeightOnlineResult table contains data related to the user's weight, body mass index value, body fat percentage, percentage of body water, muscle mass, daily calorie intake, and bone mass. The username and timestamp of each reading with the scale can also be recovered from the `TB_WeightOnlineResult` table.

UsedUserId ∨	PhoneDataID	iHealthID	MechineType	MechineDeviceID	MeasureTime	LastChangeTime	PhoneCreateTime	Result	PR	PI
Filter	Filter	Filter	Filter	Filter	Filter	Filter	Filter			Filter
0	5CF821DE...	medicaldevices2018exper@gmail.com	PO3M	5CF821DED2ED	1530829549	1530829596	1530829549	97	89	9.69999...
0	5CF821DE...	medicaldevices2018exper@gmail.com	PO3M	5CF821DED2ED	1530884863	1530884878	1530884863	96	77	8.30000...
0	5CF821DE...	medicaldevices2018exper@gmail.com	PO3M	5CF821DED2ED	1531090846	1531090859	1531090846	97	90	4.90000...
0	5CF821DE...	medicaldevices2018exper@gmail.com	PO3M	5CF821DED2ED	1531169685	1531169699	1531169685	96	80	12.3000...
0	5CF821DE...	medicaldevices2018exper@gmail.com	PO3M	5CF821DED2ED	1531259730	1531259755	1531259755	97	90	3.0

Fig. 1. Retrieval of information from TB_SPo2Result table

In addition to recovering iHealth device readings, a separate database table called `TB_Userinfo` contains data associated with the device user. This data includes the user's name, date of birth, timezone location, and email address. The iHealth MyVitals application also stores user and device data within XML files. Within these files, the patient's email address, device names, and MAC network addresses can be recovered. However, an interesting observation is the recovery of the user's authentication credentials in plaintext from the XML file called `sp_user_region_host_info.xml`. Figure 2 below, shows the recovery of the authentication access token and user password, stored in plaintext.

Fig. 2. Retrieval of plaintext password from iHealth account

The iHealth Gluco-monitoring system creates a separate folder called `jiuan.androidBg.start` to store data related to this device. However, while various databases were recovered within this parent folder, all these databases appeared to be encrypted. Hence, it is not possible to recover device readings related to the Gluco-monitoring system from its smartphone application. Breaking the encryption of the databases is considered out of scope for this research. However, user data can be recovered from the XML file called `user_info.xml`. This user data includes the patient's username, along with the device identifier that interacts with the smartphone application.

4.2 Nokia Application

Concerning the Health Mate application, data can be retrieved from a parent folder called `com.withings.wiscale2`. User and device data are primarily stored within three tables in a database called `withings-WiScale.db`. The first table of interest is called `devices` and contains data related to the Nokia Cardio Scale and BPM + devices. Information that can be recovered from this table includes the device's MAC address, timestamps related to when the device was last used, the type and model of the devices, as well as the battery level at the time of the last recording for the particular device. Figure 3 shows an example of information that can be recovered from the `devices` table.

id	associationDate	lastUseDate	modifiedDate	macAddress ⌄	firmware	timezone	battery	type	model
Filter	Filter	Filter	Filter	Filter	Filter	Filter	Filter	Filter	Filter
5595648	1541806236000	1542127729662	1542127635000	00:24:e4:5a:ee:6c	431	NULL	77	4	43
5402710	1541806407000	1542070868000	1542093243000	00:24:e4:57:12:c4	1751	America/Chicago	78	1	6

Fig. 3. Nokia device information

A second table called `measure` contains the measurements undertaken using the Nokia scale and blood pressure devices. The patient's weight, body fat, body water, pulse, bone mass, muscle mass, and body mass index, along with pulse information, systolic, and diastolic values can be recovered from this table. Each measurement includes timestamp information describing when the measurement was undertaken. It must be noted that three values associated with the Nokia Scale were not found within the `measure` table. These values are two Body Mass Index (BMI) calculations and one body fat reading.

Finally, patient-related data can be recovered from a third table called `users`. Patient data retrieved from this table include the patient's name, gender, birthday, along with the email address used during the initial application registration.

4.3 Analysis

After examining the device manufacturer's websites, all the applications evaluated in this experiment are purported to comply with HIPAA legislation. HIPAA's Privacy Rule states that "individually identifiable health information held or transmitted by a covered entity or its business associate, in any form or media, whether electronic, paper, or oral" must be protected [45]. The Privacy Rule calls this information "Protected Health Information (PHI) and includes an individual's past, present or future physical or mental health condition; the provision of healthcare to an individual; the past, present or future payment for the provision of healthcare to an individual; and common identifiers such as the patient's name, address, date of birth and social security number" [45].

The results from the analysis of the smartphone application data suggest that two (iHealth MyVitals and Health Mate) out of the three applications are potentially putting a user's information at risk. Table 2 highlights the PHI recovered from the smartphone applications evaluated in this experiment. The table shows that the iHealth MyVitals and Health Mate applications disclosed plaintext information about the patient (name and birthday), as well as health conditions (heart rates, blood pressure readings, etc.). Hence, the findings suggest that two out of three applications are, potentially, putting patient and medical information at risk from a HIPPA Privacy Rule perspective.

Table 2. HIPAA PHI stored in evaluated applications.

HIPAA requirement	iHealth MyVitals	Gluco-Smart	Health Mate
Individual's past, present or future physical or mental health condition	√	X	√
The provision of healthcare to an individual	√	X	√
Past, present, or future payment for the provision of healthcare to an individual	X	X	X
Patient's name	√	√	√
Patient's address	√	X	X
Patient's social security number	X	X	X
Patient's date of birth	√	X	√

Key: √ = Recovered from Application; X = Not Recovered from Application

Likewise, according to the HIPAA Security Rule, devices that store ePHI should consider utilizing encryption technologies of appropriate strength to protect sensitive information [46]. However, the analysis of the iHealth MyVitals and Health Mate applications revealed that these applications are storing patient and device information in plaintext. Furthermore, HIPAA also requires that safeguards are taken to protect passwords that can be used to access HIPAA-covered information [46]. However, the results from this experiment have shown that it is possible to recover the plaintext password from the MyVitals application. Hence, while all three applications claim to be HIPAA compliant, only the Android iHealth Gluco-Smart application appears to fully comply with the Security Rules requirements necessary for storing information, such as passwords, patient, and therapy details.

The examination of the above data supports the hypothesis that medical device applications, which interact with medical devices, violate the Security and Privacy rules within HIPAA. The statement holds for two out of the three applications evaluated in this research. The experimental findings reveal that patient-specific information can be retrieved from the applications including the patient's name, date of birth gender, as well as weight and height information. In addition to patient information, data related to the patient's use of the medical device can also be recovered from the medical device applications. However, the availability of this data is conditional on the specific smartphone application. For example, in terms of the iHealth MyVitals and Health Mate applications, this information included a patient's pulse rate, systolic and diastolic values, oxygen level, perfusion index, body mass index, daily calorie intake, bone mass, weight, body fat, lean mass, and body water level. Moreover, while minimal medical device usage data was recovered from the iHealth Gluco-Smart application, user details can be recovered from XML artifacts generated by the application.

5 Conclusions and Future Work

Smartphone devices are becoming increasingly pervasive in today's medical environments. As a result, there are security and privacy concerns related to the data stored and transmitted by these devices, when used in medical contexts. The findings from this initial research have demonstrated how certain smartphone applications, which interact with medical devices, violate the Security and Privacy rules within HIPAA. Information that can be recovered from these applications includes a patient's personal details and their usage of the specific medical device. This information could, in theory, be exploited by a cybercriminal who can gather intelligence about an individual's medical history, well-being, and potential ailments. Such information can then be used to develop medical profiles or combined with residual data from other smartphone applications to develop detailed patterns of user behavior.

There are several potential avenues for future research. The authors intend to expand this study to include an analysis of other medical devices and smartphone operating systems. This investigation investigates the applicability of the security and privacy concerns identified in this paper to other medical technical and environmental contexts. Research also needs to examine the degree to which data and metadata can be recovered from uninstalled medical device applications and the medical devices themselves. The insight gained from this avenue of research helps organizations to alleviate ePHI data leakage when devices are decommissioned and/or the smartphone applications are removed from a user's smartphone device. The results of future research in this area potentially provide insight into the development of relevant security measures, mitigation solutions, and the identification of necessary healthcare policy components.

Acknowledgments. This research was financially supported by the Nebraska Research Initiative (NRI). The statements, opinions, and content included in this publication do not necessarily reflect the position or the policy of the NRI, and no official endorsement should be inferred.

References

1. Krebs, P., Duncan, D.T.: Health app use among US mobile phone owners: a national survey. J. Med. Internet Res. mHealth uHealth **3**(4), (2015)
2. Perna, G.: The State of Mobile Health in Today's Practice (2018). https://www.physicianspractice.com/article/state-mobile-health-todays-practice
3. Soti Inc.: US Consumer Survey: Physicians Using Mobile Apps Seen as a Major Differentiator Amongst US Patients (2019). https://www.globenewswire.com/news-release/2019/06/06/1865254/0/en/U-S-Consumer-Survey-Physicians-Using-Mobile-Apps-Seen-as-a-Major-Differentiator-Amongst-U-S-Patients.html
4. Baumgart, D.C.: Digital advantage in the COVID-19 response: perspective from Canada's largest integrated digitalized healthcare system. NPJ Dig. Med. **3**(1), 1–4 (2020)
5. Neubeck, L., Hansen, T., Jaarsma, T., Klompstra, L., Gallagher, R.: Delivering healthcare remotely to cardiovascular patients during COVID-19: a rapid review of the evidence. Eur. J. Cardiovasc. Nurs., 1474515120924530 (2020)
6. Moorhead, S.A., Hazlett, D.E., Harrison, L., Carroll, J.K., Irwin, A., Hoving, C.: A new dimension of healthcare: systematic review of the uses, benefits, and limitations of social media for health communication. J. Med. Internet Res. **15**(4), (2013)

7. Healthcare Information and Management Systems Society. 2019: HIMSS Cybersecurity Survey (2019)
8. United States Government Accountability Office: FDA Should Expand Its Consideration of Information Security For Certain Types of Devices (2012)
9. United States Food and Drug Administration. Cybersecurity (2019). https://www.fda.gov/medical-devices/digital-health/cybersecurity
10. British Broadcasting Corporation: NHS 'Could Have Prevented' WannaCry Ransomware Attack (2017). https://www.bbc.com/news/technology-41753022
11. Van Devender, M.S., Glisson, W.B., Benton, R., Grispos, G.: Understanding de-identification of healthcare big data. In: 2017 Americas Conference on Information Systems (AMCIS 2017), Boston, USA (2017)
12. Flynn, T., Grispos, G., Glisson, W.B., Mahoney, W.: Knock! Knock! Who is there? Investigating data leakage from a medical Internet of Things hijacking attack. In: 53rd Hawaii International Conference on System Sciences, Maui, Hi, USA (2020)
13. United States Government: The Health Insurance Portability and Accountability Act. United States Government (1996)
14. United States Government: Security Standards: Administrative Safeguards (2007)
15. United States Government: Code of Federal Regulations - Title 45: Public Welfare, p. 738 (2007)
16. Grispos, G., Glisson, W.B., Cooper, P.: A bleeding digital heart: identifying residual data generation from smartphone applications interacting with medical devices. In: 52nd Hawaii International Conference on System Sciences, Maui, Hi, USA (2019)
17. Withings: BPM Connect (2019). https://www.withings.com/us/en/bpm-connect
18. iHealth: Wireless Gluco-monitoring System (2019). https://ihealthlabs.com/glucometer/wireless-smart-gluco-monitoring-system/
19. Shetty, R., Grispos, G., Choo, K.-K.R.: Are you dating danger? An interdisciplinary approach to evaluating the (in)security of android dating apps. IEEE Trans. Sustain. Comput. (2017, in Press)
20. Plachkinova, M., Andrés, S., Chatterjee, S.: A taxonomy of mHealth apps–security and privacy concerns. In: 2015 48th Hawaii International Conference on System Sciences (2015). IEEE
21. Wang, Y., Streff, K., Raman, S.: Smartphone security challenges. Computer **45**(12), 52–58 (2012)
22. Grispos, G., Glisson, W.B., Pardue, J.H., Dickson, M.: Identifying user behavior from residual data in cloud-based synchronized apps. In: Conference for Information Systems Applied Research, vol. 8, no. 2, pp. 4–14 (2014)
23. Grispos, G., Bastola, K.: Cyber autopsies: the integration of digital forensics into medical contexts. In: 2020 IEEE 33rd International Symposium on Computer-Based Medical Systems (CBMS). IEEE (2020)
24. Malasri, K., Wang, L.: Securing wireless implantable devices for healthcare: ideas and challenges. IEEE Commun. Mag. **47**(7), 74–80 (2009)
25. Li, C., Zhang, M., Raghunathan, A., Jha, N.K.: Attacking and defending a diabetes therapy system. In: Burleson, W., Carrara, S. (eds.) Security and Privacy for Implantable Medical Devices, pp. 175–193. Springer, New York (2014). https://doi.org/10.1007/978-1-4614-1674-6_8
26. Glisson, W.B., Andel, T., Campbell, M., Jacobs, M., Mayr, J., McDonald, T.: Compromising a medical mannequin. In: 21st Americas Conference on Information Systems, Puerto Rico, USA (2015)
27. Sun, W., Cai, Z., Li, Y., Liu, F., Fang, S., Wang, G.: Security and privacy in the medical Internet of Things: a review. Secur. Commun. Netw. (2018)
28. Williams, P.A., McCauley, V.: Always connected: the security challenges of the healthcare Internet of Things. In: IEEE 3rd World Forum on Internet of Things, Reston, VA, USA (2016)

29. Classen, J., Wegemer, D., Patras, P., Spink, T., Hollick, M.: Anatomy of a vulnerable fitness tracking system: dissecting the fitbit cloud, app, and firmware. Proc. ACM Interact. Mob. Wearable Ubiquitous Technol. **2**(1), 1–24 (2018)
30. Fereidooni, H., Frassetto, T., Miettinen, M., Sadeghi, A.-R., Conti, M.: Fitness trackers: fit for health but unfit for security and privacy. In: 2017 IEEE/ACM International Conference on Connected Health: Applications, Systems and Engineering Technologies, Philadelphia, PA, USA (2017)
31. Wood, D., Apthorpe, N., Feamster, N.: Cleartext data transmissions in consumer IoT medical devices. In: Proceedings of the 2017 Workshop on Internet of Things Security and Privacy. ACM (2017)
32. Miller, S., Glisson, W.B., Campbell, M., Sittig, S.: Risk analysis of residual protected health information of android telehealth apps. In: Twenty-Fifth Americas Conference on Information Systems, Cancun, Mexico (2019)
33. Kharrazi, H., Chisholm, R., VanNasdale, D., Thompson, B.: Mobile personal health records: an evaluation of features and functionality. Int. J. Med. Inf. **81**(9), 579–593 (2012)
34. Azfar, A., Choo, K.-K.R., Liu, L.: Forensic taxonomy of popular Android mHealth apps. In: 21st Americas Conference on Information Systems, Puerto Rico, USA (2015)
35. Hoog, A.: Android Forensics: Investigation, Analysis and Mobile Security for Google Android, Syngress (2011)
36. Hoog, A., Strzempka, K.: iPhone and iOS Forensics: Investigation, Analysis and Mobile Security for Apple iPhone, iPad and iOS Devices, Syngress (2011)
37. Grispos, G., Storer, T., Glisson, W.B.: A comparison of forensic evidence recovery techniques for a windows mobile smart phone. Digit. Invest. **8**(1), 23–36 (2011)
38. Levinson, A., Stackpole, B., Johnson, D.: Third party application forensics on apple mobile devices. In: 44th Hawaii International Conference on System Sciences, Kauai, HI, USA (2011)
39. Al Mutawa, N., Baggili, I., Marrington, A.: Forensic analysis of social networking applications on mobile devices. Digit. Invest. **9**, S24–S33 (2012)
40. Anglano, C.: Forensic analysis of WhatsApp Messenger on Android smartphones. Digit. Invest. **11**(3), 201–213 (2014)
41. Grispos, G., Glisson, W.B., Storer, T.: Using smartphones as a proxy for forensic evidence contained in cloud storage services. In: 46th Hawaii International Conference on System Sciences, Hawaii, USA (2013)
42. Grispos, G., Glisson, W.B., Storer, T.: Recovering residual forensic data from smartphone interactions with cloud storage providers. In: Choo, K.-K.R., Ko, R. (eds.) The Cloud Security Ecosystem, pp. 347–382. Syngress, Boston (2015)
43. Oates, B.J.: Researching Information Systems and Computing. Sage, Thousand Oaks (2005)
44. Statscounter: Mobile Operating System Market Share Worldwide (2019). https://gs.statco unter.com/os-market-share/mobile/worldwide
45. United States Department of Health and Human Services Office for Civil Rights: HIPAA Administrative Simplification - 5 CFR Parts 160, 162, and 164 (2013)
46. United States Department of Health and Human Services: HIPAA Security Guidance (2006)

Multifunctional SMART Air Cleaner

Michal Balog$^{(\boxtimes)}$ ⓘ, Angelina Iakovets, and Stella Hrehova

Technical University of Kosice, Faculty of Manufacturing Technologies With the Seat in Presov, Presov 08001, Slovak Republic
michal.balog@tuke.sk

Abstract. Environmental air quality often affects human health. Allergens, viruses, bacteria often float in the air and settle on surfaces. This situation prompts various world organizations to address this problem by means of disinfection and cleaning of premises where a person is most often. Pathogenic bacteria are often spread by airborne droplets and can persist on surfaces for a long time. The proposed study was aimed at proposing a device for a disinfecting room without harm to human health. The multifunctional SMART cleaner is based on the existing and proven properties of UV light to ensure disinfection of not only air but also surfaces. The multifunctionality of the device is represented by different modes of operation and functionality, and the intelligent control unit provides wireless communication with the detection sensor and adjustment of operating modes and cleaning intensity. The properties and parameters of individual components of the device, as well as market research made it possible to assert that the device is effective and also meets modern requirements.

Keywords: UV · UV-C · IoT · SMART · Disinfection · Sensor

1 Introduction

Disinfection has become especially important in the current situation in the world. Despite the growth in demand on disinfection devices and antiseptic due to the pandemic in recent years, air purification becomes also needed. Air cleaning is actual not only in pandemic situation but also in ordinary life. Allergens, viruses are constantly present in the air and in order to limit the spread of opposing pathogens, it is worth preemptively using air purifying devices.

Every day, employees of any enterprise spend about 7 h a day indoors. Caring for employees and visitors of the enterprise is the primary task of not only the entrepreneur but also of the state.

In connection with the development of the pandemic situation in the world, the European Committee took measures, namely the creation of an Emergency Support Instrument (ESI) [1]. In general, the ESI represents a financial lever to curb the spread of coronavirus in the EU countries. The main assistance is provided in areas such as:

© ICST Institute for Computer Sciences, Social Informatics and Telecommunications Engineering 2021
Published by Springer Nature Switzerland AG 2021. All Rights Reserved
D. Perakovic and L. Knapcikova (Eds.): FABULOUS 2021, LNICST 382, pp. 323–334, 2021.
https://doi.org/10.1007/978-3-030-78459-1_24

- providing a vaccine,
- treatment,
- testing of patients,
- assistance in the transportation of essential items, medical teams and patients,
- provision of personal protective equipment,
- training of medical personnel and exchange of experience,
- UV robots for disinfection of hospitals throughout Europe [2].

Robots have long been used in many economic fields and therefore arose the idea to use them for disinfection. It did not arise by chance, since it is very important in a difficult pandemic situation to provide fast and high-quality disinfection of surfaces, and most importantly, in hospital wards. On the European Committee's website writes that "The Commission has allocated 12 million Euros from the Emergency Support Tool for the procurement of 200 UV disinfection robots that will be delivered to hospitals across Europe. The robots can disinfect standard patient rooms with UV light in just 15 min and represent an important an asset that can help hospitals reduce the risk of infection and contain the spread of the coronavirus [2]". This type of disinfection is very effective and not new at all. For the first time, the fact that ultraviolet radiation can be used in medicine became known in 1892. Then the practice was introduced to destroy bacteria and microbes using ultraviolet light. And in 1906, the first quartz lamp for medical use was created [3]. The process of using the lamp in some countries was called "Quartzization", which meant the process of processing (disinfecting) rooms, objects, the human body with ultraviolet radiation from a quartz or bactericidal lamp. As a result, infectious microorganisms [4]. Based on the above, it can be argued that the European Commission went through the use of time-tested technologies. Robots of this type began to be used not only in healthcare, but also in warehouses and even some banks [5]. As example, one of the banks, equipped robot with 100 W ultraviolet lamps, which, according to representatives of the Sberbank Robotics Laboratory, can effectively disinfect a room with an area of 20 m^2 in 5 min. And the robot can process 2500 m^2 overnight. The disinfector operates autonomously. When entering an unknown room, he first examines it, after which he can independently navigate and move around it. When a person is detected nearby, the robot immediately turns off the ultraviolet lamps. Sberbank notes that the new robot will be useful even after the COVID-19 pandemic - in particular, during seasonal outbreaks of influenza and SARS [5, 6]. The warehouse robot was equipped with four ultraviolet lamps that shine 360°. According to the creators, the robot manages to clean a 380 m^2 warehouse in half an hour and will destroy 90% of the particles of coronavirus on surfaces [5].

It is impossible to deny that this is a great idea, but still, it is a known fact that ultraviolet dysentery lamps have a detrimental effect on people's skin. The proposed studies are aimed at finding a similar solution but under different conditions, namely disinfection in the presence of people.

2 Literature Review

The World Health Organization (WHO) claims that air pollution has become the biggest environmental health threat, with about 7 million deaths in 2012 [7]. Indoor and outdoor pollution affects health. Recent statistics on household indoor pollutants (HAP) exposure are alarming. The WHO HAP and Health Fact Sheet states that 3.8 million people die prematurely each year, including stroke, coronary heart disease, chronic obstructive pulmonary disease (COPD) and lung cancer associated with exposure to indoor air pollution [8]. The use of air cleaners and filters is one proposed strategy for improving indoor air quality [9].

There are several types of air purification that have long been known and popular:

- recuperator [10],
- conditioners with cleaning function,
- stationary air purifiers.

The main cleaning components of such devices:

- carbon filter,
- dust filter,
- ionizer,
- UV lamp.

The main purpose of all these devices is to purify and circulate the air indoors. Sublett and James, in their article "Effectiveness of Air Filters and Air Cleaners in Allergic Respiratory Diseases: A Review of the Recent Literature" write that air filtration is often recommended as a component of environmental management techniques for patients with allergic respiratory diseases [11]. It follows from this that air filtration in residential premises can be provided by WHF through a home HVAC system, PRAC, or a combination [11]. But what to do in work areas, where filter replacement will be much more frequent than in residential areas and the flow of people is much larger. Sublett and James point out that currently popular ionic devices produce ozone, irritating to breath, and in one study caused an increase in submicron particles [11], which in turn proves that ionization is not an appropriate technology for high traffic.

Due to the difficult epidemic situation, the question arises: what type of filtration or cleaning helps in the fight against SARS-CoV-2. Many scientists claim that the virus is spread by airborne droplets and that there are people who carry the virus who do not have signs of the disease, but are its distributors [12]. It is difficult for employers to provide constant testing of employees, and even more so for clients. Constant testing would bring a lot of inconvenience and frustration on both sides.

In this case, the solution is to clean surfaces and air. Cleaning of surfaces is important, as microparticles breathed out by a person and those that are spread by touch remain on surfaces in the room. Air purification will help trap airborne particles and reduce the amount of bacteria deposited on the surface, thereby reducing the likelihood of inhalation of these particles or bacteria by a person in the room.

Christiane Silke Heilingloh and a team of scientists conducted a study involving SARS-CoV-2. Scientists have investigated the susceptibility of high titer SARS-CoV-2 virus stocks to combined or separate exposure to UVA and UVC [13]. Laboratory studies have shown that SARS-CoV-2 can be inactivated by UV radiation [13].

Song Tang and a group of scientists in their studies of the covid-19 and other groups of doctors and scientists have come to the conclusion that during a pandemic it is very important to use:

– masks,
– gloves,
– disinfectors and sanitizers [14].

Such precautions have long been used by doctors, even in peacetime. Wearing masks and fear of spreading bacteria is a lot of inconvenience. It is especially difficult to provide comfortable conditions for enterprises that continue to work in the same mode. Viruses, bacteria, allergens are always present in our life, and one method of air or surface cleaning is not enough. A well-known example is the ubiquitous pathogens of intestinal gram-negative bacteria such as Salmonella, Escherichia and Shigella, especially in summer, which continue to cause severe diarrhea infections worldwide. The food pathogen Listeria monocyogenes also has a significant impact on statistics, as it tends to develop serious diseases in people with weakened immune systems. Actinobacteria of the genus Mycobacterium are also a major cause of morbidity and mortality. Despite the development of medicine, the pathogens of the Mycobacterium tuberculosis complex remain one of the most serious causes of infectious diseases worldwide.

3   Methodology

The traditional methods of disinfection currently used have their limitations. Practical problems are known associated with damage to cleaning devices or cleaning filters, finally, the development of microbial resistance due to the long-term use of chemical disinfectants such as sodium hypochlorite, ozone and H_2O_2. Mycobacteria are inherently resistant to chemical decontamination because they have an unusual cell membrane containing peptidoglycan, arabinoglycan and mycolic acid, which restricts the passage of many chemicals and drugs through the cell membrane, which contributes to the resistance of this microorganism [15, 16].

In response to the persistent challenges posed by established and emerging pathogens and to provide complementary or alternative approaches to microbiological control, there has been considerable interest in new, alternative methods of disinfection and decontamination.

The problem of disinfection and cleaning from bacteria and viruses remains relevant, since each of the previously associated methods has its own disadvantages (Table 1).

Household stationary cleaners can help the spread of some particles, but alas, with a large flow of people, they are not very effective and they also lack a mechanism for adjusting the strength of air purification. The proposed studies are aimed at offering a universal smart device for continuous air disinfection not only in hospitals and medical institutions, but also in schools, canteens, restaurants, cinemas, theaters, etc.

Table 1. The main disadvantages of existing cleaning methods [10, 11].

Cleaning element	Disadvantage
HVAC system	Main task is climate control
PRAC	Requires constant cleaning
UV-A& UV-B	Causes oxidation of proteins and lipids resulting in cell death
UV-C	Adversely affects the skin Photochemical reactions in DNA&RNA resulting in inactivation of microbes and failure to reproduce
HEPA (High Efficiency Particulate Air) Filtration	efficient only to trap particles 0.3 microns and larger

This decision was made in connection with the difficult economic situation in all economic sectors.

The main problems of all of the above facilities are:

– continuous and uneven flow of people,
– the need for disinfection even in the presence of people in the room,
– adjustment of the intensity of cleaning depending on the number of people in the room.

If to turn to real devices on the market, can be distinguished four basic principles of interior air purification (see Table 2).

Table 2. Four main principles of interior air purificators [10, 11].

Cleaning element	Parameters
HEPA filtration	- efficient to trap particles 0.3 microns and larger, - can be incorporated into central HVAC systems, - energy-intensive technology, - is not effective on many mold spores, bacteria and viruses, - requires repairing of filters
UV purification	- Disinfects by passing air through ultra-violet light - can be incorporated into central HVAC systems - cleans only those surfaces and air that is directly exposed to UV light, - do not restrict airflow, - requires replacing worn bulbs

(*continued*)

Table 2. (*continued*)

Cleaning element	Parameters
Ionization	- Creates single polarity ionization to attract particles, - the single polarity will use any nearby surface as the needed opposite polarity and dust will be settle on it, - effective workable distance 8–9 inch radius, - energy-intensive technology, - mostly ineffective against bacteria, spores and volatile organic compounds, - can interfere with radio equipment
Dust collectors/filters	- Collect particles on a metal surface contained in the unit and produces single polarity ions, - ineffective against bacteria, spores and VOC compounds, - not integrable into other systems

According to the above properties (see Table 2) of cleaning elements, it can be argued that the most suitable are UV lamps, which not only disinfect surfaces but also the air, what is especially important in conditions of raging acute respiratory diseases and pandemic. It is a well-known fact that bacteria are transmitted tactilely, by air, and also have the ability to settle on surfaces and stay there for several months, and in such cases, UV lamps are used in hospital rooms [17]. This technology is widely used not only in laboratories, but also in operating rooms where the number of bacteria is reduced by 85%, and the number of infections by 73% thanks to UV lamps [17].

4   Proposed Solution

The control of purifier filter contamination is very important in premises with a large flow of people, especially if the enterprise works in three shifts. Deactivation of pathogenic microbes by UV light is the cheapest and fastest method of the so-called surface disinfection.

For example, standard disinfectant can be diluted at a 48:1 ratio. The cost for a gallon (3,78 L) of bleach is about US dollars 2,67 (Euros 2,22). That equates to US dollars 2,67 for 48 gallons (143,846 L) of solution (3,78 L). Typical retail disinfectants cover approximately 150–250 square feet (14–23 square meters) per gallon (3,8 L). Manufacturing facilities typically occupy about 15000 square feet (1393,5 m²), which is 1393,5 L (3093,57 Euros). This significantly affects the overall cost of disinfection [18].

Under normal conditions, the working premises should be cleaned 3 times per shift. The enterprises have about 20 working days per month. Basis on this, the company will spend 3938,4 Euros per year on a 15 m² room of per year.

The proposed device serves a room with the same square, but at the same time its cost and maintenance are much cheaper and clean not only surfaces but also air. The cleaner needs to replace the lamps, where price of replacing such a lamp will be about 40

Euros. This manipulation can be made by any employee. The most sensitive component of the purifier is the UV lamp, where its working life is 8000 h, which is more than 1000 working days (over 2.8 years). Even assuming that all three lamps should be replacing at once, it will cost about 120 Euros.

Proposed device is not able completely exclude the need in cleaning surfaces by standard methods, but it able to reduce number of usual cleaning procedures, especially in room with a high level of pollution.

Construction of dust collectors, often represented by several filters (for different sized particles) embedded in the housing. This method of cleaning is not bad, but replacing filters directly depends on the amount of pollution in the air and the operating time of the device. The main problem is the lack of a filter clogging indicator (Fig. 1).

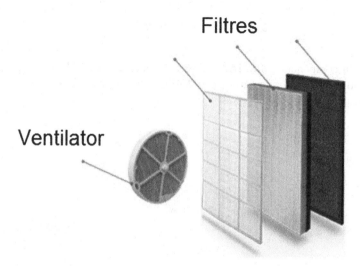

Fig. 1. General components of the HEPA air cleaner [19].

The design of filter air purifiers is represented by several filter plates and two fans or so-called "turbines" that move the air inside the air purifier structure. This design is very simple but effective.

Based on the specifics of the presented cleaners, the main requirements for cleaners that should be met:

– continuous disinfection;
– processing of the visible environment of the room and the invisible (air and surfaces);
– safety of use in the presence of people;
– effectiveness against a wide range of pathogens;
– Low operational requirements;
– The presence of a wear sensor of the working elements of the device.

To meet all the requirements, a device design was proposed (see Fig. 2).

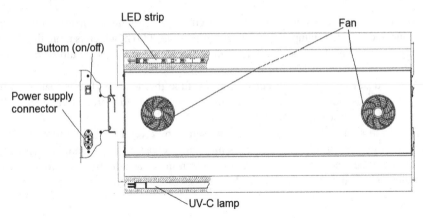

Fig. 2. Multifunctional SMART air cleaner

The main components of SMART air cleaner are: 2 fans, 3 UV-C lamps, cooling tubes, a central control unit for the device, 2 LED lighting strips and a separately mounted motion sensor (Fig. 3).

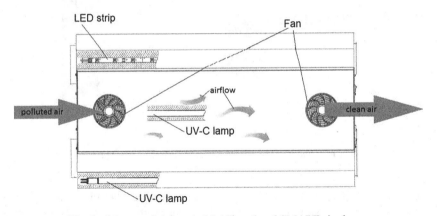

Fig. 3. Scheme of airflow in Multifunctional SMART air cleaner

One of the fans draws air into the device, the air inside the device flows near the UV lamp and is then expelled outside by the second fan. For the prototype, 16 V UVC lamps (G5) and a life cycle of 8000 working hours were chosen. This shelf life is quite competitive, since with a typical working day of 8 h/day and an average number of working days in a month of 22 days, it can be argued that the enterprise will not need to replace lamps for more than 3 years. But this is on condition that there are no drops in electricity. The fans are capable of handling 50 m^3/h at an average normal load. In order to correctly calculate the required power as well as the operating mode of the device, it was proposed to use the Smart control unit, which communicates with the detection (motion) sensor and determines the required power and frequency of switching on the device and transferring it to the surface disinfection mode.

The design of the device provides for several modes of operation:

1. LED lamp and air purifier.
2. Disenfector of surfaces.
3. Disenfector of surfaces and air.

The first mode is needed for normal office work with and/or without neighbors, i.e. provided that the employee is in the working area. In such conditions, the room is illuminated with light, and an internal UVC lamp is turned on for air disinfection.

The second mode is activated when there are no people in the room for surface disinfection. The light is off at this moment to save energy.

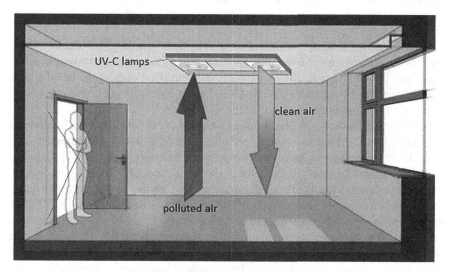

Fig. 4. Third mode illustration

The third mode (see Fig. 4.) appropriate when number of visitors was maximum and careful disinfection is needed. During third mode the LED light is turned off, but all UV-C lamps is in active mode to provide the best purification. Should be noticed, that when third mode is switched on, there should be no people in the room during disinfection.

Optimal control or switching of individual wavelengths of white, blue and UV light is ensured by the IoT smart control unit with external biosensors, sensors for detecting movement, the presence of people and the current light intensity to outdoor lighting conditions.

Device management is planned through a mobile application. This decision was associated with the spread of SMART home technologies as well as the Internet of Things. The sensor responsible for controlling the device modes was selected based on several criteria:

– - counting the number of people in the room,
– - wireless connection to the gravel device,

– - identification of people without a chamber principle in connection with the protection of personal data.

A conventional motion sensor does not detect the number of people in the room, but only reacts to movement and is not always correct. Due to the fact that there is a category of employees working at a computer and their actions, the sensor will not always be able to recognize as movements - this can switch the device to the surface disinfection mode and thereby harm a person or simply turn off the lighting in the room. In connection with this principle of operation of the sensor, it was proposed to replace it with a people counting sensor. This decision was due to the new rules introduced in many EU countries. These rules state that in connection with the pandemic, the number of people in the room is limited based on the size of the room. This rule helps not to load the cleaning device, as well as to notify employees through notifications when the number of people is already close to the boundary value.

As Khaled Al Huraimel and a group of scientists write in their article "SARS-CoV-2 in the environment: Modes of transmission, early detection and potential role of pollutions", the virus disease SARS-CoV-2 is influenced not only by the initial state of a person, but also by the quality of air [20]. This statement is applicable not only to coronavirus but also to other types of infections.

For laboratory testing was used sensor Count Max [21], which provides automated counting with infrared beam, where its accuracy up to 95% with a passage width of up to 2 m. Works regardless of changes in temperature, humidity, ambient light [22].

The horizontal infrared (IR) counter is the basic model for automating counting serving for registering the number of visitors; they are counting in two directions (entry-exit). Attendance data is accumulated in the sensor's non-volatile memory [21]. The rules say that for one customer should be allocated per 15 m^2 of the sales area of all operations in the department store intended for customers [23, 24]. Since the normal operating capacity of the device is 50m^3, it can be argued that the device will provide a comfortable working environment for four people. Thus, it was configured that when there are 4 people, the device will signal that the limit value has been reached.

5   Conclusions and Future Research

The multifunctional SMART cleaner helps to disinfect not only the air in the room but also the surfaces, as well as illuminate the room. Three modes of operation will help to effectively manage the device but also save on electricity thanks to the person counting sensor in the room. In the basic mode, it controls the optimal mixing of white and blue light in the presence of people in the room and, based on the number of people, maximizes the performance of the disinfection. The connection of the sensor and the purifier is performed by connecting to a common Internet network according to the principle of Smart Home devices. In further research, it is planned to develop a full-fledged mobile application with many functions for convenient control of the purifier. Instantly the device was controlled via the Internet resource similar to MI Home [25], which in the future will acquire more functions. In the basic mode, multifunctional SMART cleaner controls the optimal mixing of white and UV-C light in the presence of people in the room and, based on the number of people, maximizes the performance of the disinfection. At the same time, in future studies, it is planned that the device signals the status of disinfection and stores information about the power of operation in disinfection mode in a given room at time intervals in the cloud storage. Data from the control unit will be saved via the IoT communication network (Sigfox, LoraWan) on a cloud platform from multiple control units for comprehensive monitoring of the entire building and disinfection status, as well as monitoring the presence or absence of personnel.

Since the idea of smart integrated control systems is constantly evolving, it is assumed that the proposed device will provide comfortable working conditions not only during a pandemic but also in peacetime and will meet all the requirements of our time.

References

1. European Commission. Coronavirus: Commission to provide 200 disinfection robots to European hospitals. https://ec.europa.eu/digital-single-market/en/news. Accessed 1 Nov 2020
2. European Commission: Emergency Support Instrument. https://ec.europa.eu/info/. Accessed 2 Nov 2020
3. Ryabtsev, A.N.: Ultraviolet radiation. Physical encyclopedia. In: Prokhorov, A.M. (ed.) Great Russian encyclopedia. T. 5, pp. 221- 760. ISBN 5 -85270–101-7
4. Kazakh encyclopedias: T. III. ISBN 9965–9746–4–0 (2005)
5. Rachel, G.: CSAIL robot disinfects Greater Boston Food Bank. MIT News (2020). www.news.mit.edu. Accessed 15 Nov 2020
6. Makarenko, V.: Sberbank introduced a robotic disinfector to fight viruses. https://4pda.ru/2020/. Accessed 15 Nov 2020
7. Ambient (outdoor) Air Quality and Health, Fact Sheet No. 313. World Health Organization. http://www.who.int/mediacentre/factsheets/fs313/en/. Accessed 1 Nov 2020
8. Household Air Polluton and Health, Fact Sheet No. 292. World Health Organization. http://www.who.int/mediacentre/factsheets/fs292/en/. Accessed 15 Nov 2020
9. Vijayan, V.K., Paramesh, H., Salvi, S.S., Dalal, A.A.: Enhancing indoor air quality -the air filter advantage. Lung India Official Organ Indian Chest Soc. 32(5), 473–479 (2015). https://doi.org/10.4103/0970-2113.164174
10. Lemes, A.: Recuperator. https://www.pinterest.com/andrislemes/recuperator/. Accessed 15 Nov 2020
11. Sublett, J.L.: Effectiveness of air filters and air cleaners in allergic respiratory diseases: a review of the recent literature. Curr. Aller. Asthma Rep. 11(5), 395–402 (2011). https://doi.org/10.1007/s11882-011-0208-5
12. Symptoms of Coronavirus. https://www.cdc.gov/coronavirus/2019-ncov/symptoms-testing/symptoms.html. Accessed 16 Nov 2020
13. Heilingloh, C.S., et al.: Susceptibility of SARS-CoV-2 to UV irradiation. Am. J. Infect. Control. 48(10), 1273–1275 (2020). https://doi.org/10.1016/j.ajic.2020.07.031
14. Tang, S., et al.: Aerosol transmission of SARS-CoV-2 evidence prevention and control (IF 7.577). Environ. Int. 144, 1–10 (2020). https://doi.org/10.1016/j.envint.2020.106039
15. Murdoch, L.E., Maclean, M., Endarko, E., MacGregor, S.J., Anderson, J.G.: Bactericidal effects of 405 nm light exposure demonstrated by inactivation of escherichia, salmonella, shigella, listeria, and mycobacterium species in liquid suspensions and on exposed surfaces. Sci. World J. 2012, 1–8 (2012). https://doi.org/10.1100/2012/137805
16. Violet Defence. https://www.violetdefense.com/howitworks. Accessed 20 Dec 2020

17. Bečarová, K.: Light Disinfection, Freya LED Lighting (2018). www.freyaled.com.https://fre yaled.com/blog/dezinfekcia-pomocou-svetla
18. Vitale, B.: How to Calculate Your Disinfecting Cost, June 2020 https://blog.midwestind.com/ disinfecting-cost-calculator/. Accessed 25 Dec 2020
19. Vredova, V.: Clever & Clean HealthAir UV-07 air purifier. Disinfection and air purification (2020). https://market.yandex.ru/journal/overview/. Accessed 18 Nov 2020
20. Huraimel, K.A., Alhosani, M., Kunhabdulla, S., Stietiya, M.H.: SARS-CoV-2 in the environment: modes of transmission, early detection and potential role of pollutions. Sci. Total Environ. **744**, 1–10 (2020). https://doi.org/10.1016/j.scitotenv.2020.140946
21. WATCOM. https://www.watcom.ru/products/sistema_podscheta_posetiteley/. Accessed 25 Nov 2020
22. EASPRO. https://easpro.by/counters/countmax. Accessed 25 Nov 2020
23. Richterová, N.: V obchodoch platia od pondelka nové opatrenia. Takto to bude vyzerať po novom. (2020). www.noviny.sk. Accessed 21 Nov 2020
24. Public Health Office of the Slovak Republic www.uvzsr.sk
25. Google Play, Mi Home app. https://play.google.com/store/apps/details?id=com.xiaomi.sma rthome&hl=ru&gl=US. Accessed 21 Nov 2020

Sustainable Communications and Computing Infrastructures

Augmented Reality as a Tool of Increasing of Competitiveness of Enterprise

Lucia Knapčíková$^{(\boxtimes)}$ ⓘ, Jozef Husár ⓘ, Annamária Behúnová ⓘ, and Stella Hrehová ⓘ

Faculty of Manufacturing Technologies with a Seat in Prešov, Department of Industrial Engineering and Informatics, The Technical University of Košice, Bayerova 1, 080 01 Prešov, Slovak Republic
{lucia.knapcikova,jozef.husar,annamaria.behunova,
stella.hrehova}@tuke.sk

Abstract. Success in the market in today's highly competitive environment is influenced not only by the quality of products and services of a given enterprise or individual but also by the way they are promoted in the marketing sphere. Enterprises are looking for a variety of promotions, from ordinary flyers in mailboxes to large, expensive advertisements on TV screens. To attract the attention of potential customers, enterprises are forced to continually invent new ways of promotion. Advanced technology is available on the market, which almost every potential customer always has with them. Mobile marketing is now widely used, especially in the form of advertising on the Internet or in most freely available applications. The priority of the article is to increase the competitiveness of the enterprise through augmented reality. By using these technologies, the brand is presented to customers as advanced, which automatically improves its reputation in the market.

Keywords: Augmented reality · Efficiency · Digitalization

1 Introduction

Augmented Reality (AR), in computer programming, is the process of combining or "expanding" video or photos by overlapping computer-generated data in the form of 2D, 3D objects such as videos, photos, or 3D models [1]. The first augmented reality applications were "Heads-Up-Displays" (HUDs) used in military aircraft and tanks, in which information from the dashboard was projected onto the cockpit cover, through which a crew member could see the outside environment [1, 2]. Faster computer processors have made it possible to combine such displays with real-time video. The term Augmented reality (AR) was first used by Boeing researcher Tom Caudell in 1990. The first functional AR system, "Virtual Fixtures", was created in 1992 by Louis Rosenburg at the USAF Armstrong Research Laboratory, which served military personnel for virtual remote control of machines [1].

© ICST Institute for Computer Sciences, Social Informatics and Telecommunications Engineering 2021
Published by Springer Nature Switzerland AG 2021. All Rights Reserved
D. Perakovic and L. Knapcikova (Eds.): FABULOUS 2021, LNICST 382, pp. 337–349, 2021.
https://doi.org/10.1007/978-3-030-78459-1_25

1.1 Types of Augmented Reality

According to the technology used, augmented reality is divided into 4 types, namely augmented reality based on brand sensing, augmented reality without the use of a brand sensor, augmented reality based on projection and augmented reality based on superposition [3].

A. *Augmented reality based on brand scanning*
Augmented reality based on brand capture uses a camera in the device to distinguish the brand from any other object in the real world. Clear but simple patterns are used as marks (such as a QR code) because they are easy to recognize and do not require much reading power. The position and orientation at which a particular type of content or information overlaps the brand is also calculated [1, 2].

B. *Augmented reality without the use of a brand sensor*
As one of the most common types of augmented reality, it is used without a sensor (also called location, position or GPS) that does not use a tag sensor. This type of augmented reality uses GPS, a digital compass, a speedometer, or an accelerometer to make the AR software work. Behind the spread of this type of augmented reality is, in particular, the wide availability of smartphones, which contain the necessary location detection technologies [1, 2].

C. *Augmented reality based on projection*
Projection augmented reality works by projecting artificial light onto the surface of the real world. Projection-based augmented reality applications allow human interaction with augmented reality by capturing social interaction (touch) with projected light. Detection of user interaction is performed by distinguishing between an expected (or known) projection and an altered projection (caused by user interaction). Another interesting application of augmented reality projection uses laser plasma technology to project a three-dimensional interactive hologram into the air [3].

D. *Augmented reality based on superposition*
Augmented reality based on superposition either wholly or partially replaces the original view of a real object. In augmented reality based on superposition, object recognition plays a vital role because the application cannot replace the original statement with an enhanced view if it cannot recognize the object in the scene. An example of augmented reality based on superposition is the Ikea furniture catalog, which allows users to place virtual furniture in their own home using augmented reality [3].

2 Work Methodology

Augmented reality allows manufacturers to gain a competitive advantage in the fight for customers. Augmented marketing is a new trend for manufacturers to communicate with their customers through mobile applications and interactive content. AR applications can be used to promote products [4]. Manufacturers can use the app to demonstrate the actual sizes and dimensions of their products, available colors, combinations with other products, and display product prices and discounts [1, 3]. They can also educate their users by visualizing product features, usability, and assembly instructions. The possibilities of augmented reality are unlimited in this respect [1]. AR technology enables the visualization of products in the form of digital 3D models anywhere, thanks to which the customer can view the exact shapes and dimensions of the product, for example from the comfort of their home [5]. AR applications allow users to interact with proucts: "touch" them, view from different angles, take pictures, and more. Thanks to the still relative novelty, the combination of these functions allows you to create a "wow! An effect that leaves a lasting impression so that users remember the product and its manufacturer [4]. Augmented reality marketing is one of the most fun ways to introduce a product to both technically proficient and technically savvy viewers. Technological advances in AR make it easier to build applications. Customers only need a smartphone with the app running [2]. Augmented reality is fun but also useful, making it a convenient tool for marketing purposes.

2.1   Computer Graphic Objects

To use virtual or augmented reality, digital 2D or 3D objects are also needed displays on the display device. Computer graphics objects are created in 2D or 3D modelling software. The term 2D graphics represents the creation, display and manipulation of objects in two-dimensional environment [5]. Drawing programs and 2D CAD programs allow drawing objects in X-Y scale so that as if they were drawn on paper [5]. Although it is possible to draw 3D images in 2D programs, display them are static. They may be enlarged or reduced, but may not be rotated to different angles such as this is possible with 3D objects. Lighting effects cannot also be used with 2D objects. Shading is so need to create using colored fills or gradients [2, 4]. The term 3D graphics refers to the creation, display and manipulation of objects in three dimensions' environment. 3D CAD and 3D graphics programs allow you to create items in a three-dimensional environment in the X-Y-Z axes (width, height, depth). 3D objects can be rotated and displayed from all angles, with the possibility of lighting applied automatically in the rendering phase [6]. In 3D graphics with objects, they create on a three-dimensional basis, where the actual view is derived from the angle of the camera and the lights resources similar to the real world. Thanks to growing computing power, personal computers, video games with 3D graphics began to appear in 2000 [7]. It is nowadays most computers are equipped with a graphics card that handles all 3D processes. In addition to hardware and software, 3D models are required to simulate a virtual environment [7]. It can be obtained by 3D modelling in 3D modelling software, 3D scanning of real objects or by downloading finished 3D models from freely available sources on the Internet. 3D modelling is a technique in computer graphics to create a digital 3D representation any object or surface. Special software for manipulating points (vertices) is used in virtual space to create a network (collection of vertices) that make up an object [8]. These 3D objects can be generated automatically or manually by creating a deformation of a point network or other way of manipulating the vertices. 3D models are used for a variety of media, including video games, films, architecture, illustration, engineering and commercial advertising [9]. The process of 3D modeling creates a digital object that can be completely animated, which makes it a necessary process for creation character animations and special effects [7].

2.2 Hardware and Software for Augmented Reality

To use AR applications, terminal devices with a complex composition of hardware are required modules, so-called "Smart" devices. From history, the smartphone is the first mobile end the device used by AR, later also tablets [1]. In 2012, Google promoted its "Google Glass" project, and although they were not the only "smart" glasses on the market, they won thanks to marketing the most attention [4]. Since 2017, smart glasses (including the more sophisticated Google Glass) and headsets AR kits (e.g. HoloLens, Meta2, Magic Leap) get developers' attention thanks to their more complex technologies and an improved sensor. After the publication of the new necessary development AR technologies by Apple (ARKit) and Google (ARCore) as part of their operating system, the development of hardware optimized for AR by both companies (smartphones, tablets, smart glasses or headsets) has dramatically improved, and the experience has become more realistic [2]. AR software is an essential part of augmented reality. AR SDKs are used for AR software development (software development kit) or augmented reality software development kits. These tools offer features such as 3D object tracking, image recognition, SLAM (simultaneous localization and mapping), multiple monitoring and more that allow developers to exploit the potential of AR hardware. The choice of AR SDK is crucial for companies involved in AR development applications [1]. These tools AR developers can use to develop mobile applications, various systems for CAD platforms, marketing purposes and the like. SDKs are mostly designed for the exact type of hardware; however, some AR SDKs support a wide range of systems, allowing for greater flexibility in development [1–3].

2.3 Augmented Reality Used by Increasing of Competitiveness: The Process of Application

Unity software with Vuforia extension was used to create the augmented reality application from the enterprise PTC [3]. Unity software is used to create virtual scenes using the Vuforia extension can be displayed in the form of augmented reality [2]. Unity software is available in several versions. It is freely available for personal use by terms and conditions listed on the software website, for commercial purposes, the software is subject to a fee [4]. The augmented reality application was created in the student version, which is also freely available [10]. The first important step before working with this software is to install it properly [5]. The process is not complicated, but without the installation of the necessary tools and extensions, creation will not be possible applications with the possibility of presenting virtual scenes using augmented reality [7]. Before installation-specific version of Unity software, it is necessary (Fig. 1) to install Unity Hub first. Unity Hub is a standalone application that streamlines the search, download and management of Unity projects and installing different versions of Unity software and extensions [5]. After starting the Unity Hub, it is necessary to click to "Installs" – "ADD" to download a new version of the software that has not yet been installed on a given PC. When installing Unity software, there is an essential section in which you need to select a version Unity software. At the time of creating the application, the Vuforia extension is only supported in older versions of the software Unity (2018.4.18f1) [7].

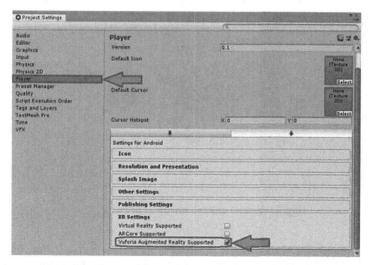

Fig. 1. Vuforia installation packet [12].

After adding AR Camera, it is possible to remove the original "Main Camera", with this camera no further work will be required. The AR camera is manipulated only when image testing needs to be tested virtual environment scenes directly in Unity without the use of an external camera. After adding the AR camera, it is necessary activation of Vuforia package support in "Project Settings". These settings are possible to get through the menu bar by clicking on "Edit" – "Project Settings". In Project Settings you need to get to Player and check "Vuforia Augmented Reality Supported" in XR Settings. The process of creating new markers consists in uploading 2D images to the Vuforia portal, which it will generate a package that needs to be imported into Unity software. This process activates new markers. After creating an account on the Vuforia portal, which can be accessed by clicking "Add Target" in Unity, it is possible to develop a database of custom markers [7, 11]. Before creating the database, itself, it is you must first create a license key to build the application using the Vuforia package. On the Vuforia portal, it is necessary to select the "Develop" option, which redirects the user to a part of the portal, where it is possible to generate a license for a given application and create your database of markers. Then by clicking on "License Manager" and "Get Development Key" a window will open, where you need to enter any license name [7, 8]. By entering the name and confirming the license, Vuforia will provide you with a license key that must be kept for use in the Unity program (Fig. 2). After successfully creating a permit for the application, it is necessary to open and copy the license generated license key and insert it into the Unity program. In Unity you need to click in "Hierarchy" – "ARCamera" and then in the "Inspector" click on "Open Vuforia Engine" Configuration.

The downloaded database must be imported into Unity by a simple double-click on the downloaded file, which will open a new window in Unity, in which you click on the "Import" option. Imported database can be used immediately. In Unity by clicking on the added ImageTarget in "Hierarchy" and in "Inspector" - "Image Target Behavior" by clicking on the "Database" option where a selection is required imported database.

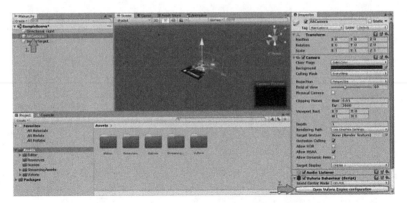

Fig. 2. Vuforia extension settings in Unity [12].

There is an option in the "Image Target Behavior" column below the database selection of individual markers located in the database, this is the procedure for addition all markers to Unity [12]. When creating promotional materials with the use of augmented reality technology is possible features overlap in different ways. One way to overlay the real view of the print marker is an overlay with another image. Such a notion is added to the marker directly. The first is necessary to create a so-called The "Quad" element in the tree directly below the "ImageTarget" that the user wants to replace according to Fig. 3.

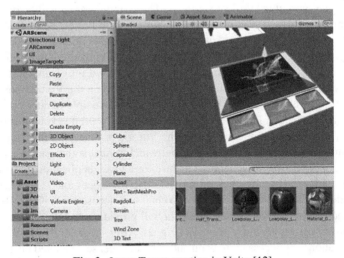

Fig. 3. ImageTarget creation in Unity [12].

After setting the "Quad" element according to the procedure above, it is necessary to add to the Unity software as well the desired image by which the user wants to replace the original marker when recognized by the application. That is made by changing the material of the "Quad" element. Then just add to this material the desired image with which the user wants to cover the original marker [11]. A picture is added to Unity simply drag from Windows Explorer to the bottom of the Unity software below the window scene display [8, 12]. Classic pictures or photos are in formats that cannot be used immediately to define the material. For these images, you need to change their texture type directly in Unity to "Sprite" and apply the changes according to Fig. 4.

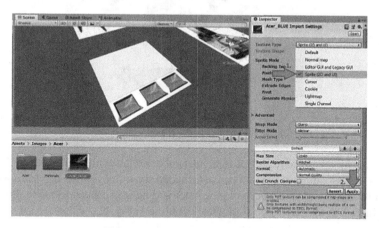

Fig. 4. "Sprite" mode in Unity [12].

The same goes for adding a video to a scene. The first is it is necessary to add a "Quad" element, and change its position, orientation and dimensions so that to take up space on the marker where the played video is displayed. This element is then adding a new "Video Player" component by selecting the feature in "Hierarchy" and clicking on "Add Component" in the "Inspector" according to Fig. 5.

Fig. 5. "Video Player" mode in Unity [12].

Unity only supports some 3D model formats such as.fbx,.dae (Collada) 3ds,.dxf and obj. These formats can be selected when saving a 3D model in 3D modelling software

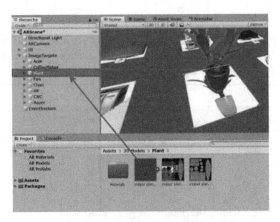

Fig. 6. 3D model insertion in Unity [12].

or when downloading from various freely available portals with a database of 3D models. After downloading the 3D model, it is necessary to move it to the bottom of the Unity software from Windows Explorer. After adding it is needed to move directly to "ImageTarget" in the "Hierarchy" project according to Fig. 6.

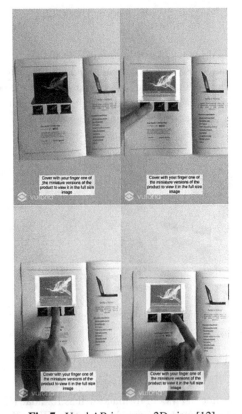

Fig. 7. Used AR images - 2D view [12].

3   Results and Discussion

The application consists of 5 scenes, in the augmented reality scene there are 8 markers, 1 basic user an environment that prompts the user to capture any marker from the product list the relevant catalogue and another 8 user environments, which are activated according to the current one scanned quality. By moving to the augmented reality scene, it is possible to continue using the application gradually by checking markers in the catalogue. The user sees only those parts of the stage, which are in the application tree below feature of the product [12]. This product used a simple replacement of the original image with a virtual image. Due to the possibility of using such a relief, it was chosen to create virtual buttons on thumbnails in 3 colour versions of the product. When scanning the marker application prompts the user to cover one of the 3 colour variants of the product with his fingers from the camera 's point of view. At each image, overlay displays the full-size variation in place of the original image product (Fig. 7).

This marker used a video player and a C # script to start or pause the video using the RayCast button. There are two buttons in place of the marker, one to start the video and the other to pause the video. These buttons are activated and deactivated alternately according to the one last pressed. When shooting product marker, a video player appears in place of the image [7]. The application informs the user to start or pause the video; you must tap the smartphone screen at the location displayed video player - for product image. Used animation, the application prompts the user to interact with the 3D model

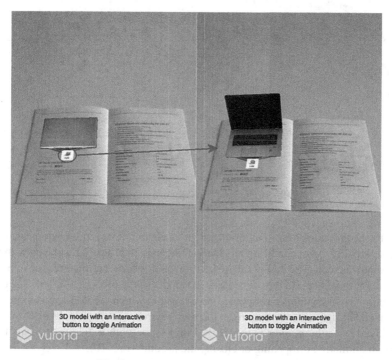

Fig. 8. Animation process used AR [12].

using a virtual one buttons (Fig. 8). After pressing the button, the animation of opening or closing according to the current state starts devices for visualizing a laptop in an open or closed form [12, 14]. It is how the customer has me a better visual overview of the product.

The virtual button can also be displayed as an animation of the button's arrival in the scene after the recognition marker. With this marker, the virtual button appears in the corner of the CNC machine with a gradual magnification in the form of an icon for more information [13, 15]. A script is used on the button to change the scene. The user does so when you press this button. It gets to the stage with more detailed information about the product (Fig. 9).

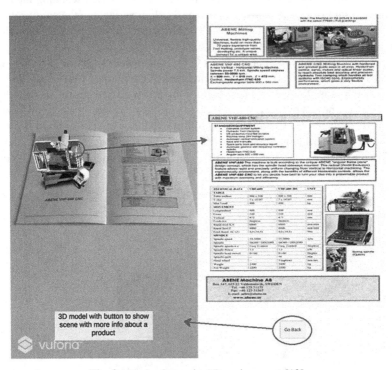

Fig. 9. Mode change in AR environment [12].

For the last product, almost all of the previous content interaction options were used augmented reality. After capturing this marker, the user interface is displayed with three buttons on the screen. The buttons at the bottom left contain a script to reduce or enlarge the model for display a real or reduced size 3D model of the product [14, 16]. The button at the bottom right contains a script to go to a scene in which the user learns more about the product. Except for these buttons in the user environment, a virtual switch will also be displayed after the marker is recognized in a scene with a 3D model. This button triggers an animation of opening or closing the product (Fig. 10).

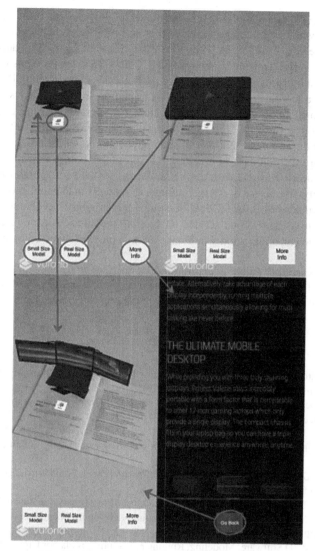

Fig. 10. Final product presentation used AR [12].

4 Conclusion

Presented research shows the possibilities of using augmented reality for promotion products by interacting with the catalogue. In addition, it offers the opportunities of interacting with the content applications using virtual, UI and RayCast buttons from changing scenes to launching 3D animations models. This type of application has a complete application in practice, but it is necessary to take into account specific the cost of using technology to develop such an application. For commercial purposes, it is essential to count on higher prices, not just wages developers, but also on the technologies used to develop the application [15]. For commercial purposes, an individual may use the Unity Software free of charge provided that his or her sales do not exceed turnover 100.000 $ in the last 12 months. A Unity Plus version is available to companies for 399 $ a year if the enterprise's revenue does not exceed 200.000 $ in the previous 12 months. If there are sales companies above, you need to purchase a version of Unity Pro for 1800 $ a year or with a monthly payment 150 $. With paid versions of Unity software, it is also possible to count on more significant customer support and various enhancements not available in free versions. [17] The Vuforia platform is also available free of charge for application development, but for finished publication applications for commercial purposes require the purchase of a license. For profitable companies up to 10 million $ per year, a Vuforia Basic license can be purchased for 42 $ per month for a standard AR functionality, for the use of a larger number of markers in the application, a Vuforia license is recommended Basic+Cloud. To store a larger number of characteristics, it is recommended to use the Cloud service on keeping models because of the amount of memory that such an application would take up on a piece of given equipment.

Acknowledgement. This article is a part result of the project KEGA 026 TUKE04/2018-Popularization of Industry 4.0 and digitization enterprises problematic as a tool for increase of technical knowledges and skills by students of secondary school.

References

1. A Brief History of Augmented Reality (+Future Trends & Impact). https://learn.g2.com/history-of-augmented-reality. Accessed 30 Sept 2020
2. AR/MR Devices. https://www.augmented-minds.com/en/augmented-reality/ar-hardware-devices/. Accessed 28 Sept 2020
3. Augmented Reality – The Past, The Present and The Future. https://www.interaction-design.org/literature/article/augmented-reality-the-past-the-present-and-the-future. Accessed 25 Sept 2020
4. Davis, J.: 3D Modeling CAD Software. https://www.3dhubs.com/knowledge-base/3d-modeling-cad-software/. Accessed 15 Oct 2020
5. Optimizing Target Detection and Tracking Stability. https://library.vuforia.com/features/images/image-targets/best-practices-for-designing-and-developing-image-based-targets.html. Accessed 21 Oct 2020
6. Petty, J.: Best 3D Software: Modeling, Rigging & Sculpting Tools For Digital Artists. https://conceptartempire.com/3d-software/. Accessed 22 Oct 2020
7. Vuforia: License Plans. https://www.ptc.com/en/products/vuforia/vuforia-engine/pricing. Accessed 23 Oct 2020
8. Vuforia: Pricing and Licensing Options. https://library.vuforia.com/articles/FAQ/Pricing-and-Deployment-Plans. Accessed 28 Oct 2020
9. McGovern, E., Moreira, G., LunaNevarez, C.: An application of virtual reality in education: can this technology enhance the quality of student´s learning experience? J. Educ. Bus. **95**(7), 490–496 (2019)
10. Gabajová, G., Furmannová, B., Rolinčinová, I.: Use of augmented and virtual reality in industral engineering. Acta Tecnol. **6**(2), 31–34 (2020)
11. Garay-Rondero, C.L., Martinez-Flores, J.L., Smith N.R., et al.: Digital supply chain model in Industry 4.0. J. Manuf. Technol. Manage. https://doi.org/10.1108/JMTM-08-2018-0280 (2019)

12. Grocholˇ, T.: Creation of promotial materials used an augmented reality environment.The sis, Faculty of Manufacturing Technologies, p.77 (2020)
13. Pellas, N., Fotaris, P., Kazanidis, I., Wells, D.: Augmenting the learning experience in primary and secondary school education: a systematic review of recent trends in augmented reality game-based learning. Virtual Reality **23**(4), 329–346 (2018). https://doi.org/10.1007/s10055-018-0347-2
14. Minler, M.D.: The state of creativity: the future of 3D printing, 4D printing and augmented reality. Qeen Mary J. Intellect. Prop. **9**(4), 503–505 (2019)
15. Trebuňa, P., et al.: 3D scanning as a modern technology for creating 3D models. Acta Tecnol. **6**(1), 21–24 (2020)
16. Marto, A., Goncalves, A.: Mobile AR: user evaluation in a cultural heritage context. Appl. Sci. Basel **9**(24), 5454 (2019)
17. Cohen Y., Faccio M., Pilati F., Yao, X.F.: Design and management of digital manufacturing and assembly systems in the Industry 4.0 era. Int. J. Adv. Manuf. Technol. **105**(9), 3565–3577 (2019)

Sustainable Constructions Supported by Ecological Smart Technologies

Marcela Spišáková⬡, Peter Mésároš, and Tomáš Mandičák^(⊠) ⬡

Faculty of Civil Engineering, Technical University of Košice, Vysokoškolská4,
042 00 Košice, Slovakia
tomas.mandicak@tuke.sk

Abstract. We are currently witnessing an increasing demand for residential, office or multifunctional buildings . Customer requirements are no focused only on the economic parameters of the construction, but also on the parameters related to the sustainability and environmental aspect of the construction. In addition, sustainable constructions can be supported by the latest smart technologies. An application of the sustainable approach to constructions is demonstrated by environmental assessment systems.

A brief analysis of knowledge in the field of construction sustainability and smart technologies supporting especially the ecological aspect of sustainability is prepared. These findings represent the theoretical basis for comparing the sustainability of construction on selected construction projects. The aim of the paper is to point out the use of ecological smart technologies that affect the sustainability of buildings. The research was carried out on selected sustainable buildings in Europe which received an outstanding rating within the environmental assessment of buildings by significant certification systems.

Keywords: Sustainability · Construction · Smart technology · Environmental assessment system · Comparison

1 Introduction

Building performance in sustainability is now a major concern of professionals in the building industry. According Cole [1] the specific definition of the term "building performance" is complex, since different actors in the building sector have differing interests and requirements in the economic, environmental and social field in sustainability. Raynsford [2] provides a detailed definition for sustainable construction - "Sustainable construction is the set of processes by which a profitable and competitive industry delivers built assets (buildings, structures, supporting infrastructure and their immediate surroundings) which: (i) enhance quality of life and offer customer satisfaction, (ii) offer flexibility and the potential to cater for user changes in the future, (iii) provide and support desirable natural and social environments, (iv) maximize the efficient use of resources."

© ICST Institute for Computer Sciences, Social Informatics and Telecommunications Engineering 2021
Published by Springer Nature Switzerland AG 2021. All Rights Reserved
D. Perakovic and L. Knapcikova (Eds.): FABULOUS 2021, LNICST 382, pp. 350–361, 2021.
https://doi.org/10.1007/978-3-030-78459-1_26

Sustainable development embraces the three broad themes of environmental, social and economic accountability, often known as the key points of sustainability." Interactions among each other of effective parameters of sustainability which are protection of environment, economic progression, and social fair are demonstrated in Fig. 1. The sustainability of construction is demonstrated through the environmental assessment of buildings.

Fig. 1. Key points of sustainability [3]

1.1 Environmental Assessment of Buildings

Currently, there are several sustainable assessment systems focused on ecological, economic, energetic, social and cultural, technical aspects of construction materials, building as a whole or building and its surroundings [4]. The three main certification schemes are the most widely used in Central Europe - BREEAM certificate (developed in United Kingdom), DGNB certificate (developed in Germany), LEED certificate (developed in the United States) [5]. In addition, a number of national certification systems are used: in Slovakia BEAS, in the Czech Republic SBToolCZ, in Austria Klima: aktiv. A common features of certification systems is that they evaluate selected building parameters in environmental, social and economic field (see Table 1). Building is certified to an assessment level that reflects its environmental, social and economic quality by meeting these criteria. The most important areas on which sustainable construction focuses are sustainable construction methods, sustainable construction materials and recycling and waste reduction [6].

The assessment of the environmental performance of buildings is mainly focused on parameters location of building, construction project management, construction project architecture, indoor environmental quality (thermal and humidity environment, light environment, indoor air quality), energy efficiency (energy for building operation, alternative systems for the use of renewable energy sources), water and waste management, user comfort, hygiene, safety, etc. [7, 8].

Table 1. Assessed parameters within certification systems [9]

Economic parameter	Social parameter	Environmental parameter
Investment costs for the construction	Visual comfort in the building interior	Materials used for construction
Operating costs	Visual comfort in the building exterior	
	Spatial building solution	
	Quality of housing	
	Health safety of the building	
	Quality of construction	Acoustic comfort in construction
	Occurrence of failures at the beginning of building use	Light comfort in building
	Occurrence of failures during building use	Air quality in the building
	Construction time	
	Thermal comfort in winter	
	Thermal comfort in summer	

1.2   Ecological Smart Technologies in Buildings

At present, the software user interface and computer hardware components are gaining more and more attention. This solution presents an integral part of our life and work. A number of past manual settings have been handled by automation. Informatics takes on a new dimension because computers start working in a stand-alone mode, where they can anticipate errors and avoid them, detect, analyze and evaluate them. The user is not involved to problem solutions. These processes, which take place in the background of the software, simplify the user's life. Software are becoming intelligent, smart because they know how to assess the situation themselves and are able to react to it. According company Siemens [10], smart technologies present "a cognitive, contextually conscious computing system that is able to make decisions without human intervention". SMART stands for acronym Self-Monitoring Analysis a Reporting Technology.

Smart technologies also hold their significant place in the field of construction. We can see smart technologies in design, construction or usage phase of buildings. Smart technologies can be used for any type of buildings.

An integral part of the new modern housing are smart technologies of controlled heating, security, camera system, shading elements, control of artificial lighting, irrigation system, air conditioning, control of various appliances as well as the electrical installation. These technologies can be controlled from a single device via wall touch screen, tablet, mobile phone, computer or TV with a network connection by software or application. Smart technologies used in buildings can be divided into [11, 12]:

- technologies for heating control (thermostats, heating controls, smart radiator heads),
- cooling control (air conditioning control and temperature sensors),

- shading control (blinds and shutters controls),
- smart technologies to ensure security (IP cameras, video intercoms, alarms, garage doors and gates, door locks),
- smart sensors and detectors (motion sensors, door opening sensors, flood sensors, fire detectors, CO_2 sensors, etc.),
- smart lighting control technology (smart bulbs),
- smart technologies in electrical installations (Smart sockets, switching relays and modules, consumption meters),
- smart irrigation technology,
- smart technologies for multimedia control (IR control devices).

Smart technologies in an ecological building perform a large number of activities and can significantly affect the condition of the building, safety, its energy consumption and many other features. Smart technologies in the building by the collected data (such as the weather) can make activities focused on reducing the temperature and elimination of heat loss; further smart irrigation technology, based on the evaluation of weather forecast, can turn the lawn irrigation. Ecological smart technologies in construction affect the indoor environment:

- thermal and humidity environment (smart technologies used for heating and cooling),
- lighting environment (smart technologies used for indoor lighting by natural or artificial light),
- indoor air quality (smart technologies used for ventilation in buildings) [7, 11].

2 Research Material and Methodology

The current trend in construction is the implementation of sustainable buildings, which are supported by smart technologies. Respect for the objectives of Agenda 21 is evidenced by the today's buildings which minimize the negative impact of constructions on environment.

The aim of the paper is to point out the use of ecological smart technologies that affect the sustainability of buildings.

2.1 Research Material

The research was carried out on selected sustainable buildings in Europe which received an outstanding rating within the environmental assessment of buildings by significant certification systems. Buildings involved in the research were selected on the basis of the following criteria:

1. building intended primarily for administrative purposes (possible additional residential purposes),
2. building was evaluated by the BREEAM assessment system and received an outstanding or excellent rating,
3. building achieves the best evaluation score in environmental aspects of sustainability, particularly focused on the quality of indoor environment,

4. building is located in Europe,
5. building is built or renovated only after year 2010,
6. building uses smart technology for their operation.

2.2 Research Methodology

The research methodology consists in the analysis and synthesis of information related to the identification of ecological smart technologies in selected buildings. Then, the number of smart solutions in the examined buildings was determined. The achieved analytical data were evaluated and the conclusions of the observation were expressed. The knowledge survey was conducted in 2019.

3 Results and Discussion

The research sample consisted of 10 office buildings, which were awarded a BREEAM certificate, specifically – 4 buildings in the Great Britain, 1 building in the Netherlands, 2 buildings in the Czech Republic and 3 buildings in Slovakia. Buildings located in the UK and the Netherlands received the highest BREEAM assessment at the time of the survey. The buildings included in the research in the Czech Republic and Slovakia achieved the highest environmental rating in these countries.

The BREEAM method for the environmental assessment of buildings built in the United Kingdom is also the most widespread. The BREEAM system evaluates many office buildings in the UK. Some buildings rated by the BREEAM certificate achieve the highest score (very good, excellent, outstanding). Only buildings that received an outstanding rating were included in the research. The BREEAM certification system is also the most widely used in the Netherlands. In the Czech Republic, buildings are environmentally assessed by the SBToolCZ [23] system adapted to the conditions of the country, but the BREEAM and LEED methods are widely used. Only buildings that were evaluated by the BREEAM system were included in the research. Unfortunately, certified buildings in the Slovak Republic do not achieve the highest level of Outstanding certification in the system of environmental assessment of buildings using the BREEAM method. The best rated building with the BREEAM system in Slovakia is the Zuckermandel project. However, it reaches a slightly lower level than the world level, specifically the level of certification very good.

3.1 Brief Description of the Analyzed Buildings – Environmentally Sustainable Solutions

20 Fenchurch Street, London, UK
Building presents, the office building in London, built in 2011, received scores 80,2% by BREEAM certification. Designers and architects set out to ensure the 38-storey tower, known as 'The Walkie Talkie' was one of the most sustainable buildings of its type in London, and have deployed a number of innovative measures throughout the design, construction and operational phases. Highlights in design approaches to environmental:

- UK's largest green wall valuable green infrastructure,
- low zero carbon (LTC) technologies – roof mounted solar PV (photo voltaic) panels,
- certified sustainable sourced concrete and structural steelwork was used,
- noise and air quality monitoring – real time monitoring of noise and dust during construction [13].

Five Pancras Square, King's Cross, London
Building obtained highest rated BREEAM Bespoke Building in the UK at 97,5% rating achieved. Environmental features involved:

- low carbon heating and electricity to the building,
- smart steps taken in the facade design to maximise daylight factors throughout the occupied areas, and to minimise artificial lighting requirements through adopting daylight linking/dimming,
- monitoring of energy and water use,
- photovoltaics to achieve zero carbon status [14].

One Angel Square, Manchester, UK
This office building in Manchester is one of the most sustainable buildings in the UK and Europe. It also confirms its environmental qualities by obtaining an excellent certification level by the BREEAM system with a score of 95,16%. Like previous buildings, building ensures its ecological sustainability by using natural resources, maximizing thermal solar gains, rainwater harvesting, greywater and rainwater recycling systems for toilet flushing and irrigation [15].

Bloomberg, London, UK
Construction was built as one of the world's highest BREEAM-rated major office buildings. In 2014 Bloomberg received a score of 99.1% in the environmental assessment. The innovation highlights involve:
   integrated ceiling panels which combine air supply, cooling, lighting and acoustic functions in an innovative petal-leaf design,

- rainwater from the roof, cooling tower blow-down water, and grey water sources, like basins and showers, is captured, treated and recycled to serve vacuum flush toilets,
- the building breathes - when ambient weather conditions are temperate, the building's distinctive bronze blades can open and close, allowing the building to operate in a "breathable" natural ventilation mode,
- smart airflow by smart CO_2 sensing controls allow air to be distributed according to the approximate number of people occupying each zone of the building at any given time [16].

The Edge, Amsterdam, the Netherlands
The Edge is the office building constructed in 2016 in Amsterdam which obtained outstanding rating 98,3% in BREEAM evaluation. A number of intelligent technologies, with their ability to adapt autonomously to the user, his requirements as well as the influence of the external environment, create intelligent workspaces without disturbing the

users they try to make as satisfied as possible in this environment, ensuring comfortable working in a productive and healthy environment. The degree of technical excellence of the Edge office building accelerates the development of sustainable buildings using intelligent technologies. The Edge consumes 70% less energy compared to buildings of the same type [17].

Tower B, Spielberk Office Center, Brno, the Czech Republic
Tower B contains a number of technological innovations that help to make it highly valued. It has a sophisticated façade that provides adequate lighting as well as protection against overheating. Ventilation and air exchange is solved using fan-coil units. Smart technologies in the building move it to a higher level of information and thus ensure its sustainable operation with energy savings [18].

Blox, Prague, the Czech Republic
A sustainable office building, which also received the highest level of certification in the environmental assessment by the BREEAM system in in Prague. The building is equipped with the latest technologies that continuously monitor the indoor environment via sensors and then perform autonomous interventions to ensure user comfort as much as possible [19].

Zuckermandel, Bratislava, Slovakia
The Zuckermandel project is the construction of a new city district which consists of the construction and renovation of the historic area in Bratislava. During the BREEAM environmental assessment, the building received an assessment – excellent [20].

Twin City, Bratislava, Slovakia
The advantages of the building include 30% energy savings due to the increased thickness of the thermal insulation of the facade and roof, triple glazing on all transparent surfaces or intelligent shading. Of course, there are also technologies in the field of ventilation with heat recovery and humidification systems or charging stations for electric vehicles, the use of rainwater and intelligent lighting [21].

Forum Business Center I, Bratislava, Slovakia
This building belonged among the first buildings in Slovakia rated by the BREEAM environmental rating system as excellent. It uses shading, ventilation or cooling technology, the building also includes a green roof made of local trees or other ecological parameters contributing to its excellent evaluation. The building, uses various devices for its operation in order to minimize manual interventions and save energy [22].

All presented buildings are shown in on Fig. 2.

3.2 Brief Description of the Analyzed Buildings – Smart Solutions

The research was not only focused on exploring ecological sustainable building solutions, but primarily on identifying smart solutions that support this aspect of construction. Then, the environmentally sustainable and smart solutions of building were compared (see Table 2).

All evaluated buildings contained the environmentally sustainable solutions. Their number and innovation was also reflected in the level of BREEAM rating:

- outstanding more than 85%,
- excellent 70%–85%,
- very good 55%–70%.

The sophisticated solution for the eco-sustainability of buildings is directly proportional to the use smart elements in constructions.

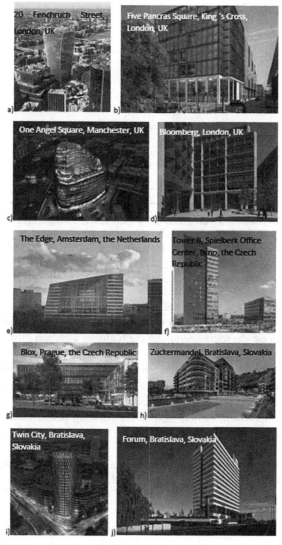

Fig. 2. Analyzed buildings with the ecological sustainable solutions: a) 20 Fenchurch Street [13], b) Five Pancras Square, King's Cross [14], c) One Angel Square [15], d) Bloomberg [16], e) The Edge [17], f) Tower B, Spielberk Office Center [18], g) Blox [19], h) Zuckermandel [20], i) Twin City [21], j) Forum Business Center I [22]

Table 2. Comparison of environmentally sustainable and smart building solutions.

Building/Country	BREEA M rating in %	Environmentally sustainable solution									Smart solution (number)
		1	2	3	4	5	6	7	8	9	
20 Fenchurch Street/UK	80,2	*	*	*	*	NA	*	*	*	*	1
Five Pancras Square/UK	97,6	*	*	*	*	*	*	*	*	*	1
One Angel Square/UK	95,16	*	*	*	*	*	*	*	*	*	3
Bloomberg/UK	99,10	*	*	*	*	*	*	*	*	*	5
The Edge/NL	98,36	*	*	*	*	*	*	*	*	*	7
Spielberk Office Center/CZ	76,8	*	*	*	*	*	NA	NA	NA	*	0
Blox/CZ	86,9	*	*	*	*	*	*	NA	NA	*	0
Zuckermandel/SK	82,3	*	*	*	*	*	*	*	*	*	3
Twin City/SK	80,19	*	*	*	*	*	NA	*	*	*	0
Forum Business Center/SK	73,0	*	*	*	*	*	NA	NA	*	*	0

Notes: 1 - heating, 2 - cooling, 3 - air exchange, 4 - shielding, 5 - lighting, 6 - renewable energy sources, 7 - photovoltaic panels, 8 - use of rain and gray water, 9 - energy saving; *- eco-sustainable solution is used; NA – data is no available; *- smart solution is used

Building *20 Fenchurch Street* boasts the first hydrogen fuel cell (as an eco-smart solution) to be installed in a commercial building. The fuel cell, which will be switched on later this summer, produces heating cooling and electricity, generating 300kW of low carbon, low emissions electricity, reducing the building's carbon dioxide emissions by at least 270 tonnes per annum.

Five Pancras Square´s smart steps taken in the facade design to maximise daylight factors throughout the occupied areas, and to minimise artificial lighting requirements through adopting daylight linking/dimming.

Another smart approaches to environmental building performance is used in *One Angel Square,* specifically:

- heat recovery from the IT systems that will also help to heat the building,
- low energy LED lighting and IT equipment and systems,
- high-efficiency passenger and service lifts.

One of the most sophisticated building in the world, *Bloomberg*, involved many smart elements:

- smart natural air exchange, where exterior blades that allow the building to breathe, and at the same time ensure its optimal shading, lighting,
- a shell ceiling that ensures optimal light distribution,

- smart use of rain and gray water,
- smart use of renewable energy sources.

The smart approach in building *The Edge* is applied in all researched areas. Environmental smart features involved:
the orientation of the building and the facade are based on the path of the sun,
smart lighting which consists of 30,000 sensors to continuously measure occupancy, movement, lighting levels, humidity and temperature, allowing it to automatically adjust energy use,

- solar panel roof which use of neighborhood level energy sourcing,
- energy reuse,
- rain water reuse,
- thermal energy storage.

Moreover, personalised workspaces by mobile application, i.e. every employee is connected to the building via an app on their smartphone. Using the application, they can find parking spaces, free desks or other colleagues, report issues to the facilities team, or even navigate within the building.

In the Czech Republic and Slovakia, the examined buildings received a lower BREEAM rating. It was also reflected in the analysis of used smart solutions. Except for building Zuckermandel, none of the evaluated buildings used the smart elements for supporting of environmentally sustainability of buildings. Building *Zuckermandel* in Bratislava used smart solutions and technologies. One of these autonomous intelligent devices is a meteorological station located on the roof of the building, which evaluates the weather and, through an intelligent system, positions the blinds so that the interior does not overheat and at the same time lets in enough light.

4 Conclusion

Sustainability of construction is currently another aspect that affects the planning of construction projects [24]. Architects and designers respect the ecological operation of office buildings, as evidenced by the excellent and outstanding results of certification by environmental assessment of buildings. Smart technologies supporting the ecological performance of buildings are able to increase the ecological potential of newly designed buildings. Smart technologies significantly save energy and resources, responsibly approach the protection of the environment and human health and significantly increase user comfort. The paper analyzed used environmentally sustainable solutions and smart solutions which supported the eco-sustainability. The survey shows that the leaders in the field of ecological smart solutions are buildings in the United Kingdom and the Netherlands. Buildings in the Czech Republic and Slovakia lagging behind in this area.

Acknowledgment. The article presents a partial research result of project APVV-17–0549.

References

1. Cole, R.J.: Emerging trend in building environmental assessment methods. Build. Res. Inf. **26**(1), 3–16 (1998)
2. Raynsford, N.: Sustainable construction: the government's role. In: Proceedings of the Institution of Civil Engineers, Civil Engineering, pp. 1622–1634. ICE Publishing (2000)
3. Sustainability – Key points of sustainability. https://jmburchall.wordpress.com/key-points-of-sustainability-2/. Accessed 06 August 2020
4. Vonka, M.: Software for certification. In: Introduction to the Issue of Environmental Assessment and Certification of Buildings According to the Principles of Sustainable Construction. National Construction Center, Brno (2012)
5. Krajcsovics, L., Pifko, H.: Sustainability Assessment of Buildings - CESBA Methodology, 1st edn. Slovak Technical University, Bratislava (2016)
6. Udomsap, A.D., Hallinger, P.: A bibliometric review of research on sustainable construction, 1994–2018. J. Clean. Prod. **254**(6), 120073 (2020)
7. Burdova, E.K., Vilcekova, S.: Sustainable building assessment tool in Slovakia. Energy Procedia **78**(3), 1829–1834 (2015)
8. Drozd, W., Leśniak, A.: Ecological wall systems as an element of sustainable development-cost issues. Sustainability **10**(7), 2234 (2018)
9. Švajlenka, J., Kozlovská, M.: Analysis of user efficiency criteria of buildings based on wood. In: Improving the Efficiency of Construction through MMC Technology, pp 80–85. TUKE, Košice (2015)
10. SIEMENS Industry, Improving Performance with Integrated Smart Buildings. https://www.downloads.siemens.com/download-center/Download.aspx?pos=download&fct=getasset&id1=A6V10601724. Accessed 02 November 2020
11. Smart home and smart, solutions for businesses. https://smarterhome.sk/sk/. Accessed 02 November 2020
12. Muresan, F.: How to use smart devices effectively in buildings? https://www.ny-engineers.com/blog/how-to-use-smart-devices-effectively-in-buildings. Accessed 02 November 2020
13. 20 Fenchurch Street, London. https://www.breeam.com/case-studies/offices/20-fenchurch-street-london/. Accessed 02 November 2020
14. Five Pancras Square, King's Cross, London. https://www.breeam.com/case-studies/mixed-use/five-pancras-square-kings-cross-london/. Accessed 02 November 2020
15. One Angel Square, Manchester. https://www.breeam.com/case-studies/offices/one-angel-square-co-operative-group-hq-manchester/. Accessed 02 November 2020
16. Bloomberg, London. https://www.breeam.com/case-studies/offices/bloomberg-london/. Accessed 02 November 2020
17. The Edge, Amsterdam. https://www.breeam.com/case-studies/offices/the-edge-amsterdam/. Accessed 02 November 2020
18. Tower B, Spielberk Office Center. https://www.ctp.eu/spielberk/. Accessed 02 November 2020
19. Blox, Prague. http://www.bloxoffices.cz/upload/blox-brochure_20141030.pdf. Accessed 02 November 2020
20. Slovak green building council. https://skgbc.eu/portal/akcie/green-business-breakfast/smart-riesenia-v-komplexe-zuckermandel/. Accessed 02 November 2020
21. Twin City, Slovakia. https://www.breeam.com/case-studies/offices/twin-city-a2-slovak-republic/. Accessed 02 November 2020
22. Forum Business Center, Bratislava. https://www.breeam.com/case-studies/offices/forum-business-center-bratislava/. Accessed 02 November 2020

23. National tool for building quality certification. https://www.sbtool.cz/. Accessed 02 November 2020
24. Gajzler, M., Zima, K.: Evaluation of planned construction projects using fuzzy logic. Int. J. Civil Eng. **15**(4), 641–652 (2017). https://doi.org/10.1007/s40999-017-0177-8

The Utilization of Renewable Energy Sources in the Construction and Maintenance of Transport Infrastructure

Patrik Šváb$^{(\boxtimes)}$ [ID], Peter Korba [ID], Michal Hovanec, Ján Lukáč, Jaroslav Hura, and Samer Abdo Saleh Al-Rabeei [ID]

Faculty of Aeronautics, Technical University of Košice, Rampová 7, 041 21 Košice, Slovakia
{patrik.svab,peter.korba,michal.hovanec,jan.lukac,jaroslav.hura, samer.abdo}@tuke.sk

Abstract. The article deals with the utilization of renewable energy sources in the construction and maintenance of transport infrastructure. In the introduction of the article, the authors present a brief introduction to this issue. The authors present a system that utilizes renewable energy sources, specifically solar energy, called the Solar Road System. The article describes the functionality of this system and selected advantages and disadvantages over conventional methods of winter road maintenance. In the third chapter, the authors point out the possible use of the solar road system in the wider scope of transport infrastructures, specifically the chapter focuses on the possibilities of using the system in airport construction, where the authors show this principle using a conceptual model of the airport. This chapter briefly describes the winter maintenance of airport operating areas. At the end of the article, the authors point out the possible directions that the development in this area will take and the issues that will need to be addressed in the future.

Keywords: Transport infrastructure · Solar road system · Renewable energy

1 Introduction

It is a well-known fact that a black surface has a high tendency to absorb sunlight and its rays. This absorption is manifested by a heated black surface. In the summer, we can observe and physically feel heat waves radiating from the overheated concrete. It is therefore not surprising that there have been some attempts to recover or utilize this heat accumulated in the concrete layer [1]. Initial efforts deal with the construction of roads from solar panels, as roads and transport infrastructure occupy a large area and the direct use of radiation by these panels. However, a problem arose with the load-bearing capacity and durability of these panels [2]. The panels would not be able to support the weight of heavy machinery and would not be able to support the weight of multitone aircraft at all. This ruled out the use of solar panels in an airport as well as road construction, as the use of thicker and more durable solar panels did not solve the problem either. Therefore, efforts to use the thermal energy accumulated in concrete and asphalt have

D. Perakovic and L. Knapcikova (Eds.): FABULOUS 2021, LNICST 382, pp. 362–373, 2021.
https://doi.org/10.1007/978-3-030-78459-1_27

been partially halted, but this alternative to using a renewable energy source has not been forgotten. In 2011, the UK government approved the budget, launching phase one in the ICAX project [3]. ICAX is an acronym that means Interseasonal Collection and Exchange. This project has focused and still is, on the use of renewable energy sources. It is therefore an environmental project that deals with the use of thermal energy from concrete. ICAX later joined the global organization E-Hub, which has the same focus as ICAX, i.e. the use of renewable energy sources, but on a global scale.

It is a combination, use, and improvement of roads, transport infrastructures so that, in addition to the primary task, they also provide the possibility to use their area for the collection of energy from renewable sources through the integration of technologies [4]. These technologies, we call them heat-collecting, were developed within this project. Specially to collect and accumulate energy. The concept of using infrastructures to collect solar energy is called Solar Road System. In several countries around the world, this system has been fully used in some places, such as car parking lots, since 2016. One of the countries is, for example, Switzerland or Denmark. At that time, it was approved after testing in external conditions and after fulfilling all the conditions and tests specified in the technical standards of the countries. The technology used to collect and collect solar energy is called an inter-season thermal transformation system [5].

1.1 Inter-season Thermal Transformation System

It is a complex system of heat collecting pipes, incorporated between the individual layers of the road, or other transport infrastructure. The first part of these pipes is located just below the top, bearing layer of the road, from where it directly absorbs the heat that was absorbed by the black surface. The second part is called thermobank. It is the part where the heat energy is dissipated by the pipes. This energy is also stored in this component of the system. It is the same as the first part made of pipes. It is an accumulator of thermal energy, where energy is stored until it is necessary to reuse it to heat the road [6]. The pipes are made of polyethylene and are placed and fixed on steel grids. The thermobank is located in the bottom layer and is embedded in sand or other material that would provide insulation from the environment. Above it is a layer of polystyrene, which serves as insulation. Above the polystyrene, insulating layer, there is also a layer of granular material, which has the task of absorbing water. This is so that it does not get into the next layer and does not cause any damage. Unlike conventional devices where any type of energy is stored, a thermobank can contain heat, thermal energy for several months. With conventional equipment, large heat leaks could occur [7].

For the earth, the surface of the earth is characterized by the fact that heat moves through the earth only very slowly. The speed of movement can be set at approximately 1 m/month. ICAX uses this knowledge to be able to store and insulate heat deep in the ground in the summer months and to use road heating from the thermobank during the winter. It is practically winter maintenance of the road. This heat transfer system was initially used to heat residential buildings during the winter months without the use of fossil fuels [8]. This has proven to be very effective, as in the hot summer months the concrete can heat up to 15 °C higher than the ambient temperature. During these months, the thermobank can be heated from its natural temperature of 10 °C to a temperature of more than 27 °C. The thermobank is controlled exclusively by a sophisticated computer system.

Heat transport is ensured by the fluid with which the individual pipes are filled. The reason why the fluid has been used as a transport medium is that water absorbs well and retains heat in an isolated environment. This cycle, the transport of heat from the concrete surface to the thermobank and vice versa, is ensured by the heat pump [9]. Such a heat pump can be powered by different types of energy. Solar-powered pumps are used, mainly because they can be powered directly by energy obtained directly from the road. It is sufficient for the computer to program the dissipation of a certain part of this energy for the needs of the heat pump. However, air-powered pumps are often used, which operate on a similar principle as air conditioners. As mentioned, pumps based on the principle of using solar energy are most often used in this system. Compared to others, such pumps are much more efficient in the winter, when they are most needed. They also produce very little noise, so they are quieter than otherwise driven pumps. The biggest advantage of solar-powered pumps is their long service life, which requires minimal service [10].

2   The Functionality of the Solar Road System

The solar road system has many uses, but it has two main functions. These functions can be summarized as heating and cooling functions. The cooling function is used in summer when the concrete or asphalt is overheated and no longer can absorb additional solar energy. Then this function is used, which does not cool the concrete in the direct sense with cold water or air but helps the concrete to cool by transferring the accumulated heat through pipes to a thermobank, where heat and heat energy are stored until the winter months. Therefore, the concrete is cooled by removing heat, and the concrete thus regains the capacity to store thermal energy, and this cycle is then repeated until the thermobanks are filled. However, this rarely happens as several are being built. In the summer months, the obtained solar energy can be used as a power supply for some buildings. In the case of an air-driven pump, which, as we have mentioned, works on a similar principle as air conditioning, the effect of an air-conditioning device can be achieved by reversing the operation of the pump. In the case of the second function, the heating, the name implies that it is used in the winter months. The heat stored in the thermobanks is used to heat the road with it. Such heating during the winter months, in the presence of a layer of snow on the road, can reliably dissolve this layer and ensure that it is safe without the use of sanding salts or other techniques. The integration of such a system into transport infrastructures was inspired by underfloor heating in residential buildings. This system has a promising future but is currently in a phase of continuous development. Its use in transport infrastructure around the world is being tested.

2.1   Advantages and Disadvantages of the System

The advantages of this system are that it draws energy from a renewable source, so there is no need to consider the possibility of its depletion. This system has no or minimal negative impact on the environment. Since it uses solar thermal energy obtained from the surrounding environment for its proper operation, technical failures are minimal. Therefore, minimal service interventions are also required to ensure the life of the system. Also, heat pumps used to transport energy from one point to another have the advantage that their use is broad-spectrum. Assuming that solar-powered pumps are used, their service life is considerably longer than for other pump types. It is also advantageous that in the summer months when there is an excess of thermal, solar energy, it is possible to use this energy exclusively to power pumps and other necessary elements of the system. It can also be used to power the systems of adjacent residential complexes, thus reducing overall overhead costs. For the winter maintenance of roads, as well as to reduce the snow layer and the formation of ice, not only heavy equipment is used, but also the method of sprinkling roads with salt.

However, this method has a negative impact on the road itself as well as on the vehicles that use it. The sanding salt helps to break down the road structure, supports the formation of various defects, as well as corrosion of the top layer of the road. As far as vehicles are concerned, sanding salt also causes corrosion of metal parts of vehicles. With the help of a solar road system, it is possible to manage winter maintenance in a way that is harmless compared to conventional means of ensuring winter maintenance. And even for vehicles using these roads. Regarding the influence of this system on the cement concrete structure itself, we also get to the disadvantage of this system. Cement concrete, but especially asphalt surfaces are prone to temperature changes. This means that in winter, during low temperatures, they shrink, and in summer, when temperatures rise, they expand. For this process not to affect the operating condition of the roads, expansion joints will be created during the construction of the road. Their task is to provide space for this expansion and contraction by the heat.

When using a solar road system, care must therefore be taken to ensure that the road and its surface heat up gradually and smoothly. If the cement concrete pavement heats up too quickly and suddenly, it could suffer a thermal shock due to sudden temperature changes. This could result in cracking of the concrete surface or other types of road defects. Therefore, care must be taken when using such a system, but it is still true that, when used correctly, it is the most effective way to maintain roads during the winter months. Another disadvantage is the increased cost of building such an area, where this efficient system would be integrated. The tubular system that forms the basis of the entire system is made of polyethylene, which is essentially a thermoplastic. The integration of such pipes costs on average 115 euros/m^2. Thus, the initial costs will increase, but these costs will ultimately be many times higher than the savings in winter maintenance.

This system with small modifications can also fulfill the power function, when it supplies energy to residential complexes, for example in the form of electricity. Another disadvantage is that in the event of a fault on the road, its repair will be considerably more difficult. This is because this pipe system is located below the surface layer of the cement concrete pavement, and thus care must be taken not to damage the pipes during the repair process, for example during milling. In the event of damage, the transport medium, in this case, the fluid, could leak, which would also mean a loss of stored energy and a total system failure. In the winter months, constant circulation of the liquid must be ensured to prevent the pipes and liquid from freezing. This could cause the pipe system to rupture. This solar road system during the installation phase of the collecting pipes can be seen in Fig. 1.

Fig. 1. Installation of solar road system collecting pipes

The circulation of this complex system is ensured by heat pumps. These pumps, therefore, play a key role in the proper functioning of the whole system. Therefore, their faultless operating condition must be ensured. The complexity of this system can be considered both an advantage and a disadvantage. However, the fact remains that with the correct use and maintenance of a flawless operating system, the system has no competition in the field of road or airport construction.

3 The Utilization in Airport Construction

The use of this system in airport construction represents a really wide range of possibilities. The biggest benefit would be this system in the winter months, during the winter maintenance of airport movement areas. With the arrival of winter, airports are entering a period when airport staff must be constantly prepared for what may happen. A lot of snow is needed to completely close an airport, but thanks to modern chemicals, huge snow removal facilities, and good planning, airports manage to keep runways (RWY) and taxiways (TXY) in a condition sufficient for safe takeoffs and landings of aircraft. However, the highest priority is to prevent ice formation at the RWY. Snow and rain can be dealt with relatively easily, as opposed to how difficult it is to get rid of an ice layer of an airfield if it is formed. It requires constant readiness and a lot of hard work. If an airport is caught in a snow event, all work on it will slow down. Runways, where aircraft on average take off regularly every 45 s, can ensure the take-off of one aircraft every 90 s in this state.

Workers must move on the tracks with increased caution due to increased sliding conditions and the RWYs must be closed regularly to clean and secure the road surface. Also regularly check the coefficient of friction to make sure that the runway is safe for the aircraft. This means that during a snowstorm, the airport"s ability to handle aircraft arrivals and departures can be reduced by up to 50%, i.e. by half. In the worst-case scenarios, even more, which is the reason for most canceled flights. Therefore, procedures and techniques like those used to ensure the condition of roads in road construction are used to ensure the operational condition of tracks.

As already mentioned, salt-based chemicals are used on roads to remove the ice layer, which is effective but causes corrosion of vehicles and roads. This must not be used at airports, as there must be no corrosion of runways or parts of the aircraft. Therefore, chemicals with special formulations are used at airports, but they are very expensive. On the other hand, they do not cause corrosion. On roads, they use snowplows to clear snow, with blades with steel edges. Such blades are cheaper, but they are not gentle on the road surface. For obvious reasons, potholes and various other failures cannot occur on the runways, so blades made of polyurethane are used. They are more expensive but much gentler on the surface of the tracks.

The airport, as well as its staff who provide winter maintenance for the airport, must consider the climatic conditions in which the airport is located and provide the means to carry out winter maintenance. A winter maintenance plan will also be drawn up, outlining the individual operations and the intervals at which they are performed. The use of cement concrete runways with an installed solar road system would therefore mean a revolution in the field of winter maintenance of the airport. In contrast to the expensive methods and means used to ensure safe and operational runways, runways with a solar system would be an effective solution to save in this area. The system is computer-controlled, so workers and machines would not have to enter the tracks, and thus the tracks would not have to be closed as in the normal procedure. Workers would only have to check computer-displayed information about individual tracks and their status. Then focus the system's attention on the individual problems accordingly. The tracks could then be heated by this system according to the set parameters. The use of the solar road system in practice on parts of the airport runway can be seen in Fig. 2.

Fig. 2. The utilization of solar road system in practice

It is obvious that the road where the solar road system is used has a clean surface, i.e. it is without the presence of a snow or ice layer. Elimination of ice formation is the most important factor in the efficiency of this system. The problem with the use of this system could arise in terms of the carrying capacity of the airport area, as gigantic machines, aircraft, move around the airport movement areas. This problem is currently being addressed, there is a certain effort by the E-hub organization to improve the load-bearing capacity of the road by using another, progressive cement-concrete mixture enriched with carbon fibers. This increases the flexibility and overall load-bearing capacity of this material.

Thermobanks can be near the collecting pipes, or they can be located remotely, for example, due to the use of geothermal options for better conservation of thermal energy. If excess heat accumulates in thermobanks during the summer months, this thermal energy can also be used in other ways than exclusively for heating airport runways. Buildings located at the airport, such as terminals, a hangar, or various airport workplaces, must be heated with fossil fuels during the winter months. When using a solar road system, part of the obtained thermal energy can be used to heat these mentioned buildings. This energy can also be used, for example, to heat water. In this case, it uses "clean" accumulated energy from renewable sources and also saves the cost of heating these buildings with fossil fuels. Such a three-dimensional conceptual model can be seen in Fig. 3.

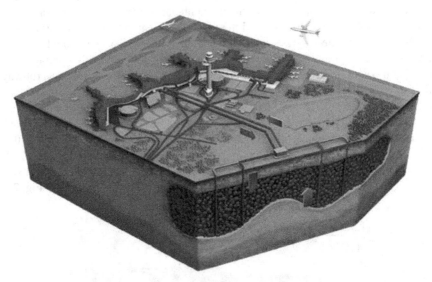

Fig. 3. 3D model of an airport with a fully integrated inter-seasonal exchange system

The location of thermobanks in the locality with geothermal activity can be seen. If the geothermal site is used correctly, the time for which thermal energy can be stored can be extended. The heat obtained through collecting rods from the airport runways utilizing another system of pipes is received from the terminal, in the direction of the arrows, to the heat pump, which ensures the circulation of the liquid. From there it gets to the thermobanks, where it can be stored. With the correct adjustment of the pump, the pump can function as an air conditioning device in the summer months, and therefore, instead of heating the terminals and adjacent buildings, it will cool them. It is more than likely that this system will have a place in the construction of airport movement areas soon. However, it still needs to be adapted to meet the specific needs of airports.

3.1 Practical Application of the System

In the case of winter maintenance of airports, the priority is to ensure the smooth and safe operation of the airport. Any operational irregularity may pose a potential threat to the smooth operation of the airport. This potential is even greater during the winter months. Therefore, the constant development in this area is noticeable in aviation. Each new technology can help airport staff and ensure its smooth operation. In aviation, safety always comes first. The department responsible for winter maintenance as may differ depending on the organization of the airport. Those winter maintenance workers at most airports with a normal hierarchy fall under the technical section of the airport. The scope and planning of winter maintenance is an important step in preparing for the winter months. It is necessary to determine the number of materials, personnel and equipment that will be used to secure it.

The weather has the biggest impact on the operation of the airport. Depending on the expected situations that may occur, scenarios are planned in advance that must be followed in order to ensure the smooth performance of winter maintenance. The staff responsible for winter maintenance must be thoroughly acquainted with these operating procedures so that, in the event of a specific scenario, each worker knows exactly what their role is. The effects of weather can vary, from heavy snow, storms and rain to icing. Each of these effects has different consequences and poses a specific threat to airport operations. To give an example of the use of a solar road system in practice, we will focus on icing.

As the riskiest stage of the flight is the take-off and landing of the aircraft, which is performed on the runway of the airport, it is necessary to ensure its fit. Any deviation from the eligible condition is a problem for smooth operation, because in the worst cases, the entire runway will be closed to restore operability, which will of course be reflected in the delay or cancellation of many flights. This type of operational irregularity can cause a so-called domino effect, where the cancellation or delay of a flight at one airport can cause operational irregularities at the airport at the destination. Regarding icing on the runway, it is necessary to define the basic factors affecting the operability of the runway. Sufficient coefficient of friction is required for correct and adequate landing braking. Briefly, the coefficient of friction is a numerical expression of the time horizon required for a complete stop of an aircraft wheel from the moment braking begins. Specific conditions are also required for the formation of icing, namely temperatures below $-3\,°C$.

If icing forms on the runway, the coefficient of friction is significantly reduced, and thus the time required for the aircraft to come to a complete stop is increased exponentially. Another problem is that when braking, the wheel may deviate from the assumed trajectory because it loses traction with the road. At large hub airports, special sensors are installed on the runways that monitor the runway surface as well as meteorological conditions. If the conditions for the formation of icing are met and if the sensors detect its formation, an alert is immediately sent to the airport coordination department. This is usually the airport dispatching department. At small regional airports, the monitoring function is performed by so-called meteorological offices. These are airport departments, which report directly to the main meteorological office of the state, or to an office at the supranational and international level. Therefore, if the conditions for icing are met and the airport does not have sensors, the dispatcher must check the coefficient of friction on the road to determine whether the safety of operation is not endangered. To give a specific example of the use of a solar road system in the airport infrastructure, we chose an airport model with a system of sensors installed to detect icing phenomena on the runway.

Therefore, the usual procedure assumes that after detecting icing and confirming a reduction in the coefficient of friction, technical staff are sent, under the guidance of a winter maintenance master, to eliminate icing on the road. This is ensured by sprinkling the road with chemicals, usually urea. Road salt is not used at airports, as it causes corrosion that is unacceptable on aircraft. It also destroys the road surface. Upon completion of this operation, the coefficient of friction on the road shall be checked again and, if within the specified range, the road shall be declared operational. If this is not the case, it is not necessary to repeat the road surface again. These activities are very time consuming. Time is a key factor in winter airport maintenance. Every action must be taken as quickly and thoroughly as possible. Any restriction on the runway results in an increased possibility of operational irregularity. For large airports, where one aircraft lands, for example, every 10 min, time is of the essence. Failure to ensure the operability of the runway is a huge problem. It should be noted that any operational irregularity has a negative impact on passenger satisfaction, but the reputation of the airport will have a negative impact on finances, where operational irregularities cause losses not only to the airport but also to the air carrier. However, experienced teams of workers under the leadership of the master of winter maintenance, i.e. the main coordinator, manage this task. However, it is not always possible to handle this situation. If a solar road system were implemented in this process, the whole process would be significantly streamlined, either in terms of time or in terms of the use of human resources.

To demonstrate the effectiveness of this system, the airport model with re-installed runway sensors for icing detection is re-selected. If the sensor detects the formation of icing, an alert is sent to the dispatching department. It is reasonable to assume that the coefficient of friction always decreases with the occurrence of icing. Subsequently, the solar road system can be started either automatically, when the system starts automatically after receiving an alarm from the sensor system, or it can be switched on manually by the person responsible for the operability of the track. These methods can be configured according to the client's requirements. In any case, after switching on the track heating using the solar road system, icing is eliminated. It is then necessary to check the coefficient of friction, and if it is sufficient, the track is declared operational. This procedure significantly saves the time required to sprinkle the track with chemicals. Another significant advantage is the minimized environmental impact of winter maintenance. When using common chemical agents to eliminate icing on the road, these agents have a negative impact on the environment. The use of a solar road system minimizes this impact. The methodology of elimination of icing phenomena using a solar road system is shown in Fig. 4.

When using this system, there is no disturbance and degradation of the track surface, as is the case with the use of chemicals, such as urea. Finally, the money spent on the purchase of these funds, the technology needed to sprinkle the track is saved and financial losses are avoided, as the potential for operational irregularities is significantly reduced.

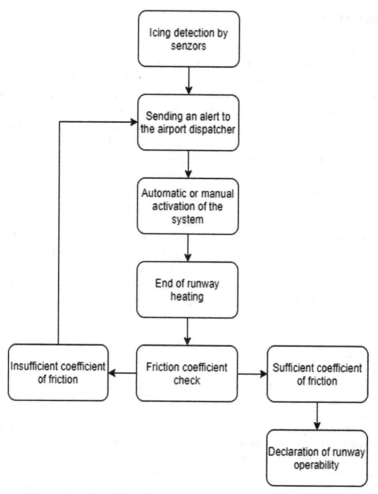

Fig. 4. The methodology of elimination of icing phenomena using a solar road system

The only problem is to ensure adequate bearing capacity of the track. However, this is the subject of current research, where it is possible to ensure the bearing capacity of the track by implementing carbon fibers in the overall structure of the road, and one of the possibilities is the implementation of nanoparticles. However, these methods require further research. It should be mentioned that the solar road system is a solution especially for the construction of new airports or the expansion of existing ones. Of course, it is also possible to modify and upgrade existing airport runways, but this would be much more costly. An adequate analysis is needed to decide on the implementation of this system into the airport infrastructure, when after its evaluation it is possible to determine the benefit of this system for a specific airport.

4 Conclusion

Technological progress is becoming more and more noticeable in everyday life. In order to improve the quality of life but also to ensure the protection of the environment and its preservation, constant development is also needed in this area. The concepts of wise cities and the ways to achieve this idea are especially at a time when the consequences of climate change are more noticeable than ever before, it is necessary to carefully assess and try to implement them. One of the components that could be to ensure sustainable development while preserving the environment in the field of transport infrastructure [11]. In the field of road and airport construction, continuous development is needed to meet the specific requirements of roads, as means of transport are constantly evolving, so are these specific means changing. One of the concepts of implementing a solar system in the roadway is that the energy collected would not be used only to ecologically ensure winter maintenance or partial supply of electricity to adjacent buildings. This concept presents the possibility of connecting the power supply of electric cars directly during their stay on the road when the accumulated solar energy would be transmitted directly to the electric cars using special panels on the road surface [12]. This could be ensured by the principle of wireless power supply, similar to the case of wireless charging of mobile phones. Such cross integration between these technologies is still the subject of future research.

References

1. Al-Ameen, Y., Ianakiev, A., Evans, R.: Thermal performance of a solar assisted horizontal ground heat exchanger. Energy **140**, 1216–1227 (2017). https://doi.org/10.1016/j.energy.2017.08.091
2. Arvidsson, A.K.: The winter model – a new way to calculate socio-economic costs depending on winter maintenance strategy. Cold Reg. Sci. Technol. **136**, 30–36 (2017). https://doi.org/10.1016/j.coldregions.2017.01.005
3. ICAX Homepage. http://www.icax.co.uk/Solar_Runways.html. Accessed on 25 Nov 2020
4. Astolfi, M., Mazzola, S., Silva, P., Macchi, E.: A synergic integration of desalination and solar energy systems in stand-alone microgrids. Desalination **419**, 169–180 (2017). https://doi.org/10.1016/j.desal.2017.05.025
5. Descamps, M.N., Leoncini, G., Vallée, M., Paulus, C.: Performance assessment of a multi-source heat production system with storage for district heating. Energy Procedia **149**, 390–399 (2018). https://doi.org/10.1016/j.egypro.2018.08.203
6. E-Hub Homepage. http://www.e-hub.org/road-solar-collector.html. Accessed on 25 Nov 2020
7. Ghorab, M.: Energy hubs optimization for smart energy network system to minimize economic and environmental impact at Canadian community. Appl. Therm. Eng. **151**, 214–230 (2019). https://doi.org/10.1016/j.applthermaleng.2019.01.107
8. Holmér, P., Ullmark, J., Göransson, L., Walter, V., Johnsson, F.: Impacts of thermal energy storage on the management of variable demand and production in electricity and district heating systems: a Swedish case study. Int. J. Sustain. Energy **39**(5), 446–464 (2020). https://doi.org/10.1080/14786451.2020.1716757
9. Luo, X., Zhu, Y., Liu, J., Liu, Y.: Design and analysis of a combined desalination and standalone CCHP (combined cooling heating and power) system integrating solar energy based on a bi-level optimization model. Sustain. Cities Soc. **43**, 166–175 (2018). https://doi.org/10.1016/j.scs.2018.08.023

10. Mirzanamadi, R., Hagentoft, C.-E., Johansson, P.: Coupling a hydronic heating pavement to a horizontal ground heat exchanger for harvesting solar energy and heating road surfaces. Renew. Energy **147**, 447–463 (2020). https://doi.org/10.1016/j.renene.2019.08.107
11. Mollenhauer, E., Christidis, A., Tsatsaronis, G.: Increasing the flexibility of combined heat and power plants with heat pumps and thermal energy storage. J. Energy Resour. Technol. **140**(2) (2017). https://doi.org/10.1115/1.4038461
12. Ramm, T., Hammel, C., Klärner, M., Kruck, A., Schrag, T.: Energy storage and integrated energy approach for district heating systems. Energy Procedia **135**, 391–397 (2017). https://doi.org/10.1016/j.egypro.2017.09.515

Evaluation Methods of Investments to Mobile Applications and Smart Technology in Construction Projects

Tomáš Mandičák📵, Peter Mésároš, Annamária Behúnová(✉) 📵, Marcel Behún, and Matúš Tkáč

Faculty of Civil Engineering, Technical University of Košice, Vysokoškolská4, 042 00 Košice, Slovakia

{tomas.mandicak,annamaria.behunova}@tuke.sk

Abstract. Smart technologies and solutions have represented an increasing growth in every industry over the last decade . Many of the smart solutions are focused on improvement with a view to sustainability. The basis of smart solutions is advanced technologies and interactive systems that respond to changed conditions. These technologies are increasingly being implemented in the field of construction and intelligent buildings or urban areas. The construction industry shows great possibilities for the implementation of smart and progressive technologies. However, construction projects represent a volume-intensive investment. The same applies to the implementation of smart solutions, which, however, can also provide savings. This needs to be evaluated very much. It is necessary to use evaluation methods of investments in these solutions. This paper is largely devoted to the evaluation methods of investments in mobile applications and smart technology in the construction industry. The research aims to conduct an overview of evaluation methods of investments to smart technology in construction projects. Research also describes examples of the use of specific smart solutions in the construction industry and urban planning. The output of the research is an overview of Evaluation methods of investments, which can be applied and used in assessing investments in advanced technologies in construction.

Keywords: Smart technology · Mobile applications · Evaluation methods of investments · Construction projects

1 Introduction

Sustainability is a new not only phenomenon, but above all, a real need of the 21st century [1]. The emphasis on sustainability is felt every day. Extensive discussions within Europe or world leaders address the issue of environmental burdens and their impact on countries' economies [2]. There is a great deal of pressure on environmentally friendly materials in every sector [3]. Construction is in the same situation. There is also pressured to reduce emissions, carbon footprints or other negative impacts of the industry

© ICST Institute for Computer Sciences, Social Informatics and Telecommunications Engineering 2021
Published by Springer Nature Switzerland AG 2021. All Rights Reserved
D. Perakovic and L. Knapcikova (Eds.): FABULOUS 2021, LNICST 382, pp. 374–385, 2021.
https://doi.org/10.1007/978-3-030-78459-1_28

in the construction segment [4]. Construction is a segment that is largely considered a major producer of waste [5]. As part of the green policy, several initiatives have been taken to reduce the volume of negative effects in this sector as well [6]. It is necessary to say that the construction sector is closely linked to other sectors. Consumption of materials largely requires addressing the issue of their production [7]. This segment is also demanding on logistics processes [8]. The implementation of a construction project requires great knowledge in the field of logistics. The challenge in this digital age is to reduce these negative impacts in construction with smart solutions and smart technologies [9]. It is the use of smart technologies that can significantly contribute to the sustainability of this segment [10]. Information and communication technologies are one of the tools that can have a positive impact on sustainability and the environment, but also on economic sustainability [11]. For this reason, it is essential to discuss the cost of the whole life cycle of a construction project [12, 13]. Progressive technologies represent new possibilities in construction, which on the other hand improve the digital skills of managers [14]. At the same time, the use of smart technologies in construction brings an increase in the quality of outputs in this segment [15].

Smart solutions in building and construction and design should lead to a reduction in environmental burdens and a sustainable economy [16]. In other words, smart technologies are also supposed to have a positive impact on the economics of building project management [17]. These technologies can effectively reduce costs and, on the other hand, contribute to better project management [18]. Therefore, the implementation of smart technologies in construction should lead to the question of how and when it will be profitable. It is the performance parameters concerning new progressive technologies that need to be monitored [19]. Investment in construction is the second-largest amount of investment in the national economy. Investments in IT solutions represent the largest volume of investments. It follows from these facts that the scale of investments in these areas is so large that it is necessary to assess these investments. Therefore, there is a basic research question on how to evaluate investments in smart technologies in construction projects. The issue of key performance indicators focuses on efficiency and performance as such. This can be measured in several ways. In the context of the perception of smart and mobile technologies in construction as an investment, it is necessary to assess and evaluate these investments from an economic point of view. The aim of this survey is to map the possibilities of methods for evaluating investments in smart technologies in the field of construction.

2 Smart Technology and Mobile Applications in Construction Projects

According to several studies, smart technologies implemented in construction are beneficial [20]. These studies highlight the benefits of implementing digital and knowledge technologies from multiple perspectives. In the context of smart technologies and the use of urban planning, several technologies are useful for solving smart cities [21]. One large group, therefore, consists of the so-called GIS technology and digital technology use for urban planning purposes. Intelligent solutions in construction and also for the city have the ability to capture real-time data that is communicated between stakeholders to optimize decision-making by using digital technology [19].

Geographic information systems (GIS) and digital technologies are based on spatial and temporal analysis of data collected into groups according to their purpose. Their goal is to model future trends and predict impacts on project implementation and the environment. These technologies are also largely based on the use of mobile devices and applications that interact. The growth of smartphones is significant, as according to the study, the use of smartphones has increased by 2% in the last year. In absolute terms, this currently represents just over 5 billion users [22].

The technology of terrestrial laser scanning and aerial photogrammetry using drones currently represents another opportunity to implement digital technologies and smart solutions in urban planning and construction. It can serve as an effective and progressive tool in the field of 3D spatial digitization of buildings and their geometric dimensions. These technologies try to display 3D buiPodklldings in detail in a digital environment, which is to be made for project documentation. These technologies automate this otherwise demanding process. The advantage is the simulation of changes itself and simple changes in planning, as it is a digital output. Laser scanners are a beneficial tool to measure buildings and urban areas, including all buildings (Fig. 1).

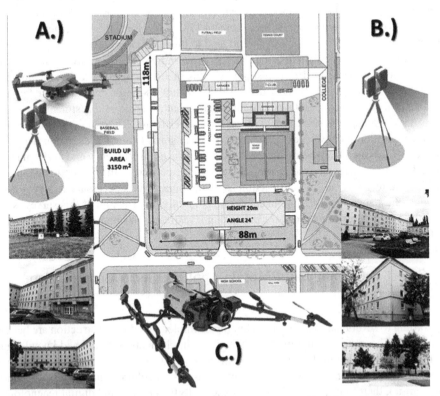

Fig. 1. Progressive methods of data collection for digital model of buildings (building – faculty of civil Engineering in Kosice)

The fact that it works and that such a smart solution can be applied in practice is confirmed by another study carried out in the city of Kosice. The picture shows the building of the Faculty of Civil Engineering, which was the reference for the given research. This building was monitored and had to be turned into project documentation and a digital model. For these purposes, three variants of data acquisition and creation of a digital point model were used. As the picture describes, one of the solutions was to obtain data via a 3D scanner. Another variation was photogrammetry and a third combination were the use of drones.

The next picture describes in more detail the capture of the roof and problematic buildings. For these purposes, AV appears to be the best solution for data collection. This study compared the suitability of the various methods (Fig. 2).

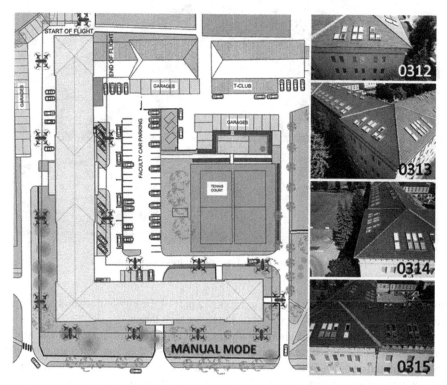

Fig. 2. 2D model and 3D model of building (roof detail)

The output of this is a fully digital model, which can be worked with in several programs (Fig. 3). Importantly, this model is an input for other technologies, especially BIM technologies, which in interaction with GIS and other mobile applications it can be an effective tool for smart solutions.

The basis is the creation of a point cloud, which can then be processed later and used in a BIM environment. This easily obtained 3D model can be considered as an initial step towards a smart solution even in the construction industry. It should be noted that

Fig. 3. Data processing from point cloud to 3D model

it is good to use an aerial 3D scanner to capture a part of the city and several buildings. It captures several objects at once, and its range is much larger.

In this study it was used similarly focused technologies in Australia. The study pointed to the suitability of addressing these smart technologies and connectivity and mobile applications [23]. The authors of the study (described in Fig. 4) showed these smart technologies connected to mobile devices and applications in practice. There is comparison of digital–physical twin at the city scale, management and integration of Building Information Modelling (BIM) and Geographic Information Systems (GIS) for a digital model of a proposed building.

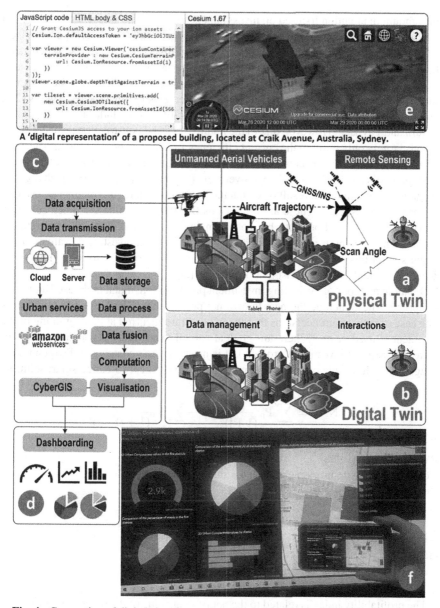

Fig. 4. Connection of digital situation, real or physical situation and mobile devices [23]

3 Evaluation Methods of Investments in Construction Projects

Evaluation of investment projects is a basic decision-making tool for project managers, who are responsible for the success of projects. This also applies to the construction industry, where the volume and scope of investments are among the largest in the country's economies. The implementation of smart and progressive technologies requires the same amount of attention focused on investment evaluation. The assessment of different projects and the selection of the optimal one can be done based on several perspectives.

On the one hand, it can be a factor of liquidity, time and risk, on the other hand, a factor of the effect that the investment brings. In the first case, they are static and dynamic investment evaluation methods [24]. In the second case, there are cost efficiency evaluation criteria, profit efficiency evaluation criteria, net cash income criteria [25]. Static methods are gaining favor due to their simplicity. This includes the Average rate of return and Payback. However, due to the nature of IT and construction projects, these methods largely only point to the current efficiency trend. They do not take into account and predict the time factor and its value. Also, the construction industry often incurs expenses in other years, which change over time (amendments to contracts, changes in project documentation as a result of which the ground is also requirements for SMART solutions and tools, etc.). These are all reasons that can determine the quick selection of a narrower number of projects, but not the main decision-making tool for investment selection. These methods are not sufficient for the purposes of investment evaluation and comparison, or other authors have worked on progress on how best to implement these evaluation methods in the assessment of projects [26].

Dynamic methods of evaluating investment projects seem much more used and more appropriate. These include the best-known net profit value (NPV). As it is only rarely in the case of investment decisions that the expenditure incurred at the beginning of the investment is used once. If there are gradual capital expenditures (which is a fact for the vast majority of investment projects), it is necessary to update capital expenditures throughout the life cycle or construction project, or intelligent so-called smart solution.

$$NPV = \sum_{n=1}^{N} P_n \frac{1}{(1+i)^{n+T}} - \sum_{t=1}^{T} K_t \frac{1}{(1+i)^t}$$

NPV - net present value.
P - cash income from investments in individual years of life.
n - individual years of life.
N - service life.
i - required return (interest rate).
K - capital expenditure.
t - individual years of construction (or SMART solution).
T - construction time (IT user time).

The profitability index is related to the net present value of the investment project. It is a relative indicator that expresses the ratio of expected discounted cash receipts from the project to initial capital expenditures [25]:

$$I_R = \frac{\sum_{n=1}^{N} P_n \frac{1}{(1+i)^n}}{K}$$

I_R - profitability index.
P - cash income from investments in n years of life.

n - individual years of life.
N - service life.
i - required return (interest rate).
K - capital expenditure.

Other authors have a different view on the calculation and comparison of investments. Previous methods took into account a pre-selected interest rate. The internal rate of return method looks for a percentage equal to the interest rate at which the project is profitable. An enterprise should accept a project if its internal rate of return is higher than the discount rate [26, 27].

$$\sum_{n=1}^{N} P_n \frac{1}{(1+i)^n} = K$$

P - cash income from investments in individual years of life.
n - individual years of life.
N - lifetime.
i - sought interest rate.
K - capital expenditure.

Another suitable method is economic value added (EVA). This represents the net return on the company's operating activities less the cost of capital. To quantify the economic added value during the entire life of the investment project, it is necessary to convert all individual EVA values and discount and add them. In the case of a positive outcome, the investment brings the benefits of implementing a smart solution [28].

$$EVA_{PV} = \sum_{n=1}^{N} \frac{NOPAT_n - WACC * C_n}{(1+i)^n}$$

EVA_{pv} – present value of economic value added.
NOPAT – main activity profit after tax.
WACC - weighted average cost of capital.
C - capital tied up in assets, necessary for the main operation of the company.
n - individual years of service life.
N - service life.
I - required return (interest rate).

Costs are a basic evaluation criterion for many projects. Therefore, this view for the implementation of smart solutions is in the first place when assessing some projects. The implementation of smart solutions in construction takes place to reduce costs in some part, or during the entire life cycle of the solution or construction project. The cost criteria for the effectiveness of investment projects can therefore include the Average Annual Cost Method and the Discounted Cost Method. The comparison of average annual costs is typical of the average annual cost method.

$$R = 0 + I * J + V$$

R – annual average costs.
O – annual depreciation.
i – required return (interest).
J – investment cost (capital expenditure).
V – other annual operating expenses.

The Discounted Cost Method is based on the same principle as the average annual cost method, but the average annual costs are replaced by the sum of the investment discounted operating costs of the individual variants over the life of the project.

$$D = J + \sum_{n=1}^{N} V_n$$

D - discounted costs.
J - investment costs.
V_n - discounted other annual operating expenses.
n - individual years of life.
N - service life.

These basic investment methods have their advantages and disadvantages. It's not possible to determine at a flat rate which is the best method. It depends on several factors and the main criteria for evaluating the investment project. Dynamic methods take into account the time factor, which in many cases will be a better alternative than static ones. When considering solutions where the main criterion will be cost, it is appropriate to use cost methods. An overview of the methods and main evaluation criteria is given in Table 1.

Table 1. An overview of the methods and main evaluation criteria [24–28]

Methods	Static method	Dynamic method	Cost method
The average rate of return	x		
Payback	x		
NPV - net present value method		x	
The profitability index		x	
The internal rate of return method		x	
EVA – economic value added		x	
R – annual average costs			x
The discounted cost method			x

4 Conclusion

Construction is a sector where there is a large volume of investment. Investment projects in the field of IT implementation (smart solutions, progressive and digital technologies) require an axial evaluation based on selected criteria. Smart solutions should bring several benefits that users (the investor) can define. Based on this, the main criteria are chosen to assess the benefits of the solution. Methods of evaluating investment projects take into account several factors. Most often, it is about time, cost and cost, which are the key performance indicators of all projects. Based on this, it is necessary to choose the right method of comparing investment plans. This survey pointed out possible methods in the selection of the investment plan and summarized their advantages, respectively, the possibilities when it is appropriate to use these methods. At the same time, the paper also provides an overview of smart solutions and mobile solutions, when it is appropriate to use one of the mentioned methods. These traditional economic methods of evaluation are, in many cases, general, but their use must be based on specific factors. Therefore, it is necessary to consider a specific investment project in new technology, analyze the benefits and define the main factor based on which they will be evaluated. This research needs to be taken further. This means trying to look for dependencies and creating a methodological model when it is appropriate to use which method.

Acknowledgment. The article presents a partial research result of project KEGA 059TUKE-4/2019 "M-learning tool for intelligent modelling of site structure parameters in a mixed reality environment".

This work was supported by the Slovak Research and Development Agency under the contract no. APVV-17- 0549.

References

1. Kridlová-Burdová, E., Selecká, E., Vilčeková, S., Burák, D., Sedláková, A.: Evaluation of Family Houses in Slovakia Using a Building Environmental Assessment System. Sustain. Bazilej – Multidiscipl. Digit. Publish. Inst. **12**(16), 1–27 (2020)
2. Behún, M., et al.: The impact of the manufacturing industry on the economic cycle of European Union countries. J. Compet. **10**(1), 23–39 (2018)
3. Knapčíková, L., et al.: Material recycling of some automobile plastics waste. Przem. Chem. **95**(9), 1716–1720 (2018)
4. Drozd, W., Leśniak, A.: Ecological wall systems as an element of sustainable development-cost issues. Sustainability **10**(7), 22–34 (2018)
5. Radziszewska-Zielina, E., Szewczyk, M.: Examples of actions that improve partnering cooperation among the participants of construction projects. IOP Conf. Ser. Mater. Sci. Eng. **25**(1), 012–051 (2017). IOP Publishing
6. Gajzler, M., Zima, K.: Evaluation of planned construction projects using fuzzy logic. Int. J. Civil Eng. **15**(4), 641–652 (2017). https://doi.org/10.1007/s40999-017-0177-8
7. Knapčíková, L., et al.: Advanced materials based on the recycled Polyvinyl Butyral (PVB). In: MMS Conference 2017. - Ghent : EAI, pp. 1–9 (2018)
8. Straka, M., Hricko, M.: Software system design for solution of effective material layout for the needs of production and logistics. Wirel. Netw. J. Mob. Commun. Comput. Inf. 1–10 (2020)

9. Mihić, M., Vukomanović, M., Završki, I.: Review of previous applications of innovative information technologies in construction health and safety. Org. Technol. Manag. Constr. **11**, 1952–1967 (2019)

10. Krajníková, K., Smetanková, J., Behúnová, A.: Green buildings and building information modelling. Strojárstvo extra **23**(9), 1–6 (2019)

11. Balog, M., et al.: Productivity fluid management as a tool for saving money in manufacturing. TEM J. **5**(2), 192–196 (2016)

12. Biolek, V., Hanák, T.: LCC estimation model: a construction material perspective. MDPI Build. SI: Life Cycle Predict. Maintenance Build. **9**, 1–19 (2019). https://doi.org/10.3390/bui ldings9080182

13. Korytarova, J., Hromadka, V.: Building life cycle economic impacts. In: Proceedings of the International Conference on Management and Service Science, Wuhan, China (2010)

14. Mesároš, P., Behúnová, A., Mandičák, T., Behún, M.: Impact of enterprise information systems on selected key performance indicators in construction project management – an empirical study. Wirel. Netw. J. Mob. Commun. Comput. Inf. (2019). ISSN 1022-0038

15. Gasparik, J., Funtik, T., Gasparik, M., Alamro, B.: Continuing increasing of quality management level in construction company using excellence model with software support. In: ISARC 2018 - 35th International Symposium on Automation and Robotics in Construction and International AEC/FM Hackathon: The Future of Building Things, Germany, pp. 207–213 (2018)

16. Radziszewska-Zielina, E.: Assessment methods of partnering relations of Polish, Slovak and Ukrainian construction enterprises with the use of fuzzy logic. Arch. Civil Eng. **1**(LVII), 87–118 (2011)

17. Kolarić, S., Vukomanovoć, M.: Potential of BIM and ERP integration in contractor construction companies. In: Conference Proceedings: 13th International Conference on Organization, Technology and Management in Construction, Zagreb, pp. 669–673 (2017)

18. Knezevic, M., Cvetkovska, M., Hanák, T.: Artificial neural networks and fuzzy neural networks for solving civil engineering problems. Hindawi, Complex. 1–2 (2018). https://doi.org/10.1155/2018/8149650

19. Gholamzadehmir, M., Del Pero, C., Buffa, S., Fedrizzi, R.: Niccolo' Aste: Adaptive-predictive control strategy for HVAC systems in smart buildings – A review. Sustain. Urban Areas **63**(2020), 102480 (2020)

20. Shirowzhan, S., Tan, W., Sepasgozar, S.M.E.: Digital twin and CyberGIS for improving connectivity and measuring the impact of infrastructure construction planning in smart cities. MDPI Int. J. Geo-Inf. **9**(240), 1–11 (2019)

21. European Commission: Commission recommendation (EU) 2019/786 of 8 May 2019 on building renovation, vol. 6, pp. 34–79 (2015)

22. Kemp, S.: Digital 2019: Global Internet Use Accelerates (2020). https://wearesocial.com/blog/2019/01/digital-2019-global-internet-use-accelerates. Accessed 15 Oct 2020

23. Shirowzhan, S., Tan,W., Sepasgozar, SME.: Digital twin and CyberGIS for improving connectivity and measuring the impact of infrastructure construction planning in smart cities. ISPRS Int. J. Geo-Inf. Spec. Issue Spat. Big Data BIM Adv. GIS Smart Transf. City Infrastr. Constr. **9**(4), 240 (2020. https://doi.org/10.3390/ijgi9040240

24. Kalouda, F.: Financial Analysis and Business Management. 2nd extended edn. Plzeň: Aleš Čeněk, ltd. Publishing (2016)

25. Valach, J.: Investment Decisions and Long-Term Financing. 3rd extended edn. Ekopress, Praha (2010)

26. Magni, C.A.: Average internal rate of return and investment decisions: a new perspective. Eng. Econ. **55**(2), 150–180 (2010)

27. Fotr, J., Souček, J.: Investment Decision Making and Project Management. Grada Publishing, Praha (2011)
28. Maříková, P., Mařík, M.: Modern Methods of Performance Evaluation and Business Valuation: Economic Added Value: Market Added Value. Ekopress, Praha (2001)

Robust Stability and Performance Investigation of Electrohydraulic Steering Control System

Alexander Mitov[1]($\boxtimes$) ⓘ, Tsonyo Slavov[2] ⓘ, Jordan Kralev[2] ⓘ, and Ilcho Angelov[1]

[1] Department of Hydroaerodynamics and Hydraulic Machines, Technical University of Sofia, Kliment Ohridski 8 blvd., 1680 Sofia, Bulgaria
{a_mitov,ilangel}@tu-sofia.bg
[2] Department of Systems and Control, Technical University of Sofia, Kliment Ohridski 8 blvd., 1680 Sofia, Bulgaria
{ts_slavov,jkralev}@tu-sofia.bg

Abstract. The article introduces a robust stability and robust performance investigation of two embedded systems for control of electrohydraulic power steering in mobile machinery . They are based on advanced control techniques - linear-quadratic *Gaussian* (LQG) controller and H-infinity controller . The synthesis of the two controllers is performed via experimentally estimated SIMO state space model. The 30% input multiplicative uncertainty is introduced in estimated model. In this manner, a dead-band of proportional spool valve position is taken into account. This dead-band is constructively implemented to provide safety requirements of electrohydraulic steering. The robust stability and robust performance analysis are done by determining a structured singular value (μ) of the both closed-loop control systems, which are represented in M-Δ structure. The workability of the both systems are verified through simulation and real world experiments on laboratory test rig.

Keywords: Robust stability · Robust performance · LQG · H_∞ · Electrohydraulic system

1 Introduction

One of the essential applications of electrohydraulic positioning servo systems is in the power steering systems of different types of mobile machines. In recent years, this application has given a strong stimulus to the development of electrohydraulic devices in the direction of its digital control [1]. On the other hand, the growing need for automation of the steering direction of mobile machines has accelerated the development of the embedded control systems that determine the behaviour of the entire electrohydraulic drive system. The controller used into the embedded system has a general importance for the steering performance [2]. Therefore, it is necessary to study the robust stability and robust performance [3, 4] of the closed-loop control system before it is implementation in the real electrohydraulic power steering (EHPS).

© ICST Institute for Computer Sciences, Social Informatics and Telecommunications Engineering 2021
Published by Springer Nature Switzerland AG 2021. All Rights Reserved
D. Perakovic and L. Knapcikova (Eds.): FABULOUS 2021, LNICST 382, pp. 386–400, 2021.
https://doi.org/10.1007/978-3-030-78459-1_29

The main goal of this article is to present the results of robust stability and robust performance investigation of two embedded systems for control of EHPS in mobile machinery. They are based on advanced control techniques - linear-quadratic *Gaussian* (LQG) controller and H-infinity controller [5, 6]. The synthesis of the two controllers is performed via experimentally estimated SIMO state space model. The 30% input multiplicative uncertainty is introduced in estimated model. In this manner, a dead-band of proportional spool valve position is taken into account. This dead-band is constructively implemented to provide safety requirements of electrohydraulic steering. The robust stability and robust performance analysis are done by determining a structured singular value μ of the both closed-loop control systems, which are represented in M-Δ structure. The workability of the both systems are verified through simulation and real world experiments on laboratory test rig.

The paper is structured as follows: Sect. 2 shows development of nominal and uncertain model of EHPS, Sect. 3 briefly present LQG and H_∞ controllers, Sect. 4 shows robust stability and robust performance investigation of the both closed-loop control systems, Sect. 5 presents experimental results for performance verification and in Sect. 6 some conclusions are given.

2 Uncertain Servo System Model

For investigation of EHPS we designed and implemented a laboratory test rig for test of different types of embedded controllers. The electrohydraulic steering unit (EHSU) introduce into the test rig is OSPEC200 LSRM [7]. The designed hydraulic circuit diagram and detailed description of the test rig system is shown in [8] and real implementation is presented in the Fig. 1.

Fig. 1. Real implementation of laboratory electrohydraulic power steering test rig.

In order to design controllers based on advanced control techniques, it is necessary to derive a linear state-space model of the plant. In this case, a black box type model of electrohydraulic power steering system was obtained through an identification procedure using experimental data set. The details on identification are presented in [9, 10]. In this section only a short representation of identified model is shown. The system can be modelled sufficiently well with third order state-space model with single input and three outputs. The input is a control action and outputs are proportional spool position y_{spool}, the measured flow rate y_{flow} consumed by the servo cylinder and the cylinder piston position y_{piston}.The first output is measured by linear variable differential transducer (LVDT), the second is measured by gear flowmeter with coupled encoder and the third output is measured with linear resistive transducer. The state-space form of the estimated plant model are

$$
\begin{aligned}
x(k+1) &= Ax(k) + Bu(k) + Ke(k) \\
y(k) &= Cx(k) + Du(k) + e(k),
\end{aligned}
\tag{1}
$$

where $x = \begin{bmatrix} x_1\ x_2\ x_3 \end{bmatrix}^T$, $y = \begin{bmatrix} y_{spool}\ y_{flow}\ y_{pos} \end{bmatrix}^T$ are the state vector and output signal, and $e = \begin{bmatrix} e_{spool}\ e_{flow}\ e_{piston} \end{bmatrix}^T$ are residuals, that are white *Gaussian* noises. The matrices of the model are

$$
A = \begin{bmatrix} -1.05 & 0.19 & 6.27 \\ -0.04 & 1 & 0.198 \\ -0.371 & 0.033 & 2.044 \end{bmatrix}, B = 10^{-3} \begin{bmatrix} -0.37 \\ -0.034 \\ -0.23 \end{bmatrix},
$$

$$
C = \begin{bmatrix} -31 & 0.67 & -6.58 \\ -0.584 & 0.007 & -0.25 \\ 0.059 & -2.019 & 0.125 \end{bmatrix}, D = 10^{-3} \begin{bmatrix} 0.117 \\ 0.014 \\ 0.0021 \end{bmatrix},
\tag{2}
$$

$$
K = \begin{bmatrix} -0.025 & -0.023 & -0.022 \\ -0.002 & 0.0066 & -0.429 \\ -0.007 & -0.01 & 0.0033 \end{bmatrix}
$$

Further, as nominal plant the deterministic part of model (2) will be regarded [11] and will be used for H_∞ controller and linear quadratic controller design. Whereas, the stochastic will be utilized to design a *Kalman* filter. To guarantee the safety working conditions of embedded electrohydraulic servo control systems, the positive overlap in proportional spool valve is imposed by standard ISO13849-1 [12], which leads to dead-band in its response. This valve determinates the direction of movement of the steering cylinder piston. From control point of view this dead-band is significant nonlinearity [13]. It can be regarded as a source of uncertainty in influence of control action to the plant. Other source of uncertainty is the neglected plant dynamics and the identification method errors. To account for all sources of uncertainty, the multiplicative uncertainty to control signal is added as is shown in Fig. 2. Thus plant model with input multiplicative uncertainty is obtained as

$$
G = G_{nom}(1 + \Delta),
\tag{3}
$$

where $|\Delta| \leq 0.3$ is bounded uncertainty linear time invariant object and

$$
G_{nom} = C(sI - A)^{-1}B
\tag{4}
$$

is the nominal plant transfer matrix. In this manner, the uncertainty in control signal may achieve 30%, which is sufficiently large.

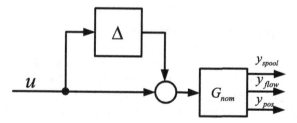

Fig. 2. Uncertain plant model.

In Figs. 3 and 4 the step responses and frequency responses for 30 random values of plant uncertainty are shown.

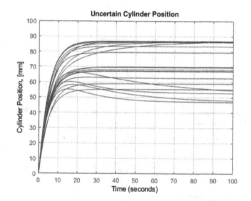

Fig. 3. Step response of the uncertain model.

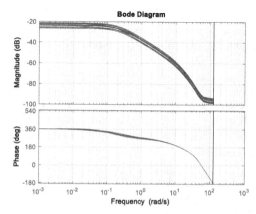

Fig. 4. Frequency response of the uncertain model.

It should be noted that the uncertainty is constant respect to the frequency, which is conservative assumption. In time domain the uncertainty is occurred in time constants and in static gain.

3   Design of LQG and H∞ Controllers

The authors have experience in the development of different LQG and H_∞ controllers for electrohydraulic steering systems based on various identification model. These developments are presented in their previous articles [14, 15].

The model (2) is used to design the LQG and H_∞ controllers. The detailed description of procedure for LQG and H∞ controllers synthesis is presented in [16, 17]. The main proposition of this article is the investigation of robust stability and robust performance of the developed embedded electrohydraulic power steering system with designed controllers. Due to that here only a brief presentation of controller design procedure is given. The scheme of designed systems is depicted in Fig. 5. The block named "Controller" represents designed LQG or H_∞ controllers.

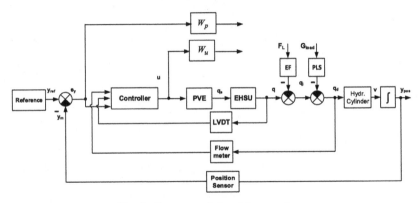

Fig. 5. Structure of closed-loop system.

To ensure performance of reference tracking the integral action LQG controller is designed. For this aim the nominal model (2) is modified as

$$e_{\text{int},pos}(k+1) = e_{\text{int},pos}(k) + T_s e_{pos}(k), \ e_{pos}(k) =_s (y_{ref}(k) - y_{pos}(k)), \quad (5)$$

where $y_{ref}(k)$ is the reference of cylinder piston position, $T_s = 0.01s$ - the sample time, $e_{\text{int},pos}(k)$ - the discrete time integral of cylinder piston position error and $e_{pos}(k)$ - the cylinder piston position error. Combining model (1) and Eq. (5) the description of augmented plant is obtained as

$$\bar{x}(k+1) = \bar{A}\bar{x}(k) + \bar{B}u(k) + \bar{G}y_{ref}(k),$$
$$y(k) = \bar{C}\bar{x}(k), \quad (6)$$

where $\bar{x}(k) = \begin{vmatrix} x(k) \\ e_{int,pos}(k) \end{vmatrix}, \bar{A} = \begin{vmatrix} A & 0 \\ -T_s C & 1 \end{vmatrix}, \bar{B} = \begin{vmatrix} B \\ 0 \end{vmatrix}, \bar{C} = \begin{vmatrix} C & 0 \end{vmatrix}, \bar{G} = \begin{vmatrix} 0 \\ T_s \end{vmatrix}$. The controller formed control signal as

$$u(k) = -K_c \hat{x}(k) - K_i e_{int,pos}(k), \tag{7}$$

where K_c and K_i are the proportional and integral parts of controller. The state estimates $\hat{x}(k)$ are computed by *Kalman* filter.

$$\hat{x}(k+1) = A\hat{x}(k) + Bu(k) + K_f(y(k+1) - CBu(k) - CA\hat{x}(k)), \tag{8}$$

where K_f is matrix Kalman filter gain. It is obtained by *MATLAB®* function *Kalman* [18]. The covariance of residual in model (2) is used in the *Kalman* filter design procedure. The obtained LQG controller minimizes performance criteria

$$J(u) = \sum_{k=0}^{\infty} \bar{x}^T(k)Q\bar{x}(k) + u^T(k)Ru(k), \tag{9}$$

where $Q = \begin{bmatrix} 1000 & 0 \\ 0 & 500C_3^T C_3 \end{bmatrix}$, $R = 100$, and C_3 is a third row of matrix C.

In order to design H_∞ controller, two weighting transfer functions W_p and W_u are introduced. They are used to specify the performance requirements for closed-loop control system. Thus the plant description used in design of H_∞ controller is

$$x_{ext}(k+1) = A_{ext}x_{ext}(k) + B_{ext}\begin{pmatrix} e \\ y_{ref} \\ u \end{pmatrix}, \begin{pmatrix} z_u \\ z_y \\ y_{cont} \end{pmatrix} = C_{ext}x_{ext} + D_{ext}\begin{pmatrix} e \\ y_{ref} \\ u \end{pmatrix}, \tag{10}$$

where $x_{ext} = [x_1, x_2, x_3, x_u, x_p]$, x_u and x_p are the states corresponding to W_p and W_u, and $y_{cont} = [y_{spool}\ y_{flow}\ e_{pos}]^T$ is the input of H_∞ controller. The controller parameters are determined by solving the mixed sensitivity optimization problem [19]

$$\min \left\| \begin{matrix} W_pS \\ W_uKS \end{matrix} \right\|_\infty < \gamma, \tag{11}$$

where $\gamma > 0$, S is the output sensitivity function and K is the controller transfer matrix. It is known that in practice a suboptimal H_∞ controller is obtained. If after optimization γ in (11) is smaller than 1, this means that the prescribed by weighting transfer functions nominal system performance is achieved. The controller design is performed for weighting functions

$$W_p = \frac{0.3(0.001s + 1)}{300s + 1}, W_u = \frac{0.001(0.3s + 1)}{0.001s + 1}. \tag{12}$$

The obtained value for γ is 0.5387, that guarantee nominal performance. The step response of nominal systems with the both controllers are depicted in Fig. 6.

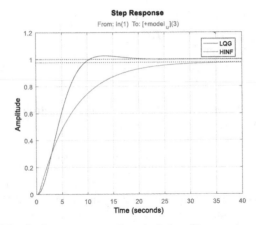

Fig. 6. Step responses of nominal closed loop systems.

4 Robust Stability and Robust Performance Investigation of Designed Control Systems

The block diagram of closed-loop system with uncertain model (3) that is used for robust stability and robust performance analysis is presented in Fig. 7. The block named K is the transfer matrix of designed LQG or H_∞ controllers. In order to investigate the robust stability [20, 21] it is convenient to transform the structure scheme of control system from Fig. 7 to standard $M - \Delta$ structure, depicted in Fig. 8. In this loop y_Δ is the uncertainty output, $z = \begin{bmatrix} z_u & z_p \end{bmatrix}^T$ is the external (performance) output and u_Δ is the uncertainty input. In case of robust stability analysis $z_u = u$ and $z_p = y_{ref} - y_{pos}$. The block named M is a lower Linear Fractional Transformation of nominal plant G_{nom} and controller K

$$M = F_l(P, K) \tag{13}$$

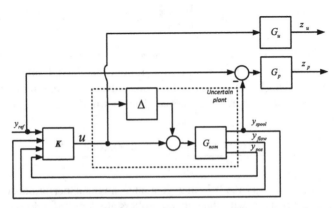

Fig. 7. Block diagram of closed-loop system with uncertain plant.

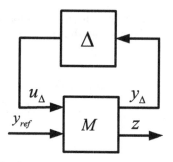

Fig. 8. M – Δ representation of EHPS.

The system depicted in Fig. 8 achieved robust stability for all Δ if and only if

$$\mu_\Delta[F_l(G_{nom}, K)] < 1, \tag{14}$$

where $\mu_\Delta[F_l(G_{nom}, K)]$ is the structure singular value of closed loop system. The robust performance of control system with the both controllers is investigated for weighting functions (11). The robust performance test is done with respect in extended uncertain structure. For the designed control system the extended uncertain structure take a form

$$\Delta_{G_{nom}} = \left\{ \begin{bmatrix} \Delta & 0 \\ 0 & \Delta_F \end{bmatrix} : \Delta_F \in C^{1\times2} \right\}, \tag{15}$$

where Δ_F is a fictitious complex uncertainty with two inputs z_u and z_p, and one output y_{ref}. The system with controller K reach robust performance if and only if

$$\mu_{\Delta_{Gnom}}[F_l(G_{nom}, K)(j\omega)] < 1, \tag{16}$$

where $\mu_{\Delta_{Gnom}}[F_l(G_{nom}, K)(j\omega)]$ is the structured singular value evaluated with respect in the extended uncertainty (15).

In Fig. 9 the limits of structured singular value (14) for both control systems are presented. It is seem that the both systems are robustly stable and robust stability margins are closed. The systems with LQG and H_∞ controllers can tolerate respectively up to 319% and 340% of the modeled uncertainty.

In Fig. 10 the bounds of structured singular value (16) for both control systems are presented. It is seem that the both systems achieved robust performance and can tolerate respectively up to 2.83 and 3.23 times lager uncertainty than modeled one.

In Fig. 11 the step responses of the both closed loop systems for 50 random values of plant uncertainty are shown. As can be seen the step responses are close to these of nominal closed loop systems (see Fig. 6), that again confirm robust performance of designed systems. The transient response of system with LQG have a negligible overshoot of approximately 5%, whereas ones of system with H_∞ controller do not have an overshoot.

In Figs. 12 and 13 the position sensitivity and position complementary sensitivity for 50 random values of plant uncertainty are shown. Again, it is seen robustness of both closed loop systems.

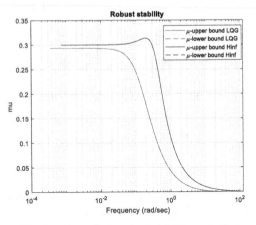

Fig. 9. μ bounds for robust stability analysis.

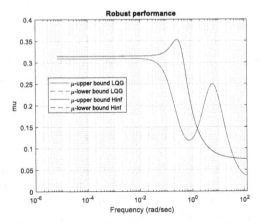

Fig. 10. μ bounds for robust performance analysis.

The disturbance attenuation for both systems are close. For instance, the disturbance with frequency of 0.01 *rad/s* will be suppressed 10 times by system with H_∞ controller and 12 times by system with LQG controller. The bandwidth of LQG system is wider than one of system with H_∞ controller.

In Fig. 14 the control signal sensitivity to noise of the designed control systems for 50 random values of plant uncertainty are shown. The LQG controller is more sensitive to noises than H_∞ controllers.

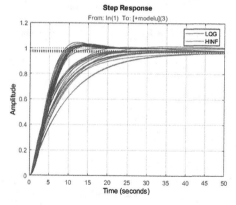

Fig. 11. Transient characteristics respect of the cylinder piston position.

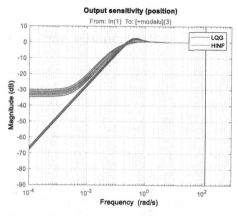

Fig. 12. The sensitivity of cylinder piston position to disturbances.

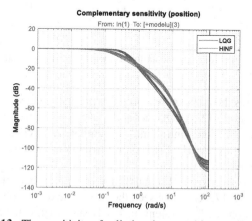

Fig. 13. The sensitivity of cylinder piston position to reference.

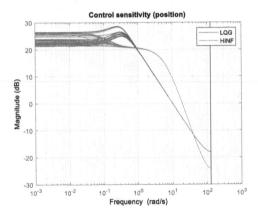

Fig. 14. Control signal to noise sensitivity.

5 Experimental Results for Performance Verification

The developed real time Simulink® structure used for experiments with LQG and H_∞ controllers is presented in the Fig. 15 [16]. The main block in model is *MATLAB® function* block which realizes the communication on the CAN channel between the microcontroller MC012-022 [22] and the workstation.

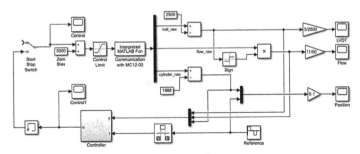

Fig. 15. Simulink® model for implementation of the LQG and H_∞ controllers in real-time.

Figure 16 compares the transient response of steering cylinder piston obtained with different type of controllers [23] (LQG and H_∞). These experiments confirm the observation from simulation that both controllers share similar performance in terms of settling time and steady state accuracy. The both controllers do not overshoot, but the LQG has a faster response in the both directions.

The comparison between control signals obtained with the both closed-loop systems are presented in the Fig. 17. As can be seen the amplitude of the control signal of LQG system is higher than one of H_∞ system. In steady state regime the H_∞ system is less oscillatory than LQG one which can be explained with its lower sensitivity to output disturbances (see Fig. 14).

Figures 18 and 19 compares the internal system values – flow rate and spool position. So we can observe that these signals are affected by both controllers and gives a possibilities for energy efficiency analysis.

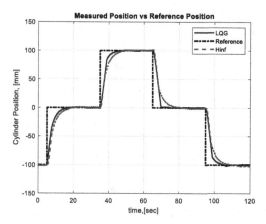

Fig. 16. Measured cylinder piston position.

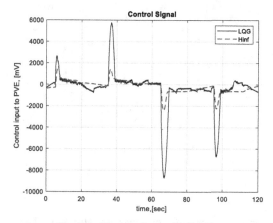

Fig. 17. Measured control signals.

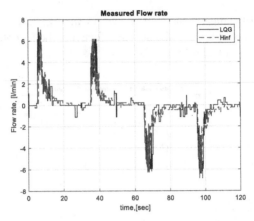

Fig. 18. Measured flow rate.

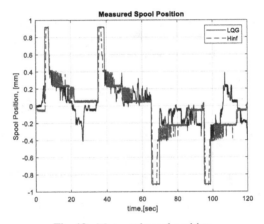

Fig. 19. Measured spool position.

6 Conclusion

The robust stability and the robust performance investigation of embedded system for control of electrohydraulic power steering based on two different advanced control strategies – linear-quadratic *Gaussian* (LQG) and H_∞ are presented in this article. The controllers are synthesized through multivariable model obtained by identification approach. The uncertainty model of EHPS is proposed, that takes into account effects of plant unmodelled dynamics, nonlinearities and measurement noises to the control system performance. This model is used for robust stability and robust performance analysis, which is done in framework of structured singular value of uncertain closed loop system. The obtained results show that the both control systems achieved robust stability and performance with similar robust stability and performance margins. The designed controllers are implemented by the PLC and are synchronized with the real-time Simulink® model over high-speed CAN channel. The Simulink® model of the controller is used for direct code generation and targeting to a particular computation platform of the EHPS test rig. The obtained experimental results present the similar performance of the both closed-loop system and confirm the results from simulation analysis of the EHPS control system with the LQG and H_∞ control techniques.

Acknowledgements. The authors would like to thank the Research and Development Sector at the Technical University of Sofia for the financial support.

References

1. Milić, V., Šltum, Ž., Essert, M.: Robust H∞ position control synthesis of an electro-hydraulic servo system. ISA Trans. **49**, 535–542 (2010)
2. Dannöhl, C., Müller, S., Ulbrich, H.: H∞-control of a rack-assisted electric power steering system. Int. J. Veh. Mech. Mob. **50**, 527–544 (2012)
3. Jin, Z., Zhang, L., Zhang, J., Khajepour, A.: Stability and optimized H∞ control of tripped and untripped vehicle rollover. Veh. Syst. Dyn. **54**, 1405–1427 (2016)
4. Wang, C., Deng, K., Zhao, W., Zhou, G., Zhou, D.: Stability control of steer by wire system based on μ synthesis robust control. Sci. China Technol. Sci. **60**, 16–26 (2017)
5. Min, Y., Quan, W., Shengjie, J.: Robust H_2/H_∞ control for the electrohydraulic steering system of a four-wheel vehicle. Math. Probl. Eng. **2014** (2014)
6. Zhao, W., Li, Y., Wang, C., Zhao, T., Gu, X.: H∞ control of novel active steering integrated with electric power steering function. J. Central South Univ. **20**, 2151–2157 (2013)
7. Danfoss: OSPE Steering valve. Tech. Inf. 11068682 (2016)
8. Angelov, I., Mitov, A.: Test bench for experimental research and identification of electro-hydraulic steering units. In: 10th International Fluid Power Conference, Dresden, Germany, pp. 225–236 (2016)
9. Mitov, A.L., Kralev, J., Slavov, T.S., Angelov, I.L.: SIMO system identification of transfer function model for electrohydraulic power steering. In: 16th International Conference on Electrical Machines, Drives and Power Systems (ELMA) , Sofia, Bulgaria, pp. 130–135 (2019)
10. Ljung, L.: System Identification: Theory for the User. 2nd edn. Prentice Hall, Englewood Cliffs (1999)
11. Proca, A., Keyhani, A.: Identification of power steering system dynamic models. Mechatronics **8**, 255–270 (1998)
12. Söderberg, A., Hedberg, J., Folkesson, P., Jacobson, J.: Safety and transport electronics – safety-related machine control systems using standard EN ISO 13849-1. In: Rise report 1, Sweden (2018)
13. Kemmetmüller, W., Müller, S., Kugi, A.: Mathematical modeling and nonlinear controller design for a novel electrohydraulic power-steering system. IEEE/ASME Trans. Mechatr. **12** (1), 85–97 (2007)
14. Slavov, Ts., Mitov, Al., Kralev, J.: Advanced embedded control of electrohydraulic power steering system. Cybern. Inf. Technol. **20** (2), 105–121 (2020)
15. Mitov, A.L., Slavov, T.S., Kralev, J., Angelov, I.L.: Comparison of robust stability for electrohydraulic steering control system based on LQG and H-infinity controller. In: 42nd International Conference on Telecommunications and Signal Processing TSP-2019, Budapest, Hungary, pp. 712–715 (2019)
16. Mitov, A.L., Kralev, J., Slavov, T.S., Angelov, I.L.: Reference tracking LQG control of electrohydraulic servo system for mobile machines. In: 10th IEEE International Conference on Intelligent Systems (IS'2020). Varna, Bulgaria, pp. 475–480 (2020)

17. Mitov, A.L., Kralev, J., Slavov, T.S, Angelov, I.L.: Design of H-infinity tracking controller for application in autonomous steering of mobile machines. In: 19th International Scientific Conference Engineering for Rural Development, Jelgava, Latvia, pp. 871–876 (2020)

18. The Mathworks Inc.: Robust Control Toolbox. User's Guide (2016)

19. Goodwin, G., Graebe, S., Salgado, M.: Control System Design. Prentice-Hall, Upper Saddle River (2001)

20. Zhou, K., Doyle, J.: Robust and Optimal Control. Prentice Hall International, Upper Saddle River (1996)

21. Petkov, P., Slavov, T.S., Kralev, J.: Design of Embedded Robust Control Systems Using MATLAB®/Simulink®. IET Control, United Kingdom (2018)

22. Sauer-Danfoss: Plus+1 Controllers MC012-020 and 022. Data Sheet 11077167, Rev DA (2013)

23. Más, F., Zhang, Q.: Mechatronics and Intelligent Systems for Off-Road Vehicles. Springer, London (2010). https://doi.org/10.1007/978-1-84996-468-5

Augmented Reality as a Tool of Increasing the Efficiency of RFID Technology

Jozef Husár[(⊠)] [iD], Lucia Knapčíková[iD], and Stella Hrehová[iD]

Faculty of Manufacturing Technologies with a seat in Prešov, Department of Industrial Engineering and Informatics, The Technical University of Košice, Bayerova 1, 080 01 Prešov, Slovak Republic
{jozef.husar,lucia.knapcikova,stella.hrehova}@tuke.sk

Abstract. The paper is focused on using the possibilities of implementing RFID technology with augmented reality. Today, it has become an element that is becoming more widely known. In this article, we gradually focus on two-second measures in two display units. The first alternative used for the measurement is the use of a UHF Bluetooth RFID reader with Smart glasses on the platform of the Android system. The second alternative is the use of industrial readers in Ethernet connection, its connection to the local wifi network and smart glasses Microsoft HoloLens 2. Both reading systems work on the principle of Ultra Hight Frequency, and therefore, different RFID tags are used in Label, industrial and metal case. For the laboratory measurements, we tested the reading distance of the RFID tag and the ability of intuitive control of applications. Based on the findings, it can be deduced that the implementation of augmented reality can help online monitoring and tracking the progress of production. As a concept, it is based on both proposals from the KANBAN system. The advantage is that suggested versions are mobile and can be directly implemented in manufacturing enterprises.

Keywords: Augmented reality · RFID · Concept of the measurement system · KANBAN · Smart glasses · Effectiveness · Competitiveness · Manufacturing

1 Introduction

The main idea of the proposed solution is based on the creation of a mobile system with which it will be possible to read radio frequency identification systems (RFID) in manufacturing companies. Based on recent experience with RFID systems, we can say that their loading is not problematic, but the problem occurs when displaying data in production. Many times it is necessary to provide a display unit that will be hardware and software compliant and can present the captured data. It opens up the possibility of using Smart glasses, which are gradually becoming known to people. These glasses work on the principle of using augmented reality and projecting the image into the work field. The fact as a concept is clear to us. It is all that we see around us undistorted and unadjusted. On the other hand, we may encounter a computer-edited and mediated reality that has been a great success in recent years. The following Fig. 1 shows the

© ICST Institute for Computer Sciences, Social Informatics and Telecommunications Engineering 2021
Published by Springer Nature Switzerland AG 2021. All Rights Reserved
D. Perakovic and L. Knapcikova (Eds.): FABULOUS 2021, LNICST 382, pp. 401–414, 2021.
https://doi.org/10.1007/978-3-030-78459-1_30

basic division of mediated reality, where the main methods include virtual reality and augmented reality [1–3].

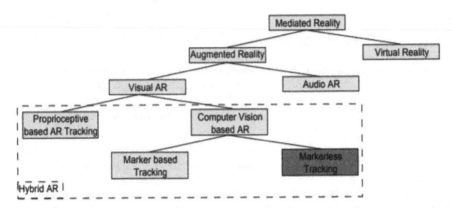

Fig. 1. Distribution of enhanced reality - distribution of mediated reality [authors own processing].

1.1 Augmented Reality

The meaning of the term "augmented" is something improved, expanded, added. In principle, the term augmented reality means a simple combination of a real and a virtual, computer-generated world. To clarify what this combination looks like, imagine a real object captured on video or a camera, where we use technology to "expand" this image in our real world with another set of digital information. Augmented reality obtains this information from various information sources using applications (off-line or on-line). In essence, this kind of reality presents us with a real (real) natural world enriched with elements of virtuality [4].

It is not easy to uniquely and generally characterize augmented reality as such. In this environment, we have the opportunity to grasp many different approaches and definitions, but to combine it into a simple characteristic, even given the ever-evolving technology, is bold. The extremely rapid development of technologies also has an impact on the development of augmented reality, both in the theoretical level and in practical use. During the constant development, the public was able to get acquainted with several personalities operating in the field of augmented reality. Prof. Steven K. Feiner, explains augmented reality as a way of the direct or indirect view of the physical environment in real-time, the elements of which are extended or added by a computer-generated sensor input, into which we include audio, video, GPS data, but also graphics [5].

Many researchers use the previous definition, but it also modifies it. One of them is the university professor Vladimir Geroimenko, who is based on Feiner's theory and tries to understand augmented reality more comprehensively. "Augmented Reality (AR) is a real-time forced perception of the real-world environment that is tightly or seamlessly integrated with computer sensory objects" [6].

Lester Madden, like many others researchers, has created his view of augmented reality and the fact that, in its simplest form, AR is the art that perfectly overlaps computer graphics and a vivid picture of the real world. Both of these worlds are very invisible [7].

Another important expert is Ronald T. Azuma, who in his work "A Survival of Augmented Reality" creates an overview of existing information found from various sources and publications until 1997, when this work was published. The generally accepted Azum definition states that the AR system contains the following properties [8]:

- Combines real and virtual objects,
- Registers (aligns) these virtual objects with the real world in three dimensions,
- Works interactively.

Canadian scientist Steve Mann, also known as the father of wearable computing, said that technology must be balanced on three axes - physical, informational and human. Also, by mixing all three, we can create an environment for users who do not select them from the physical world, but add layers of adjustments and adapt them [9].

Oliver Bimber and Ramesh Raskar present in their theory the main pillars on which AR technology is based. The basic elements include monitoring and recording, display technology and conversion, respectively a translation. Above this basic level are advanced modules, namely interaction devices and techniques, presentation and content creation. With the help of these elements, a suitable augmented reality technology can be found to serve the user [10].

Reality-virtuality continuum depicting the scale and connection between the two extremes is an interesting theory describing the environment of these realities. Before we define this scale of reality-virtuality, it is right to point out the difference and compare the augmented reality with its similar facts, as people in society often confuse it [11].

AR vs. VR

In any work on augmented reality (AR), it is necessary to mention its position in relation to virtual reality (VR). As mentioned above, the development of augmented reality and virtual reality is closely linked, but it is far from the same. Virtual reality is often defined as an artificially computer-generated simulation in which the user delves into a situation that does not contain any element from the real world. Usually, it is a pretended place that does not exist or it is a purely simulated reality. Let's compare it with AR, which usually only adds imaginary objects (digital objects, descriptions, graphics) to the real image. We find that VR is not as similar as many people think. Virtual reality, like augmented reality, has a wide range of applications. It is popular among companies providing simulators, based on the principle of virtual reality, which help employees to learn the work environment sooner. Also, almost all games use virtual reality in their concepts. Computer-connectable headsets and stand-alone headsets are a means of immersing yourself in virtual reality. The goal of both of these realities is the same, to enrich the user for a better experience [12, 13].

AR vs. MR

MR as mixed reality, in translation mixed reality, is very similar to augmented reality and is not always easy to recognize. Mixed reality refers to any combination of virtual and real existence. MR has many options and can do more things than we think. Unlike

AR, in addition to adding digital projection to the actual physical environment, in MR we can also move with them, change, i.e. create inter-actions. With the help of added elements, we can make things that can be adapted to our needs and thus shape our own environment. In a sense, mixed reality is a more interactive type of augmented reality. As with VR and AR, in mixed reality to create an experience, there must be a MR device. It is either a submersible headset (Windows MR Headset) or a holographic headset that looks like translucent glasses (Microsoft HoloLensworks). More and more, this reality is also used in practical life. Mixed reality applications are expected to help companies with engineering and design modelling in sales and even with training and education of employees and others [14].

Reality - Virtuality Continuum
The concept of Reality Virtuality Continuum (RV) was first introduced to the world in 1994. The author who developed this understanding and perception of reality is Paul Milgram. In his scientific work "Augmented Reality: A class of displays on the reality-virtuality continuum" he argues that in order to define expanded and virtual reality, they should not be understood as two opposites, but it is more appropriate to place them in a two-ended region. So we are talking about a continuous scale with two extremes. Reality-Virtuality Continuum includes all possible compositions and variations of real and virtual objects because on the one hand a purely natural real environment is defined and at the other end of the imaginary scale there is only a virtual environment, otherwise called virtuality. Figure 2 shows what areas on the Milgram scale can be created by combining reality and virtuality. Between the real physical world and the synthetic digitally created world, we find an environment of mixed reality, which is understood as an environment in which the objects of the real and virtual world are presented within one display, i.e. anywhere between the extremes of the continuum. MR thus includes augmented reality (AR), where virtual content extends the real world, but also augmented virtuality (AV), where natural objects enrich the virtual world (Fig. 2). In the first case, we observe a physical environment with added enhancements generated by the computer. In contrast, in augmented virtuality, the surrounding environment is essentially virtual but is enriched with real (not computer-generated) image data [15, 16].

It is this concept that we want to use in our design. Connecting the real world tied to augmented virtuality. To apply augmented reality in practice, we need an appropriate device with which we can experience an expanded world. AR technology is an intelligent technology and can be classified into the following categories (Fig. 3):

- HEADS UP DISPLAY

Heads-up displays were developed mainly for the Air Force and were intended to make their work easier for pilots. They were used for complex applications, e.g. flight control devices, weapon systems. A conventional HUD has three main components: a projector unit, a sight glass (combiner) and a computer (content generator). Today, however, they are mainly used in automobiles as assistance, information or navigation systems. HMD is also related to the head-up display, which works on a static basis. The head mounted display is a device placed on the head and, unlike the HUD, moves at the same time as the head moves [18].

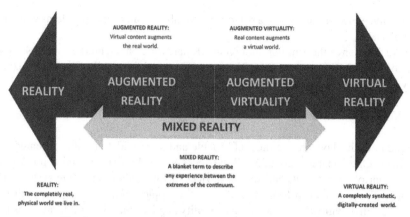

Fig. 2. Continuum reality-virtuality [authors own processing].

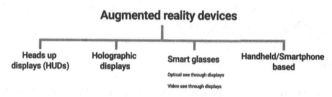

Fig. 3. Augmented reality devices scheme [16].

The holographic display shows a true 3D image easily, using a spatial light modulator. The holographic system uses a prism to connect light from the holographic display to the environment. They use light diffraction to create a three-dimensional form of an object in real space. Perhaps the biggest advantage of these displays is that they do not require any wearable device to see the AR. An example of this AR system is the Holovect device [17].

- SMART GLASSES

Recently, smart glasses are very popular in the company, which are on the market in two types. Video see-through and optical see-through glasses. HoloLens is one of the most popular devices of its kind on the market, manufactured by Microsoft. For their operation, they use many sensors and highly developed optics to add AR to the user environment. They also include several microphones, an HD camera, a light sensor and a holographic processing unit. Commands are executed by gesturing and moving the eyes. The second version of HoloLens 2 is currently on the market [19].

Magic Leap One is hardware that needs a wearable computer connected by a cable to futuristic design glasses to function. A controller with a large button and touchpad is used to control this device and interact with objects [20].

Google Glass Enterprise is a device used primarily for business. The employee activates and launches the necessary applications by voice commands. Also, these glasses provide a live video stream where a person can collaborate and solve problems with other people [21].

There are many other similar intelligent AR hardware on the market, such as: Epson Moverio, Meta 2, Spectacles, DAQRI Smart Glasses, Atheer AiR Glas-ses, Vuzix M 300, Vuzix M 100, Monitorless, and others [22, 23].

- HAND HELD DISPLAY

Hand held displays are the most affordable and most widely used augmented reality devices. One apparatus contains all the necessary technologies needed for AR. We include smartphones, tablets and similar devices that have their operating system (iOS, Android). The Apple App Store is available for Apple's iPhone and iPad with iOS, where you can download many augmented reality applications. The Android OS is used by many manufacturers of smartphones and tablets (Samsung, Huawei, Honor, LG, Xiaomi). Like Apple, they have their store called Google Play Store with augmented reality apps. Easy-to-download applications we know are ARKit, ARCore, MRKit, the famous PokemonGo game and many more [18].

1.2 The RFID System

The basic principle of operation of RFID technology is that the antenna of the RFID reader generates an electromagnetic field which has a specific distance and shape of the range. RFID tag comes within range of the electromagnetic field, and its antenna receives the transmitted signal and induction in the antenna coil induces a voltage that serves as a power source for the RFID tag. The tag microprocessor processes the signal from the reader and makes available the information about the marked object contained in the EPC code [24].

The antenna of the powered RFID tag begins to transmit a signal which the reader detects and then sends the object information to the host computer system. My articles

As with many other types of automatic identification systems, an RFID system consists of several interconnected components. The basic RFID system consists of:

- RFID tag,
- RFID antenna,
- RFID reader,
- Middleware.

2 Work Methodology

As already mentioned in the introduction to the article, the issue of augmented reality is very extensive. In our proposed concept, we use the principle of Reality - Virtuality Continuum, which means using augmented reality and reading data directly in time using smart glasses. Therefore, we focused on the presentation of individual components that we will use in our design. We deal with two possibilities of implementing RFID measurements. One is the use of Smart glasses with a direct connection using a Bluetooth

RFID reader and reading RFID tags, and the other option is to connect to a local wifi network using Smart glasses and read the data from the RFID reader from the PLC output [25].

2.1 AR Components

The first component is the *SMART glasses Epson Moverio BT 350*. Its advantage is a low purchase price, but the problem area is that they work on the android system. Therefore, the software has to be adapted to this system. It can also be considered an advantage, as creating android applications is not complicated. The problem is that these glasses can only be operated with a control tracker that is connected with a cable [23].

The Epson Moverio BT 350 glasses have the following technical parameters:

- Processor: Intel® Cherry Trail Atom ™ ×5 1.44 GHz Quad Core
- Display: Si-OLED with the resolution of 1270 × 720 pixels, stereoscopic
- Memory: 2 GB RAM, 16 GB storage + 32 GB microSD
- Camera: 5 Mpx
- Battery: 2,950 mAh Li-pol
- Connectivity: Bluetooth 4.1, Wi-Fi 802.11ac, GPS
- Operating system: Android 5.1.

The second component is the Microsoft HoloLens 2 SMART glasses. Microsoft created these on May 2, 2019. They work on Windows Holographics. Their advantage is that the glasses are autonomous, and their control is performed using hands and gestures. They contain two haptics sensors sensing the position of the hands (Fig. 4). The basic technical parameters are [26]:

- Processor: Qualcomm Snapdragon 850
- Display: See-through holographic lenses 2K 3:2
- Memory: 4-GB LPDDR4x system DRAM
- Camera: 8-MP stills, 1080p30 video
- Connectivity: Bluetooth 5, Wi-Fi: Wi-Fi 5 (802.11ac 2 × 2), GPS
- Operating system: Windows Holographic Operating System

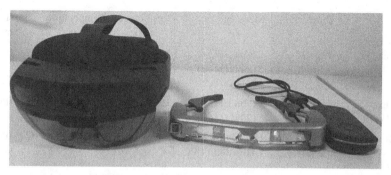

Fig. 4. Smart glasses microsoft HoloLens2 and Epson Moverio BT 350 [authors own processing].

2.2 RFID Components

The principle of dividing components into hardware and software was used to design two RFID systems. The basis of the hardware part of the RFID system is an RFID tag, which contains unique information in a unique EPC code on the marked object. Another component is an RFID reader with an antenna, which is used to read the story and then forward it for processing via intelligent software. We use two types of readers in our systems. One is mobile, and the other is a static system with an RFID reader and antenna. The software also needs to be adapted for these readers. We will use RFID explorer software for the mobile reader and Simatic web Controler for the static one [27, 28].

RFID Tags

Confidex UHF RFID tags (Fig. 5) were chosen for the proposed systems. Their advantage is IP 68 resistance and readability up to 5 m (Table 1).

Fig. 5. RFID tags [authors own processing].

Table 1. Parametre RFID tagov Confidex [authors own processing].

Type	Dimension	Memory	Read range	Temperature	IP rating
Confidex IRONSIDE Micro	27 × 27 × 5,5 mm	128bit EPC + 512 bit (M4E)	Up to 5 m	−35 °C to 85 °C	IP68
Confidex SURVIVOR™	155 × 26 × 14,5 mm	128bit EPC + 512 bit (M4E)	Up to 18 m	−35 °C to 85 °C	IP68
Confidex Links NFC &UHF	50 ×7 5 × 0,2	HF:7BytesUID, UHF 128bit EPC	Up to 5 m	−35 °C to 85 °C	IP68

Reader

For the first concept, we will use the RFID reader TSL 1128 Bluetooth® UHF, which works with Smart glasses using Bluetooth. It sends the RFID tag data to the RFID explorer software, which processes it and sends it to the database. For the second concept, we will use a Siemens SIMATIC RF685R reader with a Simatic RF620A antenna connected to a PLC 1215C (Table 2).

Table 2. Mobile and static RFID system [authors own processing].

Mobile RFID system	Static RFID system
Reader	
TSL 1128 Bluetooth® UHF	Siemens SIMATIC RF685R including anthena SIMATIC RF620A
Software	
RFID Explorer	Simatic Web Controler
Smart Glasses	
Epson Moverio BT-350	Microsoft HoloLens2

3   Results and Discussion

Based on the research and application area, we can create one complex system or two smaller, mutually separate systems (Fig. 6).

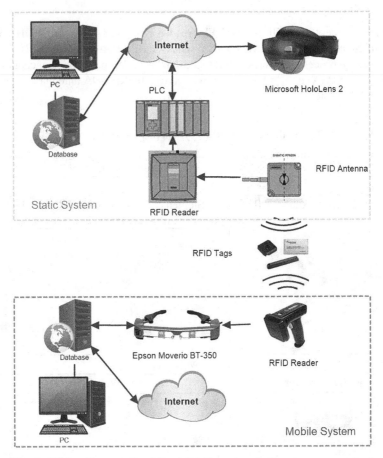

Fig. 6. Wiring diagram of mobile and static system [authors own processing].

3.1 Measurement Using a Mobile System

For this measurement, we used a TSL 1128 reader and information transfer using Epson Moverio BT-350 eyepieces. Their advantage is the simplicity of connection. For measuring and identifying the RFID tag with the EPC code, only glasses and a reading device are sufficient for us. The scanned data is transferred via wifi to a server that we set up in the program. The report export is created there. The view through the glasses and the working environment of the application shown through the remote access to the glasses is shown in Fig. 7.

The concept of a mobile reading system has its pros and cons, divided as follows:

Advantages:

- Simplicity - a system consisting of 2 components
- Mobility - allows loading anywhere in the business premises
- Low acquisition costs - the price of involvement is up to 2500 €

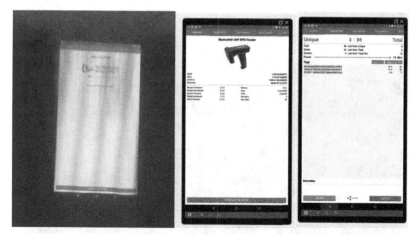

Fig. 7. Reading RFID tags using a mobile RFID system [authors own processing].

- Possibility to modify the application and outputs,
- Uploading data directly to the glasses or sending them to the database.

Disadvantages:

- Tracker control - there is no keyboard on the Smart glasses pointing device, and the glasses are controlled by a pointer
- Battery life - Smart glasses are not built for active connection of RFID reader via Bluetooth and online sending of data to the database via Wifi connection; this connection allows 1-h life.

3.2 Measurement Using a Static System

The connection of this system consists of the use of industrial components. First of all, it is a complex RFID solution in the relation of the tag-antenna-reader-PLC-display unit - wifi network. The researched workplace is the Laboratory of Lean Methods located at the Faculty of Manufacturing Technologies with a seat in Prešov of the Technical University of Košice.

In Figs. 8 and 9 we can see the individual components of the proposed static system. As shown in Fig. 9, the user has Smart glasses on and is connected to the local wifi network together with the PLC. The PLC processes all signals recorded from the reader or antenna. For simplicity and better reading, a connection to a gate mounted from an antenna and a reader between which the conveyor belt was located has been proposed. This made it possible to ensure multiple transitions of stored RFID tags between the gateway and to monitor the intensity of reading individual tags.

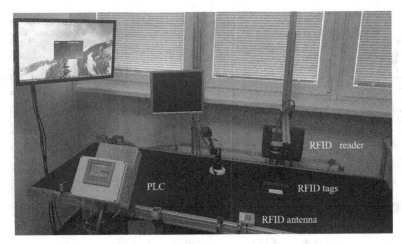

Fig. 8. The laboratory workplace [authors own processing].

Fig. 9. Control of static RFID system and working environment [authors own processing].

The concept of a static reading system has its pros and cons, divided as follows:

Advantages:

- Accuracy of information - the created gateway allowed 100% reading of all tags.
- Battery life - Microsoft HoloLens 2 glasses with a connection to wifi and standard control have an experience of about 4 h. It means that the worker is not forced to charge the glasses frequently. After connecting the power bank, it is possible to extend the duration of use.
- Hand control - is intuitive, and within 2 min, the user can quickly see. He uses gestures and a virtual keyboard at work.
- Working environment - The glasses work on the Windows Holographic operating system, this environment is similar to ordinary Windows and therefore working with it is not complicated.

Disadvantages:

- High acquisition costs - the price of involvement in at least 10 000 €
- Gesture control - sometimes, there is unnecessary click-through using the wrong gesture.
- Problems with long-term use - after a long time of using glasses in augmented reality, you need to get used to the real world.

4 Conclusion

In the presented paper, we focused on the possibilities of using Augmented reality, esp.smart glasses as a tool for performing RFID measurements. The article has designed for two systems. The first is a mobile system, and its crucial advantage is that it can identify UHF RFID tags in space, and the user can move around the production without restriction. The reader is cheap and easy to use. The second system is static. Its disadvantage is that it has a fixed reading area, which means that the user can read the scanned data anywhere and in any amount. It is sufficient to connect to a common local network. The main goal of the article is to remove standard display devices from production and replace them with smart glasses, which we confirmed on two concepts in this article.

The idea and further direction of the research team in the future are to optimize the hardware and software side for commercial purposes of manufacturing companies and to put the knowledge acquired so far into practice.

References

1. Milgram, P., Kishino, F.: A taxonomy of mixed reality visual displays. IEICE Trans. Inf. Syst. **77**(12), 1321–1329 (1994)
2. Perakovic, D., et al.: Internet of things concept for informing visually impaired persons in smart factory environments, In: Industry 4.0: Trends in Management of Intelligent Manufacturing Systems, pp. 69–86 (2019)
3. Sabolova, V., et al.: Leaning of processes and improving the working conditions of the newly created working zone. Acta Logistica **7**(4), 283–290 (2021)
4. Maxwell, K.: Augmented reality. https://www.macmillandictionary.com/buzzword/entries/augmentedreality.html. Accessed on 01 Dec 2020
5. Bimber, O.: Spatial Augmented Reality: Merging Real and Virtual Worlds. A K Peters, Wellesley (2005)
6. Geroimenko: Augmented reality technology and art: the analysis and visualization of evolving conceptual models. In: Proceeding IV '12 Proceedings of the 2012 16th International Conference on Information Visualisation, pp. 445–453 (2012)
7. Madden, L.: Professional Augmented Reality Browsers for Smartphones: Programming for Junaio, Layar, and Wikitude. Wiley Pub. Inc., Chichester, West Sussex (2011)
8. Azuma, R.T.: A survey of augmented reality. Presence-Teleoper. Virtual Environ. **6**(4), 355–385 (1997)
9. Steve, M.: The father of wearable computing. https://www.marsdd.com/news/steve-mann-augmented-reality-meta-weare-wearables. Accessed on 24 Nov 2020
10. Bimber, O., Raskar, R.: Spatial Augmented Reality: Merging Real and Virtual Worlds. A K Peters, Wellesley (2004)

11. Lei, X., et al.: TaggedAR: an RFID-based approach for recognition of multiple tagged objects in augmented reality systems. IEEE Trans. Mobile Comput. **18** (5) (2019)
12. Virtual reality vs. Augmented reality. https://www.augment.com/blog/virtual-reality-vs-augmented-reality/. Accessed on 24 Nov 2020
13. Bryksin, G.: VR vs. AR vs. MR: Differences Real-life Applications. https://www.upwork.com/hiring/for-clients/vr-vs-ar-vsmr-differences-real-life-applications. Accessed on 25 Nov 2020
14. Marr, B.: The Important Difference Between Augmented Reality And Mixed Reality. https://bernardmarr.com/default.asp?contentID=1912. Accessed on 20 Nov 2020
15. Mingram, P., et al.: Augmented reality: A class of displays on the reality-virtuality continuum. Telemanipulator and Telepresence Technologies. https://www.researchgate.net/publication/228537162_Augmented_reality_A_class_of_displays_on_the_reality-virtuality_continuum. Accessed on 24 Nov 2020
16. Reality-Virtuality Continuum. https://www.vrzone.sk/blog/reality-virtuality-continuum/. Accessed on 24 Nov 2020
17. Lin, H.-C., Yung-Hsun, W.: Augmented reality using holographic display. In: Optical Data Processing and Storage, vol. 3 (2017)
18. Kore, A.: Understanding the different types of AR devices, Uxdesign.cc, 2018. https://uxdesign.cc/augmented-reality-device-typesa7668b15bf7a. Accessed on 21 Nov 2020
19. The Best Augmented Reality Hardware in 2019. https://www.onirix.com/learn-about-ar/the-best-augmented-reality-hardwarein-2019/. Accessed on 23 Nov 2020
20. Magic Leap 1: A Thousand Breakthroughs in One. https://www.magicleap.com/magic-leap-1. Accessed on 24 Nov 2020
21. Discover Glass Enterprise Edition. https://www.google.com/glass/start/,line. Accessed on 24 Nov 2020
22. AR/MR Devices. https://www.augmented-minds.com/en/augmented-reality/arhardware-devices/. Accessed on 25 Nov 2020
23. Husar, J., Knapčikova, L: Exploitation of augmented reality in the industry 4.0 Concept for the student educational process. In: INTED2019 Proceedings, pp. 4797–4805 (2019)
24. Grabara, J., et al.: mpact of legal standards on logistics management in the context of sustainable development. Acta Logistica **7**(1), 31–37 (2020)
25. Kubac, L., et al.: RFID and augmented reality. In: 14th International Carpathian Control Conference, pp. 186–191, (2013)
26. Microsoft HoloLens 2. https://www.microsoft.com/en-us/hololens/hardware. Accessed on 26 Nov 2020
27. Kolarovski, P., et al.: Laboratory testing of active and passive UHF RFID tags. Transp. Telecommun. J. **17**(2), 144–154 (2016)
28. Hou, L., et al.: Literature review of digital twins applications in construction workforce safety. Appl. Sci. **11**(1), 1–21 (2021)

Correction to: Flash Crowd Management in Beyond 5G Systems

Valentin Rakovic, Hristijan Gjoreski, Marija Poposka,
Daniel Denkovski, and Liljana Gavrilovska

Correction to:
Chapter "Flash Crowd Management in Beyond 5G Systems"
in: D. Perakovic and L. Knapcikova (Eds.): *Future Access*
Enablers for Ubiquitous and Intelligent Infrastructures,
LNICST 382, https://doi.org/10.1007/978-3-030-78459-1_4

The original version of this book was inadvertently published with the first author surname incorrect, which has now been corrected.

The updated version of this chapter can be found at
https://doi.org/10.1007/978-3-030-78459-1_4

© ICST Institute for Computer Sciences, Social Informatics and Telecommunications Engineering 2021
Published by Springer Nature Switzerland AG 2021. All Rights Reserved
D. Perakovic and L. Knapcikova (Eds.): FABULOUS 2021, LNICST 382, p. C1, 2021.
https://doi.org/10.1007/978-3-030-78459-1_31

Author Index

Printed in the United States
by Baker & Taylor Publisher Services